ESTATE MANAGEMENT PRACTICE

ESTATE MANAGEMENT PRACTICE
(Second Edition)

by
TIM STAPLETON
M.Phil., B.Sc., F.R.I.C.S.,
Principal Lecturer, Department of Surveying, Bristol Polytechnic

1986

THE ESTATES GAZETTE LIMITED
151, Wardour Street, London W1V 4BN

First Edition 1981
Reprinted 1983
Second Edition 1986

ISBN 0 7282 0094 5

Front cover—Entrance Hall of Broad
Quay House, Bristol; developed by the
Standard Life Assurance Company.

Text set in 10/11 pt Linotron 202 Melior, printed and bound
in Great Britain at The Bath Press, Avon

"... the tenant paying the said rents hereby reserved and performing and observing the convenants herein contained shall quietly hold and ..."

Foreword to the First Edition

In commending Tim Stapleton's excellent book to you, I do so in the knowledge that it not only fills a major gap in the text books available to the professions of the land, but also deals most effectively with an area of professional activity of increasing importance.

The efficient and proper management of our scarce land resources is now recognized as a major factor in the regeneration of the commercial, manufacturing and industrial activity of this country. Similarly the effective management of our housing resources providing a basic need of society is fundamental to the well-being of the nation.

To those responsible for estate management in its widest context, this book will serve as a comprehensive aid in the execution of their traditional responsibilities requiring professional skill and knowledge of a high order.

Here we have a valuable manual written in a thoroughly readable style dealing in a practical way with the ever widening range of matters within the area of activity of the land and property manager. It is no longer sufficient to apply the traditional approach now that society demands still higher standards involving legislation, regulation and control in the field of tenure, rent, repair, health, safety, insurance and the environment.

In 1965, Michael Thorncroft wrote Principles of Estate Management, with a foreword by Sir Henry Wells, a most distinguished chartered surveyor who throughout his professional career recognized the importance of estate management as a separate discipline within our professional armoury. I know that it would have given him very great pleasure to see the appearance of this new book.

J. N. C. James, F.R.I.C.S.
Past-President of the Royal Institution of Chartered Surveyors

Preface to the First Edition

Estate Management is simultaneously a generic description of a broad range of activity and a specialist technical displine. It touches upon every aspect of the relationship between society at large and individuals who occupy or own landed property.

The effective exercise of estate management skill has to achieve a delicate balance between the acceptance of a strong historical infrastructure of law and current estates practice and the pressures of technical and social change. This has been demonstrated in a continuing debate on the most appropriate methods of education and training for estate managers. The arguments are partly rooted in misunderstanding and self-interest, they are also due to very different views about the balance between current estates practice and a perception of the education required of those entering the profession in order to solve problems of the next generation.

This book arose from a realization that compared with valuation, where specialist texts are available covering technique and statutory and investment applications, urban estate management practice is relatively poorly served with textbooks. The aim was to provide a comprehensive text with a significant practical content, and such a breadth of aim must inevitably imply sacrifices in depth. This is acknowledged, but depth has been pursued in those areas that are uniquely the province of the surveyor.

In order to meet this aim and permit ready access to defined areas of study, the text has evolved into three parts. Part I fulfils two roles; it identifies a general concept of management and then analyses the rationale and character of the principle types of estates and factors underlying their management. Part II deals with the detailed statutory and contractual setting of landlord and tenant in respect of the management of both commercial and residential property. Part III demonstrates how the formulation of estates policy leads into positive management and the means by which the surveyor can exercise his skill.

This format enables the text to form a core for estate management studies on University and Polytechnic courses and also meet the needs of the subject in the 1982 final exam syllabus of the R.I.C.S. Further reading is suggested at the end of each chapter, and the exercise involved in relating the perspective of this book to the sometimes differing approaches of this supplementary reading is an essential experience in developing a critical and constructive view of the subject. Footnotes have been avoided, for in an essentially practical subject the best footnotes are current aspects of management and the market gained from reading the appropriate journals, practical experience and forms of action learning.

It is hoped that practitioners will find Part III an interesting and stimulating commentary on positive management and Part II very much more than an *aide-mémoire* on the management of leasehold property. These two parts together contain much of the philosophy and technical background around which an estate management manual can be created as a basis for good practice.

The indebtedness of the text-book writer to others is always extensive, and many individuals have contributed generously of their time and interest to this book. To name them all is impossible, but I would mention Robin Sinclair-Taylor, of Debenham, Tewson & Chinnocks, for his contribution to parts of Chapter 9; Peter Scott, Roger Netting and Terry Cockerton for their reading and rigorous criticism of some draft chapters; and senior staff of the R.I.C.S. secretariat for their help. Also David Marsh and Peter Harrison, of J. P. Sturge & Sons, whose experience and views have enabled me to clarify my thoughts on many occasions by reminding me that we live in a practical world. Lastly my wife for her patient typing of much of the manuscript. Any fault, error or unfairness of opinion I must claim for myself.

It may be helpful to add that unless indicated to the contrary the statistics were gathered during the first two quarters of 1980. The law includes the provisions of the Housing Act 1980 and Local Government, Planning and Land Act 1980.

Tim Stapleton
November 1980

Preface to the Second Edition

The general arrangement of the text has been retained in the second edition, but significant changes have been made to the content to reflect changes in; law, practice, technology and the market place. As a result over half the text has been totally rewritten.

The first of these changes has been achieved by having regard to new cases and legislation, approximately double the number of cases have been considered (many in Chapter 6). Practice has been influenced by many factors including an emphasis on the refurbishment of inter-war office buildings and other more modern buildings (Chapter 11) and major steps on accountability and privatization in the public sector (Chapters 4 and 10).

The publication of "Pleased to Report" in 1983 has enabled Chapter 9 on Professional Practice to be revised with a much sharper focus on property management including accounts and the organization and management of the office, with assistance from the Management and Accounts departments of J. P. Sturge and Sons. The market has been subject to more detailed reporting and analysis in the last few years and so statistics have been brought up to date. The expectations and monitoring of portfolios has resulted in a much more rigorous and detailed treatment of portfolio performance from the point of view of both occupier and owner (Chapter 11).

The general character of the text is that of commercial property, and the question has been raised as to whether to keep Chapter 7 on residential property. This has been retained in order to continue with the aims of a comprehensive text and also perhaps to attempt the challenge of producing a concise treatment of residential management. Chapter 13 in the first edition has now been absorbed into the rest of the text.

Clearly the detailed investigation of a technical point is increasingly undertaken with the assistance of the growing number of specialist loose leaf encyclopedias, perhaps to be shortly replaced by VDU access to computerized information systems. It is hoped that this text, apart from conveying information, continues to provide a framework within which the basic discipline of estate management can be performed, analysed and assessed in a critical way.

Tim Stapleton
December 1985

Contents

Contents

PART I

Urban Estates

Chapter 1

The Growth of Urban Estates

1.1 Introduction

Land-ownership has over many centuries brought opportunities to influence a wide range of economic, social and political aspects not directly related to the land itself. Some estates such as those of the Church, the Crown and Livery Companies have existed since the Middle Ages with only limited changes in their land-holdings. Others have been created in a generation, due to the energy of one individual and special factors unlikely to be repeated in the foreseeable future. Urban estates have been shaped by the interaction of a number of relatively well recorded historical pressures, though different interpretations can be placed upon the motives of the parties and the merits of the outcome at various decisive stages. Economic and social development, often represented through changes in case-law and statute, have adjusted the balance of rights and duties between occupiers, owners and the general public, with serious financial consequences for the groups involved. Estate managers acting on behalf of each of the parties need to interpret the factors influencing urban property holdings in a comprehensive way, and relate these to the rationale of individual estates.

Land-use and estate management decisions on individual parcels are influenced by the history of occupation in both a physical and legal sense, each generation reacting to new opportunities and simultaneously creating new restrictions. The Ancient Monuments and Archaeological Areas Act 1979, is a pertinent reminder of the obligations attached by the nation to the recording of the past as part of the re-development process.

Estate management practice is influenced by procedures developed over many years and exercised by a profession evolved over several hundred years with all the strengths and weaknesses inherent in such groups. The success of the land-lord and tenant system has resulted in a smaller proportion of owner-occupied commercial property than elsewhere in the Western world and as a consequence highly developed procedures for the representation of the interests of both landlord and tenant and the implementation of their agreements.

The many subtle factors influencing the growth of the profession and the complex historical forces shaping urban estates can only justify limited space within the context of a study of estate management practice. A convenient, but not necessarily comprehensive approach has been used whereby up to 1945 this has been viewed more in terms of the growth of the profession and thereafter more in terms of the effects of the factors shaping urban estate management practice.

1.2 The Growth of Urban Estate Management

In Mediaeval times, the great families, the Church and the Crown placed considerable responsibility and sufficient trust as they considered prudent in their stewards, who had overall charge of the management of their estates, with bailiffs physically directing and controlling the management of individual parcels of land.

Some advice issued to stewards in the thirteenth century suggests that the principles are unchanging:

"The seneschal of lands ought to be prudent and faithful and profitable and he ought to know the law of the realm, to protect his lord's business and to instruct and give assurance to the bailiffs who are beneath him in their difficulties. He ought two or three times a year to make his rounds and visit the manors of his stewardship, and then he ought to inquire about the rents, services and customs, hidden or withdrawn, and about franchises of courts, lands ... and other things which belong to the manor and are done away with without warrant by whom and how; and if he be able let him amend these things in the right way without doing wrong to any, and if he be not, let him show it to his lord, that he may deal with it if he wish to maintain his right."

During the sixteenth century changes in social and trading conditions and the rise of a growing number of smaller landlords created an environment in which the science of the measurement, recording and presentation of boundaries was able to develop. A book of 1582 entitled, "A Discovery of Sundrie Errours and Faults Daily Committed by Land Meters" indicates that even then some criticism was being made of the work of surveyors. No doubt the author, Edward Worsop, was considered a very dangerous fellow; he even suggested training, examinations and the need for a license to practice.

By the close of the sixteenth century the rapid rise in the demand for land measurers resulted in the surveyor acquiring a reputation as an inquisitive landlord's man, much distrusted by commentators of the time. It was a logical progression from the mechanics of the making of maps and plans to their use for the purposes of the management of estates. This happened relatively slowly and it was not until the middle of the eighteenth century that business came forward in sufficient quantities and in a form which enabled practices to be created and sustained beyond the lifetime of individuals.

Throughout the seventeenth century the surveyor in his various forms was playing a relatively humble role instructed by attorneys, stewards, conveyancers and architects. During the latter part of the eighteenth century some lawyers devoted more and more time to their role as stewards managing estates and some land surveyors were successful in obtaining steadier income from regular management of the estates they surveyed.

The eighteenth century saw the start of the Enclosure movement and by 1801 a committee of the House of Commons was in favour of the appointment of a valuer as well as a surveyor in every Enclosure Bill. At the same time the Ordnance Survey was growing in importance, not without some friction between the military surveyors and civil surveyors, this state mapping service reduced the need for the private land surveyor's work on enclosures. The industrial revolution was also gaining momentum with urbanization and the construction of, first the canals, and then the railways.

The first half of the nineteenth century can be identified as the period in which the surveyor's previously chief occupation, land measurement, had superimposed upon it a much wider range of activities, all of which were due to aspects of the industrial revolution. The building of the railways required individual Acts of Parliament, their promoters became skilled in the drafting of these measures and the preparation of the necessary evidence. Their surveyors had considerable impact on the individual resident agents with whom they negotiated along the proposed route. Between 1850 and 1870 over 100,000 acres were purchased for railway purposes, similar to the activity of the motorway programme of the 1960s and early 1970s. Land agents of agricultural estates found that meeting the demand for urban growth offered greater returns than agricultural rents but by applying agricultural practice where possible, retained ownership of developed land for their client, thus creating the unique London estates.

All this activity created a considerable demand for the skilled surveyor, and whilst the eminent grew in reputation many incompetent persons sought to exercise the surveyor's skill. In the same year that the now R.I.B.A. was created, in 1834, a Land Surveyors' Club was formed in London for active promotion of the profession; they sought to exclude resident agents from membership, who were servants of a master rather than independent consultants.

In the spring of 1868 twenty surveyors met in London and by November of that year had formed the Institute of Surveyors and held their first ordinary general meeting at 12, Great George Street. Three-quarters of the original members had been involved in valuation, negotiation and arbitration for railway works but all the branches of surveying were represented within their practices. Some of their practices in both London and the provinces had been established for a century before the formation of the Institution and its member firms possessed considerable maturity.

The most eminent of the nineteenth century surveyors was John Clutton whose life spanned almost the whole century. Between 1845 and 1851 he was appointed surveyor for the Southern half of England for the Ecclesiastical Commissioners, Adviser on the Royal Forests and Crown Receiver for the Midlands and the South of England. A close second was Robert Collier Driver, who between 1860 and 1875 was responsible for a million pounds of property sales per annum. In Bristol, William Sturge was equally active, acquiring land for the Bristol and Exeter Railway, Somerset and Weymouth Railway and South Wales extension of the Great Western Railway.

The latter half of the nineteenth century saw tremendous growth in urbanization as the new municipal authorities acquired land for local urban infra-structure in much the same way as railways acquired land for the national infrastructure. The Surveyors' Institution had considerable influence on policy, legislation and administration and was mentioned in the Metropolis Management and Building Acts (Amendment) Act of 1876. The Surveyors gained a charter in 1881, which assisted them in their aims of intellectual advancement, social elevation and moral improvement.

The Institution was represented at the Congrès International des Géomètres held in Paris in 1878, where it was suggested that in order to practise surveyors should be required to obtain a government diploma; the rest of Europe accepted this principle. This did not accord with British practice, but the surveyors did set up a system of qualifying exams for new members in time to support the application for the charter.

Codes of conduct and the role of local branches were developing in the early part of the twentieth century. The Liberal Budget of 1909 posed questions on land-taxation which really only had to be faced 40 years later; though by then professional bodies had appreciated the need to avoid arguing their case on political grounds.

During the 1914–18 war agriculture and industry flourished in an effort to meet the needs of war. Speculative development of owner occupied housing, reflected the concepts of the garden city movement of the 1920s, and the start of the decline of the rented housing stock. At the same time amongst the then two dozen or so publicly quoted property companies the seeds of commercial and industrial development were being sown, the latter often based on War Department surplus. Despite 3 million unemployed in the early 1930s large office buildings were constructed in London, now the subject of major refurbishments. Industrial estates were developed in major urban centres, many of which have since been redeveloped.

With hindsight the 'twenties and 'thirties can be seen as a time when professional bodies enjoyed a period of relative stability in which to develop, particularly at branch level. The ownership of land was not a major issue and there was fragmentation of both urban and rural estates which offered new opportunities for development carried out mainly by builders utilizing traditional sources of finance. Towards the end of this period a range of social pressures in health, planning, education and welfare were building up, but their resolution was delayed until after 1945.

1.3 Education

At the end of the nineteenth century some of the luckier articled pupils were able to take advantage of the educational facilities which had arisen as an extension of the London practice of Parry, Blake and Parry. After the first war and some inter-institutional rivalry between the Chartered Auctioneers and the R.I.C.S. which did not reflect well on the latter, the College of Estate Management was formed in 1922 and absorbed the educational facilities of the above firm.

The early date at which the College was able to teach for an external degree of London University may not have been entirely unrelated to the fact that the Vice-Chancellor was the brother of Sir William Wells, a past President of the R.I.C.S. The Cambridge degree, then predominantly agricultural, was being developed at the same time. The College ran postal courses for the exams of professional bodies and by 1947 had a sizeable full-time student body. On its move to Reading in 1972 its full-time courses became an integral part of that University. The Watson Committee of 1950 recommended that the R.I.C.S. should encourage the provision of full-time courses, and technical colleges in strategic towns were encouraged to provide courses. At the 1967 R.I.C.S. Annual Conference the Deputy-Secretary at the Ministry of Education said, "I cannot believe that correspondence courses are any longer a satisfactory method for a candidate for professional status". The creation of Polytechnics in 1969 incorporating the major technical colleges which had been teaching for the R.I.C.S. exams since the 1950s enabled further growth to take place in the provision of full-time courses. By 1977 the majority of those entering the profession had qualified through full-time courses, fulfilling the prophecy of the Eve report of 10 years before. This has enabled the profession to attract some of the most able of school-leavers necessary to take it forward with confidence in its ability to handle the complex issues of the next decades. Provisions now exist for post-graduate studies, and the need, if not the means, for continuing professional development has been accepted. The development of education for the profession has been more rapid than any other comparable discipline, and this has not been without its controversy. The perception of our Victorian forebears in anticipation of the debate is illustrated by a brief extract from the views of William Sturge in 1868, in warning against a university education for young surveyors, "... the tastes and habits he will form will probably render the drudgery of a surveyor's office distasteful to him. I arrive at the conclusion that the balance is against a university education for the surveyor". This can be contrasted with the view of Jeremiah Mathews, who 2 years later was led to the conclusion that, "a university education would avoid a too premature technical training ... which warps the mind by confining it to a single channel of thought and thus renders a man incapable of understanding the motives which guide others".

1.4 Post-1945

In the post-war period fundamental changes have occurred across the whole fabric of society. Three changes have particularly influenced the way we live and as a result the demand for buildings and the way they are used:

Educational and training opportunities for young people are much greater and the young have greater mobility and purchasing power.

Many more women now go out to work, with most families having more than one income and a consequential dramatic fall in the birth rate.

A greater emphasis on the creative use of leisure time with many specialist community-based facilities.

This happened within a system of government and a planning framework with a much higher regard for social priorities and a growth of public awareness and knowledge of environmental issues. Time-consuming consultative procedures developed which in a period of high inflation rendered capital budgets of projects almost ineffective. These features have been particularly marked in the provision, funding and use of our housing stock. In the immediate post-war period and particularly the early 1950s, the quantity of housing (if not the quality) was regarded as something of a triumph. However, the problems of the tower blocks built in the last twenty years caused by the application of technology running ahead of the policy-makers' understanding of human responses has recently resulted in a more introspective view. Since the middle of the 1960s we have seen a continuous fall in housing starts, possibly due to the political parties using housing finance as a political battlefield.

The changes in housing over the last 30 years have been startling, whether measured in terms of consumers or of the nature of the fabric. Between 1951 and 1978 the proportion of one-person households doubled to 22% of the total number of households. Over the same period, the number of households without a fixed bath or sharing a bath fell from almost 50% to 4%. Also, between 1956 and 1978 the number of households with refrigerators rose from 8% to 90%.

The U.K. has had one of the greatest variations in the distribution of wealth in Western Europe. This is despite the severest redistributive income-tax, which has had some effect; for example, the proportion of wealth held by the most wealthy 1% of the population fell from 33% in 1966 to 24% in 1977. However, in 1977 the wealthiest 10% of the population still owned over 60% of the wealth, and surprisingly the poorest 50% of the population owned only 5% of the total wealth. The government's statisticians preparing "Social Trends" do not claim infallibility in absolute terms, and the issues are complicated by the patterns of social welfare and the black economy, nevertheless the overall trends are not in dispute and have long-term implications for estate management.

The taxation of unearned increment is mainly justified on social rather than revenue-earning grounds. Development Land Tax only provided a modest revenue but such taxes have an effect on land management out of all proportion to their revenue-earning potential. The stones dropped in the pond by the legislation of 1947, 1967, 1973 and 1975/76 have sent ripples into every aspect of estate management, directly influencing the development process and hence the nature of the flow of property for occupation and investment. Conflicts between demand for occupation by users and demand for investment purposes by institutions have directly contributed to the continuous cycle of boom and slump in construction and investment.

From the middle 1950s the Institutions, initially insurance companies and subsequently pension funds, have taken up direct investment in property. At the end of 1977 the aggregate property holdings of insurance companies were £7,153 million, almost double that of the pension funds, though pension funds as a whole and their property portfolios in particular are growing much faster than those of the insurance companies. In the past, over the long term, property has offered significantly better returns than gilts or equities, measured in terms of income and capital growth, though there are some worrying aspects. The market is dominated by the sentiment of no more than a dozen major funds and property is really only better than other investments if you do realize the benefit of the capital growth. What do you then buy with the proceeds? Some very large portfolios have been created with a minimum of disclosure to interested parties, containing high value properties due to new building techniques and materials permitting the construction of large floor-areas to meet user-requirements. On occasions the techniques and materials showed some unforeseen and expensive maintenance problems.

Historians with more perspective than we enjoy may well

not be impressed by any of the above as the key factor affecting estate management in the latter half of the twentieth century. The oil crisis of 1973 contained within it a de-stabilizing effect on the whole range of economic activity, bringing in its wake record interest rates, rapid inflation, particularly in construction costs, and periods during which there were falls in the standard of living of the average tax-payer. This resulted in the destructive de-gearing of industry in general and property-owning organizations in particular. Within property management the high cost of energy has raised service charges from an incidental cost to a major component of the costs of occupation. Designers are now seeking to respond with low-energy technology and the new discipline of terotechnology has emerged.

The extent to which the conservative government elected in 1979 will achieve its aim of a permanent shift in resources from the public to private sector, may not become evident for some years.

In conclusion it must be stated that of all the factors influencing investment, conventional wisdom may well be the most important. A Department of the Environment report with the inelegant title of "The Recent Course of Land Property prices and the Factors Underlying It" sought to analyse the many possible factors, but concluded in its final paragraph, "The major explanation of the property price boom which we are left with, but which is regrettably difficult to test, is that expectations about the future played a vital determining role". Putting it simply, a small number of influential opinion-formers can have a quite disproportionate effect on the market, the nature of which is a vital imput into the decision-making process in estate management.

1.5 Individual Estates

The ownership of property may be sought for many reasons. Effective estate management requires a clear knowledge and understanding of the motives of estate owners. Estates are held in order to fulfill a need; if that need is clearly enunciated then the estate manager can use his skill to manage, refurbish and develop the estate in the most desirable manner.

Interests in property are a means of storing wealth; this may be as capital asset producing no income, such as a development site, or as income from a fully developed site with an opportunity for real growth. In general trading and commercial companies property is a fixed asset and the best security against which the company can raise loans in order to further its business activities. The effect of estate management policy on the value of the assets, and hence the security offered to the investor has, in periods of unstable values resulted in guidance from professional bodies on the procedures to be adopted to give a true and fair picture of this store of wealth.

Newly formed businesses usually rent property, but there will be uncertainty as to its continued cost and occupation. Ownership offers independence but brings with it additional responsibilities and the possibility of inefficient use, due to the lack of financial discipline imposed by reviews of the cost of occupation through rent-review clauses.

The ownership of property is no longer a necessary condition for the election of representatives to government. Nevertheless it certainly remains in the eyes of many a prestigious acquisition and may bring with it social and personal advantages. Individuals can become very attached to their physical environment and the continued association of the family or business with particular land and buildings provides some certainty in a world of change, though the high maintenance costs, taxation and custodial tasks which come with heritage property impose severe burdens on owners. However, the conduct of some estates and property interests has acquired a certain notoriety, falling below the standards imposed by public opinion or the law.

The widening responsibilities undertaken by the State since 1945, subject to varying emphasis by different governments, require specialist properties, managed to meet the operational requirements of public sector bodies. The public sector is the owner of about 20% of the surface area of the U.K., though admittedly nearly half of this is the operational land of the Forestry Commission. In this respect the public sector is like any other estate owner; the English (Industrial) Estates Corporation, the Property Services Agency, water authorities and local authorities all manage estates and are subject to many of the same factors as the private sector. Apart from its specific land-ownership, the State also possesses considerable powers to influence the pattern of land use, the management of urban property and the obligations associated with the ownership of land and buildings. This concept of national estate management needs to be distinguished from the State as a group of large landowners.

1.6 The National Estate

The national estate and by implication the need for its management in national terms is one which surveyors have tended to ignore as anathema to their essentially historical private sector philosophy. It is often difficult to discover the pattern of land ownership, and town planning has tended to concentrate on what can be seen or measured—the control of land use—to the exclusion of the proprietary land unit. The concept of the management of the national estate is therefore a much greater one than the statutory planning system concerning itself primarily with controlling change of use within a county structure plan and district local plans.

Bearing in mind the position of the Crown in the eleventh century as the ultimate landlord and the role of land as a tax base, then for a country under new management, a national estate terrier, the Domesday Inquest of 1086, was an essential and obvious measure. The only other comparable survey of proprietary interests was based on the rating returns of 1872–73, when agricultural land was still subject to rating. This listed the name and address of owners of an acre or more of land; such a basis had little relevance in urban areas. The survey showed that 57% of England and 93% of Scotland was held in estates of 1,000 acres or more. Since that date until the late 1950s there was an unprecedented period of fragmentation of estates, then the financial institutions began to add direct property holdings to their portfolios. In conceptual terms their role is identical to that of the old-style charities, acting as nominees to ensure our rights to a reasonable income in old age to supplement what the State may provide. From originally being just another investor, they have become the single most important factor underlying demand in the property investment market.

But what can we discover of the nature of the national estate? The agricultural sector is probably the best documented by physical area, tenure and quality, with a very small annual percentage change in ownership. The Northfield Committee of 1979, despite making many detailed recommendations, found no fundamental defects in the existing pattern of ownership.

The diversity and size of the residential sector, representing the vast majority of the nation's store of wealth, makes it the most difficult to handle. This was made much more difficult by the advice of Secretary of State for the Environment in the summer of 1979, to 19 million rate-payers to tear up their rate return forms. However, there are some statistical sampling surveys of motivation of potential occupiers and quality of the stock. Local authority and voluntary sector housing tends to be relatively well documented.

As regards commercial and industrial property, the total cost of net acquisitions by institutions is well documented in "Financial Statistics". The Department of the Environment has collected various figures, mainly based on aggregation of the records of individual offices of the District Valuer/Valuation Officer. It has been estimated that at the end of 1981 the net capital stock of buildings, other than dwellings, in the U.K. was £300,000 million. This was equivalent in value to about 162 times the then assets of Land Securities Investment Trust and does seem rather a low figure. To the extent that exceptional progress has been made in the field of asset valuation, the aggregate of values ascribed to properties in the private sector in company annual reports may now offer a better statistical source. Though the physical extent of accommodation has been estimated in the Department's statistics, its overall quality is unknown.

There is no common basis underlying any of the statistics in respect of agricultural, residential or commercial property, and to these must be added a complex and specialist public sector estate. Parliamentary pressure on government resulted in the first annual report of the Property Services Agency in 1978. The estates of local authorities and statutory bodies had been relatively unknown outside the committee room until the 1980 Local Government Planning and Land Act introduced registers of surplus public sector land, which coincided with government pressure on public bodies to review all their operational estate.

The question which must be considered is whether government policy and implementation in respect of matters affecting land are simple individual piecemeal expedients or whether there is a measure of overall policy and an availability of information against which it may be possible to assess that policy? At this stage political issues may be raised, but not in conflict; there is a remarkable unanimity of support for the need for such an approach. Both Dr. Denman, of Cambridge University the *éminence grise* of the right in matters affecting land, and the Centre for Environment Studies, have identified the importance of proprietary interests and the lack of information.

The decade in which falls the 900th Anniversary of Domes-

day offers an opportunity for us to review the inadequate information we have on the ownership of the national estate.
Consider the contribution which a good data base could make
to the following;

easier transfer of land;
identifying trends in the pattern of land-ownership;
assisting policy decisions on land use;
determining the availability of land for development;
testing the achievements of the planning system.

In view of the problems facing the private estate owner in
assembling the information necessary to be able to take estate
decisions with confidence, so the problem facing the State in
deciding upon the correct response to perceived problems must
be immeasurably more difficult.

The First Land Utilization Survey in the 1930s, by the late
Dr. Dudley Stamp, was one of the factors leading to the introduction of the comprehensive post-war planning system. In
order to pursue the issues, various interested parties have
formed the Lands Council and are seeking to make the 1980s
the land decade, the most important single event being the
Second Land Utilization Survey.

The research departments of the major private practices have
since the late 1970s made a significant contribution in publishing market intelligence in respect of:

Micro economic studies,
Investment performance measurement,
Stocks and the utilization of commercial property,
Some tentative work on user requirements.

In addition greater awareness and confidence between academic institutions and practice, supported by the Research
Councils in helping to initiate joint research projects. These
offer the advantage of bringing together the best of the market
and client motivation of practices, with the methodology,
vigour and longer term analysis of academic research. Estate
Management has been the poorer in the past due to the inadequate research base compared with other vocational areas of
study, see 8.3.

The most rapid rate of growth of any land use in the post-war
period has been dereliction. The combination of the surveyor's
very success in creating the best financial situation for his
client, together with a planning system obsessed with the statutory plan-making process, plus a rapid rate of technological

change, laid waste to some of our major conurbations on the scale of war-time bombing, see 8.2.2.

1.7 Thesis and Definitions

The basis upon which this book is founded is that the essentially technical process of property management has superimposed upon it two further tiers of activity. First, estate management, and this means identifying the role of property within the broader overall aims of the particular entity of which the land holding forms part. In many cases property will be simply one of a number of resources of an organization, and this may require a more flexible application of estate management skills than those appropriate in a solely property-orientated management. Second, a level of public involvement in the private sector through various agencies, statutes and interest groups sufficient to justify the concept of national estate management. Linking the two, a growing sense of financial accountability in the public sector, which raises some doubts as to the validity of traditional differentiations of purpose and objective between public and private sector estate management.

It is always difficult to face up to the definitions. As a first step it is helpful to distinguish between;

Estate Management (the generic activity) defined in an R.I.C.S. Policy Review in 1974 as "All facets of the use, development and management of urban land, including the sale, purchase and letting of residential, commercial and industrial property and the management of urban estates; and advice to clients on planning"; and

Estate Management (the specialist activity) as defined by Thorncroft, "The direction and supervision of 'an interest' in landed property with the aim of securing the optimum return; this return need not always be financial but may be in terms of social benefit, status, prestige, political power or some other goal or group of goals."

This is a very helpful definition and our first two chapters are designed to enable the reader to interpret this as fully as possible, inserting his own value judgments and perceptions of estates and clients. Arnison has criticized Thorncroft's definition as springing from a totally private sector client framework and would substitute the phrase "the national estate" for "an interest" in the above definition. He goes on to identify three quite different types of personnel with a role to play in estate management. Skilled practical men (and women), accounting for the majority of those in practice, providing a service in the public or private sector, in valuing, managing or disposing of everyday property interests and property problems. A smaller, perhaps more mentally agile, group managing more complex situations, some distance removed from individual property interests, including senior partners of the larger London and provincial partnerships, senior staff in the public sector and the directors and executives of the major property and investment companies and institutions. Lastly a small group providing the innovation, the critical appraisal and reappraisal of methods, techniques and attitudes which ensure the vitality and adaptability of a profession. Perhaps there is a little of each in all of us?

Sources and Further Reading

Arnison, The Study of Estate Management, 241 EG 137.

Black, Rateable value and floor space statistics as indication of change in the building stock in commercial and industrial use, Building Research Establishment, Current Paper 52/77.

Burns, Managing the Nation's Resources, R.I.C.S. Annual Conference, 1976.

Commercial and Industrial Property Statistics 1978, D.O.E., H.M.S.O., 1979.

Farming after Northfield, C.S., July 1979.

Hammerson, The new Act and development: a reply, C.S., July 1979.

Massey and Catalano, Capital and Land, Edward Arnold, 1978.

Norton Taylor, Whose Land is it Anyway, Turnstone, 1982.

Ratcliffe, Urban Land Administration, Estates Gazette, 1978.

R.I.C.S., Survey of Published Research by Private Practices, 1982.

Rose, The Dynamics of Urban Property Development, Spon, 1985.

Scarrett, Survey of Research, Leicester Polytechnic, Annual.

Social Trends, H.M.S.O.

The Recent Course of Land and Property Prices and the Factors Underlying it, D.O.E., 1976.

The Farmland Market, Estates Gazette/Farmers' Weekly.

Thompson, Chartered Surveyors—The Growth of the Profession, Routledge and Kegan Paul, 1968.

Chapter 2

Management

2.1.1 Introduction

Management of any type, whether of property or of any other resource or process, is concerned with what happens between the main decision-making structure, whether it be the board of a company, trustees, an appointed commission or an elected authority, and the performance of the operational task. In the case of a small business or partnership, since there will be little delegation, there need be little formal control other than that achieved by the normal flow of correspondence. One of the main functions of management is the control of devolved responsibility. Many small organizations without such devolved responsibility achieve their success or failure solely on the personal qualities and skills of their proprietors. This is not to say that such organizations will not find the tools of management useful, rather that a detailed functional approach to management may not be very relevant. To the extent that a larger proportion of property is now being managed within large organizations, the case for a study of management in its own right becomes stronger. Management has been defined by Allsopp as:

"The selection of goals and the planning, procurement, organization, co-ordination and control of the necessary resources for their achievement. Management is concerned with the dynamics of circumstance and activity and is generally motivated by the need to economise in the use of resources and time in achieving pre-determined objectives. In commerce, management is concerned with efficiency in the conversion of opportunity and resources into wealth."

The operational heart of this can be expressed as converting policy into action, leading to the questions:

What policy?
What action and by whom?
Is it the right action?

Much of the remainder of this book is concerned with applying these questions to estates and individual properties. This is achieved in Part I by an analysis of the different kinds of estates, in Part II by decision-making in the management of leases and in Part III by decision-making in relation to estates. There are many interpretations of management and its theories have developed within business management as an essentially product-orientated approach, with management having somewhat combative implications within the industrial relations field. In order that a study of management makes a positive contribution to estate management, considerable care needs to be taken not to go too far down the business management route. Business management is becoming more a social process with an emphasis on people management within large organizations producing a standard product in very large quantities, indeed, a growing capacity to over-produce in many technological fields, whereas estate management is concerned primarily with the stock of a heterogeneous specialized asset; people are important, but the numbers in all but a handful of organizations are relatively small, and the task is one where standard procedures can only be applied with the greatest of care, education and training. In fact many of the problems that arise require a combination of perceptive originality and experience and at any one time only a limited number of individuals will be in a position to exercise such qualities. Quite apart from the diversity of the types of property and estates, the organizations which carry out the management function have very different characteristics in terms of rationale, size, mode of operation and accountability.

To summarize, the problem would seem to be agreeing upon some general functions of management and relating these to property, bearing in mind that the education of the majority of surveyors up to the mid-1970s has tended to concentrate on skills of how best to carry out specific instructions rather than contributing to the writing of instructions. Also, other than in specialist property organizations, surveyors have at times been reticent in actively integrating the estate within the overall management function and structure of the parent organization.

On the consensus of a number of authorities considered by Thorncroft it is proposed to examine the general functions as; planning, organizing, co-ordinating and controlling.

The application of these general functions of management to property is not without its difficulties or its critics. This is partly due to considerable misunderstandings and also a fairly standard human failing amongst professionals of a dislike of their expert opinion being challenged, particularly at an interface with another discipline. If the general principles of management can be broadly stated then this enables the individual surveyor to apply them to any aspect of estate management, utilizing his own experience to the full. Appendix A contains a flow-chart illustrating some broad aspects of management within a large corporate organization.

2.1.2 Planning

This relates to the work of the policy-making group within the organization, concerned with forecasting on different timescales and the analysis of all the underlying factors affecting the organization's activities or potential activities and determining any necessary responses. A few, or even one leading personality may create policy, alternatively there may be a corporate approach. In whatever way it is produced or structured or communicated, the planning function having determined policy should then be expressed as a management brief, up-dated with the benefit of further information that arises from regular monitoring of performance. This is considered in Part III, which has as its theme positive management, and particularly by Chapters 8 and 11.

One recent problem is the need to plan further and further ahead, due to the lengthening gestation period of projects of every type, but the factors underlying the decision seems to be changing more quickly and more significantly than past experience is readily able to assimilate. This then leads, not necessarily to a counsel of despair but to opportunist planning, which can be efficient in its individual execution but less effective in its overall impact. This is likely to result in the planning process becoming more important than the plan itself; that is to say the process of planning is justified as the best way of ensuring that all factors are considered and agreements made as to the weight to put upon them and as a consequence their effect on decisions of the policy-making body.

2.1.3 Organizing and Co-ordinating

This is concerned with setting up a structure to perform the management brief, and there are several approaches. It may be a case of the executive manager receiving a brief and using his experience and knowledge of his staff and resources, deploying them to meet that brief. Alternatively, where an opportunity exists for change or some new venture, a number of issues can be identified:

Specialist or generalist organization?
Centralized or decentralized organization?
Effectiveness or efficiency?

The last of these is particularly interesting. Put simply, efficiency is concerned with ensuring that each particular operation is carried out to yield the most desirable cost/value ratio. Whereas effectiveness implies standing back from the operation, ensuring the objective is clear and then determining which of several alternative methods is most able to meet that objective. Discussions of this type tend to result in rather heated meetings, a sure sign that personalities and issues have become inter-linked. The above usually has to be carried out within an existing organizational structure with its own management style, threshold of responsiveness to change, pattern of resources and staffing.

This leads into the third function of management, the co-ordinating of staff and resources into the most effective means of operation, integrating effort. This is closely related to the selection and motivation of staff and that almost indefinable atmosphere which does exist in efficient, effective and well managed organizations. A study of the way that policy once formulated is disseminated throughout the organization, and the way that the right information reaches policy-makers can go some way to establishing the importance of the co-ordinating function. Specifically this depends upon communication, both the means of communication and the effectiveness with which the information is handled and directed to those most able to use it.

2.1.4 Control

Control is only necessary if there has been delegation and this leads to the conclusion that the smaller the unit of accountability or profit centre the less relevant is a structured pattern of management.

Assuming a sufficiently large organization for the four functions of management to be distinct, then effective control is more than the receipt of reports, however detailed and accurate they may be. It is the measurement of the performance indicated by the information in the reports against planned or desired objectives. The means that are necessary to achieve effective control will vary significantly between different management situations. What is essential is that monitoring methods, give appropriate feedback to the policy-makers as they enter the next stage of their planning with more information and so up-date the brief.

At its simplest and possibly worst, the brief may be no more than a company's annual report with an analysis of the past year and a prospective of the future. It could be much more, not just a management tool but part of the system of motivation that ensures that a member of the organization never needs to ask, "what should I be doing?" nor wonder whether he has done it right, for at the end of the day, the only real management tool we have is those who work around us.

2.2.1 The Relationship of Management to Property

The most useful contribution of general management to property is the theory of "Management by Objectives", developed in the early 1960s. The case for such a theory has been stated by Druger as:

"What the business enterprise needs is a principle of management that will give full scope to individual strength and responsibility and at the same time, common direction of vision and effort, establish teamwork and harmonize the goals of the individual with the common weal. The only principle that can do this is management by objectives and self control."

The process consists of:

Management formulates strategic plan by defining corporate aims and objectives in the short, medium and long term.

Action and resources are co-ordinated within a tactical plan.

Individual units then prepare means of implementation, with realistic and measurable performance requirements for individuals.

Regular monitoring and review is undertaken on an appropriate frequency. This is set out in diagrammatic form in Appendix A, and is readily applicable to any large estate management organization. It is also relevant to the refurbishment cycle of any large commercial building, such as a shopping centre or major multi-let office building.

Four distinctive types of estate management can be identified:

The management of the proprietary unit exercised by: directors, elected members, trustees, partners, public servants, receivers or others in whom ownership is vested. In any organization in which property is not the primary purpose, the main skills will be those of corporate management with an emphasis on business and financial management.

The management of the estate management organization, requiring the application of business and personnel management skills within a particular professional setting. In the case of property investment companies and specialist professional practices, this second type of management will be almost indistinguishable from management of the corporate organization, and is particularly covered in this chapter.

The management of specific:

Estates / portfolios—with operational or investment objectives.

Areas —geographical areas.

Functions —types of professional activities.

The management of individual properties, and Part II is concerned exclusively with contractual and statutory aspects of the occupation of leasehold property, with Part III concentrating on a wider range of activities.

The great majority of the training and practice of estate managers—(over 90%?) is concerned with the last of these four, though lack of understanding of the other three may relegate the practitioner to the status of a technician. Indeed the R.I.C.S. published a report in 1985, entitled "Competition and the Chartered Surveyor" identified practice management as the key issue.

Considerable care has been taken to describe these four activities as types rather than levels of management—levels suggest some intrinsic merit in progression from one level to the next. This may well be the case for some individuals, but having regard to the different sizes of estates organizations and the financial importance of the correct specialist advice upon detailed aspects of property management, no career paths or education and training implications are implicit in the order in which these four types of management have been analysed.

Three examples may illustrate some of the points in this chapter. The first relates to a large private practice, the second to a large operation estate in the public sector and the third to an estates department in commerce.

Private Practice

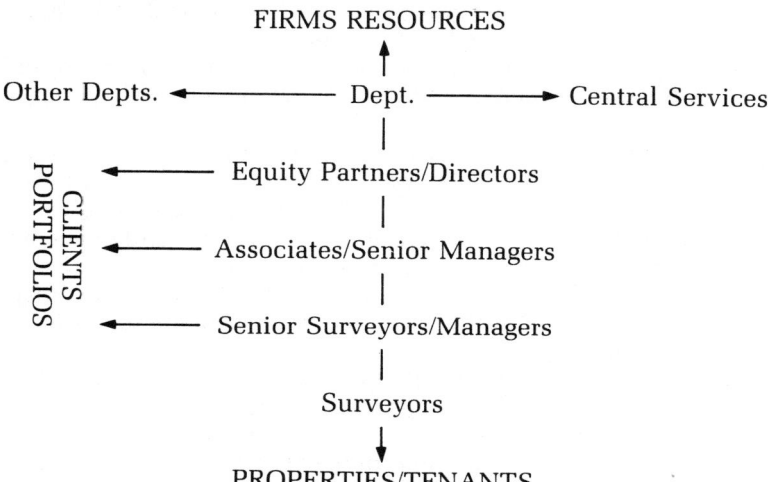

FIRMS RESOURCES

↑

Other Depts. ◄——————— Dept. ———————► Central Services

|

CLIENTS PORTFOLIOS ◄——————— Equity Partners/Directors

|

◄——————— Associates/Senior Managers

|

◄——————— Senior Surveyors/Managers

|

Surveyors

↓

PROPERTIES/TENANTS

Public Sector

British Rail Property Board

BOARD
Chairman—MD, Disposals, Management, Development, Finance.

REGION
Regional Director
Assistant Directors—Disposals, Management, Development.

|

Principal Surveyor

|

Senior Surveyor

|

Surveyors

Commerce

In 1984 the Prudential reorganized its estates department, which manages 2,500 properties with 10,000 tenancies, into the Estates Division of Prudential Portfolio Managers Limited, with a professional staff of over 100, consisting of eight groups:

Investment—purchase and sales of property, market intelligence and valuations.

Development—project management of rebuilding and refurbishment schemes, site assembly for major development
projects, appointment of developers.

Agency—new lettings, lease renewals, rent reviews, rental
intelligence, liaison with solicitors on changes in lease
clauses.

Management—day to day management, service charges,
monitoring of lease clauses, landlords consent. Monitoring
performance of properties and general estates data base.

Land Agency—direct management or appointment of agents,
acquisitions, disposals and improvements.

Architects—design and construction of new buildings,
obtaining of planning consent, management of building
contract.

Building Surveyors—major repair and refurbishment work,
structural surveys of potential acquisitions.

Engineers and Works—design and specification of plant and
machinery, supervise maintenance programmes, audit of
building efficiency including energy usage.

The whole is co-ordinated by a fund management group which
takes instructions from the various investment portfolios, who
are regarded as clients, and arranges and monitors the supply
of services by the various technical groups above.

2.2.2 The Estate's Setting

Chapter 1 traced the historical growth of urban estates and
introduced examples of the various factors determining the
shape and pattern of property ownership and the use and
development of land. These can be classified as follows:

The social climate in which there is greater accountability
for the effect individual or corporate decisions have on the
community. Various practices in the commercial, and particularly the residential, fields have been judged, not by the courts,
but by public opinion, and found defective. The knowledge
and influence of the Fourth Estate in technical fields is strong
and extensive research programmes have been carried out by
various agencies into aspects of land management and land
use. The effect of the social climate will vary, depending upon
the identity of the estate but is effect on the motivation of
staff and the response of tenants and other interested parties
should not be under-estimated.

Political change has characterized the post-war period and
no more so than during the previous decade. The property mar-

ket in its various forms as investment asset, product of the construction industry and provider of services to the population at home or work is particularly susceptible to changes in political thought. Some legislation is politically inspired in both its creation and demise as can be seen by the Community Land Act in England. Others—Capital Transfer Tax— blend into acceptability. More fundamental changes, such as entry into the E.E.C., have within them the seeds of long-term changes in our understanding of property rights.

Statutory change has put flesh on to political ideology so much so in the case of the Community Land Act as to cause its death through obesity. The most significant changes have not been of primarily property legislation but of secondary legislation affecting the quality of the environment and employment and business practice. This has resulted in much closer liaison between surveyors, solicitors and accountants.

The frighteningly bad economic performance of the U.K. in the 1960s and 1970s has resulted in remedies which have looked more like self-inflicted wounds. Consequently long-term estate management plans have been severely distorted by high interest rates and high cost inflation, and some periods of falling or static property values. Apparently rapid rises in values need to be measured in real value terms against longer time-intervals which allow for the periods of depressed values.

Physical and technical factors related to higher expectations amongst tenants and some serious failures of both materials and techniques have caused major maintenance problems early in the life of buildings. Inner city decay caused partly by the success of the planning policies of the 1960s and the over-all scale of industrial activity has resulted in thousands of acres of wasteland which, due to complex institutional factors, seem to many to present almost insoluable problems.

The aggregate effect of rapid change in all the above parameters of estate management have created strains on the traditional pattern of land-holding, resulting in substantial sales and acquisitions of property and the merger and demise of once flourishing organizations.

2.2.3 Staffing

The estates staff will enjoy the benefit of a number of cohesive forces which will help the team to achieve the desired goals. They will be able to identify with a physical estate and the professionally qualified staff and those aspiring to that status will have a common body of knowledge and expertise. Some care is necessary in the way senior non-professional staff relate to recently qualified staff, the former often contributing a considerable depth of experience across a narrow front of the management task; the latter approaching the situation with an almost opposite mode of thought whilst the clerical staff tends to take its standards from the management. The balance between professional, technical and clerical staff reflects the management style of different organizations, but generally the larger the organization, the larger the proportion of support staff. Some estates operate with an entirely white-collar staff, in others, rather like an iceberg, there is a much greater blue-collar staff performing a direct-labour role. The more notorious of these are found in urban authorities in the North and Scotland, whose activities have been questioned on grounds of both effectiveness and efficiency. Some direct labour staff for continuing small maintenance tasks can usually be justified but whether dealing with direct or contract labour a high standard of supervision is necessary, even if this requires professional staff taking the place of the once ubiquitous foreman.

2.2.4 The Portfolio

The effective management of the portfolio will require substantial contributions from other disciplines; lawyers, accountants, architects and other specialists within the construction industry. The portfolio may vary from an owner-occupier estate in industry, to an investment estate in the financial sector, to mainly leasehold occupations by a high street trading company. They will all be subject to the same underlying factors, but the weight to be attached to each and the different time-scales involved, will result in a wide variety of response to changes in estates policy. A portfolio consisting of retail leasehold occupations can be changed relatively quickly by assignment or sub-letting in response to changes in the company's marketing policy, whereas the portfolio of an institutional investor is much more difficult to change without disturbing confidence in the fund. Ideally this should be changed by redirecting the annual inflow of funds rather than by a rapid restructuring of the stock of investment properties.

The portfolio may be physically diverse, a collection of properties meeting the client's functional needs in much the same way as plant or machinery. This must be distinguished from the compact urban estate which, at its most concentrated, is similar to an agricultural estate within its own "ring fence". Such estates in the private sector are normally of several hundred years standing, since they are now almost impossible to create without compulsory purchase powers. Very often they arose from the ownership of the land in its previous agricultural use prior to the urban growth of the 19th century, creating an opportunity for more than the aggregate management of a number of individual properties. The strict enforcement of covenants results in an environmental quality far higher than the most successful application of planning legislation by the local authority. Opportunities for marriage value will occur and in due course it may be feasible to carry out large-scale redevelopment.

Such an estate has a morphology consisting of phase of:

Pre-development
Development
Technical efficiency
Middle life
Old age
Refurbishment or redevelopment

Judicious expenditure by the owner on regular maintenance, improvement or change of use may freeze or temporarily reverse any one of these stages. Local planning policy in general and listed building legislation in particular can significantly affect the life of individual buildings or the estate. Other legislation such as the Leasehold Reform Act can challenge the whole integrity of residential estates.

As redevelopment or refurbishment comes closer, considerable thought is required in order to obtain the best return from the existing estate without causing any problems in respect of the implementation and phasing of the works of renewal.

Finally the portfolio must be managed in a manner consistent with the general ethos and role of the proprietary interests. There are many reasons, philanthropy, self-interest or pigheadedness, for not pursuing prudent estate management advice. It is the client's prerogative to disregard professional advice; it is the adviser's prerogative to give that advice, if necessary forcefully and frequently.

2.2.5 The Property

Since the management of individual properties accounts for much the greater part of time spent by surveyors in practising

estate management skills, these skills are the most highly developed. However, some property may be leased, some owner-
occupied and some held for investment purposes.

Each of these requires a different approach to both overall
management and detailed implementation of policy with the
support of an appropriate records system. If required, some
comparability can be achieved by making internal arrangements for owner-occupied property, such that the freehold is
held within the group/parent, and operating companies or
departments can be charged a market rent. A standard proforma for property records is unlikely to be able to capture,
in a convenient way, all the necessary information for each
of the three types of interests.

2.2.6 The Occupier

Assuming that the greater part of management is carried out
by or on behalf of landlords directly of occupying tenants, then
the surveyors have tended to create and perpetuate the myth
that estate management can be de-personalized, in a way rather
like that of the doctor trained not to get personally involved
with his patient. However, this does not imply that there is
not a real need to understand personal reactions, motivations
and responses in order effectively to manage the landlord's
interest. It is each individual tenant who is the real source
of rental income and the quality of the covenant; property
is merely the means by which we measure the quantum of
the liability.

The importance of tenant mix in achieving a balanced pattern of trading, and so a favourable investment yield on a shopping centre, is just one example of management of the occupier.
It is not just a matter of implementation of user covenants
but also of creating respect and mutual trust between landlord
and tenant. As service charges become an increasing proportion
of the cost of occupation, they have the capacity to use up
much of the time of managing agents on relatively minor and
occasionally frustrating disputes. The landlord's agent should
look for a good working relationship with the tenant, particularly as in some circumstances the covenant requires him to
make determinations between landlord and tenant.

In the field of housing, the occupier's needs are paramount.
Housing is a basic human requirement; there is therefore, an
obligation on society to take decisions at the highest level
on the standards to be achieved in housing and ensure that

those standards are met. Public and voluntary sector housing are so distinct in character, specialist in function and detailed in content as to be subjects in their own right. The powerful interventionist role of statute in protecting the position of private residential tenants is considered in Chapter 7 and can be contrasted with the provisions for tenants of commercial property in Chapter 6.

2.2.7 The Users

Quite apart from the tenant, many other persons may properly be upon the premises, clients and customers specifically invited, trade representatives, employees of specialist service companies with responsibilities for the maintenance of the building or equipment and officers of central or local government with rights of entry.

Over a long period, common law, more recently partly overtaken by statute law, has created duties on landlord and tenant for the physical and environmental safety of such visitors to property. In addition landlord or tenant may wish to influence the conduct or opinion of such visitors for property or trading purposes. The covered shopping centre creates a requirement for complex safety and security systems together with a wide range of services for the customers invited on to the premises. The same is true of transport interchanges or specialist recreational facilities such as historic houses with in excess of half-a-million visitors a year. Estate managers need to give more thought to the implications of their responsibilities as managers of facilities used by large numbers of the public.

These include:

An excellent knowledge of the practical implications of the relevant law. A well trained security staff on the private property.

The use of technology—
Closed-circuit TV,
Video recording,
Monitoring of all access points,
Environmental monitoring.
Regularly tested emergency procedures.

2.3.1 The Estate Management Process

The application of the general functions of management to urban estates can be seen as a process, the complexity of which, and frequency with which it is repeated, is appropriate to the nature of each individual estate. Lack of awareness of such a process does not mean that it is not occurring but that it may be occurring informally or in an *ad hoc* way. The smaller the estate the easier it will be to regard each decision as unique. That may make that decision easier but prevent the establishment of accepted procedures. The strong personalities of some proprietary interests may well feel threatened by the suggestion that each decision is not unique but capable of understanding and analysis within a structured process of management.

2.3.2 Strategy and Tactics

A written statement of some broadly based goals will enable the policy-makers to give emphasis and weight between these and so react to changes in underlying factors. The problems facing long-term planning have already been identified, so the estate manager, having received the strategy and advised upon its formulation, should anticipate and encourage its regular review.

Whilst there may be a unanimity of opinion by the estate owner, whether an individual, board or elected members, as to the goal or goals to be pursued, the estate manager has a more difficult task. Alternative tactics will exist, all of which can achieve that goal. For the balance of an investment portfolio can be changed in a variety of ways:

Change in pattern of new acquisitions
Disposals and new acquisitions
Refurbishment or redevelopment
Change of use of existing properties
Take-over of another portfolio

The time-scale involved may be the crucial factor in selecting the most appropriate tactic, together with a perception of the response of interested parties. The choice of the preferred tactic tests all the qualities of the estate manager; judgment, knowledge, technical expertise, financial acumen and personnel management.

2.3.3 Implementation

This is the field in which the estate management staff will have had most training and experience. If the selection of the preferred tactic is followed by a clear and concise brief, and assuming staff of reasonable technical competence are available within an organizational structure appropriate for the task then implementation should be the least difficult part of the process. It can be assisted by the availability of an estate management manual and access to specialist advice.

The content and regular review of the manual is a major function of the senior estates staff; it is common in the larger property companies, partnerships and public sector departments. The manual will set out standard statutory, contract and management procedures and identify sources of information for exceptions. The act of producing the manual and its regular review will provide senior staff with the opportunity to clarify their own approach. This text-book is not a manual, though it is hoped some of its content could assist senior staff in determining the type of manual and some of the content appropriate to their estate's needs. The sources from which specialist advice may be obtained can take many forms, but this is not just a matter of sources, it is rather one of adopting a positive approach to the problem-solving, and this is claimed to be one of the differences between the education of the graduate and those taking the professional examinations. Finally, the personal qualities of the staff involved must be stressed; considerable responsibility is devolved to individuals. Integrity and negotiating skill in discussion with those representing property interests and third parties can be developed through education and training but it must be said that to some it comes naturally and in others it is difficult to detect.

This implies a heavy responsibility on those in education to consider very carefully the real motivation of students whose entry to the profession is facilitated through university and polytechnic courses.

2.3.4 Control

Whilst the information contained in a regular system of reports is interesting, it is only useful when measured against some objective, either quantitative or qualitative performance criteria. Since control follows from delegation, the pattern of responsibility will indicate the necessary form of control. Information must be collected and then presented in such a form that the decision-maker can reach conclusions on action at various levels of both policy and implementation.

Martin in "Shopping Centre Management" concludes that

the most effective managers tend to be those who delegate (not abdicate) the administrative functions first and the human relations functions last.

The application of computer systems to estate management now offers the estate manager the opportunity to change the whole clerical system and is considered in Chapter 9. For as little as the cost of a reasonable motor-car, a mini-computer and printer can:

issue rent demands;
maintain clients accounts;
allocate and apportion service charges;
account for arrears;
operate a forward diary.

This can be done with a visible record to satisfy the most cautious of the staff in the accounts office. Problems can be identified quicker and performance be analysed in a more rigorous way. Information for regular review by policy-makers is more readily available and more work can be handled by the same staff. This does require a substantial commitment by the existing staff and considerable care is required in the way the concept, the technology and the system are introduced.

To summarize, the first two chapters have shown the historical development of estate management and the application of the broad functions of management to urban estates. Of the many features of estates, their economic rationale is more fundamental than any other characteristics, therefore the following chapters adopt this basis for their classification and more detailed study and analysis.

Sources and Further Reading

Allsopp, Management in the Professions, Business Books, 1979.
Thorncroft, Principles of Estate Management, Estates Gazette, 1965.
Ratcliffe, Urban Land Administration, Estates Gazette, 1978.
Martin, Shopping Centre Management, Spon, 1982.
Matthews, The Management Organization—Paper V in The Management of Urban Property, C.E.M., 1972.
Garnett, Motivating People in Professional Organizations, R.I.C.S. Annual Conference, 1979.
Glendinning, Management by Objectives in Local Government, Knight, 1973.
Readman, Fiscal and Economic Change—Britain on the Brink, R.I.C.S. Annual Conference, 1979.
R.I.C.S., Competition and the Chartered Surveyor, 1985.

Chapter 3

Private Sector Estates

3.1 Nature of the Estates

Estate management practice has developed within the private sector over several hundred years, but it is only over the last two decades that property has changed from a passive resource to a highly marketable commodity. The estates in which it is managed vary in size from Land Securities Investment Trust, with a portfolio valuation of over £2,000 million, to that of the small residential landlord. Their extent may be as diverse as that of clearing banks with a branch in every high street or as concentrated as a high value block in the City. Though they are diverse in terms of the type of property held and the legal status of the proprietary interest, there are a number of common features which unify private sector estates:

The use of financial criteria in measuring performance and the preparation of annual reports and accounts which have to fulfil minimum requirements. The introduction of accounting standards and the asset regulations of the professional bodies have introduced a discipline into the treatment of the fixed assets in these accounts.

Accountability to a defined group, in a company the shareholders, though in practice this may be one or two major institutions. In institutions, and particularly pension funds, some managers have adopted the approach of beneficent Victorian philanthropists in keeping the contributors and members ignorant of matters beyond their comprehension. The Wilson committee has made detailed recommendations on ways of improving accountability. The National Association of Pensions Funds has put pressure on its member funds to provide proper information for interested parties and the R.I.C.S. has prepared a guidance note on the valuation of pension fund portfolios.

Either liability to tax in some form on income and capital or exemption from tax, both situations significantly affecting the acquisitions policy and portfolio management.

Property may be the *raison d'être* of a private sector organization or just one of a number of resources which has to be marshalled and co-ordinated to carry out the trading activity. In a property company the management of the portfolio is the primary, indeed sole activity. In an Institution property is one of several alternative means of achieving the aims of the fund. In commerce and industry, very often occupying the Institution's investment portfolios, property is a cost to be kept as low as possible consistent with meeting the trading requirements.

Over the last few years there have been changes between these three main types of private sector estate owners. Firstly, Institutions have acquired significant blocks of shares in individual property companies; for example, Clerical Medical and General hold 24% of the shares of Brixton Estates, similarly the Prudential have a 7·7% holding in Land Securities. Secondly, individual properties move from one sector to another, the economic crisis of 1973/4 led to the destructive degearing of a number of property companies, whose assets were taken over by the Institutions. There is no clear information on the size of this change nationally, but a study of Bristol has shown a major change in the ownership of office developments completed between 1970 and 1978:

Funding/Ownership	as at date of development	as at 1978
Pension funds	18·5%	30%
Insurance companies	22·5%	43%
Contractors/property companies	41%	15%
Owner-occupiers	18%	12%

This represented almost three million square feet of space with a market value of £250 million. Much the greater part was developed to meet an assumed speculative demand, with over one million square feet completed in 1974. At the end of 1980 there was, for the first time since 1972, a shortage with rents of £5 per square foot. The pattern of occupation at that date was:

Public Sector	38%
Insurance and Financial	29%
Professional	7%
Other Commercial/Industrial	26%
	100%

By 1984 there was a temporary over supply with 1·5 million square feet available and rents at a plateau of £6 per square foot.

This can be compared with a survey of Reading by Richard Ellis in 1983, which showed a very similar pattern of occupation:

Public Sector	38%
Insurance and Financial	25%
Professional	12%
Other Commercial / Industrial	25%
	100%

In Reading, there was a relationship between the character of the occupier and the size of the unit:

SIZE	*MAJOR OCCUPIERS*
Under 10,000 ft²	— Professional
10,000 ft² to 20,000 ft²	— Financial and Insurance
20,000 ft² to 50,000 ft²	— Public Sector
Over 50,000 ft²	— Other Commercial/Industrial and Public Sector

This suggests that the Institutions are investing in themselves to a very significant extent. Further and perhaps more worrying, the insurance community is likely to be significantly affected by micro-processors, and there are indications of a steady fall in the aggregate space demands of the public sector. With 60% of the decade's demand coming from two users vulnerable to change, there is a case for examining, in a critical way, current designs for new office buildings.

3.2.1 The Institutions

The investment and portfolio management work of the Institutions is a matter of continuing discussion between stockbrokers, investment analysts and surveyors, both in-house and consultants. Most large London partnerships claim to act for at least 10 funds and the best known firms certainly each regularly act for well over 20 funds. This has some interesting implications. When the telephone rings and an investment proposition is considered and found acceptable, which fund acquires, or does it depend on who happens to be in the office that day? Alternatively it may well be in the interests of one of the funds managed by the firm to sell an investment and another to purchase, in order to improve the balance of both funds, but such a transaction may look just a little too neat.

Investment portfolio management represents only a small proportion of the total work of general practice surveyors, but it is almost certainly that part upon which they will be judged by other professions, and it is incumbent upon the profession to ensure that it has the technical expertise and intellectual rigour not only to take the right decisions but to demonstrate the validity of the assumptions upon which those decisions are based.

Property only has a role to play in Institutional investment in as much as it can "deliver the goods", that is to say, in the future produce an overall result equivalent to 2% over the yield on gilts to compensate for the property "hassle factor". Though some insurance companies such as the Norwich Union have had property portfolios since before 1950, the majority have emerged since the late 1960s and typically represent 10% to 15% of the overall portfolio. The management of the property portfolio cannot be seen in isolation; the property manager must involve himself in the overall objectives of the fund and in so doing contribute to general management. Acknowledgement of the merits of the acquisition of gilts when they are yielding 14% may enable him to speak with more strength when he feels the right moment has arrived for a major property acquisition.

A property portfolio may be analysed against a number of different criteria, using number of properties, capital value or rental value as the unit of comparison. Typical criteria include: type of property, type of tenants, age of buildings, tenure, location, pattern of rent-reviews, and distribution of value. There is no ideal balanced portfolio and even if it could be devised it would need to change. This would happen in any case as the relative values of the properties changed under market conditions. The following are some examples:

	Offices	Shops	Industrial	Agriculture
1972 average of the 7 largest property unit trusts	50%	17%	27%	0%
1972 poll of managers' most desirable portfolio	70%	20%	10%	0%
1982 Michael Laurie E.I.U. Index	56%	26%	18%	0%
1982 U.S.A. Pension Funds	56%	18%	25%	1%[x]

	Offices	Shops	Industrial	Agricul-ture
1983 D.T.C. Pension Funds	51%	23%	19%	7%[+]
B.H.S. average of 50 funds 1985	55%–65%	25%–35%	5%–20%	0%
B.H.S. most desirable portfolio 1985	30%–40%	30%–50%	5%–20%	0%

Note x residential
+ miscellaneous.

The desired shift between 1972 and 1985 from offices to shops is striking. The balance of the portfolio and its performance is developed further in Chapter 11, but possibly more important than the balance of properties making up the portfolio is the positive management of the portfolio, continually seeking out opportunities for increasing the return on the capital invested.

In looking for factors which demonstrate the difference in technique in the management of gilts, equities and property, the most obvious is the high value and individual nature of each property investment, but this can be overcome by investment through property unit trusts. A much more significant fact is the annual average rate of turnover of the three types of investment. In 1978 the annual turnover of property assets was around 2%, with equities at 11% and gilts at 81%. This is partly due to the costs of transfer but also to the different roles which each investment plays in the overall portfolio policy. Property interests also offer an opportunity for improvement, by means of judicious expenditure, changes in tenure and change of use.

Turnover Ratios

	Prop	Gilts	Equities
Pension Funds			
1980	1·5%	48%	11%
1983	3·2%	56%	22%
Insurance Cos			
1980	1·5%	79%	14%
1983	3·1%	76%	20%

Work for Institutional investors can be divided between acquisitions and increasingly disposals, and continuing portfolio management, both of which require the support of good records systems. Considerable folklore has become associated with the former as the pursuit of prime properties drove yields during 1979 to 10 points below the return of gilts. This demonstrates such a belief in an exceptional rate of rental growth for a long period of time, as to transcend most of the world's religions. The yields used can be justified by what is being paid in the market as a large amount of money chases a small amount of prime property. The shortage of prime properties is to some extent inevitable for if such property were readily available it would lose its scarcity factor. The relative decline of property companies means that they are unable to carry out sufficient development to meet the Institutions' requirements, and as a result Institutions have carried out developments themselves or in conjunction with property companies in whom they have a substantial interest. Other sources of investments include the purchase of the property assets of trading concerns through lease-backs, or the funding of a particular retailing organization's development programme, though this brings with it a covenant risk. The large shareholdings which Institutions have built up in property companies enable them to move to a take-over, transferring the properties from the equity holding to direct property investment. Such action may require some subsequent rationalization to obtain a balanced portfolio.

It is all a matter of confidence. The amount of property traded each year is such a small proportion of the stock that relatively slight changes in underlying factors have a magnified effect on the market in the small annual flow, and hence the valuation of the entire investment stock. Experience of 1973/4 and other periods of crisis has shown that the only time that large amounts of investment property are likely to come onto the market is when the market itself is depressed. At such a time asset valuations in the previous year's annual report by the most respected of City firms are of little more than historic interest.

In order to give scale to the general features of Institutions, some statistics have been gathered. They should be interpreted with the greatest of care, and the reader is advised to use the latest quarterly edition of Financial Statistics or a company annual report for any analysis. Changes in the market value of equities or gilts or property can result in what appear to be major changes in investment policy when in fact the underlying assets have changed very little. Government statistics are collected in terms of capital values, yet the most important feature for Institutions is income-flow, particularly projected income-flow in the medium-term. Little reliable published information is available on the balance of portfolio income-flows.

3.2.2 Insurance Companies

Apart from a few specialist companies, insurance companies are involved in a wide range of business interests. A substantial part of their business is in long-term liabilities and this is one of the justifications for property investment. The ten largest companies are identified below with information on the size of total funds in 1983 and, in order to demonstrate their links with property companies, an example of their larger holdings in publicly quoted property companies:

Insurance Co.	Total Funds	Property Companies
	£m	
Prudential	11,658	16% of Chesterfield
		8% of Land Securities
		5% of Beazer
Legal and General	5,507	13% of Greatcoat
		15% of London Prov Shops
Norwich Union	4,638	15% of Standard Securities
		10% of Land Investors
Commercial Union	3,187	
G.R.E.	2,463	Bid for Aquis 1984
Scottish Widows	2,291	—
Standard Life	2,229	24% of Hammersons
Eagle Star	1,816	5% of MEPC
		8% of Allied Securities
Sun Life	1,751	8% of Samuel Property
Co-op Insurance	1,411	10% of United Real

Note, total funds refer to life assurance and pension money only.

The largest insurance company, the Prudential had property assets of £2·5 bn in 1982 and a development and refurbishment programme of £200 million. This included 1.1 million square feet of industrial space and 0·6 million of office space outside Central London. During the year the company disposed of £200 million of assets in order to capitalize on marriage value and improve the quality of the portfolios. (This was part of a shift in the proportion of real property in the portfolio from 30% to 25%.)

At the same time small growing funds with a modest exposure in the direct property market formed a pool of potential purchasers. Such funds need to inject considerable property management expertise into tenurial and physical restructuring in order to justify the purchase.

To the extent that they hold shares in property companies and property is part of the asset base of all their other share holdings, Institutions have rather wider property interests than is suggested by the figures for their direct property port-folios:

Market Value of Long-term and General Funds (£m)

At end of year	Total funds	Direct property portfolio
	£m	£m
1976	29,949	5,584
1977	41,527	7,153
1978	46,829	9,244
1979	52,262	11,282
1980	65,262	13,642
1981	74,302	16,596
1982	96,099	17,545
1983	114,554	19,259
1984 net acq.	8,263	744
1985 Q1 net acq.	1,931	197

3.2.3 Pension Funds

Large pension funds are a recent phenomena and with their tax-exempt status and specific client orientation are a much more specialist type of organization than insurance companies. The nationalized industries, with very large numbers of employees, are now the major investors and there is evidence that the larger investors tend to have a greater proportion of property in their overall portfolio. Two factors influencing the overall investment policy are the age-structure of the members of the fund, which set up cyclical waves of pensions liability, and structural changes in the pensions industry due to legisla-tion or social change. The local authority funds consist of the County funds, in 1984 the largest included:

	Total	Property	Property
	£m	£m	%
G.L.C.	716	138	19
West Midlands	680	68	10
G.M.C.	686	93	14
Strathclyde R.C.	750	43	6

The abolition of metropolitan counties will have implications for these funds.

From 1974 their portfolio balance was restricted by a minimum requirement of 25% in gilts and a maximum of 25% in property and overseas investments combined. This was relaxed by statutory instrument in 1983, at a time when private sector funds were investing less in property in real terms than in previous years. Some of the smaller funds are too small to invest directly in property with a sufficient spread of risk and economy of management expenses and they invest via property unit trusts, including £130 million in L.A.M.I.T.

The other public sector funds are very different in character, with the majority of members represented by only seven funds, with assets at April 1984 of:

	Total	*Property*	*Property*
	£m	£m	%
National Coal Board	5,000	637	13
British Telecom	4,600	880	19
Electricity Supply	3,000	753	25
Post Office	2,750	571	21
British Railways	2,550	414	16
British Steel	2,150	613	29
British Gas	2,050	348	17

The private sector funds are much more diverse and include hundreds of individual companies' pensions schemes. The largest of these include, as at 1984:

	Total Funds	*Property*	*Property*
	£m	£m	%
British Petroleum	1,591	432	27
I.C.I.	1,656	253	15
Imperial Group	939	408	43
Lloyds Bank	1,013	134	13
Nat West Bank	1,408	239	17
Shell	1,540	275	18
Unilever	1,022	248	24

Unlike the statutory undertakers, no funds dominate the market and most of the funds are each less than £10 million in value. The smaller funds can only invest in property in a prudent and economic way through the property unit trusts rather than a directly held property portfolio.

Market Value of Funds (£m)

Local Authorities

At 31 March	Total Funds	Property U.T.s	Property
1978	3,867	115	159
1979	5,135	137	232
1980	6,890	172	387
1981	8,061	248	493
1982	11,358	343	613
1983	14,274	400	692
1984 net acq.	1,373	32	97
1985 Q1 net acq.	337	13	30

Other Public Sector

At end of year	Total Funds	Property U.T.s	Property
1978	10,582	186	2,305
1979	13,408	259	2,533
1980	15,505	289	3,448
1981	18,362	340	4,074
1982	23,964	337	4,676
1983	29,346	276	4,737
1984 net acq.	2,671	(1)	236
1985 Q1 net acq.	654	(11)	44

Private Sector

At end of year	Total Funds	Property U.T.s	Property
1978	20,253	594	2,394
1979	23,622	772	3,248
1980	31,543	916	4,374
1981	36,921	994	5,093
1982	48,869	1,270	5,244
1983	62,532	1,357	5,588
1984 net acq.	4,522	13	362
1985 Q1 net acq.	1,399	(17)	55

3.2.4 Property Unit Trusts

Property unit trusts are not available to the public, only to particular funds, and they enable small and medium-sized pension funds to have the benefit of investment in a balanced property portfolio. The four largest in 1977 and their portfolio size are set out below:

	1977 £m	1982 £m
Fleming	80	274
Hanover	46	94
Lazard	88	179
Pension Fund (P.F.P.U.T.)	157	254

The total value of Property Unit Trusts in 1982 was of the order of £1,700 million. A medium-sized fund is the aptly titled Property Unit Trust for Public and General Superannuation Schemes, whose portfolio value rose from £17·2 million in 1977 to £24·8 million in 1979. At that latter date its portfolio comprised: 33·1% offices, 22·5% agricultural land, 16·5% shops, 15·6% industrials and 12·3% cash. The agricultural element of the portfolio was much above that of Institutional funds in general.

The net sales of units (£m) in recent years are as follows:

	Pension Funds	Charities	Total
1976	59·2	0·6	59·8
1977	157·0	1·2	158·2
1978	95·4	0·9	96·4
1979	100·5	0·5	101·0
1980	112·5	0·6	113·1
1981	210·0	1·2	211·2
1982	58·0	1·0	59·0

3.2.5 Property Bonds

Property bonds are strictly an arm of insurance companies and have already been incorporated within the insurance company statistics. The largest, the Abbey Life Property Fund, had a value of £600 million in 1983. They have acquired a distinct character and to the extent that they permit the individual member of the public to invest almost directly in commercial property and reflect new marketing techniques by the industry, their importance is greater than their portfolio size might suggest. Legally they are insurance policies backed not by the traditional range of portfolio investments of insurance companies but solely by property. They also provide more detailed disclosure of their underlying assets than ordinary insurance companies. Devised in the late 1960s, only one failed in the 1974 crash and that fund has now re-imbursed bond-holders.

Recent annual reports of the funds have provided less information than they did some years ago. The funds managed by the Property Growth Assurance Company are amongst the most informative, and their agricultural fund offers a remarkable opportunity for individuals to invest in agricultural land. In 1981 this was backed by 46 farms occupying over 13,000 acres with a value of £16 million. The vast majority of the farms were within 50 miles of the Wash and committed to arable farming. Some 750 acres farmed in-hand with farming profits of £120 per acre going to the fund, 3,250 acres in partnership and the remainder let on tenancies with 3 yearly reviews in England and 5 yearly in Scotland. The company's commercial property fund stood at £36 million in 1981 and the property portfolio consisted of: offices 54%, shops 26%, and industrials 20%. Of all the tenancy agreements, 74% were on five-year reviews and 65% of the tenancies had a review in the period 1982 to 1984 inclusive.

In conclusion the 76 Bonds in existence in 1983 had a total value of approximately £1,500 million.

3.3.1 Property Companies

The more robust of the property companies, which does not necessarily mean the largest, had recovered from the 1973/4 crash by 1980 and began acquiring land for major new development and redevelopment projects. By 1983 the banks had outstanding loans to property companies of £3,300 million; as much as at the height of the crisis in the mid 1970s. Property companies are primarily either investment companies, developing in order to build up their own portfolio, or development companies, to whom land and buildings are stock in trade. In the former the properties are in the nature of capital, in the latter, trading stock. As a result the overall method of operation, funding, taxation and accounts will show a number of differences.

The sensitive nature of the development process can be seen in the more sophisticated project appraisal and feasibility techniques that are now being used. The projects have a long gestation period and construction works cannot commence until a series of critically interlinked preliminary phases have been completed. The most important aspect of the overall management of a property company is relating the characteristics of individual projects to the characteristics of the company. At its simplest this means that just because a development opportunity is likely to be sought after by the market as a whole its appropriateness for a particular company will depend upon the aggregate implications of projects to which the company is already committed, specifically, the size and balance of short- and long-term debt and the projected incomes within the portfolio over the next few years.

At the end of 1972 property companies were deeply committed to projects meeting an apparently unquenchable demand for investment properties, supported by valuations based on anticipated rents and funded by a profligacy generated by government and the banks. The economic crisis of 1973/4 coincided with what was already slowly being recognized as an over-supply in terms of potential occupiers. The painful process of re-adjustment took most companies five years and a few, including Town and City, suffered severely from the effects of destructive degearing with disposals and rental income being totally absorbed for ten years in restructuring the debt.

Movements in share prices tend to over-accentuate the realities, with sentiment reacting strongly to both changes in the factors underlying the profitability of property companies in general and the particular circumstances of individual companies. For example, one particular property can dominate a portfolio as was the case in 1977, when the valuation of Plantation House at the perhaps full figure of £51 million was the keystone to the re-financing of British Land. Rapid changes in share prices do not assist the general well-being of companies and both the strong and the weak can easily find themselves the subject of take-over bids by Institutions. The catalyst for this already exists in the substantial shareholdings which the major Institutions hold in nearly all quoted companies. Some Institutions have their own property companies. By their very nature these are not quoted companies but have grown to become a significant type of property company. During the 1970s four publicly quoted property companies went into liquidation and 38 were taken over by Institutions or other property companies.

3.3.2 Annual Reports

The annual reports of the publicly quoted companies demonstrate a varying degree of disclosure to shareholders and interested parties. Some show a positive attempt by the directors to give the real owners of the companies, the shareholders, a true and fair view of the state of affairs of their company. Few give as much information as that found in the annual reports of the property bonds but over the last few years more companies have provided, in addition to the statutory requirements, information on:

Portfolio analysis—user
       tenure
       geographical spread
       value bands
       rent-review projections
5 and 10 year summaries
Lists of major properties
Basis of valuation and depreciation
Shareholder analysis

The Chairman's report and the notes to the accounts offer opportunity for comment on key issues, such as the application of depreciation concepts, which have a more fundamental effect on property companies than other types of companies. The British Property Federation exists to enable the companies to lobby with one voice on matters which affect them generally such as depreciation and the widening impact of professional, national and E.E.C. guidance/directive on company and property matters.

A small proportion of company reports seem almost to take pleasure in failing to provide adequate information to the shareholders. One of the larger companies used to enter its properties at cost with no independent valuation and stated that its policy is to exclude the reversionary value of the portfolio. The auditors, by stating that the historical cost convention had been adopted, were then able to approve the accounts. The long overdue current cost accounting standard as amended for property companies, has corrected this, but one wonders at the motivation and responsibility of a small minority of those charged with the stewardship of publicly quoted property companies.

3.3.3 Property Company Analysis

Whilst the substantial aim of the text is the effective management of the individual properties in a portfolio, it would be wrong not to recognize that property companies are part of the equity market. Hence the proprietory rights in the aggregate portfolio, in the form of shares traded, is in the province of the stock brokers and their analysts. The distinguished financial journalist Michael Brett has considered this interface in detail in "Valuation and Investment Appraisal", edited by Clive Darlow, and Milnes has taken an accountant's view in "Property Company Accounts".

It is important to note that property shares tend to have a high P.E. ratio compared with other specialist equity sectors. In considering P.E. ratios, price is the market's reaction to events, whereas earnings (on an agreed basis) are closer to an accounting fact. Care is needed where earnings are influenced by an exceptional factor and share price is influenced more by expectations as to future earnings rather than historic accounts. In property valuation terms, P.E. ratio is a similar concept to Y.P.

The yield on a share, dividend: share price, is a similar concept to yield on a property, net rental income: capital value. The problem is that the route from the company's profit through to the dividend actually paid can be tortuous. As a result from year to year the dividend may be greater than, or less than the profits.

Property companies are perhaps unique in that they are backed by numerous assets which are of a tangible nature. Each asset is capable of being sold separately, and after deferred contingent tax payments as necessary, the aggregate net proceeds will (in theory) exceed the market capitalization. Laing and Cruickshank have estimated that between the start of 1983 and the end of 1984 the average discount to asset value fell from 37% to 21%, sufficient alone to increase share prices by 25% over those two years. You cannot, unlike rental income, buy anything with a capital valuation, until it is realized.

An analysis of any type of general trading company is incomplete unless a check is made upon it to establish whether beneath the figures there may be a latent and dormant potential property company. That is to say underperforming freehold and long leasehold property assets, which could be divorced from their operational user, without destroying the operational users activity as a viable general trading activity—in short what was once, perhaps unfairly, called asset stripping.

There are many Accounting Ratios which are calculated directly from the standard information found in the annual accounts of all companies. Their appropriateness and importance varies between the different specialist equity markets. One of the most important for property companies is the ratio of resources to debt, which may be considered in capital or revenue terms. Perhaps the simplest to consider in the balance sheet is capital valuation: debt ratio; if less than 1, then bankruptcy seems inevitable! Typically the ratio of debt: share-holders funds is a measure of the "gearing", indicating the extent of the exposure to risk. (To the extent that for all practical purposes Property Bonds, and Property Unit Trusts do not borrow money then their inherent stability is apparent).

The same principle may have more immediate effect on the profit and loss account, where the annual equivalents of debt and capital value, that is to say interest payments and net income respectively, can be compared.

It must be clearly understood that the relationship between capital and annual gearing is not symmetrical. Since variations in interest rate affecting variable rate loans or short term fixed interest loans result in changes in the annual interest payment, even though the capital debt is unchanged. Also, the refurbishment of a portfolio may reduce income due to voids and hence worsen the ratio, but this may be only a temporary, and welcome, indication of the improving quality of the underlying assets.

3.3.4 Case Studies

Land Securities and M.E.P.C. are the two largest property companies, with a substantial overseas portfolio. Some aspects of their annual reports can be compared to show:

	Land Securities March 1984	M.E.P.C. September 1983
	£m	£m
Book value of properties	2,188	1,120
Borrowings	265	363
Total income	138	102
Income before tax	84	65
Employees with salary in excess of £30,000	8	4

Portfolio Balance	Land Securities by capital	M.E.P.C. by capital	by income
offices	60·7%	58·3%	59·5%
shops	36·6%	22·6%	25·0%
industrial	2·7%	11·4%	13·4%

These two companies alone represent about one third of the total assets of all publicly quoted property companies and the largest 10 companies together represent about two thirds of the total assets of the 88 publicly quoted property companies. The significance of a few properties is apparent in M.E.P.C., where 5% of the properties, each worth over £5 million, account for 60% of the total value of the portfolio.

The following summary shows the effect of the turbulent 1970s on the key indicators of the financial profile of Land Securities.

	Independent valuation	Borrowings	Revenue
	£m	£m	£m
1971	682	364	36
1973	1,126	418	42
1975	916	463	49
1977	849	443	60
1979	1,187	335	76
1981	1,667	292	104
1983	2,027	283	131

The Grosvenor Estate illustrates the diversity of activities found within property companies. It consists of the West End estate, the Cheshire Estate, Grosvenor Estates Commercial Development, Ltd., and currently the most active part, the Vancouver-based Canadian Public Company Grosvenor International Holdings. All four of these exist to provide funds to support various family trusts; the majority of the income is, of course diverted to the Inland Revenue and tax-planning is as important as the feasibility and funding of individual schemes.

The West End estate consists of 100 acres of Mayfair and 200 acres of Belgravia, where a balance has to be struck between residential, office and shop use, having regard to the pressures of the Belgravia Leaseholders Association, the planning authority, in the form of Westminster City Council, and the estate's own aspirations, bearing in mind its experience of planning through leasehold covenants. The Cheshire estate is perhaps the most diverse, consisting of extensive agricultural interests in both farming and forestry, together with the Grosvenor Hotel and shopping precinct in Chester, developed jointly with Laings. This is an example of the work of Grosvenor Estates Commercial Developments Ltd., which exists primarily to develop sites not forming part of the traditional Grosvenor estate. Comprehensive shopping developments have been completed in a number of towns, pre-funded by major institutions:

Northampton	P.O.S.S. Fund
Runcorn and Chester	Sun Life
Lewisham	I.C.I. Pension Fund
Staines	B.P. Pension Fund

The shop portfolio comprises about two and a half million ft², this includes 150,000 ft² in Cheltenham and the Grafton Centre at Cambridge, which opened October 1983, providing 300,000 ft², including a department store of 100,000 ft², Site assembly was complex as the Kite area of Cambridge had a tortuous 20 year planning history.

The portfolio also contains around one million ft² of offices, and there is a growing involvement in industrial development on a 120 acre site at Gillingham, and an inner city site at Sheffield.

The overseas estate, originally based in Canada, now includes properties in Honolulu, Australia and California. The possibility of being able to invest overseas with a proven and known developer has not been lost on the U.K. institutions, to the mutual benefit of the estate and the pension funds who are now involved.

There is no doubt that the Grosvenor estate possesses numerous advantages; considerable in-house financial resources, which offer a first-class covenant, major historic land-holdings, experience and a reputation for good design. The extra ingredient is, according to Jimmy James, a trustee and previously surveyor and chief agent, one of the great secrets of estate management and it is, "to leave something on the table for the lessee so as to encourage him to spend money and involve himself in the property".

Property companies have tended to operate with a relatively small co-ordinating and accounting staff with the minimum amount of direct labour. Land Securities employ less than 400 full-time staff, of whom 60% are administrative or clerical. Leading London and Provincial partnerships are closely involved in all aspects of the companies' developments, in some cases acting as project managers. Much of the day-to-day management of tenancies is also carried out by these firms, against the trend in commerce and industry for in-house management. The companies have shown a remarkable resilience to the problems of the 1970s and seem likely to continue in a relatively stable state for the foreseeable future. One change that has occurred is a wider distribution of development risk, with Institutions accepting risk and in return receiving equity participation. The management of risk is now being approached in a more explicit way, applying sophisticated analytical techniques from areas of financial management.

3.4.1 Commerce and Industry

The largest area of growth for the employment of surveyors over the last few years has occurred through the creation and expansion of in-house estates departments in trading companies. Employment sector statistics of chartered surveyors show:

	1973	1984
Private practice	48%	45%
Public sector	30%	25%
Commerce	9%	15%
Retired	13%	14%

The main types of trading companies are retail chains, financial services, manufacturing including food processing, and the complex brewing, catering hotel and leisure industry. An interesting development has been the formation of the Association of Corporate Real Estate Executives (A.C.R.E.) which consists of representatives from 25 of the leading companies across a wide range of commercial and industrial activities. The Multiple Shops Federation has existed for many years and has been active in property matters, particularly rating, but its range of membership is narrow compared with that of A.C.R.E. A Property Managers Association (P.M.A.) has also been formed by the surveyors of some medium-sized retail/wholesale companies.

Both Jenkins and Wheeler have reached similar conclusions on the factors leading to the emergence of in-house estates departments and the distinctive character of the work, balancing and integrating property decisions within the overall objectives of the trading company. Broadly, the reasons for the creation of estates departments are all associated with the growth of the company. In smaller companies the finance director or company secretary is usually responsible for property matters, from time to time instructing surveyor on an *ad hoc* basis to advise or act in respect of property matters. As the company grows in size and the personalities of key individuals develop, one or more firms is likely to be called upon in a more regular way to advise upon both property aspects arising from the growth of the company and its existing property interests. At this stage the company will be handling quite a large number of documents relating to its property. More complex issues beyond the experience of existing administrative staff are presenting themselves and property matters are a subject of daily discussion at a senior level in the company. As the company matures, more significant legal interests are taken in premises from which the company operates, and property represents a growing proportion of the net assets of the company, subject to detailed accounting standards. Further expansion is only possible by the take-over of existing companies or diversification into other areas of activities, requiring different types of property from that traditionally occupied by the company. At this stage it will be possible to justify the appointment of an estate manager on grounds of both the fees being paid to consultants, the quality of work and need for informal advice within the company. The problem is finding an individual with the range of experience and personal qualities to fill this role previously carried out by a professional practice. As the company expands further, the estates department grows and acquires the breadth and depth of a professional practice.

In large companies, particularly multiple retailers, a complete organization can be formed consisting of architects, quantity surveyors, property managers and other specialist staff, creating a multi-disciplinary team able to design layouts and bring into use new units in the least possible time within the fast moving retail market.

The estate managers in commerce and industry presents something of an enigma to the profession. Clearly they are making their mark in terms of numbers, levels of responsibility and involvement in corporate management. In 1983 R.I.C.S. statistics showed that 9% of the G.P. Division worked in commerce or industry, excluding Property Companies where a further 3% were to be found.

During 1980 G.K.N., Britain's largest international engineering group, created a property department and advertised for a manager at c. £20,000. Many estates departments created in the last few years are now headed by senior executives who contribute to the management of the whole trading enterprise and frequently report to a property director. In 1982 an Imperial Group subsidiary advertised for a Director of Property Development at c. £30,000, requiring creativity and an entrepreneurial approach to exploit the assets to the full.

The growth of these departments can only be at the expense of some private practices who adopt a somewhat ambivalent attitude, very pleased to be instructed but aware that however good a job they think they do, as circumstances change, the instructions may be transient. As companies are taken over or merge, or as departments change, so the work may expand or disappear over-night. These departments in representing major multi-national clients are the patrons of many large practices who carry out substantial work on their behalf as retained surveyors. Whilst in many of the relationships both parties are very satisfied with the arrangements, it is quite common to hear private practice criticize in-house departments for being over-staffed and out of touch and for the departments to express considerable concern about delays in their retained surveyors' reports and excessive fees.

Surveyors in commerce and industry tend to deal with a specialized type of property, most marked in the licensed trade, but require a breadth of knowledge in order to assess the impact of the whole range of factors which affect their premises, though the operational requirements of their employer can limit the implementation of what might otherwise be quite prudent estate management objectives. In acting for a single client, in aggregate they represent many of the tenants who occupy the investment portfolios of the institutions, hence their perception of property as a cost to their business is very different from that of the insurance companies and pension funds.

There has been some suggestion in the past of undue emphasis on investment and development both in practice and in professional and academic examinations to the detriment of the interests of corporate owners and occupiers. The introduction in 1982 of a management component into the final examinations of the R.I.C.S. and the growing interest in the profession in the formulation and implementation of positive management for operational estates shows this is no longer the case.

3.4.2 The Tasks

The two main activities of the in-house estates department are acquisiton/disposal and day-to-day management. The programme of acquisitions, or in some cases development, is derived from the corporate trading strategy. This is extremely important for companies in direct contact with the public, where site selection influences turnover and physical appearance contributes to the company's identity in the eyes of the public.

The property department's knowledge of the property market and alternative means of financing acquisitions and development will make a significant contribution to the overall profitability of the company. Close liaison to the marketing department is essential in order to get the best value from the property market commensurate with trading needs. For a surveyor who wishes to develop his career with a company, an involvement in trading or general management may be the only way open, though relatively few choose this route. The property itself may be owner-occupied or rented and within a large company there will inevitably be some lettings of accommodation retained or sub-let for various reasons. Much of the regular management work will consist of rent-reviews, renewal of leases, maintenance, rating and the growing number of administrative responsibilities attached to the occupation of property.

This will require an efficient records system, which is not just a passive store of information but is able to make a positive contribution to the overall management of the company. As portfolios increase in size and lease terms become more complex, the rise in the total cost of employing reliable clerical staff and fall in cost of micro-processors will result in companies introducing computerized record systems. Company annual report now include much more information on property; the accounting standards on current cost accounting and depreciation together with Assets Guidance Notes prepared by both the R.I.C.S. and I.S.V.A. represent a major additional task for the property manager, who will be concerned to obtain the highest quality of mandatory and discretionary property information provided in the annual report.

The internal surveyor can be put under pressure by the company, contrary to his professional judgment. For example, under current cost accounting, the depreciated replacement cost can often give a higher figure than market value for semi-specialized assets. It may suit the company to instruct the internal surveyor to adopt a basis against the advice he offers, which could give rise to an interesting situation on a subsequent external valuation. It will certainly test the qualities of the internal surveyor, who should discuss this with his professional body.

The means by which the estate management function can make a proper contribution to corporate management will depend partly on the formal pattern of responsibility between senior executives and directors and partly on the way in which property works for the company. In some companies, the property is held in the group and internally charged market rents enable the management to see each site as a profit centre. This can have embarrassing results when a site manager insists that the group surveyor has fixed too high an internal rent and threatens to instruct an agent to act against the group surveyor on behalf of his own profit centre.

3.4.3 In house or Consultants?

It is unusual to find an estates department which carries out every aspect of the management of the company's property. The reasons for this will be partly the way in which the company and its estates department have developed over the years, and there is seldom a conscious review of the allocation of tasks within and outside the company. However, there is some general agreement on the factors which result in the employment of consultant surveyors, either on an *ad hoc* basis or in a retained capacity:

The geographical spread of the portfolio may be such that it would be financially inefficient to deal with some or all the properties from one office.

Certain specialist skills may be required infrequently and it is unrealistic to expect staff to have that expertise.

The cost of obtaining the keeping up-to-date the range and quality of certain types of market evidence and information may be beyond the scope of an in-house estates department.

In certain circumstances an external report or valuation may be better for the particular task that has to be undertaken. Strictly, it may appear better in the eyes of third parties, whether it is intrinsically better or worse is another matter.

The quality of work involved, or the speed with which it must be done, may be quite outside the capacity of the size of the establishment.

A commercial market fee basis which may be used to price the "value added" of the estates department.

The estate manager will therefore be closely involved, probably with a director, in the agreeing some general policy on the selection and appointment of external surveyors. Quite apart from the work they do, there is no doubt that contact between internal and external surveyors benefits the internal surveyors through discussion with fellow professionals with experience of property aspects of a number of different companies. The external surveyors, particularly if operating on a retained basis, need to seek out means of obtaining a close contact with the client and his business. All industries seem to have their own technical press, and a day spent reading the last few months of the trade journal will immediately alert the external surveyor to the trade issues likely to affect the management of the company's property interests. One of the criticisms made of external surveyors is that they have difficulty in accepting the relevance of the questions being asked and the service role of property within a corporate trading organization. A problem facing retained surveyors on their appointment is digesting the mass of property records which have been arranged in a system for the company's use in a form not very helpful for the retained surveyors. This can only be overcome by assistants spending several weeks on the extraction of information. It is essential to obtain the enthusiastic co-operation of the one or two key "moles" in the company who are a mine of information on the background to the property and plant. The agreed fee basis for retained surveyors will be significantly less than for individual *ad hoc* instructions, particularly on the larger higher-value units of occupation.

3.4.4 Trading Companies

Classification of the types of companies involved is not easy; the only formal national groupings are the Multiple Shops Federation, A.C.R.E. and P.M.A. As a general principle the closer the activities of a trading company are to the public, the more important is the selection of sites and the physical quality of the accommodation and such property will be readily marketable. The less contact a company has with the public, the less important is the siting of the property which will tend to have the character of assets valued on the depreciated replacement cost basis. Further, the "faster" or more fashion-conscious the trade, the more likely it is that premises will be leased rather than owner-occupied.

Of the four categories identified earlier in 3.4.1, the retail chains are perhaps the most distinctive and most sensitive to location. Thus their property is a fundamental factor underlying both turnover and profits and due to the high value of the units, those companies with a significant number of freeholds find property represents most of their net assets. In 1982 Marks and Spencer's portfolio stood at over £1,000 million and Sainsbury's at £438 million. Major changes have occurred within the retail chains; units are getting bigger and smaller units are being closed. In order to grow, large companies have had to diversify, not always successfully, and one-stop, edge of town shopping is being taken very seriously.

Some of these points can be illustrated in the pattern of trading and type of stores occupied by Tesco, with a property portfolio worth £426 million in 1981. Between 1977 and 1982 the company spent £440 million on expansion and closed 273 small stores which made some contribution to the cost of the development programme.

Tesco also entered into sale and leasebacks on stores at:

Acton	
East Grimstead	
Gloucester	
Leamington	With Royal
Lowestoft	Insurance
Newbury	in 1980
Penzance	for £21·43 million
St. Albans	
Southend	
Yeovil	

Bishops Stortford	
Dorking	With Civil
Hove	Aviation Pension
Ipswich	Fund in 1982
Kings Lynn	for £6·435 million
Lymington (2)	

The following table shows the shift in emphasis from small to large units by number of shops and percentage of the total net sales area:

	Under 10,000 ft²		10,000 ft²– 25,000 ft²		over 25,000 ft²	
	No.	%	No.	%	No.	%
1973	664	60	102	36	6	4
1975	616	51	113	38	16	11
1977	562	43	121	35	32	23
1979	401	33	123	33	47	34
1981	337	25	151	35	66	40
1982	313	23	156	35	75	42

In 1985 Tesco announced plans to add about ½ million ft²
of new selling space each year by opening 12–14 superstores
a year at an annual cost of £200 million.

Larger units can be obtained over a period of years in established shopping streets by buying in adjacent interests and
refurbishing in stages or, as major shopping centres are developed, paying the market rent and getting the best pitch available, or fighting a way through the planning minefield to open
a new store on the edge of town with substantial carparking.
This is an example of the need for very close co-operation
between the estate manager and the trading team as a strategy
is developed for the best allocation of funds between the competing projects. Taken to the limit, the edge-of-town development results in a hypermarket with 100,000 ft² of sales and
parking for up to 2,000 cars as developed by Carrefour or the
Brent Cross shopping centre, demonstrating a unique combination of site, size, quality and catchment area. This challenge
to the traditional High Street, coupled with a severe price
war and exceptionally high prices being paid by occupiers and
Institutions for the few 100% pitches that become available
forced more independent retailers out of business.

Events at Woolworth during the early 1980s demonstrate
the ebb and flow in the retail trade as they sold properties
and purchased companies in order to restructure its pattern
of trading.

The old management with a portfolio valued in 1982 at £484
million started selling stores in 1982, which realized £27 million. The following year 17 were sold, realizing £36 million.
At the start of 1984 about a dozen large stores were available
in the market and about 20 smaller stores, the largest such
as the stores at Liverpool or Edinburgh each worth a figure
approaching £10 million. During the year 32 stores were sold
to the Heron Corporation for £50 million, who undertook a
break up. Two other stores including Oxford Street were sold
for £20 million and a further 30 were on the market. At the
end of that year the group was trading from about 860 stores.

During the same period they made a substantial advance
into D.I.Y. by the purchase in 1982 of Dodge City and B and
Q, providing over 100 units with a floor area of 2·5 million
ft². This was followed in 1984 by the purchase of Comet, by
outbidding Harris Queensway. B and Q was the largest D.I.Y.
retailer in 1985 with 160 units providing 4·6 million ft². In
order to grow, retail groups have embraced retail warehouse
locations and whilst initially regarded with suspicion by the

Institutions by 1983 they were prepared to fund such schemes. The operators fall into two main groups; D.I.Y., such as W. H. Smith Do-It-All, and Great Mills Superstores (a subsidiary of R.M.C.) and Furniture and Furnishings dominated by M.F.I., with 122 stores and Queensway with 84. The latter group require prominent units of 30,000 to 40,000 ft² with a minimum of 60 car spaces. (A further group which tend to be in inner city locations are stores, such as Comet, selling electrical goods.)

The fundamental change taking place in retailing in the mid 1980s is demonstrated by the out of town link between Tesco and Marks and Spencer. Also Sainsburys have linked with British Home Stores and in 1985 A.S.D.A. and M.F.I. combined, enabling them to trade out of 8 million ft², they were reported to be seeking a further 100 stores. If this momentum were to continue to the second half of the decade, the resulting retail parks will raise questions as to the future role of many traditional High Streets. Linking the retail sector and the financial services sector, the impact of the building societies is apparent in every High Street. Many societies have doubled the number of branches during the 1970s, often using vacant bank premises which were surplus to requirements following the mergers which resulted in the four main joint stock banks. Whereas the banks are subject to the Companies Acts, the building societies are subject to different requirements and revaluations of assets happen infrequently, though new legislation is expected in 1986. The property assets of the four main banks and the last complete or partial revaluation date are set out below:

	The Bank	The Group
	£m	£m
Lloyds (1981, 2, 3)	439	673
Barclays (1982)	624	1,095
Midland (1983)	413	960
National Westminster (1981)	825	1,058

In terms of the number of units in their estates, each of the banks, with around 3,500 branches and other ancillary accommodation, occupy a large estate. Typically 80% of the value of their assets are attributable to freeholds. The estates are relatively static, with a small number of disposals arising from the slow rationalization of the estate following the mergers of the late 1960s. Due to the specialist nature of bank occupation, the costs of fitting out and equipment are high, much of this expenditure will be the responsibility of the premises department.

The building societies, unlike the banks, conducted a major expansion programme in the late 1970s and early 1980s. In 1979 the Halifax, the second largest society, opened 21 new branches; the Leeds, the fifth largest society, opened 43 new branches, and in 1978 the Nationwide opened 52 new offices. Each of these societies then had about 400 branches. Judging by the annual reports, revaluations seem something of a rarity, though a book-cost of between £40 million and £50 million seemed quite typical for each of their portfolios. Unlike banks, who have more ancillary operations to utilize the floors over banking halls, the building societies operate from the ground floor unit. Those that have pursued a freehold portfolio have become landlords in respect of the occupation of the upper floors and some societies have in this a substantial income, of a similar character to property investment companies. The building societies seem very aware of the significance of their sites for advertising purposes and it is possible that the high prices paid for premises can partly be justified on the grounds of advertising hoardings and of keeping the other people out, though this is not a recommended method of valuation. The expansion slowed down in the mid 1980s, and as a result of mergers some societies closed more offices than they opened.

The manufacturing sector, including the food processing industry, is the least site sensitive of the four major sectors and accounts for about half of the membership of A.C.R.E., including: Courtauld, G.E.C., Imperial Foods, Dunlop, Reed, Unilever (and hopefully I.C.I.). The estates are relatively static, growth only occurring on the take-over of other companies and the occasional major new manufacturing plant. Due to technical change, large obsolete premises have to be sold, presenting difficult valuations and marketing problems, quite apart from the social implications in a town where the company employed several hundred staff.

Most of the modern warehousing premises on industrial estates used by the companies for distribution purposes are owned by Institutions, almost all the rest of the property is owner-occupied, and costs in one form or another are the basis for management work. Much of the management work is concerned with maintenance, repair, adaptation and new building. Sites are developed more and more intensively, since this means greater productivity from the fixed assets, often resulting in poor circulation and different types of buildings with varying lives. As technical processes develop, requiring large plant, parts of the site may be re-developed several times. The character of the asset being totally different from general purpose office buildings and warehouses, the estate management process is more a physical than a financial task. Property records emphasize costs and maintenance programmes with none of the complexity of leases and property is not central to the over-all profitability of the enterprise.

Unilever is one of the world's largest groups, employing 275,000 staff in 75 countries, and in 1983 £572 million of capital works were approved. Their accounts show land and buildings at £849 million, whereas plant and machinery was £1484 million. I.C.I. employ 120,000, over half in the U.K., with land and buildings of £1,106 million (ignoring oil concessions) and plant and machinery of £4,952 million. There are two significant points: firstly, the way plant and machinery dominates property is a clear sign of an owner-occupied estate, and secondly, within the context of the overall accounts, there is a somewhat disinterested view of property.

It is in this sector that the assets guidance notes have created particular new tasks for the in-house estate manager. Many of the properties will be specialist, requiring a depreciated replacement cost approach for entry in the balance sheet. Patently they will have a limited life and this can be shown most clearly with buildings associated with the extraction of minerals, which have a proven reserve and hence rate of use. As current cost accounting replaces historic costs, the estate managers will have to review his approach to work for the balance sheet, though great comfort can be gained from the accountant's concept of materiality, which is concerned with the sensitivity of the final figure to changes in the components.

The licensed, hotel and catering and leisure sector exhibits the particular feature of the trade and the property assets combining to create a site-sensitive goodwill. A brewery sell their product in two markets—licensed houses and off-licences, and the closer the brewery comes to a 100% monopoly of the trade outlets, the less incentive there is to spend any money on improving the property, since any additional custom will be drawn from another of the company's houses. Thus the only sites worth developing are in areas where the brewery has little representation. Similarly the major respresentation will fight such an application for a licence with considerable vigour. Watney Mann and Truman, which is part of Grand Metropolitan, operates 7,000 public houses and 7 breweries, with 30 depots in strategic locations.

Turnover rents are common for public houses with banded percentages and deficiency payments, and this results in complex agreements, requiring the support of a comprehensive property records system. The estate manager must be sensitive to a number of special features:

The vertical integration of the brewing business and the complex problems of relating the large single-site manufacturing process and distribution system to the individual landlords.

The weekly, monthly and annual cash-flow budgets of the licensed trade creating a short-term trading position which is difficult to relate to the longer-term view of property as an asset providing future growth.

The significance of the personality of the management of the licensed premises, with the ability to render ineffective the most carefully prepared property analysis of the situation.

At the same time the estate manager, with his knowledge of the area, may be able to contribute information and analysis on the medium-term trade potential within the area and so influence the changes that occur within what is usually an old-established licensed estate.

The growth of a recognizable leisure sector, potentially capable of analysis is a recent phenomena, an approach to classification is as follows:

Urban (intensive)
  Squash
  Swimming
  Skating
  Snooker   In various combinations as sports centres
  Tennis
  Gym
  Dance

High Street
  Amusement centres
  Betting
  Bingo

Rural (extensive)
  Golf
  Holiday centres

Caravan / Camping
Marinas
Country parks
Leisure / Theme parks
Sporting (hunting, shooting, fishing)
Endeavour recreation

Spectator
  Racing
  Team competitions   } Stadiums
  Museums
  Heritage property   } Buildings

Provision is by a highly complex range of alternatives based upon the private, public and voluntary sectors, but in the context of this chapter, the management of the above by the first mentioned sector, will have particular regard to:

Smoothing of user by market segmentation and differential pricing to avoid peaking.
Multiple, non conflicting user.
Design for minimum staffing levels.
Monitoring of staff performance, user, revenue and expenditure to determine an optimum relationship.
The use of concessions to provide specialist facilities.
The balance between theme and supportive activities.
Visitor / user / friend / customer / member identification and marketing techniques.

Intensive problems are being encountered in the valuation and appraisal of such properties in distinguishing the trade element, dependent as it is upon business management, from the property element.

3.5 Personal and Special Capacity

Individuals hold interests in land and buildings, other than private domestic dwellings in various forms; shares in private property companies, partnerships, sole traders and various trusts. The estate manager will advise on the most convenient and tax-efficient form in which the property should be held, having regard to the long-term aims of the owners. Individuals are particularly aware of the impact of taxation, due to the directness of its effect, and in order to mitigate tax liabilities, transactions, projects and the receipt of income may be arranged in an economically inefficient way so as to obtain the greatest net-of-tax return. Despite advice, recommendations may not be accepted, due to the owner's expectations, and elements of inertia and uncertainty can offset the opportunities for positive management. Decisions can be delayed until the company or family unit are forced to take action, for example, when business assets are still held by the retired generation of a family business on whose death capital transfer liabilities are created which could easily have been avoided.

Special legal status can be attached to the management of the estates of companies or individuals. When a company falls to ill health then the responsibility for the management of the company may be formally removed to parties with that special legal status.

A receiver may be appointed under the Companies Acts by a debenture holder who wishes to have control of a company in order to obtain repayment of the outstanding debt. Once appointed though the directors stay in office, their powers are suspended for the period of the receivership, and the company may be able to continue to trade.

The above must be distinguished from the role of a liquidator whose raison d'être is the termination of the company's existence. This may arise under a voluntary winding up; here a majority of the directors must make a statement that the company will be able to pay its debts within 12 months, the shareholders then appoint a liquidator, where upon the directors have no power over the company.

Alternatively the creditors or shareholders can petition the court to make a receiving order. If the court is satisfied that the debtor has no substantial defence then a receiving order is made and the Official Receiver takes control. This can be followed by:

A statement of affairs by the debtor
Meeting of creditors
Appointment of a special manager of the Company
Public examination of the debtor
An adjudication order

After which the debtor's property passes to his trustee in bankruptcy and the debtor incurs the disqualifications of a bankrupt. A trustee may within 12 months of his appointment seek leave of the court to disclaim a lease entered into by the bankrupt.

The type of skill and judgement that is required was illustrated in the property market following the crash of 1974. Too active marketing of the assets of many property companies would have further depressed values generally, and the leading accountancy practices and surveyors involved in this work were able to show creditors that a steady and orderly marketing of companies and assets was in the best interests of all the parties.

The death of individuals results in the operation of the functions of personal representatives whose duties are principally to:

Gather together and realize the assets of the deceased, and make any necessary investments.

Pay the debts of the deceased, the administration expenses and the Capital Transfer Tax

Distribute the balance amongst the beneficiaries according to the terms of the Will or the rules of intestacy.

Personal representatives may be either executors appointed under the Will, or in the case of those who died intestate, administrators whose appointment arises when letters of administration have been granted. The powers of management of personal representatives are set out in section 39 of the Administration of Estates Act 1925. As a result surveyors may be instructed to advise upon valuation for capital transfer tax purposes and the appropriate method of disposal for property.

Trustees may be appointed in many different circumstances by:

The settlor,

The beneficiaries',

A person granted that power by deed or under the Trustee Act 1925,

The court.

The surveyor may be involved in acting as a trustee or taking instructions from trustees of several district types:

Personal representatives acting as trustees.

A family trust.

A trust for sale as the vehicle for managing joint ownership.

A charitable trust.

A wide range of statutory powers are given to trustees by the Trustee Act 1925, including under section 23 the right to appoint solicitors, bankers, surveyors and similar agents; and under the Law of Property Act 1925, section 29 which allows trustees for sale of land to delegate their powers to solicitors, accountants, surveyors and other agents.

68	*Estate Management Practice*

The investment power of trustees are prescribed as to those securities in which they are permitted to invest under the Trustee Act 1961 and any other securities specifically author- ized in the trust deed, as a result the power to invest in real property is limited; though trustees for sale of land are given power under the Law of Property Act 1925 to buy land with proceeds and capital money under the Settled Land Act 1925 may be used to purchase freeholds or leaseholds with more than 60 years unexpired.

Changes in the law governing the rights and duties of trus- tees and personal representatives were recommended in 1982 in the 23rd report of the Law Commission including all trustees being able to buy freehold or leasehold investments (but not development properties), subject to obtaining appropriate pro- fessional advice.

In acting in a special capacity or advising such a client, the surveyor will only be able to provide the best service to a client if he has a clear appreciation of the powers, duties and con- straints attached to the legal status. A request to study the formal documents creating the status may initially receive a rather surprised reaction but in almost every case, the client will see the importance of receiving advice in the correct context. It will also demonstrate the need for close liaison between solicitors, accountants and surveyors in adopting a co-ordinated approach to the estate.

Sources and Further Reading

Darlow, Valuation and Investment Appraisal, Estates Gazette, 1983.

Davey, Profile of a Faceless Landlord, C.S., January 1979.

Financial Statistics, Government Statistical Service, H.M.S.O., quar- terly.

Hanson, The Form and Content of Property Company Reports, The Valuer, Jan./Feb., 1978.

Jenkins, The Role of the Property Manager, The Management of Urban Property, C.E.M., 1972.

Jenkins, Whence the Chartered Surveyor as a Professional Advisor, Keynote address, R.I.C.S. Annual Conference 1984.

Massey and Catalano, Capital and Land, Edward Arnold, 1978.

Milner, Property Company Accounts, The Institute of Chartered Accountants, 1978.

Mintel Retail Intelligence Report on Shopbuilding, Sites and Rents, Annual.

Money into Property, Debenham, Tewson and Chinnocks, Annual.

National Association of Pension Funds' Year Book, Annual.

Penfold, Doing What Comes Naturally for the Grosvenors 251 E.G. 846.

Pension Funds and Their Advisers, Annual.

Plender, That's the Way the Money Goes, Deutsch, 1982.

Property Companies' Financial Data, Estates Gazette, Weekly.

Review of the Functioning of Financial Institutions, Wilson Committee, H.M.S.O., 1980.

The Office Market in Bristol, Richard Ellis / Lalonde, 1979.

Westick, Property Valuation and Accounts; The Institute of Chartered Accountants, 1980.

Wheeler, A Property Manager in a Commercial Trading Company, R.I.C.S. Annual Conference, 1979.

Will Local Authority Pension Funds Now Buy More Property, CS, 13.1.83.

Chapter 4

Public Sector Estates

4.1 Introduction

Public sector estates have grown as the role performed by the public sector has developed, particularly over the last 35 years. The estates can be distinguished from those of the private sector by a structure of accountability to the public through various officers responsible directly or indirectly to elected members, and by the specialized nature of a substantial part of the estate which meets social and public needs. The predecessors of some of to-day's local authorities built up substantial urban estates over several hundred years, most notably the Corporation of the City of London. Whereas the Land Authority for Wales, which was only created in 1975, as essentially a land trading organization, already holds nearly 1,000 acres of development land.

The public sector estate extends to almost one fifth of the area of the U.K. No comprehensive asset valuation has ever been attempted, but due to the area occupied by the Forestry Commission, its value is undoubtedly very much less than that proportion of the surface area. Central government occupies about 8% of the total area, and much of its non-forestry estate is managed by the Property Services Agency.

Local authority estates cover 7% of the surface area, the majority of which is used for housing purposes. Nationalized industries occupy 2·5% of the surface area, most of this being the operational land of transport and public utilities. Lastly, various conservation and specialist agencies of the QUANGO type occupy a further 1·5%.

As at, 1985, R.I.C.S. statistics showed a total of 5,500 general practice surveyors employed in the public sector. About 2,200 were employed in central government including 1,850 in the office of the District Valuer and Valuation Officer of the Inland Revenue, concerned with specific valuation work rather than estate management, and most of the remainder working in the Property Services Agency. About 2,700 were employed in local government, the G.L.C. estates department accounting for about 10% of the total. A further 600 worked in the nationalized industries and various statutory bodies.

71

There is some similarity between public sector estates and the estates of commerce and industry, for each provides a service to enable the occupier/owner to carry out their primary, non-property-orientated activity. Urban land for public sector purposes tends to be acquired well ahead of perceived need, and even when land has been acquired there has been a history of delayed starts to capital programmes. Due to demographic changes and technological developments, some needs have changed quite dramatically. Land acquired for schools in the early 1970s is not needed, due to the fall in the birth rate, North Sea gas has resulted in obsolete gas works in inner city areas, and the changing strategic situation permits the disposal of surplus defence lands.

The estates function within the operational estates of the public sector (and perhaps also commerce and industry) was summarized by the Chief Works Officer in the D.H.S.S. in 1980 as:

Describing the size and nature of the land and buildings required for the delivery of health care.

Acquiring and disposing of property as circumstances require, within the procedures of the estates manual and approvals system.

Using and maintaining the estate while it is required for health care.

Complying with all statutory and legal requirements.

Doubts have been raised as to the vigour with which statutory authorities review their land needs and the speed with which surplus land has been marketed. There are several reasons for this, a natural inertia against disposals, and in the past various time-consuming administrative procedures had to be completed. Some elected authorities have as a matter of policy pursued the acquisition of land within their area. The Conservative government elected in 1979 saw property not just as a necessary resource for performing the functions of government but as a valuable asset capable of providing funds for the public sector. The ways individual public bodies interpreted and reacted to the policy was influenced by political aspects, the character of the estate and the balance between the merits of freehold and leasehold disposals. Many of these same issues were raised in a different context in local government under the Community Land Act 1975. There is a growing entrepreneurial philosophy within public sector estates, which together with changes in their management and administration have made them much more responsive to change.

4.2 The Property Services Agency

The P.S.A. was formed in 1972, but its constituent parts had existed for several hundred years. Over the years small discrete central government estates had been amalgamated; the Ministry of Public Buildings and Works was formed in 1963 and this became part of the Department of the Environment on its formation in 1970. Outside advice was taken on how to structure the physical resources of land, buildings, supplies and the supporting technical staff. It was agreed to set up a semi-autonomous agency within the D.O.E. with substantial managerial freedom in its day-to-day affairs, which is rather different from the strong influence of elected members in the management of many local authority estates.

The P.S.A. consists of those functions already within the D.O.E. concerned with physical resources of central government, together with the Defence Lands Service transferred from the Ministry of Defence. Four basic kinds of services are provided:

Estate Management; the provision and management of land and buildings to meet the needs of many different public sector clients.

New Works; the provision of services for the design and management of construction works.

Maintenance of all kinds of structures and plant.

Supplies; the provision of all types of equipment from office furniture to cars.

As the civil estate in the U.K. alone comprises over 10,000 holdings widely scattered and some very extensive in area, the whole operation has to be broken down into a number of manageable units and a decision-making structure. In order to manage the wide range of technical skills, ensure that clients' needs are carefully analysed and responded to effectively, and operate in convenient units, the organization consists of headquarters directorates concerned with clients' requirements and the overall management of the staff and resources and operational regions. England forms eight regions, with Wales structured as a region and Scotland with a hybrid organization. With respect to the maintenance function, each region consists of several areas and then districts, and it is within the works sections of the regions that the great majority of the staff are to be found. Leslie Chapman's book "Your Disobedient Servant" offers a constructive and critical analysis of the Southern Regional Works Section and has been the cause of much discussion.

The first annual report of the P.S.A. was published in 1978 and this was undoubtedly partly due to pressure from several directions for adequate disclosure. The second annual report contains a brief statement of the P.S.A.'s general aim, "to meet its clients' requirements efficiently, economically and in accordance with the Government's policies for the conservation and improvement of the environment. In the light of these policies the Agency aims to enhance standards of design in new buildings and other works within its responsibility".

The predominant type of property in the Civil Estate is offices, and outside London the majority of these are the local offices of the Department of Health and Social Security, the Department of Employment and the Inland Revenue. The merits of freeholds are appreciated but public expenditure cuts limit the new development that can be undertaken. Only about 30% of the London offices are freehold; outside London the figure is about 40%. Linked to this was the Hardman Report, accepted by the Government in 1974, which aimed to transfer 30,000 civil service posts from London and release 5 million ft^2 of leased office space. In 1979 the Conservative Government set in motion a comprehensive review of the civil service manpower; this inevitably included reviewing function, location and resources, and both decentralization and new projects are being overtaken by events. For example, the P.S.A. itself was programmed to move to Middlesbrough, but will now remain in Croydon.

The rental cost of the office estate is a function of the general market in the type of offices occupied by government departments and the pattern of rent-reviews. In 1981/2 rents and service charges cost £197 million, with £524 million spent on new work and £579 million on maintenance.

One of the problems that has arisen is ensuring a consistent method of measurement. Statistics in the first report were based upon a number of different practices. The second report is based on what is called "Agent's Letting Area", that is to say, usable area including corridors but excluding all other circulation areas and cloak-rooms and lavatories. Direct comparison between the two reports is clearly unrealistic but the variation in the figures in the table for the Civil Estate (see Appendix B) is remarkable, and only a small part can be explained by the change in the character of the estate over only one year. If policy decisions in earlier years have been based on statistics now known to have been inconsistent, then this can hardly inspire confidence in any of the parties involved.

A major disposals policy has now been implemented and one of the most valuable sites, 1·7 acres of Bloomsbury, was auctioned by Weatherall, Green and Smith in 1980. The site was acquired piecemeal between 1961 and 1974 for the new British Library, but this is now to be built in St. Pancras. The auction attracted leading developers as most of the leases had only a few years to run and a price of £7·44 million was paid by London Trust Company with Hammersons as the underbidders.

In addition to government departments the P.S.A. has over a 100 repayment clients, including the Manpower Services Commission, British Telecom (prior to privatization) and the various Research Councils and Establishments.

The greater part of the Defence estate is situated in the U.K. and one-third is overseas, most of which is in Germany. There are five overseas regional offices and land in the U.K. is dealt with through the existing regional offices. Apart from meeting the extensive and specialist needs of the Forces of the U.K., estate management and works are carried out for N.A.T.O. and for the United States Air Force.

At the peak of the 1939–45 war, Service requirements extended to 11,500,000 acres but in a review of Defence Lands in 1947 it was estimated that 1,027,200 acres were required. Between 1961/62 and 1971/72 191,000 acres of land were disposed of and at the latter date negotiations were in progress on 880 individual sales with a total area of 21,500 acres. By 1971 the Ministry of Defence holdings of land and foreshore had fallen to 662,000 acres and a Defence Lands Committee was appointed to review the holding of land by the Armed Forces to make recommendations as to what changes should be made in these holdings and in improved access for the public, having regard to recreation, amenity or other uses which might be made of the land. This was, therefore, an extensive, rural conservation-orientated review, very different from the urban development-site-based review provided for in the Local Government Planning and Land Act 1980.

This has been assisted by the removal in 1979 of the Government's administrative ring-fence system whereby surplus Defence lands had to be offered to any other part of central or local government before being placed on the market. In 1984 there were 85,900 married quarters, of which the surprisingly high number of 14,500 were vacant. Many of the houses are in isolated areas and depend upon a larger functioning Service establishment for social and technical infrastructure. Their disposal may, therefore, offer some problems. A number of large maintenance and storage depots, several of around 20 acres in size, are also available and are particularly suitable for refurbishment and development for industrial and warehousing purposes.

The Diplomatic Estate which extends to 97 countries is managed from the U.K. by 11 surveyors who are seconded from the P.S.A. to the Foreign and Commonwealth Office.

The P.S.A. represents a tremendous management task, with a total staff in 1981/82 of 29,000 serving a very wide range of clients. The professional estate management staff of 270 represent about 14% of all the professional staff and have the support of around 250 technical staff. It should now be apparent why, with the best of intentions and a high calibre of professional staff, decisions on estate matters cannot proceed very speedily. Most of the clients are very large organizations, and estate matters are closely related to changes for the staff, which require detailed consultation with staff representatives. Linked to this there is uncertainty and changes in policy at the highest level in government, and during the 1970s several major cut-backs in finance for capital works.

Accountability has become a general issue and this has shown itself in a number of different ways, parliamentary, as distinct from government, investigations through the Public Accounts and Public Expenditure Committees, and some of the exchanges have been extensively reported, the majority arising initially from comments in Leslie Chapman's book. Within the Civil Service, the P.S.A. is responsible to both the D.O.E. and the Treasury for the extent and effectiveness of its expenditure.

To the extent that the Chief Executive, with the rank of Second Permanent Secretary, and his management group are placed in a position of accountability, they therefore develop accountable management within the Directorates of the P.S.A. and in the operational regions.

In 1982 a businessman, Alfred Montague was appointed Chief Executive. He sought to introduce various measures to encourage efficiency:

Charging all occupiers for the market rent of their accommodation, in 1984/5 £680 m was paid under this system.

Reviews of accommodation needs and resources on a town by town basis. For example between 1979 and 1988 it was planned to reduce London Office estate from 21·5 million ft^2 to 17·2 million ft^2 of which currently only 40% is owner-occupied.

The use of consultants and contractors which also permits the testing of internal costs.
Shorter lines of communication and greater accountability for budgets and resources.
Greater autonomy for the defence estate, perhaps recognized by the appointment of Healey and Baker to advise on the M.O.D. estate in 1984.

The volume and value of the estates work undertaken by the P.S.A. in 1981–82 is set out below:

Type	Civil		Defence		Repayment	
	Cases	Value	Cases	Value	Cases	Value
		£m		£m		£m
Purchases	85	3·02	39	2·28	138	7·27
New lease	354	2·63	89	0·27	96	2·91
Renewal/ review	952	30·57	738	3·50	242	6·02
Lettings	649	2·64	651	0·90	76	0·17
Disposals	468	17·73	647	34·02	175	3·83
Valuations	135	94·23	134	204·00	147	41·00

It has been estimated that the value at 1983 prices of the civil estate was £6 billion and the defence estate was £7 billion.

In conclusion mention should be made of the Dalton Committee which reported in 1984 on its terms of reference, "To examine the functions other than rating valuation, of valuers now employed by the Valuation Office of the Inland Revenue and by other government departments, local authorities, the general public and other bodies, for valuations and advice; and to recommend how these needs can best be met in an efficient and cost-effective manner". The committee recommended the setting up of a comprehensive Government Valuation and Estates Services, whose head should be the Chief Valuer, Inland Revenue, (the head of the P.S.A. resigned about one month before the report was published. He was replaced by a career Civil Servant). No fundamental operational changes were proposed, though it was recommended that wherever possible charges should be made for the services provided.

4.3.1 State Agencies

In order to perform the many tasks facing the public sector in a complex urban society and achieve a balance between autonomy and accountability, various agencies have been created. The title of QUANGO (Quasi Autonomous Non/National Gov-

ernmental Agency) has recently been formulated to describe
this specie of bureaucracy. It has been suggested that, depending on your definition, between 2,000 and 3,000 exist, and
appointments to such bodies lie within the gift of the appropriate Minister. Strenuous efforts are being made to reduce
their number, though this is more easily achieved with advisory bodies than operational agencies such as statutory undertakers. A small number of the QUANGOs are specifically
estates or property orientated, and several of the largest statutory undertakers possess estates in excess of 100,000 acres.

QUANGOs can be classified as to the type of function they
perform or by the Department of Government to which they
are responsible. For convenience those with substantial land-
holdings are listed below in alphabetical order;

Associated British Ports (privatized 1983)
British Airports Authority (privatization 1986?)
British Airways (privatization 1986?)
British Broadcasting Corporation
British Gas (privatization 1986)
British National Oil Corporation
British Rail Property Board
British Steel
British Telecom (privatized 1984)
British Waterways
Electricity Authorities
English (Industrial) Estates Corporation
Health Authorities
Land Authority for Wales
London Regional Transport
National Bus Company
National Coal Board
National Freight Corporation (privatized 1983)
Nature Conservancy
New Town Development Corporations
Police Authorities
Post Office
Scottish Development Agency
Universities
Water Authorities
Welsh Development Agency

Two quite different subgroups can be distinguished, the statutory undertakers or public utilities and a newer group of
quasi-commercial agencies.

Estimates of their total land-holding vary, partly due to problems of definition, but around 4% of the surface area of the U.K. is not an unreasonable opinion.

4.3.2 Statutory Undertakers

Responsible to central government are a range of statutory bodies providing the infrastructure necessary for a highly developed urban society, principally energy and communications, and these are commonly called statutory undertakers. Much of their land is operational land occupied by sophisticated and specialist plant, and some of this may become surplus to requirements as has happened to the Gas Board's land once used for the manufacture and storage of town gas. Other land is indistinguishable from that generally available in the market, such as showrooms or general warehousing and maintenance depots.

The largest estate in this group is that of the Coal Board, with 250,000 acres, but the most important in terms of a valuable and complex urban estate is that managed by British Rail Property Board, which extends to 191,000 acres. The full extent and nature of many of these estates is unclear, since only a few of the annual reports of the various bodies contain any analysis of their property holdings. In the Commons in April, 1979, Mr. Allaun asked the Secretary of State for Transport, "How many acres of land are owned by British Railways, London Transport, other surface inland transport undertakings and statutory docks and harbour undertakings respectively and how much of each acreage is surplus to requirements and is being offered for sale as development land?" The Minister provided the following information but was unable to answer the other points:

British Railways Board	200,000 acres
British Transport Docks Board	12,500 acres
National Freight Corporation	2,250 acres
National Bus Company	650 acres
London Transport Executive	4,000 acres

4.3.3 British Rail

As one of the ten largest landowners in the country and an employer of over 1,000 staff, the British Rail Property Board is not only an important landowner but also perhaps the best example of a complex and specialist estate with considerable development potential. The estate is classified as either operational land, required for use or possible use for railway purposes, or non-operational and available for disposal. The Property Board was formed in 1969 and between 1970 and 1981 inclusive contributed, in rental and capital receipts, £435 million to British Railways.

Land within the operational estate can never be sold but can be leased and, if circumstances change, transferred to the non-operational estate. In 1983 gross income from lettings totalled £71 million. An important area for future income-growth is a fresh approach to station trading. The first Smith's bookstall on a station opened in 1848; by 1935 there were over a thousand but since then there has been a steady decline which has now halted. Stations offer extraordinarily high pedestrian flows, around 200,000 persons per day at London termini. Good layouts in what is now called "barrier line trading", occupied by tenants specializing in particular trades, can achieve a weekly turnover of £25,000 per unit. The use of turnover rents results in a joint endeavour by landlord and tenant to boost sales to their mutual advantage. Waterloo station barrier line now includes; W. H. Smith (bookshop and record shop), chemists, heelbar, leather goods, employment bureau, ice cream parlour and fruiterers.

Land which has been designated as non-operational cannot through its use for railway purposes make a financial contribution to the primary function of the railways but can be sold or let. In 1978 these 30,000 acres were valued on an existing use basis at £182 million. Ownership of non-operational land, together with disused tunnels, bridges, viaducts, embankments and retaining walls, carries with it some onerous expenditures necessary to ensure the safety of the public and the stability of the land of adjoining owners. In addition nearly 500 buildings are listed as being of historic interest and to some extent the Railways have the same problems as the Church as the unwilling custodians of historic but functionally obsolete buildings. The burden of the upkeep of its historic buildings has been estimated by the Railways as requiring £100 million to bring them into a state of good repair. As a result, they are prepared to give away historic buildings to local authorities and amenity groups.

Much of the surplus land is the route of old branch lines and where possible sales are made to adjoining owners or local authorities. One of the problems is long leases containing impractical clauses. For example, the Railways have some nineteenth century 999 year leases in which they covenant to return the demise to the freeholder complete with an operating railway system.

Disposals were likely to peak in 1984 and thereafter both capital and income receipts may fall as the estate will diminish, reflecting the effect of the disposal policy required by the 1979 Conservative government.

On sales in urban areas the Board was very exposed to Development Land Tax, since with nineteenth century acquisition costs and low current use values, the base values in the tax calculations were all low. Further one annual tranche of exemption across the whole estate was used up in the first transaction of the tax year.

For their large development projects based on stations the Board may need a special Act of Parliament, for example the British Railways (Liverpool Street Station) Act 1983. This enabled Rosehaugh Stanhope to start on a £250 million scheme to rebuild Liverpool Street Station and build 1·25 m ft² of offices and 30,000 ft² of shops. British Rail will receive an initial purchase price for each phase, followed by a deferred overage payment. The aggregate of the initial purchase prices is £75 million.

In 1983 the Board completed schemes with a total floor area of 900,000 ft² and started 25 schemes covering 1·25 million ft² with £75 million of private sector investment. Perhaps the most impressive scheme completed in 1984 was the 250,000 ft² Victoria Plaza office building with its three attria.

In pursuing its development programme the Board is faced with highly complex problems of;

Road and rail communication
Services
Listed buildings
Special legislation

If these can be overcome then Fenchurch Street, Kings Cross and Marylebone stations in London and Snow Hill in Birmingham will all be subject to major schemes.

The estate is now managed from seven regional offices and a London H.Q. A typical regional office employs a 100 or so staff, with responsibility for the management of a rent roll of 20,000 items. Each region is split into a number of areas, with an area surveyor and a team of 10 to 15 staff dealing with the day-to-day management. In addition there are specialist teams dealing with sales and development, and appropriate technical support from building surveyors and other specialists.

The total rent roll extends to 110,000 items and rent demands and arrears are now dealt with by a central computer. Regions are sent summaries of outstanding arrears and must supply the computer with details of any changes in the tenancy agreements. The vast majority of the rentals relate to small charges for rights to cross railway land, where as the heart of the commercial property portfolio is contained in just a few hundred leases. The Board does, of course, make a contribution to the revenue of the railways as a whole and their successful equity participation in future projects is therefore a benefit to every tax-payer.

During 1980 as part of its policy of disposal of public sector assets the Government announced a plan to set up a holding company for some subsidiary activities of British Rail, including shipping, hotels and property. If this is implemented by a flotation on the Stock Exchange then the character and mode of operation of the Property Board will tend towards that of a specialized property company. This could create pressures for the more rapid transfer of land from operational to non-operational status. The Board's approach to the detailed management of its portfolio is already very commercial, as developers seeking drainage and other rights over the Board's land in order to release land for development have discovered. The Board take the view, correctly, that this is analogous to the principles elucidated in *Stokes* v. *Cambridge*, 1961, and seek what they regard as an appropriate proportion of the development value realized as a result of the grant of rights.

In 1985 the Monopolies and Mergers Commission reported on the Board with 43 recommendations for improvements of the "could do better" nature.

4.3.4 Quasi-Commercial Estates

A number of social and economic factors have led the public sector into taking some major development initiatives. Arising from the unemployment of the 1930s, industrial estates were created in the assisted areas and post-war planning produced the New Towns, providing a new environment for over one million people. The extent of these programmes at any particular time is influenced as much by political issues affecting policy as technical or economic factors influencing detailed implementation.

The New Towns, which now number 28, must not be seen as solely a public sector concept. The first two New Towns,

Letchworth and Welwyn, were private sector activities, and in 1963 Letchworth was successful in getting its assets transferred to what is in effect a trust, Letchworth Garden City Corporation.

Since their inception the New Towns had received capital advances up to 1979 of over £2,500 million and in addition to their social and community services, the total assets include;

350,000 houses
9 million m² of industrial space
1·3 million m² of office space
1·2 million m² of shop space

Each town was developed from a mainly rural setting by an autonomous statutory body. With a comprehensive approach to the balanced development of a whole new community, Milton Keynes is currently the most active, where £29 million has been spent on the largest covered shopping centre in the U.K. and extensive industrial estates are being built in a very attractive location. Reductions in national population projections have had their effect on the target populations and development programmes, with the result that during the 1980s more second generation towns are likely to achieve a relatively stable character.

By the early 1960s it was clear that the first generation of New Towns were moving towards a balanced and completed state. As a result the Commission for New Towns was created in 1961 to manage their assets but it was later agreed that housing and neighbourhood shopping would be transferred to the district councils and only the commercial and industrial estates would go to the Commission.

The Conservative government of 1979 re-opened the whole issue with a policy decision to sell off £100 million of commercial and industrial assets per annum, and between April 1979 and September 1981 £212 millions of disposals were made. There are complex political, social, economic and estate management arguments as to which is the best type of landlord for these assets. Good estate management would favour one landlord able to plan through leasehold covenant and adopt a comprehensive approach to improvement and ultimately renewal and redevelopment. However, the temptation to sell piecemeal to Institutions as a way of obtaining capital without selling gilts with an obligation to service the debt proved too great.

The Urban Development Corporations proposed in the Local Government, Planning and Land Act 1980 are the application of New Town methodology to secure the regeneration of urban areas. The first two are London Docklands and Liverpool, with an initial maximum capital loan of £200 million which can be raised by order to £400 million. This is quite distinct from the borrowing limit of the Commission for New Towns which funds the new towns programme. The Urban Development Corporations are granted very wide powers to acquire, hold, manage, reclaim and dispose of land, to carry out building operations and carry out the functions of statutory undertakers. They will not be operating like New Towns in greenfield locations but in areas with an existing range of local government services. The Act enables the Secretary of State to make a vesting declaration in respect of land of local authorities or public bodies in the area, transferring the property to the urban development corporation.

The New Towns and Urban Development Corporations Act 1985 is designed to assist the winding up of new towns and amend the funding of the UDCs.

In response to the depression of the 1930s the government formed North-Eastern Trading Estates in 1936 on a 700 acre site at Gateshead with the long-term aim of building 400 factories capable of providing work for 15,000 employees. The Team Valley Trading Estate now employs a workforce of 17,000 and there are still 100 acres undeveloped. In 1960 the English Industrial Estates Corporation was formed, incorporating all three of the Government's industrial estates in the assisted areas.

At the end of March, 1984 the portfolio extended to 30 million ft^2 with a rental income of £15·6 million and a capital value (cost) of £242 million, a revaluation was in hand in 1985. In 1983/4, 1,182 units were let with a floor area of 3 million ft^2 (approx) but 472 units were vacated by tenants with a floor area of 2 million ft^2 (approx).

The Corporation does not see itself in competition with the private sector but complementary to the role of the private developer. The emphasis is on manufacturing employment rather than meeting the needs of warehousing and service industry. Further initiatives are being taken to develop inner city sites which the private sector may find unattractive in financial terms but which offer a very real social return.

The Industry Act 1980 permitted the Corporation to adopt a more entreprenurial approach, as a result Legal and General, Barclays Bank and the Coal Board Pension Fund provided £25 million of development finance, supported by rental guarantees from the corporation.

The Industrial Development Act 1985 amended the English Industrial Estate Act 1981 by enabling the corporation to, provide advisory services to tenants, obtain grants from the E.E.C. and borrow from the general money markets. In the same year the Corporation proposed a £350 million scheme to redevelop Chatham Dockyard.

The complexity of the types of QUANGOs involved in land management and development is demonstrated by the arrangement in Wales. The Welsh Development Agency was formed in 1975, taking over the responsibilities of the Welsh Industrial Estates Corporation. It now employs a staff of 470 and is concerned with three areas of activity; direct investment in industry, environmental improvement and the development of industrial estates. The latter is their main activity and in 1979 they acquired 552 acres and had a land bank of 1,000 acres, a further 500 acres being under negotiation.

The majority of their developments are small advance factories, particularly in areas affected by steel closures. The first programme was announced in April, 1977, and between then and May, 1978, 310 units had been authorized and 52 had been completed. The average size of the units was about 6,000 ft^2 and some were only 1,500 ft^2.

The Secretary of State has approved a corporate plan from 1984 to 1990 with a shift from spending on advance factories to site infrastructure.

In addition to the above and totally separate in every respect is the Land Authority for Wales, which has identified itself as filling a vacuum between the allocators of land for development and the developers of land. It believes it has established a clear role for a commercially viable public organization working within the planning structure but concerned solely with the acquisition, management and disposal of land for industrial, commercial and residential development. In order to clarify what appears to be an overlapping of function, the Authority is an entrepreneur in bare land and does not have a budget for construction. The Conservative government do not expect its future scale to exceed that of 1979. In September, 1979, the Authority had acquired 1,600 acres and disposed of 600 and it estimated that its net worth, that is to say the value of land holdings less outstanding debts, was about £5 million, clearly a successful commercial enterprise. However, it must be remembered that both bodies had been able to buy land net-of-tax, which up to June, 1979 was a very important concession. The Land Authority for Wales estimated that one-third of its net worth was attributable to this benefit.

4.4.1 Local Government

The growth of local government as the means of providing services to meet local needs as determined within financial constraints by locally elected members has given a distinctive character to local authority estates.

Local government is big business in terms of the services provided and the resources it controls; housing, education, social services, highways, recreation and in some authorities municipal docks, airports, industrial estates, shopping centres and wholesale markets.

The small districts in rural areas provide housing but beyond that their estate may include little more than ownership of various office buildings and ancillary accommodation to perform their statutory duties. Whereas the large urban districts comprising cities of several hundred thousand population, such as Sheffield, Leicester and Bristol are each the largest landowners within their urban areas, involved in commercial property management and entrepreneurial projects in addition to providing estates services to the locally provided social infrastructure.

The Bains report identified the importance of the estate management surveyors in the allocation of resources in local government;

"Land and buildings are among the most expensive and scarce resources of a local authority and the efficient management of these resources is a matter of first importance. In many authorities the management of existing land and buildings will be a substantial task, which, coupled with the acquisition and disposal programme, may well justify the existence of a separate major department closely linked to the land utilisation sub-committee of the policy and resources committee. We have in mind particularly authorities with a substantial investment in land and buildings and also authorities with large town/city centre redevelopment programmes in hand."

"Each authority should create and maintain a central record of all estate owned, and should co-ordinate all forward land acquisition and disposal proposals in order to maximise the use of existing estate. In particular consideration should be given, wherever possible, to the combination of separate acquisition and building proposals on to one site, in order to achieve savings in building costs and in common services and for the convenience of the public."

"Through their land utilisation sub-committee authorities should also consider carefully and keep under review the economic use of existing property. Changing local circumstances may suggest that it would be more economic to sell or redevelop existing sites and rebuild on a different site where the demand can equally well be met. The possibility of combining commercial and public uses should not be overlooked."

Local government is not one comprehensive structure. For the moment in London, the Greater London Council is allocated a strategic role, in relation to the London boroughs, though both have some difficulty in determining the practical implications of such a division of responsibility, and the Inner London Education Authority exists in a unique single function role. In the remainder of England, in the shire counties, former all-purpose county boroughs now co-exist with the same effective status as rural districts within large, and in some cases new counties, whilst in the largest urban conurbations metropolitan counties and districts have a different pattern of responsibilities. Local government in Scotland is based on regional authorities and even in Wales, where the structure appears similar to that of England, the Land Authority for Wales carries out functions throughout the principality once vested in counties and districts in England.

The various re-organizations of local government presented problems in the re-allocation of property and estates staff to serve the redistributed pattern of responsibilities. In Scotland the re-organization was considered so fundamental as to require a Property Commission to determine disputes in the allocation of property.

Over 7,000 disputes were referred to the Commission but only 24 of these resulted in a formal hearing. Re-organization raised strong passions and despite the passage of time it seems to have permanently affected the approach of elected members in some urban districts suffering injured civic pride.

4.4.2 England

Apart from the agricultural smallholdings in the shire counties which extend to approximately 425,000 acres, the three largest specialist statutory estates in local government are housing, social services and education. Their importance is reflected in their budgets and staff, which dominate their respective authorities. The estates departments service their needs as clients in a rather similar way to the in-house estates departments of commerce and industry. On the other hand there is a property management and an entrepreneurial role where the estates department takes a lead, earning an income for the council and influencing the visual character and economic structure of the area, often the most important means of achieving positive planning.

The estates surveyor works within overall policies created by a complex framework of individual elected members, committees and the corporate management of senior officers. The following job description of the chief officer of a city estates department illustrates these points and the wide range of professional duties:

Professional Responsibilities

Advises the Council, Committees, Chief Officers and Heads of Departments on all aspects of land and property interests, including mortgages and loans, prepares the relevant reports and valuations and represents the Council, when necessary, at Tribunals and Public Inquiries.

Provides professional support and expertise to the City Council's economic development policy and, in particular, gives high priority support to the Industrial Development Officer, including practical assistance where necessary.

Undertakes the negotiations by way of purchase, lease or other arrangements for all land and property required by the Council, and claims for compensation related to property, including work for "agency" services.

Negotiates the disposal by way of sale, lease or other arrangements for all land and property surplus to the Council's requirements.

Undertakes the efficient management and related maintenance of the Council's Corporate Estate, Central Shopping Area, Commercial and Industrial Estates, the Markets and other land and property held for general or redevelopment purposes; with particular emphasis and sensitivity to new industrial developments and nursery units, especially where they support the development of small firms.

Undertakes the maintenance of such Public Buildings and

the management and/or maintenance of such other buildings, land and property as may from time to time be the responsibility of the Department.

Operates a continuous review of the Council's overall land holding, their land and property requirements. As part of the corporate activity, identifies and promotes the redevelopment potential of the Council's land interests in conformity with their Economic Development and planning strategies.

Maintains a complete record of the Council's interests in land and property, maintains and updates the relevant Ordnance Survey map records and other documents, keeps adequate records and files of the Department's activities and proper books of account, and undertakes the "referencing" of private ownerships.

Maintains and updates valuations of the Council's properties for fire insurance purposes, to accord with the City Treasurer's requirements.

Prepares estimates of revenue and expenditure in connection with the Department's activities for the information of the Council, Committees and Management Team.

Maintains an effective working relationship and joint approach with other public Authorities and in particular with the private sector, to assist in the efficient operation of the Council's functions and the attainment of the City's aims, objectives and economic prosperity.

Departmental Management Responsibilities

Controls the activities of the Department and expenditure of the Departmental budget, to meet approved targets, programmes and services.

Reviews the performance of Departmental staff at regular intervals and advises on appropriate training.

Manages and organizes the staff of the Department in order to meet defined objectives.

Delegates appropriate responsibility to Senior staff, consistent with effective decision making, whilst retaining overall accountability.

Subject to the policies of the appropriate Committee, selects and appoints Departmental staff.

Ensures compliance with statutory obligations and Council policy governing the safety, health and welfare of Departmental staff and their visitors.

Undertakes such other duties consistent with the appointment as may be required by the appropriate Committee or the Chief Executive.

Corporate Management Responsibilities

Participates fully in the corporate management process as a member of the Chief Officers' Management Team, including the provision of professional advice and expertise as well as contributing to the activities and business of the Team generally.

Discharges the duties and responsibilities of the post with due regard to the principles of Corporate Management and the policies of the Council.

In counties and districts with a substantial urban base, implementation of these responsibilities can require between 20 and 50 qualified estate management staff, with appropriate technical support. Much would depend on the extent of the investment estate and the involvement in maintenance, particularly of the housing stock. Some idea of the scale of the estate can be seen in a typical county with 3,000 holdings and a total fire insurance re-instatement value of £1,000 million. During a year there were 485 acquisitions and 106 applications for planning approval related to the corporate estate. The departments of the authority together occupied about 250,000 ft² of offices. One of the organizational problems is whether to structure estates departments on a geographical basis, allowing staff to identify closely with their area, or on a functional basis related to the type of work, enabling the staff to further develop their professional expertise. In addition it is important that the main programme committees are attended by experienced officers knowledgeable in the detail of estates matters which influence the provision of services. The effect of these factors can result in a multi-tier structure requiring a high level of personal as well as professional skill in its senior members.

During the early 1980s a new trend amongst County Councils was the creation of a comprehensive property department bringing together:

Architecture—Design, Electrical, Mechanical and Structural Engineers
Building—Quantity and Building Surveying
Estates—Valuation and Property Management
Land—Land Agency and Agriculture

This was recognized by their Chief Officers setting up COPROP in 1984 as a forum for discussion for the 17 counties in England and Wales which then had this structure and the others expected to adopt it.

In small districts particularly in rural areas estates matters tend to be the responsibility of the chief executive or planning department, with consultants advising from time to time. Authorities may call in the District Valuer, who provides a consultancy service. This is often suitable for specific valuation advance, but that office has limited experience of continuing estate management work, which is carried out on behalf of central government by the Property Services Agency. Any long-term project is better carried out by a suitable private practice with experience of this type of consultancy work, particularly if there is an involvement with Institutional funding.

4.4.3 Greater London

In its role as a strategic authority the G.L.C. has not found its relationship with all the 32 London boroughs very easy, and when different political parties have been involved there have been periods of very limited co-operation. Many projects require close co-operation between the two authorities in both the formulation of the plans and the implementation on the ground through the acquisition, management and disposal of sites. Failures tend to be better reported than successes and the inability of the boroughs and the G.L.C. to resolve political differences which have delayed progress on the redevelopment of Docklands has led to the statutory initiatives to create the Docklands Urban Development Corporation. Though its status is similar to that of a New Town corporation, the present financial climate and character of the area will require a different philosophy and approach. Another statutory body, the Lea Valley Regional Park Authority, was created not out of default but of necessity to give effect to an ambitious plan for a linear water-based recreation facility, serving a principally urban community. The Park Authority has representatives from the G.L.C., London boroughs, county and districts, and has been remarkably effective in the restoration of derelict land and the provision and management of intensively used recreational facilities.

The G.L.C. estates department serves the programme committees concerned with: housing, transportation, planning, arts and leisure, health and safety and general services, together with the requirements of the Inner London Education Authority. In the case of the largest projects such as Covent Garden, Thamesmead, St. Katherines and the Thames flood barrier, special skills have had to be pioneered within the context of multi-disciplinary teams.

In the late 1960s and early 1970s very large compulsory purchase programmes were being completed involving the statutory procedures and where necessary the relocation of existing occupiers as well as the supervision of the works on site and management of the completed schemes. In order to get closer to the public, temporary site offices were set up and staffed in the evenings. The authority has also been active outside the G.L.C. area, acquiring several thousand homes and developing sites in coastal areas suitable for G.L.C. tenants of retirement age in order to release key housing for those in need in central London. The success of the town development programmes may be in part responsible for the lack of certain types of employment opportunities in some inner urban areas and initiatives are now being taken to recreate industrial opportunities.

In the early 1970s the Department spent around £30 million per annum on the acquisition of land and buildings, in 1974/75 this rose to £79 million, but it fell in the latter part of the decade. One of the best documented and most active periods was between 1970 and 1973 and during that time:

    20,000 transactions were recorded,
    4,000 properties reviewed for fire insurance purposes,
    34,000 homes were surveyed for loans with a total value of
        £172 million,
    11,000 homes were sold to tenants,
    1,700 acres were acquired,
    544 acres were sold for £22 million,
    and £18·5 million was collected in rent from commercial
    property, including 3,000 shops.

The massive programmes of compulsory acquisition are now over, partly due to the lack of finance for both revenue and capital purposes, and partly to a lack of confidence that wholesale re-development can offer an adequate aggregate financial and social return for the costs involved.

It is perhaps inevitable that there should be a high turnover of young professional staff in the Department due to the general range of opportunities in London and the differentials at different ages between the remuneration packages in the public and private sectors within central London. The professional approach adopted by the G.L.C. to staff development has a long tradition, as this extract from the London County Council Staff Gazette of 1900 indicates:

"The municipal officer's education is not completed when he has left school or college, and as some of the profoundest economical and social questions are being worked out in the problems which every day arrest the attention of municipal government it is evident that officers, to be abreast of the work required of them, must be students as well as officers ... and a professional officer is doubly important if besides being a specialist in his own profession, he knows some of the influences which have produced his work and which in turn his work is likely to produce."

The abolition of the G.L.C. and Metropolitan Counties will have implications for their operational and investment assets—to be the responsibility of their Residuary Bodies. This is particularly so where the G.L.C. Covenant has guaranteed rent as part of the funding of a scheme.

4.4.4 Positive Management

The management of local authority estates is influenced by the particular holdings and geographical boundaries of the authority and the detailed management must have regard to statutory requirements such as section 123 of the Local Government Act, although many of the former constraints upon disposals of land and property by local authorities have been removed.

In a period of financial stringency, limited economic growth and some gloomy projections of technological unemployment, the entrepreneurial estate of the authority can take on an important role. Firstly, by its management in the interests of the rate-payers, as central government seeks to reduce the proportion of its contribution to local government finance additional sources of revenue and capital are essential in order to maintain the existing provision of services without unacceptable increases in the rate poundage.

In order to benefit from the urban infrastructure that they provide authorities need a land bank which can be brought forward for development either by the council itself or by a developer on a ground lease. Whether land should be sold to realize the maximum capital value or leased at current open market rent is a matter of investment policy and the view of the elected members as to their responsibilities to current rate-payers and future rate-payers, with the benefit of the impartial advice of the estates surveyor.

Secondly, the estates department has a major contribution to make towards positive planning. It can assist the planning department in advising on cost and value implications of its policies and the likely reaction of the private sector to various possible planning briefs. As the largest land-owner in the area, the estates department can make plans reality by implementation on local authority sites, which may encourage the private sector. This will require a relatively subtle working relationship between the two departments, in which conclusions can be reached on any conflicts between social planning objectives and entrepreneurial estates objectives. This area of activity is one in which the planning and development surveyor is making a major contribution in seeking to bridge the gap between planners and developers.

Thirdly, the estates department is uniquely placed to take initiatives in the fields of industrial and economic development. This can be done by assisting and consolidating the existing industry and the encouragement of natural growth by the provision of nursery units, though the enthusiasm of the planners for high-quality layouts and landscaping will have to be curbed if the pioneering industrialists are to be able to afford the rents. In fact it may be better to create nursery units by refurbishment of existing buildings in the older industrial quarter of the town than by provision on peripheral industrial estates. The attraction of new industries is an altogether more complex task. It requires the corporate marketing of the character of the town in the best possible light together with an imaginative and attractive response to any leads.

These points are well illustrated by Leicester City Council. By Local Act of Parliament in 1968 they consolidated the Corporate Estate "for the benefit, improvement or development of the City". The fund with a capital value of £40 million and an annual surplus of income of over £1 million does not mirror a typical institutional fund. There are a longer number of secondary properties and high management obligations, but since the properties are within the City, management expertise can be applied on an intensive basis.

In emphasizing the commercial role of the estates department it must be recognized that this can only be carried out within a local government framework. The estates department must respect the political constitution of the authority and the importance of implementing the statutory functions but in its general management of the commercial estate it should adopt an approach to the market close to that of a large and responsible property company or institution. It will not always be possible to separate the political, the commercial and economic factors. Political aspects and statutory provisions can place pressures on both individual departments and the corporate management of the authority by senior officers. This was apparent with the Community Land Act 1975 and the Local Government, Planning and Land Act 1980. The latter affects many of the powers and duties of local authorities.

Sources and Further Reading

Bains Report, The New Local Authorities: Management and Structure, H.M.S.O., 1972.
British Rail, Annual Reports.
Chapman, Your Disobediant Servant, Chatto and Windus, 1978.
Chartered Surveyors in the Public Service, R.I.C.S., 1975.
Dalton Committee, H.M.S.O., 1984.
Land for London, G.L.C., 1973.
Office Accommodation—A Multi-departmental Review of the Manage- of Government Office Accommodation, Cabinet Office, 1985.
Report of Defence Lands Committee 1971–73 H.M.S.O., 1973.
Roberts, Managing the corporate estate of Leicester City Council, Property Management, Volume 2, No. 3.
Selling Surplus Public Property, Supplement to C.S., April, 1980.
Simpson, Turning Railway Stations into Covered Shopping Centres, C.S., January, 1980.
Smith, The Role of the Chartered Surveyor in Public Service over the next Decade, R.I.C.S. Annual Conference, 1979.
Surveying in the Eighties, Appendix C, R.I.C.S., 1980.
Town and County Planning, February/March, 1979.
Trends, Occasional Bulletin, G.L.C. Valuation and Estates Department.
Welsh Development Agency, Annual Reports.

Chapter 5

Charities

5.1 Historical Development and the Charity Commissioners

From the early Middle Ages the wealthy and worthy have endowed various bodies with assets for specified charitable purposes. The motives of these benefactors varied, in some cases it may have eased their consciences, others may have seen it as easing their way to heaven, and others made their gifts in the very best sense out of charity. Over the years and centuries the assets rose or fell in value and were changed, the specified purposes of the charity became more or less relevant, and the whole institutional and social environment appeared quite different to succeeding generations of trustees.

The importance attached by society to charities is shown by several hundred years of specific statutory provisions and, perhaps most important from the point of view of the management of the charitable funds, exemption from taxation. Widespread malpractices by trustees in the nineteenth century led to the establishment of the Charity Commissioners in 1853, and their present supervisory function is governed by the Charities Act 1960.

Charities are involved in real property in three distinct ways:

The largest charities have been endowed with substantial property investments and land once agricultural is now the site of many commercial developments.

The charities in carrying through their purposes need to occupy both general and specialist property. This is an operational use similar to that of any occupier of property, but much of the property will be owner-occupied, arising from gifts of many years ago.

A small number of charities are in the specific business of the preservation of land and buildings, characterized by the National Trust.

The history of charities is an integral part of our social history as the core from which the whole of the Welfare State has developed. The founding and endowment of the Ox-bridge colleges in the fourteenth century and hospitals, as early as 1215 in the case of St. Thomas's, has resulted in their ownership of substantial agricultural and commercial property holdings. To these can be added the City Livery Companies and Merchants' Guilds of the older provincial cities. The largest charitable estate is that of the Church Commissioners, and there remains the Crown Estate, almost defying classification but in many respects exhibiting management characteristics similar to those of the largest charities. All the above have some special features but they possess sufficient common features, such as their antiquity and close involvement with the Establishment, to be called collectively the old or traditional institutions.

It is important to distinguish charities from private trusts; the former benefit the public at large or a section of the community, can exist in perpetuity and do not fail if their objectives become frustrated. The Charities Act of 1960 replaced many previous overlapping public and private Acts of Parliament and the Charity Commissioners now operate under its provisions in promoting the effective use of charitable resources by encouraging the development of better methods of administration, by giving trustees information, advice and checking abuses. About 147,000 charities are registered, but a small number are exempt, including most of the old institutions, specifically the Church and the Ox-bridge colleges. With respect to the investment property of registered charities, under section 29 of the Charities Act 1960, the Commissioners' approval is required for disposal, purchases or exchanges, and about 2,500 orders are given each year for these purposes. Before giving their approval the Commissioners require independent professional advice from a surveyor acting solely for the charity. It is the Commissioners' practice to require trustees who have received an offer they wish to accept to publish notice of the price offered and inviting higher offers, in fact higher offers were received in 20% of cases, with additional proceeds of over £500,000 in 1983. Registered charities cannot invest directly in land, but if their endowments include land they are permitted to re-invest the proceeds of any disposal of such endowed land for the same purposes. The Commissioners are not opposed to a change in the law to permit charities to invest directly in land in addition to the existing broad and narrow categories of investment currently available to trustees, see 3.5.

From the point of view of the character and management of their property investments the larger land-owning charities, the old institutions, can be distinguished from the new institutional investors in a number of ways:

They have been in existence for several centuries and the most important, such as the Church, have acquired their own statutory setting for the management of both their investment and operational land or are subject to supervision by the Charity Commissioners.

Property has been added to the investment portfolio in a rather random way in the past by bequests and there has tended to be a presumption against sale. Until recently portfolios have not been planned or managed with quite the vigour adopted by the new institutions.

The relatively modest inflow of new funds, unlike pension funds, means that in order to carry out development it may be necessary to sell some of the portfolio to realize sufficient finance, or alternatively, and more likely, the charity will grant a ground lease, participating in the development value by rent-reviews.

There is overall, a cautious investment policy, with less opportunity for large profits and losses, further the limited disclosure requirements means that transactions and investment performance are not so often reported in the technical press. The cautious investment approach is reflected in small or negligible debts, hence little or no gearing, resulting in greater stability than that of property companies.

There are specific allocated purposes for the revenue from investments which can influence the investment strategy.

Charities, as part of their *raison d'être*, imply a commitment to some patent standards of morality, and this can influence the type of property/tenants which the trustees will find acceptable. Further, tenants may seek to make a negotiating factor out of this aspect. The Church Commissioners seem very sensitive to this type of criticism of their residential management.

Exemption from tax, apart from V.A.T., is almost absolute, the only exception was a temporary liability to Development Land Tax. This has implications on the attractiveness of particular investments which carry onerous tax implications for typical investors.

They have a higher proportion of their assets in property than the new financial institutions and particularly in agricultural land which is now proving to be well placed as greenfield industrial sites.

5.2 The Church Commissioners

For hundreds of years the estate of the church was held by individual cathedrals, chapters, dioceses, bishops, parishes and other ecclesiastical units. During the nineteenth century the Ecclesiastical Commissioners acquired more of these assets and by 1891 they had an income of over £1 million. The present structure of the Church Commissioners was created by the Church Commissioners Measure of 1947 and the major role of the investment funds is to meet clergy stipends. Their expenditure on contributions to stipends, pensions and clergy houses account for approximately 90% of their investment income. The investment policy is to obtain the best current income consistent with maintaining the real value of the assets but they do bring ethical and social as well as financial criteria to bear on their investment policies and practices. Property has been making a growing contribution to the income of the Commissioners. In 1970 Stock Exchange investments provided £12·6 million and property £8·4 million. By 1983 this had changed to £32·3 million and £37·9 million respectively. Over the years within the property portfolio there has been some disposal of agricultural and residential property which has assisted the funding of commercial development projects.

Assets	1979		1983	
	Capital value	Income	Capital value	Income
Agricultural	£122·5 m	£3·2 m	£217.2 m	£6.5 m
Commercial				
Offices	266·6	10·8	382·7	17.6
Shops	56·1	1·8	78·5	5·2
Warehouses	42·9	2·4	56·5	4·5
Minerals	2·6	0·4	0*	0*
Residential	91·0	3·5	169·8	4·6
Other (sites, etc.)	7·0	0	0	0
Totals	584·9	22·1	904·7	38·4

* Included in agricultural.

The commercial property has its origins in historical episcopal and chapter estates now occupying some key sites in London, and during the 1960s and 1970s a considerable amount of development work was carried out. Recently the emphasis has changed to portfolio management and rearrangement of leases. Adjustments to the funding and pattern of ownership of three large office buildings in London has increased the capital value of the buildings and the income to the Commissioners.

In 1956 the Commissioners formed Church Estate Development and Improvements Company as a holding company, and it has been very active as a means of carrying out projects jointly with other companies. In the 1960s it owned shares in 26 property companies, but due to the tax liability on company dividends this is now unattractive and the interests are being re-structured so that income is received directly as rent rather than as dividends payable from company profits subject to tax. In 1978 10 companies were involved and in 1979 only 8, with a value of £16 million. These interests are incorporated within the schedule of property assets.

The agricultural property extends to 173,000 acres and includes nearly 500 farms. There is a steady programme of portfolio management which includes sales of land for development purposes and acquisitions to consolidate existing estates. In addition there is a major programme of capital expenditure in excess of £1 million per annum on improvements. These factors account for the high average rent per acre in 1983 of £47·28 which can be contrasted with the average rent of Glebe lands of little more than half this sum.

Over recent years the residential estate has been the source of considerable problems. It comprises three distinct types of property the Octavia Hill estates providing cheap housing for 1,900 tenants in inner London Boroughs south of the river, the Maida Vale estate of 2,800 houses and flats attracting middle-class tenants, including the Little Venice area and the Hyde Park estate of high-quality refurbishment and new flats which are meant for the luxury end of the market. For some years they have been reducing their stake in residential property but they, "... do not however think it right nor of benefit to their beneficiaries, or to their tenants, nor to proper standards of public debate and behaviour for them to withdraw precipitately from their responsibilities and inheritance. Nor in view of their statutory liabilities for the pay, pensions and housing of the clergy, are they prepared to let their property at less than a fair rent or to dispose of it at less than a fair price." Sales on 375 properties were agreed on the Maida Vale estate in 1983, at a total price of £27 million.

Quite apart from the investments vested in the Commissioners, there are some 20,000 holdings of Glebe land which were transferred from the parishes to the Diocesan Boards of Finance in 1978. It must be said that often in the past the management of these assets has been at best ineffective and at times non-existent. The total income is of the order of £2 million, 70% of which is attributable to 6,600 parcels of agricultural land occupying over 100,000 acres. It will take several years for a full review and rationalization of the Glebe to be completed, but many of the individual interests are quite unsuitable as investments and quite uneconomic in terms of effective management. It is reasonable to expect that over the next few years there will be substantial disposals. In 1983 663 parcels were sold for £8·8 million.

In addition to its investment properties, the Church has an extensive operational estate consisting mainly of churches and houses. The location and character of many of these buildings is inappropriate to the current needs of the church and in conjunction with the dioceses there is an extensive programme of disposals. In the year ending 1983, 308 houses were sold at an average price of £64,000, 76 houses were built at an average construction cost of £76,000 and 105 houses were purchased. During the 1970s, 905 churches were declared redundant under the Pastoral Measure of 1968. Their exemption from listed building control has been a matter of controversy. The fate of redundant churches generates strong emotions, considerable success has been achieved in finding alternative uses including arts centres, offices, museums, warehouses, worship by other religious bodies, residential, sport and masonic hall. Of those 905, 317 have been found an alternative use, the future of 147 is still unresolved, 199 have been demolished and 136 preserved.

5.3 The Crown

The Domesday Inquest of 1086 showed that the Crown owned one-fifth of the entire kingdom. The present Crown estate has evolved as a result of complex statutory arrangements and possesses a unique status which almost defies classification. The Crown estate must be distinguished from the private crown estate; the former is the public property of the crown, held in "right of the crown", the latter the property owned privately by the Queen, including Sandringham and Balmoral. In 1760 the crown surrendered the Crown estate in return for a civil list payment. Since 1810 it has been administered by a board of commissioners and the present Crown Estate Commissioners hold office under the Crown Estate Act 1961.

In recent years surplus revenue of over £5 million per annum

Charities   103

has been paid to the Treasury, which is greater than the cost
of the civil list. Perhaps the best description of the practical
character of the estate is a nationalized property company,
though it can be distinguished from other estates on the following grounds:

Exempt from certain legislation. For example prior to the
Housing Act 1980 tenants did not enjoy security under the
Rent Acts, though in 1966 the Commissioners said that they
would, "act where-ever possible in such a way that crown
tenants will not be worse off than those of a good private
landlord".
Not subject to taxation.
The estate has no specific obligations to meet, though surplus income goes into the Treasury.
The estate performs no statutory function and the duty
of the Commissioners is to maintain the Crown Estate as
an estate in land (with such cash or investments as may
be required for the discharge of their functions) and to maintain and enhance its value and the return obtained from
it, but with due regard to the requirements of good management.
The estate is not in receipt of other sources of income
and the emphasis is therefore on portfolio management
rather than acquisitions.

About half the total rental income comes from the urban assets,
though the remainder of the estate is very extensive, including
260,000 acres of agricultural land, the Windsor estate and
rights to minerals and the foreshore and sea bed. With the
exception of industrial estates totalling 45 acres in Taunton
and Bingham, almost all the value of the urban estate is located
in London and much of this is in the nature of ancient posses-
sions of the sixteenth century. The character of the commercial
urban estate is most unusual; the rental income, 1971, £4 million, 1976, £6·4 million, 1979, £15·3 million, suggests a relatively small estate, in fact the estate is extensive but let on
long leases. Thus, as a ground landlord enforcing lease covenants the estate is far more important than the aggregate rent
roll suggests. The commercial estate includes freehold interests in the City, Oxford Street, Regent Street, Kensington High
Street, Haymarket, St. James's, Pall Mall, Trafalgar Square, Victoria Street and Park Lane.
The residential property covers the whole spectrum of the
market. At one end the Regents Park estate consists of high-

quality flats and villas, at the other, a number of fair rent flats and houses provide much needed accommodation close to the centre of London.

Development can either be instigated by tenants who have the benefit of a long lease or by the Crown estate as landlord. In both cases the sensitive nature of the location of most of the estate is likely to result in substantial planning problems. The estate, unlike the Institutions, is not in receipt of income from other sources, so either development has to be funded from capital receipts or carried out by the private sector. The largest scheme for many years has been the re-development of the 27 acres Millbank estate. The initial brief was prepared in 1969 and was subject to very extensive planning consultations. Work has started on some sites and steady progress is being made in what will be an important re-development in terms of both London and the Crown estate. During 1978/79 the Church Commissioners sold to the estate 1·4 acres of land to complete the major acquisition necessary to carry through a comprehensive scheme. When completed in 1985, there will be over 300,000 ft^2 of offices and residential property, including 400 tenancies covered by the fair rent legislation.

The main Crown estate is not quite unique, for the Duchy of Cornwall is similar in character, with 130,000 acres of agricultural land and 44 acres in Kennington including 850 tenancies and the Oval cricket ground. For completeness, the estate of the Duchy of Lancaster should also be mentioned, which includes 45,000 acres of agricultural land.

5.4 Other Investment Estates

The colleges, hospitals, livery companies and municipal charities can take a longer-term view than property companies but lack the financial resources of the new Institutions. By definition most of their assets are old having been bequeathed as farmland, possibly developed in the nineteenth century, redeveloped in the 1920s and subject to feasibility studies for a second re-development towards the end of this century. The portfolios are often not so large as to be capable of balance in the sense of the large Institutional funds and each fund thus acquires its own character. Almost all the larger funds contain a substantial proportion of farmland. In 1978 Massey and Catelano estimated that five charities or quasi-charities held something over 2 million acres, in the following percentages of the total area of the U.K. as agricultural investments

The Crown Estate	0·48%
The Monarchy	0·30%
The Church Commissioners	0·28%
Ox-bridge colleges	0·34%
Other Charities	2·60%

To see this in context, this can be compared with the work of the Northfield Committee (1978) and Steel (1983) on the holdings of the Financial Institutions. Northfield estimated the Institutions held 530,000 acres, Steele, four years later, estimated this had risen to 880,000 acres worth £1,148 million, held as follows:

Pension Funds	£415 m
Insurance Companies	£585 m
Property Unit Trusts	£148 m

Information of the estates of charities is not generally available as the trustees are accountable only unto themselves. The Ox-bridge colleges hold in total about 200,000 acres of agricultural land within their total property portfolio. Trinity College, Cambridge, is probably one of the wealthier colleges, in 1971 its total portfolio of investments was worth £23 million, producing an income of £1·5 million. The property sector of the portfolio consisted of 255 houses, 76 shops, 15 warehouses and 16,000 acres of agricultural land. The College has also been active in dealing in land for development in Suffolk and Kent, with a reputed profit of £2 million. Other universities and the endowed teaching hospitals have some major land-holdings in London and also a total of 20,000 acres of agricultural land.

Some of the landowning charities are registered with the Charity Commissioners and it is possible to inspect various documents and returns, but these provide only a partial view. The municipal charities arising from schemes of amalgamation are amongst the largest landowners in a number of towns and are closely involved in re-development proposals as ground landlords. There is an Association of Land Owning Charities, in which the Ox-bridge colleges are prominent.

5.5 Operational Estates

The property of charities which is used for charitable purposes rather than investment purposes is usually owner-occupied. This is rather similar in principle to the property of manufacturing industry where the estate manager is mainly concerned

with maintenance and repair. If the premises were endowed
and built at a time when labour was cheap, say in the 1920s,
such buildings now require heavy maintenance programmes
as components require renewal. Furthermore the overall design
is wasteful of space and probably showing signs of technical
obsolescence.

Where income from the endowment is insufficient to maintain the operational property, then the trustees will need to
enter discussions with the Charity Commissioners to determine how their own affairs can be rearranged or changes which
are being made to other charities could be used to their advantage. The Ox-bridge colleges, though in receipt of substantial
investment incomes, are also faced like the Church with the
upkeep of historic buildings. The largest colleges each require
several hundred thousand pounds per year from their investment income to maintain their mediaeval courts and chapels.

A small number of charities, most notably the National
Trust, have as their prime purpose the preservation of historic
buildings. The National Trust is very sensitive to the fact that
it is funded from private sources but with the status of a charity
and the attraction to donors of exemption from capital gains
tax and capital transfer tax it is in a relatively privileged position.

Heritage property offers the opportunity to study the public,
private and voluntary (charity) sectors performing very similar
tasks. The old Ministry of Public Buildings and Works, with
its responsibility for ancient monuments, previously part of
the Department of the Environment, was, during 1983, recon-
stituted as the Historic Buildings and Monuments Commission, with a grant-in-aid of £52 million. In order to support
their activities they started a subscription scheme whereby
members of "English Heritage" enjoy free access to the Commission's 400 sites including properties such as Stonehenge
and the Tower of London which attract more visitors than
the most ambitious private sector facilities.

Private stately homes, designed to keep the public as far
away as possible, but opened to keep the tax man away and
to attract as many of the public as possible, are now a business
in their own right. This has been shown by the purchase of
Warwick Castle by Madame Tussauds, who would, no doubt,
be a bidder for the Tower of London if the Government's disposals policy were pursued to its logical conclusion.

The National Trust, with over one million members, is committed to the preservation of both land and buildings and not

just the grandest of buildings; smaller domestic buildings now form the basis of a holiday cottage letting portfolio consisting of several hundred properties. Their total ownership now extends to 500,000 acres, the vast majority of this being of high scenic value but low agricultural value.

The motivation, objectives and mode of operation of each of the three sectors (public, private and voluntary) of heritage property vary and it is usually apparent from quite small features which type of management is supervising the property. Also each operates under a different financial regime and a somewhat random method of property allocation, influenced as much by the availability of funds (see 12.5.4) as by a ranking of architectural or historical features. Pricing policy is influenced by both general factors and the particular features of individual properties. Nevertheless the end result in all three sectors is the preservation of heritage property and its enjoyment by in excess of 35 million visitors a year. Also probably a greater variety of property and effectiveness than if any one of these sectors were given overall supervisory powers to the exclusion of the other two. Comparative statistical evidence is not very easy to use but in 1975 the position was as follows:

The D.O.E. received 15·5 million visitors paying approximately 13p per head at the 240 properties under its control. Two-thirds of the visitors were accounted for by only 24 properties, a number of them located in London.

Private stately homes are less easily assessed. It has been estimated that the three largest jointly had as great an income as all the D.O.E. sites with one-tenth of the number of visitors. The most popular half-dozen houses, each attracted about half-a-million visitors.

The National Trust received 4·2 million visitors at their several hundred properties (visits to bare land are not recorded), with almost 0·5 million members paying a (then) annual subscription of £3, accounting for nearly 1 million visits.

Since 1976 the aggregate number of visitors to each sector has steadily risen but in the private sector they have been divided between a growing number of competing properties, with the result that some individual properties have suffered a fall in numbers. The vagaries of the weather on certain key week-ends also introduces a distortion into the figures which can mask more fundamental changes in visitor behaviour.

Sources and Further Reading

Charity Commissioners, Annual Reports.
Church Commissioners, Annual Reports.
Crown Estate, Annual Reports.
Massey and Catalano, Capital and Land, Arnold, 1978.
National Trust, Annual Reports.
Norton-Taylor, Whose Land is it Anyway, Turnstone, 1982.
Report of the Committee of Inquiry into the Acquisition and Occupancy of Agricultural Land. Cmnd. 7599, H.M.S.O., 1979.
Stapleton, Funding Recreational Development, 251 E G 841.
Steele, Financial Institutions, Their investments and their agricultural land ownership, Reading University, 1983.

PART II

Lease Management

Chapter 6

Commercial Property

6.1 Introduction

The activities and procedures dealt with in this chapter represent the major part of the work of estate managers. The subject has not been approached from either a legal or valuation standpoint but one which endeavours to identify decisions the estate manager needs to take in relation to individual leases, and the factors to be considered. Only a limited amount of case-law has been mentioned, as copious and rigorous legal texts exist. The most respected of these, Woodfall, is now produced in loose-leaf encyclopaedia form in its quest to keep abreast of the case-law. The valuations required are not complex but are best approached within the discipline of a clearly developed conceptual base rather than as *ad hoc* aspects of estate management.

The primary legislation, that is to say that legislation concerned primarily with the ordering of the relationship between landlord and tenant of business property, is found in the Landlord and Tenant Acts of 1927 and 1954, the latter as amended by the Law of Property Act 1969.

In the post-war period, and particularly since the start of the 1970s, there has been a plethora of secondary legislation and administrative procedures which have significantly affected the position of occupiers, and to a lesser extent owners, of commercial property. It is intended to summarize all the primary legislation, but as regards the secondary legislation, its existence will be identified but not pursued.

The last half of the chapter concerns itself with the interpretation and implementation of covenants, emphasizing those aspects where particular estate management skills are required. It should be made clear that a comprehensive and detailed legal treatment of such important covenants as those of repair or rent review can only be obtained from a specialist legal text and the necessary advice from the legal profession.

6.2.1 Landlord and Tenant Acts

Two principal Acts and an amending Act create the statutory

111

framework. The Landlord and Tenant Act 1927, Part I, and the Landlord and Tenant Act 1954, Part III, deal with compensation for tenant's improvements at the end of the lease. Part II of the 1954 Act sets out a detailed code of rights and duties at the termination of tenancies, and a number of amendments were made by the Law of Property Act 1969, following a report by the Law Commission.

The aims of the legislation are to ensure that commercial landlord and tenant relationships work well, that the parties are treated fairly and that there is encouragement to maintain and enhance the physical fabric. As was said by Goulding J. in 1979, "Parliament did not by this legislation intend to petrify the economy of business premises. I think rather that the intention was to leave the market to develop freely subject only to the amending protective policy of the Act." In fact, of the applications made under the Act only approximately 5% result in the court making an order as to the terms of a new tenancy or refusing to grant a new tenancy. The County Court hears cases where the rateable value is less then £5,000, other cases are heard by the High Court.

The application of the legislation to business tenants under section 23 has been interpreted broadly to the benefit of tenants in the occupation of a holding carrying out a wide range of activities. The extent of this illustrated by *Groveside Properties Ltd.* v. *Westminster Medical School*, 1983 where a flat leased by the school was occupied by four medical students. The Court accepted that a major medical school was a business activity and that part of this business was the fostering of a collegeate spirit, which the flat assisted. Certain tenancies have been excluded by section 43, including those not exceeding six months unless they contain ... provision for extension beyond six months or the tenant has been in occupation for a total period exceeding twelve months. Also section 38 provides that on a joint application to the Court by the two parties, the Court may approve an agreement excluding the provisions of sections 24 to 28, this is being used more widely.

Some of the problems of comprehension and interpretation of the statutory provisions, particularly where there is a consequentiallity of events, can be overcome by the application of decision-making techniques. The Building Economics Bureau has produced a useful flow-chart through the legislation, though (as with any application of new techniques to an existing situation) it does require a certain flexibility of approach in its practical application. A simplified flow-chart is set out in appendix C.

An essential requirement for the operation of statutory provisions of this type is motivation by the parties to initiate and respond to notices within the prescribed time tables. Towards the end of a lease, a mesne landlord between a freehold or long leasehold and a tenant in occupation is under little incentive to operate the system. The Act provides in section 44 and Schedule 6 for the concept of a competent landlord, being the landlord with the most immediate interest for a term greater than 14 months at the date of the relevant notice. There can only ever be one competent landlord and only he can operate the statutory procedures for terminating tenancies.

6.2.2 Security of Tenure

Section 24 provides that no periodic tenancy or tenancy for a fixed term exceeding six months of a holding to which the Act applies shall come to an end unless terminated in accordance with the Act. The only ways that the tenancy can be terminated are:

By one of the common law methods, notice to quit by the tenant or surrender or forfeiture.

By one of the special forms of statutory notice:

Tenant's notice to terminate under section 27.

Landlord's notice to terminate under section 25.

Tenant's request for a new tenancy under section 26.

By the landlord and tenant agreeing to the grant of a new tenancy, whereby the current tenancy terminates on the date of commencement of the new tenancy.

The action to bring to an end a tenancy to which Part II of the Act applies can be taken by either landlord or tenant. A landlord's notice under section 25 must be served within the period of six months to 12 months prior to the specified date of termination. Such a notice is invalid unless it requires the tenant to notify the landlord within two months whether or not he is prepared to give up possession. The landlord's notice must also state whether the landlord would oppose the tenant's application to the Court for a new tenancy and if so the grounds upon which the landlord would oppose the application.

A tenant for a term of years certain exceeding one year who has not received a section 25 notice from his landlord may request a new tenancy by serving a notice under section 26 in the period six months to 12 months before the expiry of the original tenancy, and in some circumstances it can be advantageous for the tenant to take the initiative in this way.

A landlord who delays service of his section 25 notice may be pre-empted by the tenants' section 26 notice, requesting a new tenancy and specifying a renewal date, 12 months hence, despite the contractual term expiring sooner. In this way the tenant gains up to six months at the existing historic rent.

If the tenant has served a section 26 notice, the landlord cannot serve a section 25 notice, but may within two months serve a counter-notice on the tenant specifying the grounds upon which he will oppose the tenant's application either as to the renewal itself or the proposed terms.

The form of these various notices are to be found in the Landlord and Tenant Act 1954 Part II (Notices) Regulations S.I. 1957 No. 1 157, S.I. 1967 No. 1831 and a quite extensive consolidation in S.I. 1983 No. 133, the latter extending to 70 pages. This more than confirms the author's opinion that the service of these notices is a matter for solicitors, particularly as in *Robert Baxendale Ltd.* v. *Davstone*, 1982, the Court of Appeal reversed the decision of the County Court in permitting an extension of the time limit under County Court Rules Order 13, rule 5.

The interpretation of the various "x" months statutory notices was considered in *Dodds* v. *Walker*, 1981. This confirmed the general rule that where a notice is given in months, the period of the notice ends on the day of the month which bears the same number as that on which the notice is given. Where the initiating event date month is higher than the last day of the terminating month, then that last day is the terminating date. Hence a response on 31 January to a notice served on 30 September was out of time.

During the lengthy negotiations for renewal circumstances may change, or the tenant may become aware of the strength of the landlord's grounds for opposition. As a result, the tenant may wish to withdraw his application. In the County Court the tenant can withdraw under C.C.R. Order 18, rule 1, without leave of the court. In the High Court the tenant can withdraw under R.S.C. Order 21, rule 3 and as amended by S.I. 1982 No. 1786, this discontinuance may be without leave of the court.

Notices under sections 25 and 26, whilst initiated by the different parties and commencing with different procedures, are but two mutually exclusive routes to the same destination;

the right of the tenant to make an application, under section 29, to the Court within two to four months of the original notice for a new tenancy. The success of the legislation can be judged by the very small number of cases that result in a hearing, and the system has been accepted by professional advisers as generally fair and equitable. The parties, aware of a secured access to the Court are generally able to reach agreement. If the landlord has taken no action and the tenant wishes to terminate his fixed term or continuing tenancy then he can serve notice in accordance with section 27.

6.2.3 Landlord's Opposition to Application for a New Tenancy

There are seven grounds specified in section 30 upon which the landlord may successfully oppose the tenant's request for a new tenancy. Some are based upon the tenant's failure to perform covenants, others on the landlord's intentions. In the latter case the tenant may successfully oppose the landlord's intentions through section 31(a) or qualify for compensation on quitting in accordance with section 37, as no blame can be attached to him.

Surveyors will be called upon to give expert evidence for the parties in a hearing before the Court and much of that evidence will be related to one or more of the grounds of section 30(1):

a. Breach of repairing obligation. The landlord will have to show that this is of a serious nature and the Court may accept an undertaking by the tenant to remedy the breach.

b. Persistent delay in payment of rent.

c. Other serious breach of covenant or any other reason connected with the tenant's use or management of the holding. This grants substantial discretion to the court.

d. The landlord is willing and able to provide suitable alternative accommodation on reasonable terms to meet the tenant's requirements, including the protection of goodwill.

e. Possession is required of the subtenancy in order to let the premises as a whole which are currently let in parts and could be let more advantageously as a whole. This ground will only be relevant when the interest of the tenant's immediate landlord is shortly to end. Only then will the superior landlord have the status of a "competent" landlord.

f. The landlord intends to demolish or re-construct or carry out substantial works of construction and he could not reasonably do so without obtaining possession. In *Betty's Cafe Ltd.* v. *Phillips Furnishing Stores Ltd.*, 1958, it was shown that the intention must be established at the time of the hearing, and this can be shown by the stage to which contract documentation has progressed.

The work of demolition or re-construction must involve either the whole of the premises or a substantial part. In *Atkinson* v. *Bettison*, 1955, works on just the ground floor of a three-storey building were held not to qualify.

Works of construction that have been held to qualify include the:

Installation of a new staircase,
Larger lifts and new toilets,
Concreting of an open area,
Installation of tie rods.

Prior to 1969 the landlord could be successful even if he only required part of the premises or required them for a limited period of time. Section 31(A) now provides that if the tenant is prepared under the new lease to give the landlord access and/or take a new tenancy of an economically separable part of the holding, then the tenant can defeat the landlord's application. By implication, a landlord could design his scheme so that it causes maximum interference for the maximum period of time and so defeat the tenant's counter claim.

The work entailed for both landlord and tenant in responding to or initiating matters related to sections:

31A 1(a)   Access in order to carry out works.
31A 1(b)   New tenancy of economically separable parts.

is likely to be both extensive and expensive, so that in all but the most valuable property this is an encouragement to negotiation.

The terms of the existing lease to be renewed need careful study, if as in *Heath* v. *Drown*, 1973, the lease contains clauses giving the landlord wide powers to enter and carry out works, he will have to prove his proposals cannot be accommodated within these provisions.

g. The landlord intends to occupy the premises either for business or residential purposes, but the landlord must

have held the superior interest for at least five years. In
Cam Gears v. Cunningham, 1981, the tenant occupied a
car park in connection with their occupation of nearby
premises. The landlord wished to occupy the holding by
erecting a building and facilities for M.O.T. testing of cars,
this was accepted by the Court.

The case of Chez Gerald v. Greene, 1983, where the landlords claimed they wished to occupy the premises to run
a restaurant, illustrated the typical issues where the
Court has to consider whether the landlords ideas have;
(to quote the elegant phrasing of Asquith L.J.), "Moved
out of the zone of contemplation—out of the sphere of
the tentative, the provisional and the exploratory—into
the valley of decision." This can be demonstrated by:

A resolution in the minutes of the Company.
The raising of finance.
The acquisition of specialist trading expertise.
The financial appraisal of the project.
Consideration of planning and other requirements.

An interesting situation can arise when the lessee is
also the planning authority as in, Westminster City Council v. British Waterways Board, 1983. Westminster were
using the property as a cleansing depot and indicated
they would not give planning permission to the Board
who wished to use it for Waterways purposes. The court
held that planning permission probably would be granted
on appeal, and that the Board genuinely intended to carry
out its proposals; the House of Lords confirmed the Board
was entitled to occupation. If the Court is not satisfied
on grounds e, f or g, but would have been satisfied if
the date for termination had been up to a year later, it
must make a declaration to that effect without an order
for a new tenancy.

If the Court sees the proposals as more distant, it may agree
to the new lease containing a break clause or being shorter
than would normally be granted, as in Wig Creations v. Colour
Film Services, 1969. In Adams v. Green, 1978, the Court noted
that if a break clause was a disadvantage to the tenant, his
rent should be reduced to reflect this. The court was particularly helpful to the landlord in Amika Motors Ltd. v. Colebrook
Holdings Ltd., 1982, where in recognition of the landlord's
intention to develop, the court granted a five year term with
a break after three years.

6.2.4 Interim Rents

From the date the contractual tenancy ends to the date the terms of a new tenancy are determined by the Court or finally agreed between the two parties can be a long period. Tenants were able to delay final agreement for many months or even years and during this time only the old rent could be recovered by the landlord. To deal with this mischief the Law of Property Act 1969 introduced a section 24(a) enabling the landlord to make an application to the Court for an interim rent after he has given notice under section 25 to terminate the tenancy or the tenant has requested a new tenancy under section 26.

The interim rent is payable from the date of the landlord's application under section 24(a) or the date specified in the landlord's or the tenant's notice, whichever is the later. Thus in *Stream Properties v. Davies*, 1972, the landlord gave notice in September, 1970, to end the continued tenancy on 25 March, 1971. In December, 1970, the tenant applied to the court under section 29 for a new tenancy. In November, 1971, the landlord applied under section 24(a) for the determination of an interim rent and it was held that the interim rent was payable from November, 1971. In *English Exporters (London) Ltd. v. Eldonwall Ltd.*, 1973, the date of the section 24(a) application was 29 December, 1971, and the date specified in the tenant's section 29 application was 1 March, 1972, so this later date applied. In this case the decision was given on 13 November, 1972. Six weeks is allowed for appeal, and in accordance with section 64 the new tenancy cannot start earlier than three months after the Court's decision as to the grant of the new tenancy. The interim rent was payable from 1 March, 1972, to 1 April, 1973, when the new tenancy began. Section 24(a) cannot be said to be a total success.

The interim rent will usually be fixed at the hearing which also determines the new rent. The interim rent is to be backdated to the ascertained interim commencement date. This valuation is retrospective, whereas the new rent can take account of things likely to happen up to the date when the new term will commence. The interim rent is that on an assumed annual tenancy. If the arguments are accepted that tenants should pay a premium on market value for reviews of periods longer than five years, then an annual tenancy is worth rather less than the general level of market evidence. The terms of the new tenancy may be different from those of the old tenancy; the interim rent is to be fixed in terms of the old tenancy whereas the new rent reflects the terms of the new tenancy. Lastly, and most confusing of all, the interim rent must have regard to the old rent. In *Fawke v. Viscount Chelsea*, 1979, the Court of Appeal accepted that this implied a cushioning effect, though in that case they reflected the failure by the landlord to carry out repairing covenants which resulted in serious dry-rot damage.

Where there are no problems of breach of covenant, then the decisions of the courts tend to give a discount for interim rent of 10% to 30% of that amount determined as the new rent. The scale of discretion which the section gives to the judge as valuer is considerable, therefore the role of the expert witness is crucial. The interim rent element of the evidence cannot be dismissed as less important than that for the new rent. It may only apply for a few months, but the opportunity it provides for demonstrating the application of sound valuation experience and the ways it can be distinguished from the new rent may enable the Court to assess the quality of the expert evidence and so strengthen or weaken the effect of the expert's evidence on the Court's decision on both rents.

6.2.5 The New Tenancy

Arising from the earlier procedures, the Court may under section 29 make an order for a new tenancy. This raises a number of issues which, if not agreed upon between the landlord and tenant, present the court with the task of determining all the terms of a new tenancy, the most important of which is the rent.

The Act provides in section 34 that it shall be the rent that the holding might reasonably be expected to be let at in the open market by a willing lessor, disregarding:

any effect on rental of the tenant's previous occupation;
any goodwill attached to the premises;
any effect on rent of improvements referred to below;
any value attributable to a licence to sell intoxicating liquor if it appears to the Court that the licence belongs to the tenant.

Improvements are to be disregarded if carried out other than as an obligation of the lease and either carried out during the tenancy about to terminate or completed not more than 21 years before the application for a new tenancy, and the tenant and user have qualified under the Act during that period of time.

The issue of how valuers should give effect to this apparently simple legal instruction on improvements has been considered in *G.R.E.A. Real Property Investments Ltd.* v. *Williams*, 1979. The tenant's valuer argued that the premises should be valued as if the tenant's works did not exist and this should be done by deducting from the annual value of the complete premises the annual equivalent of the current cost of the tenant's improvements. The landlord's valuer argued that the same ratio of value for unimproved and improved values that existed at the start of the lease should subsist throughout the whole period of the tenant's occupation. Though this was a consultative case stated from a rent review arbitration, Forbes, J., considered this in its broadest context and provided the following guidelines:

> The tenant is to be credited with the rental equivalent of the improvements.
>
> The improvements are to be assumed to have been paid for when they were done and assessed as a wasting asset.
>
> The improvements should be valued as existing as at the review (renewal) date and not completed at that date.

Later that year he heard *Estates Projects* v. *Greenwich London Borough*, 1979, which concerned four former houses used as shops on the ground floor and offices on the upper floors. The Court was not enthusiastic about the methods adopted by landlord, tenant or arbitrator but indicated qualified support for the relative proportion of values at the start of the lease, which had been used by the landlord in the previous case.

Where the improvements are a replacement of some previous buildings, structures or site works, rather than an addition, then the landlord will wish to enjoy the hypothetical value which those demolished premises would have had if they had still existed. The importance of detailed records including photographs cannot be overstressed.

It has also been suggested that the landlord should enjoy the rental value (if any) attributable to the potential of the unimproved property for its suitability for making improvements.

Care should be taken to avoid the problem that arose in *Euston Centre Properties* v. *H. and J. Wilson*, 1983, where "the tenant" under an agreement for a lease carried out works. It was subsequently held that during the agreement for lease the "tenant" only had the status of licensee and hence could not enjoy the statutory improvements disregard.

The Court is given a discretion in section 33 to grant a tenancy for a term not exceeding 14 years. This, together with the provisions for the effect of improvements upon rentals, has some interesting implications for negotiations between landlord and tenant.

Consider the following circumstances, bearing in mind that section 34(2)(a) and the 1954 Act provides that the 21 year disregard runs from the date of statutory application for the new tenancy (up to 12 months before the end of the tenancy).

Lease A   Lease B   Lease C

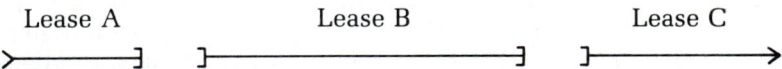

If improvements are completed eight years before the end of lease A and if the tenant can obtain in lease B a term of 14 years or less, then there will be statutory improvements disregard at the start of both lease B and lease C. Hence there is an incentive for the tenant to pursue the exercise of his rights before the court (who cannot grant a term for more than 14 years). By contrast the landlord should (out of court) grant lease B for as short a period as possible, in excess of 15 years; in order that the 21 year disregard is avoided at the start of lease C, enabling the landlord to reap the benefit of the improvements.

Alternatively if improvements are completed nine years before the end of lease A the landlord wants lease B to be for 14 years and so lease C can commence outside the 21 year disregard. Whereas the tenant wants either a term of 13 years for lease B, so that lease C commences within the 21 year statutory disregard, or as long as possible lease term B, to delay the start of lease C.

There is ample scope here for some significant tactical negotiation in respect of the rental value of different length leases, quite unrelated to the frequency of rent reviews. In *CBS UK Ltd* v. *London Scottish Properties*, 1985 the landlord was seeking a 14 year term, but the tenant only required a lease for $2\frac{1}{2}$ years, which was granted by the court.

In default of agreement between the two parties section 35 enables the Court to determinate any other matters and they shall have regard to the terms of the current tenancy and to all relevant circumstances.

This leaves considerable discretion to the court, as was demonstrated in *Cairnplace Ltd.* v. *CBL (Property Investments)*

Co. Ltd., 1983. The current tenancy had a provision whereby on assignment the landlords could require two directors of the assignee company to guarantee performance of the obligations under the lease for the remainder of the term.

The landlords sought a provision in the new lease requiring the tenants to provide sureties. The tenants challenged this on two grounds, firstly that sureties should be dealt with by section 41A(b) and secondly that the jurisdiction did not extend to third parties. The Court of Appeal confirmed the landlords request saying, "there may be many other circumstances, differing widely from those in the instant case, in which it would be fair and responsible for the court to determine that there should be guarantors of the tenant's obligations in the new lease".

Assuming that one of these relevant circumstances is the terms being agreed in the market at the date of the new tenancy, then landlords may endeavour to make significant changes to the terms of the old lease.

In *Card Shops Ltd.* v. *Davies*, 1971, the Court refused on renewal of the tenancy to replace a qualified covenant against assignment with an absolute restriction since it would significantly restrict the tenant's future ability to realize goodwill on an assignment.

In *Charles Clements (London) Ltd.* v. *Rank City Wall*, 1978, there was a restriction of use to cutlers, (a trade in which the tenants had been engaged for many years) which the landlord wanted to relax. It was agreed that the difference in rental value was £1,750 p.a., and the Court held that it was not right to impose the relaxation on an unwilling tenant.

Institutions now look for a "clear" lease, that is to say one where either the tenant is responsible for all outgoings, or the landlord, whilst responsible for outgoings, is able to recoup their full cost in a comprehensive service charge. If a landlord can alter the terms of a lease on renewal of a tenancy this can reduce the yield by in excess of 1% and significantly increase the value of his interest, for only a relatively modest reduction in the rental to reflect the more onerous obligations. In the case of *O'May and Others* v. *City of London Real Property Co. Ltd.*, 1979, the landlord was initially successful in introducing a comprehensive service charge in the new lease, with provision for a sinking fund for capital items. The Court adopted four tests which had to be satisfied before amending the terms of the old lease:

Has the party demanding the change shown a good reason?

Will the party resisting the change be adequately compensated?
Will the adjustment materially impair the conduct of the tenant's business?
Is the variation fair and reasonable between the parties?

The case was subsequently heard in the Court of Appeal in 1980, where the tests were approved but the Court did not accept that the second test was satisfied. They did not feel that a 5% reduction in rent passing was adequate compensation for a short-term tenant taking on an indeterminate risk which should properly be borne by the freeholder or a long leaseholder, this was confirmed by the House of Lords.

Though these criteria were used for a change in the repairing obligations, they are equally applicable to changes in other terms of the lease and demonstrate the flexibility built into the legislation, and one of the reasons for its success.

One of the most helpful determinations under the Act and be found in *Newey and Eyre Ltd. v. J. Curtis and Son Ltd.*, 1984, this considered in relation to warehouse premises the similarities and differences of comparables:

Access
Floor area
Rent review period
Sitting tenant v. vacant possession
Repair covenants
Relativities of values between floors
Age and layout
User clause
Improvements
Premiums and upwards only reviews

The Court fixed a rent of £13,000, which analysed out at £2·40 ft.[2] for ground floor warehousing, the lease provided for landlord's repair and restriction on user to the storage of electrical goods.

In most instances landlords and tenants reach agreement without recourse to the courts and a tenant agreeing to these types of changes in lease-terms will ensure that the rental is adjusted accordingly. Further, the effect of the lower capitalization rate creates a situation similar to marriage value, and the tenant may well seek a share of the value added to the landlord's interest. This will be strongly resisted by landlords, but is a useful negotiating point for tenants' surveyors.

The Act also provides in section 32 for the Court to determine the property comprised under the new tenancy. In almost every case this will be unchanged but where the tenant is prepared to accept part only and the Court rejects section 31A, (1)(b) landlord's grounds of opposition, the tenancy shall be that smaller part.

If the Court orders that a new tenancy be granted, the tenant has 14 days within which to apply for the order to be revoked, presumably in case he changes his mind on learning what the terms of the new tenancy are going to be.

6.2.6 Compensation on Quitting

If the landlord is successful in satisfying the Court upon one of the seven grounds in section 30, then section 31 provides that the Court shall not grant a new tenancy. However, whilst some of the grounds are based on the tenant's breach of covenant, others are based solely on the landlord's initiatives and no blame can attach to the tenant. A landlord who is successful under section 30, paragraphs e, f and g, will in accordance with section 37 have to pay compensation, on a basis which possesses only the merit of certainty. The compensation is 6 × the rateable value if the tenant has been in occupation for more than 14 years and 3 × the rateable value for any shorter period. Where the landlord patently has a good case it would be a total waste of the tenant's time to apply for a new tenancy, and the section as amended provides that the tenant does not need to apply for a new tenancy in order to protect his right to compensation.

A problem arose in *Edicron Ltd*. v. *William Whitely Ltd*., 1983, in defining the holding upon which the rateable value multiplier should be based. Here the tenant re-occupied a portion of the premises which had previously been sublet between the service of the section 25 notice and after putting in an application for a new tenancy but before the expiry of the section 25 notice. The tenant subsequently discontinued his application for a new tenancy and under section 64 the tenancy expired three months thereafter. The court held that the date of the service of the section 25 or section 26 notice defined the extent of the holding, as a result compensation at $4\frac{1}{2}$ × rateable value was obtained on part which had not been occupied for 14 years. Whereas in *Cardshop Ltd*. v. *John Lewis Properties Ltd*., 1982, the date for determining the multiplier that applies is the date the tenant quit.

Finally tenants, who receive the statutory compensation, will be pleased to know that it is not charged to Capital Gains Tax. The Court of Appeal in *Drummond* v. *Brown*, 1984, held that the payment was not "a capital sum derived from an asset ... in particular a capital sum received by way of compensation for any kind of damage or injury to assets or for the loss destruction or dissipation of assets" as provided in the Capital Gains Tax Act 1979. Rather it was simply a sum which Parliament said should be paid, the decision is perhaps generous to the tax payer.

The arbitrary nature of the compensation when rating revaluations are infrequent and inflation running at a high level is quite unsatisfactory. The Local Government Planning and Land Act 1980 enables the Secretary of State to vary the multiplier by statutory instrument, this may well be used at the next rating revaluation.

6.2.7 Compensation for Improvements

If tenants are to improve their business premises then various incentives are required, and these include adequate compensation for the tenant quitting on the termination of the tenancy. The tenant will only qualify under Part I of the Landlord and Tenant Act, 1927 if, prior to the commencement of the works, he serves notice on the landlord, who has three months in which to object. If there is no objection and the landlord does not offer to do the works himself then the tenant can carry out the works. If the landlord objects then the matter can be determined by the Court. The Court must be satisfied that any improvement is of such a nature as to add to the letting value of the holding at the termination of the tenancy, is reasonable and suitable, and does not diminish the value of any other property belonging to the landlord.

It is thought, somewhat surprisingly, that *Deerfield Travel Services Ltd.* v. *Leathersellers Company*, 1982, was the first case to give guidance on what constitutes sufficient notice by the tenant, under section 3 of the Act. The Court held that a series of documents served by the tenants did constitute proper notice and that the landlord's responses did not constitute an objection within three months. Hence the court could certify the works carried out were proper improvements. The compensation shall not exceed the smaller of; the net addition of the value of the holding as a whole which is the direct result of the improvement, or the reasonable cost of carrying out the improvement less the cost, if any, of putting the improvements into a reasonable state of repair.

The effect of the improvements on the value of the premises is influenced by the landlord's subsequent intentions. If these include demolition, structural alterations, refurbishment or change of use, then these will be reflected in the basis of compensation, to the detriment of the tenant. In practice the 1927 Act procedures are seldom initiated by tenants. In shop property many so-called improvements are of a trade rather than a property character and most leases provide that at the end of the term the tenant shall restore the premises to their original condition.

6.3.1 Secondary Legislation

The common law relationship between landlord and tenant is set out in the lease, which should be a comprehensive contract between the parties. In fact the lease may not cover every eventuality and it also has superimposed upon it the Landlord and Tenant Acts. Both the lease and the Landlord and Tenant Acts are concerned with the legal rights, powers and duties between the two parties directly concerned with the use and occupation of the demised premises.

Social, technical and economic change and the ineffectiveness of written agreements have shown the need for a much wider pattern of rights and duties between individuals, and between individuals and the State. In relation to property, the law of tort, particularly nuisance, waste, negligence and trespass, represent a substantial pattern of rights and duties in respect of third parties. Some wrongful acts may constitute both a breach of contract and a tort, and in such circumstances the plaintiff may choose the basis for his action. In recent years statute law has tended to take over the role previously played by the law of tort in protecting third parties and seeking to ensure that the public at large are not subject to various dangerous conditions or undesirable practices. These provisions represent a substantial volume of secondary legislation and are either of a general environmental type or directed at a specified group of persons; owner, occupier, owner-occupier or the employer. Unless there is some indication to the contrary, they tend to be directed at whoever is in possession of the premises.

6.3.2 General Environmental Measures

The pattern of public health legislation and planning legislation, together with some housing legislation, grants to local authorities substantial overall control of the environment. In some fields it is a technical matter of measurement of quality, in others a qualitative opinion of safety, health or visual amenity. Within the breadth of the environment law some of the provisions are concerned with the creation and maintenance of the infrastructure of services which permit the existence of intensively developed urban areas. Others refer to the pattern of rights and duties between the community as a whole, represented by the local authority, and the owner and occupiers of individual properties. In a few cases the infringement of this pattern of rights and duties may constitute a public nuisance and the local authority may be able to exercise its powers under the Public Health Act 1961 to deal with dangerous structures and carry out works if the owner fails to take the necessary action.

The depth and complexity of the provisions can be seen within the Sweet and Maxwell "Local Government Law Encyclopedias". Here "Environmental Health", in three volumes, and "Planning", in four volumes, each contain over 60 statutes dealing with the quality of the environment and the physical condition and use of land and buildings.

The manager of urban estates will from time to time have to deal with the effects of this type of statutory provision exercised by local authorities or various government agencies with which he has had no previous contact, and despite many years of experience, may be unaware of their detailed content. It is invaluable to have access to and the ability to use the various reference and research systems which are increasingly becoming available An attitude of mind favourable to the interpretation of new statutory and administrative material is an essential requirement for those now entering the profession.

6.3.3 Liability to Specific Third Parties

Third parties originally enjoyed rights under common law, but statute law has developed to enhance these rights. Common law is not static and developments in statute law have often been followed by a wider interpretation of the common law.

The occupiers of premises fronting a highway are under a particular duty at common law to ensure that their property is not a danger to persons using the highway. Similarly there is a liability to owners and occupiers of adjoining property; this may relate either to the condition or the user of the premises. A third and most important liability of occupiers is to persons coming on to the premises. If such persons are on the premises as a result of a contract to provide some form of services then the Unfair Contracts Term Act 1977 prevents the exclusion of negligence for business liability.

The Occupiers Liability Act 1957 applies to all visitors who come on to the premises with the express or implied permission of the occupier or in exercise of some statutory right. It imposes a duty on the occupier to take care to see that the visitor will be reasonably safe in using the premises for the purposes for which he was invited or permitted to be there. The position of trespassers was much improved by section 1 of the Occupiers Liability Act 1984. The occupier who has reasonable grounds to believe a third party may be in the vicinity of some danger, must take such care as is reasonable to ensure that he does not suffer injury. Section 2 of the Act reverses an effect of the Unfair Contracts Term Act 1977, by enabling those who permit access to land for recreational or educational purposes to seek to exclude liability for any injuries.

The 1957 Act also dealt with the rights of visitors who had accidents due to the failure of the landlord to carry out his repairing obligations. Whilst this was effective in respect of the common parts, it was not very effective in respect of the demised premises, due to the implied covenant that the tenant must have given the landlord notice of the defect. As a result this was replaced by section 4 of the Defective Premises Act 1972. This provides that a landlord under an obligation to repair owes a duty of care to all persons likely to be affected. The duty arises not only when the landlord is aware of the disrepair but also when he ought reasonably to have known, and reserving a right to inspect would seem to imply the latter condition as satisfied.

Lastly, as between adjoining owners, problems can arise in respect of party walls, as regards support, weather protection and consequential defects and decay. In *Bradburn v. Lindsay*, 1983, one of a pair of Victorian properties was demolished. The occupier of the remaining property claimed under negligence and nuisance he had lost support but more particularly dry rot had spread from the demolished building and exposure to the weather was causing further decay. It was held that the plaintiffs were entitled to:

Have the exposed wall treated with dry rot prevention.
Recover costs of treating dry rot.

Have the exposed wall buttressed and furnished in appropriate rendering.

The Local Authority can take the initiatives under section 29 of the Public Health Act 1961, as amended by the Local Government Act 1982. They can require a person undertaking demolition to:

Shore up any adjacent building.
Weatherproof surfaces of an adjacent building exposed by the demolition.
Repair and make good any damages to an adjacent building.

There is a right of appeal on the basis that the adjacent owner should contribute.

The Law of Property Act 1925, and in London the London Building Acts (Amendment) Act 1939, create a pattern of rights and duties, with provision for notices and the determination of disputes, the aim being not unnecessarily to restrict development, redevelopment and refurbishment.

6.3.4 Employers

Quite distinct from their liabilities as occupiers, occupiers also have responsibilities in their role as employers. This responsibility has built up from various statutory provisions, starting with the Employers Liability Act of 1880. The Health and Safety at Work Act 1974 brings to an end the previous piecemeal approach and presents a framework within which a comprehensive code can develop, enforced by a single safety authority. Over a period of time each of the specialist Acts and their Inspectorates are being integrated within the new Health and Safety Executive. Failure to meet some requirements is treated as a criminal rather than a civil offence and one of the most important requirements is a safety statement putting on record the employer's policy and organization for safety and welfare. The real teeth of the Act are the powers to make detailed regulations supported by codes of practice to assist in their effective implementation.

The two most important specialist statutory provisions are the Factories Act of 1961 and the Offices, Shops and Railway Premises Act of 1963. Both Acts adopt the widest possible defintion of the types of premises which are covered. The requirements include: minimum working space, minimum temperatures, minimum sanitary conveniences, standards of ventilation and lighting, access, safety of machinery and specialist arrangements in connection with noxious or dangerous materials. The Fire Precautions Act 1971 originally applied to premises not covered by the Offices, Shops and Railway Premises Act and the Factories Act, but the Health and Safety at Work Act 1974 has applied this Act more widely. It is primarily concerned with the need for fire certificates and the means by which they may be enforced and consequential works for fire-protection. The Act has a particularly severe effect on some of the older private hotels where the costs of carrying out the works far exceeded the financial resources of the operator and significantly diminished the value of the property.

A designation order under section 1 of the 1971 Act requires buildings in which more than 20 persons are employed to have a fire certificate. The certificate contains:

The use covered by the certificate.
The means of escape.
Maintenance of the means of escape.
The means of fighting fire.
The means of giving warning.
Particulars as to dangerous materials.

A certificate may impose matters such as:

Ensuring escape is free from obstruction.
Maintenance of equipment.
Instructions to employees.
Limitations on persons in the building.
Anything else the fire authority consider appropriate.

The 1976 modification of the regulations place the onus of compliance with the certificate in the case of multi-occupied buildings with the owner, and by implication his agent.

In practice the granting of a fire certificate will be conditional upon the testing of alarms and precautions, safety equipment and the keeping of a log book.

A person in default (the owner) may, if convicted be liable to an unlimited fine and / or two years imprisonment.

Under the Health and Safety at Work Act 1974 if an inspector finds there has been a contravention of the Act he may serve an improvement notice (section 21) a prohibition notice (section 22) or take proceedings in the magistrates court (section 33). If the occupier wishes to appeal against an improvement notice perhaps because the cost of works would be unreasonably high for the resulting benefit then he can appeal to an industrial tribunal within 21 days. It may be possible to negotiate a solution with the inspector or the tribunal may cancel, affirm or amend the notice.

In *Westminster City Council* v. *Select Management*, 1984, the council were successful in imposing improvement notices on the property managers in a block of flats. It was held that whilst each flat qualified as domestic premises; the common parts, lifts and stairs, were non-domestic premises and made available as a place of work for the use of persons who came to repair and maintain the premises. Accordingly, the person with control of the non-domestic premises, had a duty to ensure, as far as was reasonably practicable, that they were safe and without risks to health.

A prohibition notice is more serious, this can direct that certain activities cannot take place unless the specified works are carried out. An appeal does not suspend the effect of the notice.

The essential grounds for the two appeals referred to above is that it is not "reasonably practical" to comply with the inspector's requirements. This implies a subjective practical judgment seeking to balance cost against the level and frequency of the risk that the inspector claims is a breach of the legislation.

Various activities require licences from the local licensing justices or a government agency or need to be registered with the local authority. For example, to obtain a licence to sell intoxicating drink you must apply to the justices' clerk, the police, the local authority, and the fire brigade and provide details of the proposed licensee and the premises. In addition to full and off licences, a residential licence or a restaurant licence may be obtained, and all licences need to be renewed annually. The licensing justices also grant licences for betting shops and this involves the applicant in preparing plans of the area, identifying other betting shops and seeking to show the necessary demand for additional premises. Applications to the licensing justices may well be challenged by those already in the trade in that area.

Local authorities are responsible for the registration of many specialist uses including scrap metal, pet shops, stables and employment agencies. Certain special agencies, such as the Gaming Board, issue licences to gaming clubs, and during 1979 Ladbrokes lost gaming licences for their most prestigious gaming clubs in London and this resulted in a fall in the price of their shares. The valuation of premises subject to the annual renewal of a licence is particularly difficult, and can only be undertaken after detailed research into the general nature of the trade, the standing of the operator or proprietor and the reputation of the particular premises.

6.4.1 Commercial Leases

The interpretation of leases lies at the very heart of urban property management. The estate manager is involved in the interpretation and implementation of covenants in existing leases drafted many years ago and also in advising on the drafting of new leases. The length of leases and the unpredictable changes in the requirements of the business community and of the property market are liable to result in problems quite unforeseeable at the time a document was drafted. A relatively small number of important cases have over the last few years played a major role in the interpretation of covenants, especially rent-reviews in times of rapid inflation. Appendix D contains a model rent-review clause, first recommended for use jointly by the Law Society and the R.I.C.S. in 1979.

In 1975 the Law Commission published a Report on Obligations of Landlords and Tenants which contained a draft Bill entitled Landlord and Tenant (Implied Covenants) Bill. Some of the covenants relate solely to residential tenancies but the majority relate to all types of property. The main thrust is in respect of repairs, and if this were ever enacted then the common law as to implied covenants and the Housing Act 1961, sections 31 and 32, would be superseded.

Ten years later the Law Commission published two further reports; covenants restricting dispositions, alterations and change of use, (No. 141) and forfeiture of tenancies (No. 142). The first report distinguishes between:

Absolute covenants—a complete undertaking not to . . .
Qualified covenants—not to . . . with landlord's consent.
Fully qualified covenants—not to . . . without landlord's consent, which is not to be unreasonably withheld.

The report recommends that the absolute covenant against disposition should not be permitted, but could continue for alteration and user covenants, and that qualified covenants should never be allowed, only fully qualified covenants, with some clarification of the reasonableness test.

The second report proposes that grounds for forfeiture would constitute a termination order event, which would present a court with three alternatives:

The making of an absolute order.
The making of a remedial order.
Refusing to make an order.

In order to produce more equity there is a proposal for the
tenant to have the right to make an application for an order
where the landlord has been in breach of his obligations.
If enacted, the provisions would only apply to tenancies
created after the commencement of the Act, and for many years
there would be both the current system and the codified law
running in parallel.

Most leases are renewals of existing tenancies and negotiations will commence on the basis of the terms of the current
lease, within the framework set out by statute law. In the case
of a letting to a new tenant, the surveyor should, if he considers
it necessary, obtain references from an appropriate source and,
particularly when the prospective tenant is a relatively newly
formed private company, a guarantor for the rent.

When agreement has been reached in principle for a new
lease, heads of agreements are prepared by the lessor's surveyor,
and the lessor's solicitor prepares a draft lease giving effect
to that agreement and including all the normal lease covenants.
Careful study of the draft lease by the surveyor to ensure its
ability to give practical effect to the parties' intentions should
ensure that at least the early years of the term should be trou-
ble-free. The lessor will be anxious to ensure that the lease
goes as far as possible towards what has been called "inflation
proofing" his income from the property. The lessee's negotiating position will be influenced by the extent to which it is
a buyers' or sellers' market and the lessor's desire to implement
a standard form of lease.

Lastly attention should be drawn to the shortest Act on
the Statute Book, the Cost of Leases Act 1958 which in its
entirety consists of section 1, "Notwithstanding any custom
to the contrary, a party to a lease shall unless the parties there
to agree otherwise in writing be under no obligation to pay
the whole or any part of any other party's solicitors costs in
the lease."

This was considered in *Cairnplace Ltd.* v. *CBL (Property
Investment) Company Ltd.*, 1983, where the tenant successfully
appealed against the judgment at first instance. The court
had originally interpreted section 35 of the 1954 Act which
covers the other terms of the lease as enabling it to make the
tenant responsible for the landlord's cost in accordance with

custom. However the Court of Appeal held that statute over-ruled custom, since if it did not there would have been no purpose in enacting the legislation.

6.4.2 The Demise

This should be clear and unambiguous with reference to appropriately coloured plans attached to the lease. When photo-copying plans showing fairly complex physical boundaries, care must be taken that the copy is carefully coloured-up in the same way. It is usual for a schedule of rights and a schedule of reservations to be set out in detail at the end of the lease.

In certain very limited cases the rights attaching to the occupation of the demised premises can be increased by the tenant. The Law of Property Act 1925, section 84(1), enables the owner or the tenant, under a lease of more than 40 years of which more than 25 years have expired, to apply to the Lands Tribunal for the modification or discharge of a restrictive covenant. If the Tribunal grant consent they may direct the applicant to pay compensation to any person entitled to the benefit of the covenant.

In 1984 the Law Commission published Report No. 127 "Transfer of Land: The Law of Positive and Restrictive Covenants" which concluded that there was a need for a fundamental revision of such covenants. Their proposals were set out in a draft Land Obligations Bill.

The tenant in using the premises may attach to them various chattels which then become fixtures. Following *New Zealand Government Property Corporation v. H.M. and S. Ltd.*, 1981, it is necessary to distinguish between: fixtures put in by the tenant for the purposes of their trade, and those installed as part of the structure, which become landlords fixtures. The Court held that the rental benefit of the former could not, except by express agreement, become part of the demised premises and so were not improvements in the context of section 34 of the 1954 Landlord and Tenant Act.

6.4.2a Rent and Guarantors

The rent, whether fixed or stepped, and frequency of payment, on old or modern quarter days will be stated, together with the rate of interest on overdue rent.

Any rent-free period for fitting out, any premium and any works should be stated with conditions which must be met.

The service charge will be identified and its payment specified as additional or further rent. Although the detail of the rent-review will be set out in a separate schedule, the dates for review, together with upwards/downwards provisions, must be referred to, and it is helpful to require a memorandum to be attached to the lease after every review.

References will have been taken out in the case of less substantial tenants or enquiries made to establish that the tenant is indeed the claimed subsidiary of a "blue chip" covenant.

It may be necessary, in order to be able to recommend a tenant to the landlord, to obtain personal or corporate guarantees. The complexity of issues which may arise in respect of the liability of guarantors is illustrated by *Selous Street Properties* v. *Oronel Fabrics Ltd.*, 1984, the facts are complicated:

Selous let to Oronel (of whom Morgan was a guarantor) in 1973 for 21 years.
Oronel assigned to Highlight Sports in 1973, who gave a direct covenant to Selous.
Highlight Sports assigned to Sunbird Fashions in 1976, who gave a direct covenant to Selous.
Sunbird Fashions assigned to Cavatina Holdings in 1976.
Karniol stood surety for the performance by Sunbird and with Sunbird for the performance by Cavatina.

Selous made a claim for £110,000 of rent arrears arising from a rent review in 1980. Oronel and Morgan argued that due to the effect of a licence given by Selous to Highlight in respect of retrospective consent for minor improvements they were excluded from their obligations. The Court did not accept this since case law went against Oronel (the tenant) and whilst Morgan (the guarantor) would normally have been discharged by the variation, the detailed wording of the surety prevented this.

Whatever legal rights may be, their implementation depends upon the identification of a party able to discharge them. The judge had to consider rights of subrogation; he accepted that though the original lessee and assignee are both liable to the lessor, the assignee is primarily liable. Thus Cavatina were primarily liable and so obliged to indemnify Oronel (Karniol was also obliged to indemnify Oronel). Thus once Oronel had paid the arrears, they would be entitled to be subrugated to Selous rights. It was also held that as Morgan could not be in a worse position than Oronel he had a right to be indemnified by Cavatina and Karniol.

A tenant seeking to avoid these long term problems has several routes open to him including:

Release on assignment, (indeed *Pinemain* v. *Welbeck International*, 1984, suggests that for an assignee to enforce a surety guarantee, the benefit must be expressly assigned to him).
Short leases.
Options to break.
Options to renew.

The last two of these are considered below. However the real question is whether, as under Scottish Law, the tenant's liability should end upon his assignment of his property interest?

6.4.2b Options

The term of the lease is a matter of current practice. Normal occupation leases are frequently for 20 or 25 years with reviews every five years. Longer or shorter leases can be granted, but the same objective of longer or shorter periods of occupation can also be achieved by options within a standard lease.

A lessee may seek an option to break the lease at intermediate dates and this can include the payment of a fine; a lessor usually only agrees to this when the building has proved difficult to let, since the effect on the investment value of his interest can be severe. However American and European based multi-nationals are used to shorter lease terms, and invariably require options to break. The attractiveness of their covenant usually overcomes any hesitation the lessor may have on account of the uncertain long-term income, though this poses some interesting valuation problems.

Quite distinct from the statutory rights to a new tenancy, leases can contain an option to renew on similar terms. Landlords should beware of the risks of creating a perpetually renewable lease, which the Law of Property Act 1922 converts to a term of 2,000 years. Where an option is given, the clause should specifically exclude the option provision from the terms of the new lease. Tenants seeking to exercise the option will need to ensure, in accordance with *Kitney* v. *Greater London Properties*, 1984, that they have performed all the covenants.

A landlord's attempt to frustrate the tenant's exercise of an option was considered by the House of Lords in *Sudbrook Trading Estate Ltd.* v. *Eggleton and Another*, 1982. Here the clause in an option (to purchase) provided that the price was to be agreed between valuers appointed separately by the land-lord and tenant, and in default by an umpire, appointed by the valuers.

The lessors refused to appoint their valuer on the basis of precedent that as long as the agreement was incomplete the court could not order specific performance. The House of Lords overruled all the precedent since 1807 and ordered that the valuations be made and the property conveyed.

Upon the exercise of the option, the parties will be anxious to determine which terms, if any, can be altered and brought into line with current practice. In the early 1980s there were several cases on one aspect of options to renew, at the heart of the valuers expertise, concerned with the approach to a 21 year frequency of review. In *National Westminster Bank Ltd. v. BSC Footwear Ltd.*, 1981, the Court of Appeal considered an option to renew for a further term of 21 years, "at the then prevailing market rent". At first instance the judge had accepted the landlord's contention that this could be interpreted as prevailing market conditions, and so the arbitrator could determine a rent for three or five years and provide machinery for the rest of the 21 year term. The Court of Appeal allowed the tenant's appeal and ordered that the arbitrator was to determine a single rent which was to be payable throughout the term of the new lease.

This decision was followed in *Bracknell Development Corporation v. Greenlees Lennards Ltd.*, 1981, despite a bold attempt by the landlord to introduce the doctrine of frustration, as held to apply to leases in *National Carriers Ltd. v. Panalpina (Northern) Ltd.*, 1981, on the basis of the impossibility for an arbitrator to determine a "full and fair" market rent for the whole period. The judge accepted expert evidence, not displaced in cross examination, that an arbitrator would be able to determine a single rent for a period of 21 years in accordance with the clause.

These two cases appear conclusive law that no new rent review or variation can be inserted in the contractually renewed lease. In *Lear v. Blizzard*, 1983, the court failed to award any uplift for a 21 year term, though this should not be taken as a general rule, but relevant only to facts of that case, a somewhat secondary investment; the decision has been subject to criticism.

The sparcity of the wording of the option clause often causes uncertainty as to how improvements are to be treated. In *Thomas Bates v. Wyndham Lingerie Ltd.*, 1981, where the court ordered recitification of a contractually renewed lease which failed to provide for an arbitrator to determine rent in default of agreement on review, the clause referred to "such rents as shall have been agreed between the lessor and the lessee". The Court was able to distinguish this from *Ponsford v. HMS Aerosols Ltd.*, 1978, where there was no reference to agreement between the parties and so improvements could be disregarded.

An important lessor's option is a redevelopment clause. This provides that at specific dates during a normal occupation lease the lessor, on giving the required notice and if necessary being able to satisfy the courts, the lessor will be able to get possession for the purposes of redevelopment. This will not only depress rents but also limit the quality of the covenant. However, it does preserve some income from the property and avoid any empty-rate charges. What may be more important is that it preserves some reasonable economic activity in areas which can easily become blighted or derelict many years before the redevelopment project is commenced.

6.4.3 Repair

Of all lease covenants, those of repair are most capable of variety of phraseology. They may need to cover the standard in which the property is let, is to be kept, and is to be given up. Responsibility will need to be apportioned between the parties and procedures set out for the purposes of inspection and the giving of necessary notices.

The responsibility of the parties is not solely a matter of contract. The parties may find that due to the common law or statute they become responsible for a variety of unfortunate events that befall third parties as a result of the condition of the property, and adequate third party insurance is essential.

In the case of a single occupier, a modern lease will usually be on a full-repairing basis. In the case of multi-occupation a variety of different patterns of obligations exist. Considerable difficulty has been experienced in law in distinguishing between repair and renewal. The case of *Ravenseft Properties Ltd. v. Davstone*, 1979, hinged on the interpretation of the tenant's obligation to "...repair, renew, uphold, etc..." The practical matter to be resolved was who should pay for replacing defective cladding at a cost of £55,000. The lessee's defence was that this was caused by an inherent defect. This was rejected by the Court, who held that if an inherent defect relates to the whole building, then the lessor is responsible, but if related to a subsidiary part of the demised premises the lessee is responsible.

Many phrases are used to indicate the obligation:

in repair,
in good repair,
in good and tenantable repair,
in good and substantial repair,
in structural repair.

Only the last of these contains a reduced burden. The standard of repair work required is that to reflect the state, condition and character of the property at the commencement of the lease. This raises the question as to the anticipated life of the repair on say a flat roof where cracks may be capable of remedy for a limited period by filling as opposed to a complete new covering. In *Manor House Drive Ltd. v. Shahbazian*, 1965, it was held that a patching repair was acceptable.

A tenant is not obliged to return to the landlord a wholly different property to that demised. Thus in *Halliard Property Co. Ltd. v. Nicholas Clarke Investments Ltd.*, 1983, the court held that the covenant to repair did not extend to re-building in accordance with modern bye laws, a jerry built extension of $4\frac{1}{2}$ inch brick work which fell down.

In order to strengthen their hand landlords can introduce a tenants covenant, "to rebuild, replace, and renew whenever necessary in accordance with best modern practice, the whole or any part of the demised premises that may be or become beyond repair".

A prudent lessee should have a full structural survey carried out by an experienced building surveyor with necessary specialist assistance.

This is equally true of a newly-constructed building, and the surveyor should also be instructed to give an estimate of the likely repair costs of the building, and if this is in any way unusual, seek a commensurate balancing reduction in the rental. Instead of a full-repairing lease, a building may be let under what may loosely be called an internal repairing lease. This is usually the case in a modern lease of a multi-tenanted building where there are service charge arrangements. Also, on occasions older leases of single-occupier buildings were on this basis, and landlords wishing to alter the terms of the lease will have to satisfy the four tests in the *O'May* case, which were approved by the Court of Appeal.

Under internal repairing leases the main expenditure by the tenant is usually painting and decorating to a required standard at specified intervals, and in the last year of the lease the landlord will find it useful to be able to state the colour for the final year, since this may help a subsequent letting.

There are a number of points along the spectrum which allocate repairing obligations between the parties. In *Smedley* v. *Chumley and Hawke Ltd.*, 1981, the tenant covenanted to repair the interior and exterior and the landlord covenanted to keep the main walls and roof in good structural repair and condition. The foundations were found to be defective due to a lack of piling under part of the concrete raft. The landlord claimed the problem arose from a defect of design and that the remedial work would be an improvement of the premises originally demised to the tenant and so he was not liable for the repair. The Court held that the only way for the landlord to meet his obligation was to carry out full remedial work.

In the case of a short-term letting, or the letting of premises in relatively poor order, particularly if they are blighted by some redevelopment or refurbishment proposals, then the landlord has to approach the matter in a very different way if he hopes to receive anything other than a nominal net income from the tenant, though even this would be better than nothing, since if the premises are unoccupied there may also be a liability to pay empty-rates. A phrase such as, "to leave the premises in as good a state of repair as they were at the time of the letting, fair wear and tear accepted" will meet the interests of the two parties. There are many cases concerning the practical implications of this phrase and a useful summary is found in *Miller* v. *Burt*, 1918: "The tenant is responsible for repairs necessary to maintain the premises in the same state as when he took them. If, however, wind and weather had a greater effect upon the premises, having regard to their character, than if the premises had been sound the tenant is not bound so to repair as to meet the extra effect of the dilapidation so caused." In *Regis Property* v. *Dudley*, 1959, it was held that, "... it does not mean that if there is a defect originally proceeding from reasonable wear and tear the tenant is released from his obligation to keep in good repair and condition everything which it may be possible to trace to that defect."

In the case of a fair wear and tear clause a schedule of condition at the start of the lease, attached to the lease, will establish a bench mark for the life of the lease. The surveyor should bear in mind that the document may not be referred to until the end of the lease and adopt an overall style appropriate to those circumstances. Problems can arise generally in respect of repairs when the lessor has covenanted to undertake work but fails to do so and it is a matter of urgency to protect the lessee's personal property. If the lessee, without giving notice, voluntarily does the work then in law the lessee cannot recover the costs, though there is nothing to stop his trying. If the lessee gives the landlord notice and the landlord fails to do the work, then *Lee-Parker v. Izzet*, 1971, indicates that the cost of the works can be recovered by a reduced rent-payment.

6.4.4 Lessee's Breach of Covenant to Repair

A claim for damages for breach of covenant to repair is usually brought at the end of the lease where, due to a lessee's breach, the lessor has suffered a loss in the value of his reversion. Assuming regular but not frequent inspections by the lessor's surveyor, the lessee should have been made aware of any failures to perform covenants during the lease by notice or interim schedules of dilapidations.

The provisions of the Leasehold Property (Repairs) Act 1938 provide relief against enforcement of the covenant to repair in the case of leases granted for a term of more than seven years when three or more years remain unexpired.

The Act provides that before commencing an action for damages, the lessor shall serve on the lessee a section 146 notice, to which the lessee may respond by claiming the benefit of the Act.

The Court is only to permit enforcement of the covenant if the lessor can prove one of the following:

Immediate remedy is necessary to prevent substantial diminution in the value of the reversion.

Immediate remedy is necessary to give effect to legislation.

Where the lessee does not occupy the whole property, immediate remedy is required in the interests of another occupier.

The breach is capable of immediate remedy at relatively small cost compared with the consequences of postponement.

A few months before the end of the lease, the lessor's surveyor, in accordance with the provisions for entry in the lease, should prepare a schedule of dilapidations in order to determine the extent of damages, if any, sustained by his client. The loss is the cost of carrying out the the necessary work and any subsequent loss of rent. This provides an opportunity for the lessee to carry out the work or challenge the schedule. The lessor's surveyor should be clear as to his client's intentions as to the subsequent use of the building.

Section 18 of the Landlord and Tenant Act 1927 sets a ceiling figure on any damages that may be recovered. The damages cannot exceed the amount by which the value of the landlord's reversion is diminished by the breach. Taken to its ultimate, if the lessor intends to demolish at the end of the lease or undertake substantial refurbishment, the breach of covenant will not have damaged his reversion, and no damages can be claimed.

The lessee's surveyor will need to advise upon the reasonableness of the schedule, both the physical items and the costs attached to them. The lessor's intentions in respect of the building, particularly the possibility of refurbishment, must be considered to establish the ceiling value to the claim. In the case of a fair wear and tear clause, the interpretation of the original schedule of condition is likely to create ample opportunity for a large difference of opinion as to the size of a claim for damages. Any attempt in the landlord's schedule to include inherent defects specifying work which will improve the building should be strongly challenged by the tenant.

The final result will usually be arrived at by agreement between the two surveyors and both will probably enter the negotiation with a little to give away. Should either adopt an inflexible attitude, there may be provision in the lease for arbitration. Alternatively the matter will have to be referred to the courts, and this is probably a field in which the skill of the lawyers is least well suited.

Valuation surveyors will be required to advise upon the statutory ceiling value to the claim for damages. This requires an estimation of the value of the lessor's interest with a fully implemented repairing covenant, less the value of the interest in the physical condition as found, and it is only fair to say that such a calculation is as much a negotiation as is that between the building surveyors.

An increasingly common question is the extent to which the cost of the necessary work alone is recoverable. In *Drummond v. S. and U. Stores Ltd.*, 1981, where there was no clear evidence on the effect on the value of the reversion, the Court awarded to the landlord a substantial part of the cost of repairs. The Court also awarded three months loss of rent to cover the period for carrying out the works.

As an alternative to the preparation of a schedule of dilapidations and damages at the end of a lease, the lessor may exercise his rights under the lease to enter the premises and carry out repairs if the tenant has failed to execute them after due notice.

In really urgent cases the lessor may have no option other to simply take action under this provision. Lessor's surveyors must warn their clients that the costs are irrecoverable unless the full statutory procedures are complied with and this will not be possible.

In *SEDEC Investments* v. *Tanner*, 1982, the lessors discovered stonework on the front of the building was falling on the pavement, they exercised their right of entry to carry out emergency work and subsequently served a section 146 notice requiring compensation, to which the lessees replied by claiming the benefit of the 1938 Act. The court held that a section 146 notice served by the lessor after the breach was remedied was invalid, and hence no damages could be claimed. However in *Hamilton* v. *Martell Securities*, 1984, it was held that where a tenant failed to comply with a repairing covenant in a lease which expressly conferred on the landlord the right to enter the demised premises, to carry out repairs and recover the cost from the tenant, an action brought by the landlord to recover such costs is a claim for a debt due under the lease and the 1938 Act does not apply. This was approved in *Colchester Estates* v. *Carlton Industries PLC*, 1984.

There is also specific performance. In the past the courts have been unwilling to order specific performance of repairs, due to the need for detailed supervision. In most cases damages alone were considered an adequate remedy, though in *Francis* v. *Cowcliffe*, 1977, specific performance was awarded in respect of the replacement of a defective lift.

One of the most spectacular cases has been the problems of the New Scotland Yard Building in Victoria, the granite panel cladding of which was cracked. In *Land Securities* v. *Receiver for the Metropolitan Police*, 1983, the lessor sued for forfeiture in order to obtain interpretation of the repairing covenant. The lessees sought declarations of the court that their proposal to replace granite with steel cladding would be an improvement; which had implications for the lessors. The lessees sued the architects, consulting engineers, developer and the G.L.C. for negligence; the cost of replacement could affect the damages.

6.4.5 Improvements

Most leases contain an absolute or conditional covenant by the lessee not to make any alterations to the demised premises. Very often internal partitioning is permitted, as long as the premises are restored to their original condition at the end of the lease. This can be used to advantage by the lessor as the costs of purchasing and fitting partitioning are high and once removed the partitioning has little second-hand value. If the lessor waives his right to require the making good of the demised premises at the end of the lease, the lessee saves the cost of the work and the lessor can then let partitioned office space for more than open space. Only the more prestigious companies are prepared to have specialist-designed partitioning layout to meet their own occupational requirements.

The lessor may have good reasons for preventing alterations, for example, to protect the quality and features of the particular building or estate of which it forms part. Also such activity by a tenant could have qualified as the commencement of a project of material development and create a liability on the lessor to pay development land tax with no prospect of additional income for many years after the date for payment.

The lessor may be quite willing to carry out alterations suggested by the lessee and in return for an appropriate increase in rent they can reach an agreement and amend the lease accordingly. It may seem easy to agree a certain annual percentage payment of the cost of the works. This should be approached cautiously, to ensure that the effect of rent reviews has been considered. Taking a long-term view, the lessor's best interest would be served by taking a value approach and the lessee's by taking a cost approach. The arguments and factors involved were examined in *G.R.E.A. Real Property Investments* v. *Williams*, 1979, see 6.2.5.

Where a lessee wishes to make improvements, the 1927 Act provides for a procedure of notices and rights which balance the interests of the two parties. If the lessee does carry out the improvements then there is provision for compensation for the improvements on quitting. The Act also provides in section 19(2) that if the lease states that the works cannot be done without the lessor's consent, then that consent cannot be unreasonably withheld, though the landlord can obtain payment of a reasonable sum in respect of the diminution in value of the premises or other property in his ownership.

Lambert v. *F. W. Woolworth and Co. Ltd.*, 1938, provides some detailed interpretation:

The question of whether the works are improvements is to be considered from the point of view of the tenant.
Generally the onus of proving unreasonableness is on the tenant.
The Court can determine whether the sum required by the landlord is too great.
Alterations may be improvements if they enable the tenant to use the demised premises and the adjoining premises together more conveniently, although they may not improve the demised premises alone.

Several statutes provide for the making of compulsory improvements, and can prevent the use of the property until these are carried out. Most of these powers are now covered by the Health and Safety at Work Act. Leases contain a clause placing the liability for this type of work on the lessee, but this may not be fair when the lease has a limited term to run and compensation on quitting may be totally inadequate. In, for example, the Fire Precautions Act 1971 the Court is given power to apportion the cost of works equitably between the two parties. This does not mean it is necessary to go to the courts, since the parties may be able to reach agreement by negotiation. Apart from reducing the capital cost to the tenant, in due course it will also prevent him paying rent upon his own capital costs.

6.4.6 Insurance

Insurance has become an industry in its own right, the following are amongst the questions which need to be answered by the property manager.
Normal reinstatement basis, or some lesser amount based on indemnity where reconstruction of old and obsolete buildings would be uneconomic?
If normal reinstatement basis, have all the characteristics of the building and the factors influencing its reinstatement been considered, including:

limited access;
site clearance;
architectural detail;
changes in building regulations, statutes, bye laws;
services.

What arrangements have been made to allow for inflation between valuations, and to reflect the period of delay, before completion of the reinstatement?

What risks are to be covered?

fire;
special, engineering and other perils;
loss of rent, reflecting reviews;
invalidation by tenant's breach of covenant.

What arrangements have been made to cover liability to third parties and employees?

Who is responsible for undertaking the insurance obligation, how is the cost of premiums to be reimbursed and is there adequate exchange of information between interested parties?

Some idea of how badly matters may go is shown by *Beacon Carpets Ltd.* v. *Kirby and Another*, 1984. The landlords covenanted to insure the premises, together with a sum to cover two years loss of rent in full value in the joint names of lessor and lessee and that in the case of the destruction of the premises they would, with all convenient speed, layout all moneys received in respect of such insurance in rebuilding.

The landlords insured the building for £30,000 plus £3,000 to cover rent and fees, the policy named the insured as the landlords and the tenants for their respective rights and interests. The premises were destroyed by fire in 1977 and £26,484 was available for reconstruction, though reinstatement would have cost £50,000. In 1978 the tenants said they no longer wished to occupy any new building and the site remained vacant. In 1979 the tenants surrendered their lease to the landlord, the two parties shared the insurance proceeds equally and the landlord sold the site for £20,000. By their own acts they had released the clause from operation.

The Court of Appeal were somewhat unhappy at the way the parties had moved away from the pleadings at first instance. They allowed an appeal by the Beacon Carpet from the Judge at first instance who had awarded £2 nominal damages and said that the insurance money belonged to the two parties in the ratio of the value of their interests immediately before the fire. An increasing number of leases contain a clause of this type, that is to say, if the premises are not rebuilt within a specified time period (three to five years depending upon the building) then the insurance money is to be shared in the ratio of the value of the parties interests immediately before the event.

6.4.7 Service Charges

The growing complexity and quality of environmental services in modern property, particularly air-conditioned offices and enclosed shopping malls has resulted in service charges of quite startling proportions. A major element of service charges is energy in one form or another and labour, the costs of both rising more rapidly than the rate of inflation. Service charges rising at 10% p.a. compound are not unusual and represent a growing proportion of the costs of occupation, see 9.1.5.

It is normal to have a covenant by the lessee to pay service charge as additional rent and a lessor's covenant to provide the services in accordance with a comprehensive schedule consisting of two parts; firstly procedure for the apportionment of the charge, and secondly the full extent of the services to be provided.

With fixed payments rendered impracticable by inflation, and unrealistic due to new or different techniques over the long term, some experiments have been made in holiday time sharing market with indexation based on a typical year. However an estimate based on the previous year actual costs has become almost universal. This needs to be allocated between the contributors and leases have tended to adopt one of the following:

Specific percentages in the documents; do they aggregate to 100%?

Floor areas with the use of an agreed measuring code, in shops it is possible to have some formula so that large shops are charged less than their floor area proportion.

Rateable Values, in *Moorcroft Estates* v. *Doxford*, 1979, there was a reference to the ratio of the rateable value of the demises premises to the rateable value of the whole. During the lease the assessments of various parts of the building changed. It was held that for the purposes of apportionment, the rateable value ratios should be those existing at the date each expenditure was incurred.

Use made of the services, logical but impractical.

Rental value at a particular date.

In all the above methods care needs to be taken with voids, landlords occupation, improvements and extensions. The effect of extensions and improvements was highlighted in *Pole Properties* v. *Feinberg*, 1981, see 7.4, where the court re-wrote the lease.

The services to be provided in a modern clause typically include:

Lighting and cleaning of common parts.
Cleaning windows of the common parts.
Heating, cooling and ventilating the building.
Repair, maintenance and renewal of fire extinguishers.
Provision, maintenance and repair of fire alarms.
Security systems and emergency lighting.
Provision, maintenance and repair of lifts.
Furnishings and fittings of common parts.
Provision and renewal of rubbish bins.
Painting and decorating the common parts.
Painting, decorating and washing down the exterior of the building.
Repair, renewal and painting of window frames.
Repair, maintenance and renewal of boundary fences.
Inspection, cleansing, maintenance and repair of all conduits and all associated apparatus.
Inspection, maintenance and repair of sprinkler system.
Display of names of occupiers of the building.
Facilities for the use of the landlord's staff.
Compliance with statutory provisions in relation to fire or other hazards.
Employment of staff for the efficient management of the building and provision of accommodation and necessary equipment and conditions of service.
Payment of general and water rates on the common parts.
Payment of insurance premiums.
Repair and maintenance of the structure.
Management costs of the services.

Some of these items are not regular annual expenditure but relatively infrequent, particularly in the case of the replacement of plant and machinery. In order that tenants contribute fairly over the life of the building, sinking funds may be set up in an appropriate form for major items of plant and reserve funds for regular maintenance. These funds can be held by independent trustees which will satisfy the lessees as to the proper accounting of the funds.

Whilst initially attractive, such funds pose a number of problems and some landlords have concluded that their administration and taxation implications are unacceptable. The tenant will be anxious to ensure that contributions to the fund are treated as an expense just like rent, (hence lease clause, "as additional rent") the landlord will seek to avoid taxation of the fund and its accumulation of interest. Unfortunately, both positions are not tenable, and the landlord will have to pay schedule A income tax on the annual contributions to the fund. When expenses are incurred the landlord will be able to claim these against all the income from the property that year and carry forward any excess against rental income in later years.

If the fund is not referred to as "additional rent" then strictly contributions should be taxed as a trade under schedule D Case I, which is likely to be less attractive than Schedule A.

Alternatively a trust can be set up as a separate taxable entity, the contributions to the trust would not be taxed, but the resulting income from the investment is liable to tax technically as a trust, but possibly as an unincorporated association. The tenants may have difficulty in obtaining relief from tax on his contribution, since it can be argued the money has not been spent, rather allocated for a purpose. The trust will offer the advantage of protecting the tenant from the landlord's dealing in the fund, or his insolvency as in *Re Chelsea Cloisters Ltd., 1981*. A fund in the form of a trust may fall foul of Capital Transfer Tax. The reader may already be forming a view about the merits of such funds.

In 1982 an R.I.C.S. working party suggested a formula whereby at the end of each year the contribution from the start of that year and previous years is paid back to the tenant, and the sum credited to the landlord. Then when a real expense arised the landlord calls upon such portion of the credit as is needed to pay that expense. It is thought this may meet the respective tax requirements of both parties.

Tenants may raise queries on various aspects of the substance of service charges including:

Whether the schedule of services includes improvements or enhancements, the cost of which should be borne by the landlord?
Whether what the landlord wishes to include in the charge is covered by the schedule of services?
If is is covered, is it necessary?
If it is necessary, is the procedure appropriate? In *Bander Property Holdings v. J. S. Darwen (Successors) Ltd., 1968*, it was held that the landlord need not adopt the cheapest method available of supplying the service. Further as long as it is reasonable to do so, the landlord can elect to do a permanent job rather than just "patching up", as in *Manor House Drive Ltd. v. Shahbazian, 1965*.

If it is appropriate, is the procedure carried out and supervised correctly?
If it is correctly carried out is the cost incurred reasonable?
Finchborne v. *Rodrigues*, 1976, is authority for the proposition that the landlord can only recover from the tenant such costs as are fair and reasonable.

The lessor's main concern will be the comprehensiveness of the clause and during the 1970s they moved to a commanding position on services charges both as to the approach to the items included and restrictions on the lessee's opportunity for effective criticism. Some leases contain a final phrase in the schedule of services provided to include, "provision of any other service or facility and the making of any other payment which may reasonably be required for the efficient running of the building, the comfort of the lessees and the efficient running of the services areas", together with a provision that the decision of the lessor's surveyor shall be final on any matters of provision, liability of apportionment. This does seem to be somewhat weighted in favour of the landlord.

Perhaps the most important case in this field is *Concorde Graphics Ltd.* v. *Andromeda Investments S.A.*, 1982. Concorde Graphics were the tenants of one floor of a multi-storey industrial building, the service charge was provided for in a relatively brief clause in the lease referring to a rateable or due proportion of the cost of various items, with disputes to be settled by the landlord's surveyor whose decision was to be final and binding on the parties. The landlords and managing agents changed and the service charge increased three-fold due to a change in management policy and procedures. The tenant queried; the inclusion of some items in the account, the cost of other items including the managing agents fee, and the basis of apportionment.

The Court held that whilst the landlord's managing agents had made a demand for the service charge on the tenants in that capacity, the function of the landlord's surveyor in the clause was essentially arbitral.

Although he is the landlord's agent he must act impartially and hold the balance equally between the landlord and the tenant, notwithstanding that the landlord is his principal and paymaster. His position is no more delicate than the architect required to issue certificates under the standard R.I.B.A. contract. The managing agents were unable to perform this function, the Court declined to accept the tenant's proposal that the whole clause had failed and the Court should step in, but pointed out that the problem had arisen because the landlord had appointed a firm of surveyors to act both as surveyors and managing agents, and that the landlords should appoint some other surveyors.

The lessee should not be surprised to find that the lessor's costs arising from the arbitration are an additional item in the service charge. Service charges include managing agents' fees and under these circumstances it is only fair that when management is on an in-house basis a sum similar to that charged by managing agents should be included. In periods of inflation, even if service charges are payable quarterly in advance, from the lessor's point of view last year's accounts are not a proper basis. It would seem reasonable to include provision for payment quarterly in advance on last year's accounts appropriately indexed, say on the wholesale price index, to avoid a permanent cash-flow problem.

In the case of covered shopping centres, the Tenants' Association may provide a forum for comment and discussion of service charges, which is not available in respect of other types of property. It is as well to remember that the tenants' perception of service charges is a cost of the services provided, the most obvious of these are the daily and weekly cycle of simple physical activities on site, see Appendix F. It is not unknown for charges to be one-third or half of the rent and rising annually, presenting very real challenges to the most skilled of property managers. The most likely opportunity for limiting service charges is an agreed trade-off of quality for cost, though over a period of time this could damage the attractiveness of the investment. Over the long-term this will result in pressure for low energy design and construction and in the short-term for regular review of the energy budget, to avoid heating empty accommodation or heating to temperatures in excess of quite acceptable working conditions, see 11.5.3.

6.4.8 User

There are two kinds of user clauses, those that refer to the use of the premises in general planning terms and secondary clauses which relate to the way that use is conducted. Most leases contain a specific user clause, such as "offices" or "shop" and this will be further restricted in some cases, such as a shop to a particular trade, though this, as indeed any other clause in a lease, can be varied with the agreement of both parties.

Unlike improvement and assignment or sub-letting, there is no implied covenant that consent cannot unreasonably be withheld but in the case of a conditional covenant section 19(3) of the 1927 Act prevents the landlord from taking a fine or premium if he does grant consent.

Planning law may provide some guidance on the interpretation of the specified use but there is no presumption of a mirror image of interpretation between the two fields.

In *Anglia Building Society* v. *Sheffield City Council*, 1982, the lease contained a clause restricting the user to "a travel and employment bureau and theatre ticket agency", consent not to be unreasonably withheld. The tenants, Alfred Marks (employment agency) wished to assign to Anglia Building Society. The landlords argued that a higher rent would be obtained from a "Class 1" retail user. The tenants argued that the premises were already in a service use. The Court held, by analogy with *Bromley Park Garden Estates* v. *Moss*, 1982, that the landlord was seeking a collateral advantage and that consent was unreasonably withheld.

The user clause must be considered with great care at rent-review. Though the clause may suit the lessor's overall property management aims, restrictive user may depress open market rental. To be fair to the lessee a rent-review clause should state the specific restrictive user as a factor to be considered. If it is silent there is a presumption that it is to be included. Only if expressly excluded and there is provision for a more general user clause to be used for the purposes of the calculation should the lessor get the best of both worlds.

However, in *The Law Land Company Ltd.* v. *The Consumers Association Ltd.*, 1980, the Court of Appeal had to decide a conflict between a generally drawn rent review clause emphasizing an open market basis, and a specific user clause to the particular tenant in occupation. The Court held that it was not the parties' intention that the rental should vary according to the tenant's ability to pay as this would have been unworkable, and the open market basis prevailed with no reduction for the specific user.

A change of use can interact with statutory provisions with some alarming results. A tenant seeking planning permission for a change of use could set in motion compulsory purchase procedures under the now repealed Community Land Act or a change of use could act as the commencement of a project of material development under development land tax. As a consequence both the lessor and lessee could become liable for the payment of tax even though it may have been many years before the lessor had an opportunity to obtain additional rental under the lease.

Secondary user covenants tend to be of two types, those relating to hours of use and those to the general wellbeing of the building, the lessees or the lessor. Normal hours of business are usually specified and in office leases the delivery of goods is required to take place outside those hours. This is particularly true of furniture and partitioning, which can seriously inconvenience other users of the building.

The general wellbeing of the other tenants can be covered by what are in effect private bye-laws relating to the use made of common parts, and specifically excluding their use, for example, as waiting areas or for display purposes. The building and the lessor's interest can be protected by covenants limiting the installation of specialist heavy business machines and activity likely to prejudice the provisions of the insurance policy. Lessees of office buildings who are involved internationally in certain specialist fields or in data-handling may need to work irregular hours, and it is better that this be expressly provided for than to rely on generous verbal assurances in the solicitor's office.

This leads into security or in a more positive sense, safety. Enclosed shopping centres have the most comprehensive and demanding requirements and thus are a good example in order to identify the principal factors:

Control of vehicular access—hours of use for the public and service vehicles.
Control of shoppers at entry and in the centre.
Control of retailers in the use of the premises.
Control of vandalism and shop lifting.
Liaison with emergency services.
Management of in house staff.
Application of new technology; electronic pass cards, closed circuit T.V. with recording facilities.
Testing of emergency procedures.
Supervision of plant and machine contractors dealing with fire alarm, fire prevention and fire fighting equipment.
Anticipation of special risks.

6.4.9 Assignment and Sub-letting

It is possible to classify clauses as containing:

No restriction against assignment.
An absolute covenant against assignment.
A qualified covenant against assignment.
An express proviso that consent cannot be unreasonably withheld (but note 1927 Act section 19(1)(a)).
A covenant by the tenant to offer a surrender to the landlord before assigning.

Each of these is worthy of attention in respect of the broader management implications from the point of view of landlords and the specific operational requirements of tenants.

An absolute covenant places the tenant in a very difficult position and the value of his interest is subject to a very substantial discount. If the lease contains a covenant not to assign without landlords consent, then section 19(1)(a) of the Landlord and Tenant Act 1927 implies a term that this is not to be unreasonably withheld.

In *Bickel* v. *Duke of Westminster*, 1977, Lord Denning said "I do not think the court can or should determine by strict rules the grounds on which a landlord may, or may not, reasonably refuse his consent. He is not limited by the contract to any particular grounds. Nor should the courts limit him." In broad terms, the refusal must relate to either the character of the proposed assignee or to the effect of an assignment on rental or capital values. It has been held unreasonable to refuse consent on the basis that if a licence to assign was granted the lessor would lose a good tenant of another of his properties. Also in *Killick* v. *Second Covent Garden Property Co.*, 1973, it was held to be unreasonable of the lessor to refuse consent because he feared there would be a change of use (contrary to a further covenant in the lease) since the consent would not preclude the lessor enforcing the user covenant.

In *Bromley Park Garden Estates Ltd.* v. *Moss*, 1982, the Court of Appeal has limited the landlord's grounds for refusing consent. The tenant of a flat over a restaurant wished to assign, the landlords refused consent saying it was not their policy to permit assignments of residential property and they would accept a surrender. In fact, it was their hope that the tenant of the ground floor restaurant would surrender and take a new lease of the ground and first floor, increasing the value of the freeholder's interest. The Court held that the landlords were not entitled to refuse consent in order to achieve a collateral advantage (the furtherance of their investment plans) which was wholly unconnected with the terms of the lease. The fact that their purpose was in accordance with good estate management did not make the refusal reasonable.

Lessors have sought to avoid the reasonableness test by making a proviso that as a condition of the consent the lessee must offer to surrender his lease, this was accepted in *Bocardo S.A.* v. *S. & M. Hotels Ltd.*, 1979. However, in *Allnatt London Properties Ltd.* v. *Newton*, 1980, such an agreement was held to be void under section 38(1) of the 1954 Act.

The judgment was somewhat convoluted, but it appears that a tenant wishing to assign should:

Offer to surrender in accordance with the clause.
If the offer is rejected, request consent.
If the offer is accepted, inform the landlord that the agreement is invalid.
Then request consent.

One way a landlord can still try to restrict assignment without an absolute covenant is to introduce a restrictive user clause, this is likely to depress rental values.

Where a building lease for more than 40 years contains a qualified covenant against assignment or sub-letting then section 19(1)(b) of the 1927 Act provides that consent need not be obtained as long as the lease has seven or more years to run and the landlord is given notice in writing within six months of the transaction; this does not apply to leases granted by public bodies.

Finally, an unlawful assignee, that is to say where consent has not been granted, may seek relief as in *James* v. *Southern Launderettes*, 1985, though the Court in granting relief directed that the assignee should pay the landlord's cost.

6.4.10 Forfeiture

The ultimate remedy available to a lessor when a lessee fails to meet the covenants in the lease is to exercise a right of re-entry. The courts, with the aid of statute, have sought to limit the use of this remedy by looking for any act by the lessor which constitutes a waiver, requiring particular procedures to be followed and granting relief.

If there has been a breach of a condition of the lease, then the lessor's right of re-entry arises automatically. If there is a breach of covenant then a right of re-entry must have been expressly reserved in the lease. The lessor can demonstrate his intention to forfeit the lease for the breach of a covenant by serving a writ for possession. The right of re-entry can be lost by some act which acknowledges the continuance of the tenancy. A demand for rent, or acceptance of rent due after the breach, with the knowledge that the breach has occurred, is the most patent form of waiver and stop-rent safeguards must be built into the accounting procedures of managing agents.

The doctrine of waiver needs to be interpreted in different ways for "once and for all" breaches such as assignment or alterations and "continuing" breaches, typically user or repairs. In the latter case waiver through, for example, acceptance of rent applies only to past breaches. In *Cooper v. Henderson*, 1982, the landlord continued to accept rent knowing that the tenant was using the property for residential purposes in breach of covenant to use them for business purposes only. The Court of Appeal granted forfeiture as this was a continuing breach. The landlord may lose his right to forfeiture through estoppel, where he makes some positive action to accept the breach.

For breaches other than the non-payment of rent, the Law of Property Act 1925, section 146, prevents the enforcement of a right of re-entry unless the lessor serves a notice on the lessee specifying the breach, requiring a remedy if this is possible, and the payment of compensation. Only if the lessee fails to take action in a reasonable period of time can the lessor commence proceedings.

If the breach concerns a covenant to repair then the section 146 notice must give effect to the provisions of the Leasehold Property (Repairs) Act 1938. This requires the notice to state that within 28 days the lessee may serve a counter-notice claiming the benefit of the Act. In these circumstances, in leases of more than seven years with more than three years to run, forfeiture can only occur with approval of the Court, see 6.4.4.

This can be contrasted with the Law of Property Act 1925, section 147, which only provides relief in some limited circumstances in respect of internal decorative repair. The relief is claimed by a lessee on application to the court, which considers all the circumstances of the case, including the unexpired term. The lessor is under no obligation to advise the lessee of his rights under section 147. If a lessee fails to take the necessary action after the service of a notice in accordance with section 146 and the lessor seeks to enforce his rights of re-entry, the lessee can apply to the Court for discretionary relief. This can

be granted upon various conditions, including time limits and
the payment of the lessor's costs.

A sub-tenant can apply to the Court for an order vesting
in him the parts of the property that he occupies for the residue
of the sub-tenancy, and so be protected from the misconduct
of his mesne landlord which has resulted in the exercise of
a right of re-entry.

In *Cadogan v. Dimovic*, 1984, the landlords had obtained
judgment in a forfeiture action for breach of repairing covenants in the main lease. It was held that the court had jurisdiction under section 146(4) of the 1925 Act to make a vesting
order for a new term of part of the accommodation occupied
by a sub-tenant, even though the contractual term had ended
before the application for relief.

In *GMS Syndicates Ltd. v. Gary Elliott Ltd. and Others*, 1980,
the landlords alleged immoral use of the basement by the sub-
tenants of the basement. Gary Elliott, the lessee of the ground
floor and basement, who occupied the ground floor shop, were
granted partial relief from forfeiture by the Court, restricting
the order for possession in favour of the freeholder, to the basement.

In the case of non-payment of rent, the lessor has a wider
range of remedies. He can exercise distress on the lessee's goods
(see 9.1.4) or sue on the covenant or, as is more likely, seek
to exercise a right of re-entry reserved in the lease. There is
no need for a section 146 notice, but the common law requires
a formal procedure to be adopted. This can be avoided by the
lease stating that rent is to be paid without demand. The basis
upon which the courts will grant relief for non-payment of
rents is found in section 38 of the Supreme Court Act 1981.

The right of the sub-lessee to protect his interest on threat
of forfeiture of the head lease is found in section 146(4). The
Court may make an order vesting for the whole term, or part
of it, the property comprised in the lease, or part of it.

It is common to find a provision in a lease for forfeiture if
the lessee becomes bankrupt. However, the Law of Property
Act 1925 section 146(10) provides relief and in effect a trustee
in bankruptcy or liquidator has a year in which to find a purchaser and obtain the value of the profit rent. This was considered in detail in *Official Custodian of Charities v. Parway
Estates Developments Ltd.*, 1984.

In conclusion, *Peninsular Maritime Ltd. v. Padseal*, 1981, has
left the law on the enforceability of covenants after the service
of landlord's writ for forfeiture in considerable confusion. It

appears that the landlord cannot enforce the tenant's covenants but the tenant seeking relief from forfeiture can enforce
the landlord's covenants.

6.4.11 Rent-reviews

The impact of inflation together with the search for growth
by the institutional investors has concentrated interest on the
interpretation of rent-review clauses. The 1976 and subsequent
Blundell Memorial Lectures have made a major contribution
in this field by providing a vehicle for the wide dissemination
and discussion of rent-reviews and other lease covenants, identifying the close liaison necessary between lawyers and surveyors in their drafting and interpretation. The aim being to
ensure that the clause is comprehensive in its content, conclusive in its interpretation and practical in its implementation.
In 1979 the R.I.C.S. and the Law Society published a draft
model rent-review clause and recommended its use wherever
possible in business leases. This was revised in 1980 and is
set out in Appendix D, (further revised in 1986).

    Reference should also be made to the I.S.V.A. model clause
published in 1984, these differ in numerous respects:

Feature	R.I.C.S.	I.S.V.A.
Review date	frequency pattern	specific dates
Rental basis	having regard to open market	specific open market
The occupation	let as a whole	—
Premium	without a premium	—
Tenant	to a willing tenant	reasonably expected to let to a willing tenant
Hypothetical term	the original term	unexpired term with a minimum of 10 years
Fitting out / use	fit for immediate occupation and use	fully fitted out and equipped, ready for immediate use
Planning	—	benefit of consent available for occupier
Tenants voluntary improvements	full disregard	fair allowance
Compulsory improvements	neither address	the range of situations
Other disregards	explicit goodwill sub-tenants	implicit goodwill lawful undertenants

See Appendix D.

Feature	R.I.C.S.	I.S.V.A
Tenants fitting	—	specific disregard
Upwards only	upwards/downwards	upwards only
Presidential appointment	R.I.C.S. arbitrator or expert	I.S.V.A. arbitrator
Intermediate review	—	automatic after statutory interference

The significance of many of the above will become apparent during the remainder of this chapter.

In *Compton Group Ltd.* v. *Estates Gazette*, 1977, the court stated, "The construction of the review provision is a question of law, which must be determined by the court in order that surveyors may know what is to be the subject-matter which they are required to value. It is not the function of the Court to give the surveyors direction as to how they shall make their valuations that is to say what factors to take into account and what weight to give to them."

Whatever the phraseology of the particular clause in the lease, the four most important elements are: frequency, basis, procedure and arbitration. These are considered below.

(a) *Frequency*

Older leases, that is to say those dating from before the early 1960s, contained rent-reviews at far less frequent intervals than current practice, where five years is normal and under favourable conditions three years can be achieved. Assuming that five-year reviews are the basis in the market, then all other periods, whether shorter or longer, can be regarded as non-standard. Since the whole rationale behind the relatively low yield on property compared with that on Government Stock (the reverse yield gap) is the prospect of growth in income, then a longer rent-review period offers the lessee protection from a higher rent at the normal review interval and in some cases has an additional value. Lessees have sought to reject this argument; retailers in particular say they must compete in the High Street and each year's trade must be judged on an equal footing. A higher rent based on the benefits of not having a review in five years' time has to be paid out of the current year's profits. To the extent that both cases have a ring of truth the estate manager is able to make either case on behalf of different clients with a degree of conviction. Taking five-year reviews as standard there was evidence by agreement or arbitration of uplifts on rent of 5% having been obtained on seven years reviews, 10% to 15% on 14 year reviews and 15% to 20% on 21 year reviews, in respect of good quality investment properties in the first half of the 1980s.

In the latter case an uplift of 31% can be justified, applying equated yield techniques and projected annual rental growth of 5%. Various tables, graphs and computer programs exist to assist such calculations but what can be achieved on the day is often more a reflection of the negotiating strength of the two parties or the background of the arbitrator than of the strength of theoretical models.

Using Donaldsons' Tables (based upon annual in arrear rents, and growth in perpetuity) and assuming an investment with five-yearly reviews is a 7% risk, the following table can be drawn up on the basis of anticipated annual rental growth at first 5% and then 10%. The table indicates the theoretically correct yield to be used in capitalizing incomes for non-standard terms.

Annual rental growth	*Frequency of review*				
	3 years	5 years	7 years	14 years	25 years
5%	6·7%	7%	7·3%	8·2%	9·4%
10%	6·5%	7%	7·6%	9·4%	11·9%

If the investment is an 11% risk then repeating the procedure:

5%	10·6%	11%	11·4%	12·7%	14·0%
10%	10·2%	11%	11·8%	14·3%	17·0%

Clearly the lower the expected rate of rental growth the less significant is the effect of varying rent-review frequency on the choice of an appropriate yield which maintains the investor's true return. The range of potential applications of such tables, when carefully used, has perhaps not been fully appreciated by those in practice when faced with a non-standard frequency of review. Those who regularly advise lessees will see little merit in either the concept or the detailed content of the tables.

In *Pugh* v. *Smith Industries*, 1982, an independent valuer was faced with a review clause which required a "full yearly open market rent", excluding the provisions of the clause. He gave an award in the alternative, firstly assuming the rent would be fixed for the whole 20 year term at £36,750 and secondly assuming five year reviews (the normal market basis) at £30,600. The court held that the only possible legal interpretation was that of the first alternative; very much against the interests of the tenants. A similar conclusion was reached in *Safeway Food Stores* v. *Bandenway Ltd.*, 1983, where the Court held that the assumed fixed term rent was for 69 years. In *National Westminster Bank* v. *A.Y.M.M.C.*, 1984, the Court was faced with a clause, "other than the provisions relating to the amount of rent payable" and held that this too precluded the assumption of rent reviews during the assumed term at review; this decision has been widely questioned.

Alternatively the lessor can encourage the lessee to agree to standard review frequency and offer a premium or its annual equivalent in compensation. This can prove a useful course of action, enabling the new income to be capitalized at a lower yield, enhancing the investment value of the lessor's interest. This observed change in the frequency of reviews has resulted in a new type of clause, review of review, whereby in longer leases the frequency of the review will itself be reviewed at say 20 or 25 year intervals to the then current market pattern, with provision for arbitration.

By contrast a poor investment property, showing signs of functional, social or financial obsolescence, subject to an F.R.I. lease, may well command less rent on a long fixed term review than on a typical open market five year review basis.

Finally there is the problem of a contractual, rather than statutory renewal clause, see 6.4.2b. The wording is usually along the lines of: a renewal, for one more term only on the same terms as the existing lease excluding the right to renew, at open market rental value. Landlords have sought to insert normal frequency rent reviews, in order to more easily interpret open market value, when these did not exist in the original lease. The courts held in *BSC Footwear* v. *National Westminster Bank*, 1981, that this was not to be implied and that the arbitrator should determine, "the then prevailing market rent", reflecting the long period until the rent could next be varied.

(b) *Basis*

Most leases seek to establish a rent at review date at the then current open market value. Various phrases may be used: fair rent, reasonable rent, rack rent, and they may be further qualified as to the status of a willing lessor and/or lessee. Any phrase other than "open market rental value" can cause problems in interpretation. It is essential to create a background within the lease similar to that created by the Landlord and Tenant Act 1954 at the start of a new lease, incorporating provisions in the spirit of those found in sections 32 and 35 of the Act. These will include:

1. Intent of the parties.
2. Improvements.
3. User.
4. Term remaining.

Briefly, it can be said the the review clause, creates its own hypothetical lease and this is illustrated below:

1. In *Evans (Leeds) Ltd.* v. *English Electric Company Ltd.*, 1978, the lease used section 34 in the definition of market rental but added the assumption that there was a willing lessee.

The arbitrator found for a maximum of £515,000 p.a. and a minimum of £290,000 p.a. depending upon the interpretation of the clause. The court found in favour of the landlord, "the willing lessee will be unaffected by liquidity problems, government or other pressures. ... In a word his profile may or may not fit that of English Electric Company."

2. Silence of the clause in the matter of improvements resulted in the House of Lords decision in *Ponsford and Others* v. *HMS (Aerosols) Ltd.*, 1978, that the tenant's rent at review included the value of improvements carried out by the tenant which were not a condition of the lease. This was due to the rent being described as "assessed as a reasonable rent of the demised premises". In order to avoid this problem the review clause should specify either that improvements are to be disregarded throughout the lease or identify a time period for which they are to be disregarded. If during the lease the lessee wishes to carry out extensive improvements which require a longer pay back period, then by agreement the license granted by the lessor to carry out the works could extend the lease or the period of time before which the lessor would be able to reflect the improvements in the rent.

A convenient shorthand has been developed whereby if the clause stresses agreement between the parties, a "subjective" test is to be adapted, having regard to all the factors which would influence the parties in a negotiation; whereas if the clause refers to a reasonable rent for the demised premises an "objective" test is adapted which results in a rent based on the premises as existing at the relevant date, including improvements.

3. If the lease includes any unusual or onerous covenants, specialist user clauses or options to break it must be clear how

these are to be treated as factors influencing the basis for the review. In *The Law Land Company Ltd.* v. *The Consumers Association Ltd.*, 1980, the Court of Appeal faced with a conflict between a general open market review clause and a restricted user clause in the lease to the specific tenant, rejected any reduction in the open market basis as unworkable.

In *Plinth Properties* v. *Mott Hay and Anderson*, 1979, the use was restricted to consulting engineers' offices and the landlord had an absolute right to withhold consent for a change of use. The Court determined that at the review date the restricted value of the premises was £89,200 p.a. but that on normal lease terms, permitting relaxation to other uses with the typical covenant that consent was not to be unreasonably withheld, the rental value was £130,455.

A case of similar character, with the benefit going in the other direction, was *Bovis Group Pension Fund Ltd.* v. *GC Flooring and Furnishing Ltd.*, 1983. The rent review clause referred to a letting for office purposes. In fact only two floors were used as showrooms and stockrooms and there was no planning permission for the building as a whole to be used purely as offices. It was agreed that the rent in terms of solely office use was £85,000 and in terms of the actual use of the property was £75,000. The Court held that the arbitrator should disregard the actual use and assume the entire demise was used as offices. Also in *Trusthouse Forte Albany Hotels Ltd.* v.*Daejan Investments*, 1980, the Court accepted a clause which substituted shopping for the actual hotel uses.

In *UDS Tailoring* v. *BL Holdings Ltd.*, 1981, a restricted user to, "men's and women's bespoke and ready to wear tailors", was held by the court to merit a 10% reduction from unrestricted open market value.

4. Rent-review clauses usually specify the term to be assumed remaining until the end of the notional lease; if the lease is silent, then this can only be the actual term remaining. As this gets shorter it could depress open market rent, but *Pivot Properties Ltd.* v. *Secretary of State for the Environment*, 1980, established that the parties would anticipate renewal in accordance with the Landlord and Tenant Act 1954, if on the facts such renewal would be possible. This resulted in the higher of the alternative rents of £2·925 million and £2·1 million being adopted.

All these factors were relevant in *99 Bishopsgate Ltd* v. *Prudential Assurance Co.*, 1984. The most crucial aspect was how to give effect to the rental basis of vacant possession in a building of 300,000 ft², on a 98 year lease with 7 year reviews.

Both parties initially valued on a floor by floor basis to arrive at a rent of £7·451 m p.a., the tenant then claimed three deductions; a 10% allowance for size, 20% for length of the lease and 16 months rent free over 7 years. The arbitrator had only granted the first of these with an award of £6·7 m. However, he had also made an alternative award which recognized the rent free argument, but spread the allowance over 14 years (the likely period of a subletting) in the sum of £6·065 m p.a. The tenant appealed, and the alternative award was accepted by the High Court and confirmed by the Court of Appeal.

(c) *Index, Turnover, Upwards/Downwards*

An alternative basis for review, particularly in the case of more unusual types of property or locations, is the use of an index. For example greenfield campus-style offices or a hyper-market where there is no market evidence could be indexed to other property rentals such as the average current open market rent on several named buildings or an adjacent modern warehouse unit. Such factors will affect the yield on the investment. Rent reviews can also be set at fixed sums for the future, and only hindsight will enable the parties to determine the merit of their decisons.

Rent-reviews lead into indexation, but indexation is not just an alternative means of handling the effect of inflation within property investment, it can profoundly alter the whole pattern of operation of the landlord and tenant system. Profit rent and market rent become nebulous concepts, leading to very real problems in applying both landlord and tenant legislation and traditional property management techniques to the investment.

In France and Belgium rentals are indexed to a cost-index with, in effect, a review to the true market at longer intervals. Each year the rent is adjusted to the cost-index, but every three years the tenant has a right to break. Thus if true open market rent is below the cost-indexed rent, the lessee's threat to exercise his option to break should encourage the landlord to revert to true open market rent.

In the U.K. Slough Estates have obtained indexation to the retail price index. In 1983 the company offered its tenants the free option to convert to normal three year review market rents, less than half elected so to do. Specialist industrial premises, more in the nature of plant than true buildings, have been let on a retail price index, reviewed annually and reviewed to market rent every five years offering real value security, as long as the tenant's covenant is satisfactory.

The development of covered shopping centres with a controlled environment and sophisticated services and management, has presented an opportunity for turnover rents which are used widely in North America.

Typically the rental consist of a minimum base rent, payable quarterly in advance in the normal way, with a turnover rent exceeding that figure. This requires a definition and authentication of turnover with varying percentages for different trades, for example:

Variety stores	2% to 4%
Food	2% to 6%
Electrical and household	6% to 7%
Restaurants	6% to 10%
Shoes and jewellery	9% to 13%

The advantages to landlords include:

Lettings can be finalized earlier.
Annual growth.
Awareness of tenants trading activities.

The disadvantage to landlords include:

The need to develop new relationships between landlord and tenant.
Problems with the Landlord and Tenant Acts.
Problems with funding.

It is also necessary to amend the normal lease clauses dealing with assignment, user and rent review.

The growth during the later 1960s of upwards-only reviews certainly protected the investor's income but its fairness has been questioned. When a lease ends and a new lease is granted the rent will be at the open market level irrespective of whether rents have risen or fallen. Is the rent-review simply a lessor's clause or part of an entire exercise to ensure that reality and fairness is present during the lease in the same way that the Landlord and Tenant Acts operate at the termination and grant of a new lease? In *Stylo Shoes v. Manchester Royal Exchange*, 1967, the Court in determining the terms of a new lease ordered that the review by upwards/downwards. This was followed in *Janes (Gowns) Ltd. v. Harlow Development Corporation*, 1979, where the judgment reads: "I am not satisfied on the evidence before me that the insertion of rent review clauses for review in one direction only have affected the rents which have been payable and accordingly I think that the appropriate course to take is to insert a rent review clause in this lease to provide for variation in either direction but to make no consequential adjustment to the rent."

(d) Procedure

Generally the rent-review clause will require the landlord to trigger its operation by the service of a notice at a certain date or within a certain period in a particular form, and it may require a rent to be specified. Some leases require the lessee to reply within a specified period of time to the lessor's notice, otherwise the lessee is assumed to have accepted the rent specified in the lessor's notice.

Inevitably cases arose where a lessor's notice was served late. In 1977 the House of Lords made a fundamental change to the significance of time in rent-reviews. The effect of *United Scientific Holdings Ltd.* v. *Burnley Borough Council* and *Cheapside Land and Development Co. Ltd.* v. *Messels Services Ltd.*, can be summarized as follows:

1. Time, *prima facie*, is not of the essence of rent-review provisions, so lessors may serve notice late, but the rent when determined has effect retrospectively.
2. The parties may make time of the essence in the contract and the courts will support this, otherwise time is not of the essence. An example of this is found in the "deeming" provisions in *Henry Smith's Charity* v. *AWADA Trading and Promotions*, 1983.
3. In *Drebbond Ltd.* v. *Horsham District Council*, 1978, the lease provided that the lessor could require arbitration to determine a new rent by the service of a notice on the lessee within three months of the lessor's notice initiating the rent review, "but not otherwise". It was held that this phrase had by implication made time of the essence and the lessor, being out of time, failed in an application that the matter be referred to an arbitrator.
4. By contrast in *Touche Ross and Co.* v. *Secretary of State for the Environment*, 1982, the Court of Appeal held that a provision that, in the absence of agreement, the matter should be referred to a surveyor, "as soon as practicable, but in any event not later than three months.,.." did not have to be strictly complied with, as part of the timetable was out of the control of the parties.

5. The conduct of the parties can make time of the essence.
6. In a situation where there is an option to break at the same time as a rent review, time is to be of the essence of the contract, because the tenant might have exercised the option if he had been aware of the new rental. Despite ingeneous arguments to the contrary the Court of Appeal confirmed this in *Al Saloom* v. *Shirley James Travel Service Ltd.*, 1981, and *Coventry City Council* v. *J. Hepworth and Son Ltd.*, 1982.

It has taken several years for the full implications of the decision to be felt. This is illustrated by a series of cases seeking to test what period of delay might make time of the essence. This has been brought to a conclusion by *Amherst* v. *James Walker Goldsmith and Silversmith Ltd.*, 1983, where it was held that if time was not of the essence, the right of a landlord to trigger a review could not be destroyed by mere delay however lengthy. A very practical point, where there has been a long delay, is the equity of the landlord enforcing a clause for interest on back rent as well as the back rent itself, it depends upon the value placed on landlord and tenant relationships, see *James* v. *Heim Gallery (London) Ltd.*, 1980. If the lease is silent on the date when the back dated rent review becomes payable, then *South Tottenham Land Securities Ltd.* v. *R. A. Millett*, 1983, provides that it shall be the quarter day following the award.

If time is of the essence, then it is necessary to consider whether the conduct of the parties meets the criteria set out in the lease. In *Horserace Totalization Board* v. *Reliance*, 1982, it was held that a tenant's counter notice which: referred to the period for reference to arbitration, objected to the landlord's proposed increase and asked the landlord to supply evidence, was not sufficiently explicit that the tenant was electing for arbitration rather than negotiation to satisfy the clause in the lease, hence the tenant's rights were lost.

A lease may contain a clause of both types, as in *Esso Petroleum* v. *Anthony Gibbs Financial Services*, 1983, where a rent review notice could be served by the landlords 12 months either side of the rent review date of 6 July, 1978. If no such review took place the landlords could serve a month's notice, to review the rent at any time before the next set review in 1984. It was held that "subject to lease", "without prejudice" negotiations between the surveyors were not an exercise of the earlier fixed date review.

Mistakes are likely to be costly; in *Centrovincial Estates PLC v. Merchant Investors Assurance*, 1983, a solicitor's letter offered the defendant tenant a rent from the review date of £65,000, which the tenant accepted. A few days later the solicitor telephoned to say the offer should have read £126,000, it was held that the contract had been concluded at the lower figure.

The greatest of care is necessary in the drafting of notices. The landlord's trigger notice must be unequivocally recognized as such, rather than the mere opening of negotiations. The tenant's counter notice must clearly state an election for arbitration rather than indicating some protest at the suggested rent or appearing to negotiate.

(e) *Arbitration*

This had developed across the whole range of commercial activities as the civilized way of settling disputes, whereby the parties agreed to a third person in whom they have confidence to settle the dispute, and to abide by the decision.

Before dealing with the determination of a rent-review by an arbitrator it is essential to distinguish the arbitrator from the independent expert. The arbitration is a legal proceeding under the Arbitration Acts and the arbitrator reaches a decision on the basis of evidence put before him, usually at a formal hearing. He can call for the discovery of documents and he interprets the evidence. His decision is enforceable as if it were a judgment of the court. Though he is not liable for negligence, the Court can set the judgment aside on the grounds of misconduct. The independent expert is appointed jointly by the two parties to carry out a normal valuation and to give his own opinion on the matter to be decided. He may have regard to evidence submitted, he may have a hearing and adopt what he considers the most appropriate procedure. His decision is not enforceable directly by the courts and he is liable for action for negligence, see *Palacath Ltd. v. Flanagan*, 1985. The independent expert may, if he wishes, proceed in the same way as an arbitrator, though the following procedures are specifically those of an arbitrator.

The rent-review clause will provide for the appointment of an arbitrator, usually by the President of the R.I.C.S. Before accepting such an appointment the arbitrator should satisfy himself of his competence and ability to resolve the dispute, and this could involve correspondence with the parties.

In *Thomas Bates and Son Ltd. v. Wyndhams (Lingerie) Ltd.*,

1980, the rent review made no provision for arbitration in default of agreement between the parties. The Court having satisfied itself that the omission was a mistake and on the particular facts, ordered rectification by the insertation of a provision for arbitration.

Once the arbitrator has accepted the appointment he must ensure that in any communication both parties are treated in an identical way. Having obtained confirmation from the parties that they accept his appointment, the arbitrator will issue directions to the parties setting out requirements and a timetable for pleadings, consisting of: Claim, Defence and Reply and arrangement for expert evidence and costs. The procedure of the hearing is entirely at the discretion of the arbitrator: if necessary he is able to obtain a legal opinion. When he inspects the property he should ensure that both parties are given an opportunity to accompany him.

At the hearing the parties may be represented by lawyers with surveyors giving expert evidence, or surveyors alone. The law regarding expert evidence is complex and was made clear by Mr. Justice Megarry in *English Exporters (London) Ltd.* v. *Eldonwall Ltd.*, 1973. The arbitrator can accept direct evidence, that is to say comparables that the surveyor or his firm has dealt with, but any other evidence should only be admitted if supported by authenticated details of the property and a copy of the lease, or alternatively agreed between the parties.

This has been developed in *Segama NV* v. *Penny Le Roy Ltd.*, 1983. The lease defined the market rent as meaning "yearly rental value of the demised premises having regard to the rental values current at the relevant time for similar property ... let with vacant possession." In accordance with *Melwood Units* v. *Commissioner of Main Roads*, 1979, the Court held that the arbitrator was entitled to hear evidence of rents agreed after the review date, though the greater the lapse of time the progressively more unreliable the evidence would become. The point was made that the same would be true of rent agreed before the relevant review date.

The Court also held that where the clause refers to vacant possession it is quite proper for the arbitrator to have regard to evidence of rents agreed with sitting tenants, though the arbitrator may think it appropriate to adjust such rentals.

In reaching his decision the arbitrator must only have regard to the evidence submitted, though the weight he gives to evidence will be conditioned by his own experience, which was the reason for his appointment. In *Fox and Others* v. *PG Well-*

fair Ltd., 1982, only one party gave evidence before the arbitrator, and in his mind the arbitrator rejected most of this. The Court held that in doing this silently he was introducing his own evidence and as there was no cross examination none of the evidence was tested. Lord Denning said the arbitrator had misconducted himself and the award was set aside.

The R.I.C.S. Guidance Notes suggest the award should contain the following:

The parties and the subject property.
The arbitration appointment—
The agreement to submit to arbitration.
The date of appointment.
The method of appointment.
The instrument of appointment.
The issue.
The decision on costs.
Signature and date.
One of more of the following may be included—
The preliminary hearing and procedures.
A reference to agreed facts.
The date and place of the hearing.
The attendance at the hearing or written representations.
A reference to the inspection of the property and any comparables.

A reasoned award should be given if one of the parties requests it; the arbitrator should accede unless he can think of no good reason for doing so, if both parties make the request, he should comply.

The publication of the award is closely related to the costs and fees. There are the costs of the reference, inclusive of all the costs incurred by the parties and the award, and the costs of the award itself which includes the arbitrator's fee. Prior to the issue of his award the arbitrator will specify how the costs should be paid and he will not release his award until his costs are paid. As the lessor has the most to gain he may well pay all the costs of the award to obtain the arbitrator's decison. The service charge clause may deal with the allocation of costs between the parties. Alternatively the arbitration clause may refer to the payment of costs.

The Arbitration Acts of 1950 and 1979 provide an essential background upon matters of procedure and set out the relationship between the Court and the arbitrator acting in a quasi-judicial capacity. Section 27 of the 1950 Act gives the Court power to extend any strict time limits. Its application to rent reviews was first considered in *Chartered Trust* v. *Maylands Green Estate Co. Ltd.*, 1984, where the tenant failed to demonstrate the degree of undue hardship arising from a time of the essence clause necessary for the Court to grant relief. The Arbitration Act 1979 has made several changes; the previous forms of judicial review are replaced by two new simplified procedures.

Section 1 allows for an appeal on a point of law arising out of the award. In the absence of the consent of all the parties the Court cannot give leave to appeal unless it is satisfied that the resolution of the legal issue, "could substantially affect the rights of one or more of the parties." In *Duvan Estates Ltd.* v. *Rosette Sunshine Savories Ltd.*, 1981, the Court held that the fact that the arbitrator had looked at facts and figures arising after the review date was only of marginal effect and did not intervene.

Section 2 gives the Court jurisdiction to determine questions of law which arise during the course of the arbitration. The Court will only consider this if made with the consent of the arbitrator or concurrence of the parties and the decision might produce a substantial saving in cost and substantially affect the rights of the parties. In *Chapman* v. *Charlwood Alliance Properties Ltd.*, 1981, the Court was not satisfied that all the hurdles could be jumped.

As many as 20,000 arbitrators per annum have been appointed by the President of the R.I.C.S. and a surveyor involved in estate management should expect to be involved in arbitration from time to time. Though arbitrations are private some are referred to the courts as a case stated, usually to interpret lease covenants. However in *Belvedere House* v. *King*, 1981, one of the parties to a rent review sued (unsuccessfully) a surveyor acting as an independent expert. The judgment contains some useful comments on technique and the interpretation of comparables.

Sources and Further Reading

Adams Rent Review, 1981, Oyez.
Adams, Statutory Renewal Terms, 251 E.G. 1045.
Adams and Sinclair Taylor, Insurance of Leased Premises, R.I.C.S.
Aldridge, Letting Business Property, Oyez, 1978.
Bernstein, Handbook of Rent Review, Sweet and Maxwell, 1981.

Blundell Memorial Lectures:
  1976. Bernstein and Wheeler, Rent Review Provisions in Leases, 238 E.G. 473.
  1977. Colyer, Inflation-Proof Leases I, 242 E.G. 943.
    Brewer, Inflation-Proof Leases II, 242 E.G. 1037.
  1978. Prior and Harding, Service Charges in Leases.
  1979. Bernstein and Hill, Valuing the Incomparable, 251 E.G. 147.
  1980. Priday and Hoyes, Improvements and Redevelopment, 255 E.G. 229, 333.
  1984. Reynolds, Liability of Lessee and Sureties on Assignment.
Bowie, The Reverse Yield Gap, 267 E.G. 138.
Brand and Williams, The Neighbours Obligations, 269 E.G. 200.
Donaldsons' Investment Tables, compiled by P. Marshall, 1977.
Evans, The Law of Landlord and Tenant, Butterworths, 1974.
Flowchart Through Business Tenancies, Building Economics Bureau, 1978.
Fox-Andrews, Business Tenancies, Estates Gazette, 1978.
Freedman and Fogel, Rent Reviews, R.I.C.S./I.S.V.A. Clauses, 272 E.G. 496.
Hooper, Letting Shops on Percentage Rents, C.S., December, 1970.
Meaney, Rent Reviews I and II, 264 E.G. 117, 225.
Metcalf and Stubbs, Surveyor as Arbitrator and Expert Witness, C.S., May, 1975.
Murdoch, Rent Review Notices, 269 E.G. 297.
Service Charges, Jones Lang Wotton, Estates Times, 19.10.84.
Smith, Necessary Protection for a Landlord, 252 E.G. 474.
Smith, Valuation of Lease determinable on Bankruptcy, C.S. May, 1976.
Stapleton, Lease Term Bargaining, Land Management Research Conference, Spon, 1984.
Stapleton, Options to Renew, 269 E.G. 1232.
Stapleton, Options to Break, 275 E.G. 788.
Stapleton, Landlords Consent, 272 E.G. 1136.
Turnover Rents, Gerald Eve/R.I.C.S., 1984.
Warren, Rent Review Analysis, 1983, 3/4 R.R.L.R.
West, Law of Dilapidations, Estates Gazette, 1979.
Whittaker, The Changing Function of Service Charges in Shopping Centres and Office Buildings, C.S., June, 1979.
Williams, Interpreting the interim rent provisions, 271 E.G. 1058.

Chapter 7

Residential Property

7.1 The Housing Stock

The urbanization of the nineteenth century and sharply divided political philosophies for much of the twentieth century have resulted in residential property suffering from more legislation than any other subject. A core of Public Health, Town Planning, Housing and Rent Acts has been supplemented by separate Acts dealing with specialized areas such as rating and leasehold reform. As observed in the Department of the Environment's Consultation Paper of 1977, "... there can be no doubt that the complexity and obscurity of the Acts are a source of frustration and anxiety to landlords, tenants and those responsible for administering and interpreting the legislation".

The nature of the housing stock can be analysed in terms of many different criteria; age, condition, occupancy or tenure, and is subject to changes due to economic, demographic and political factors which affect both the existing stock and the net annual flow.

Until quite recently the public, private and voluntary sectors have existed as relatively self-contained concepts, subject to different forms of control and subsidy. During the latter part of the 1970s the relative subsidies enjoyed by owner-occupiers and local authority tenants and the sale of council housing became important political and social issues.

The Housing Act 1980 has changed many of the conditions underlying the provision and occupation of public sector housing and replaces the authorities' discretionary right to sell with, for the vast majority of tenants, a mandatory right to buy. For the occupiers that remain in the public sector as secure tenants, Chapter II of Part I provides the framework for a more equitable relationship between landlord and tenant. Tenants now enjoy security of tenure and the terms of occupation permit sub-letting and encourage improvement, together with the right to information and consultation.

Owner-occupation rose from around 10% of the stock in 1914 to 63% in 1984 and a reasonable estimate of the maximum possible percentage by the year 2000 is 70%. In 1980 local authority and New Town housing accounted for about 32% of the stock, higher than that in any other country in Western Europe; the remainder of the stock, around 13%, was attributable to the private sector and housing associations. Despite the growth of housing associations, between 1970 and 1978 the number of homes in this final group fell by about one million.

Given that about half local authority households are in receipt of some form of welfare payment and that not all tenants wish to become owner-occupiers, then it would be technically possible over a generation to see 70% owner-occupation. The sale of council houses is not just a matter of numbers, there are complex social and financial implications. Care must be taken to strike a fair balance between the rights of individual occupiers as sitting tenants and those of the general public in terms of the effect of sales on the financing of local government. Perhaps the most important group and those with the least voice are those in need of housing in particular areas who can see a reduction in the stock available to let. In 1980 only one third the number of local authority houses were started compared with the number in 1970.

It can already be shown in areas where houses have been sold that the most attractive and easily maintained properties are purchased by the tenants and as a result the average management and maintenance costs of the remaining public sector houses increase. In Birmingham between 1966 and 1975 the Council sold about 10,000 homes, but only four of these were flats.

The purchase of housing is encouraged in Part I Chapter 1 of the Act by a discount on open market value after three years' occupation of 33%, rising by 1% per annum thereafter to a maximum of 50%. The Housing and Building Control Act 1984 decreased the period of qualification to two years and increased the maximum discount to 60%, (rise to 70% discount likely). The same Act extended the right to buy to properties of which the authority only owned a leasehold interest; greater than 21 years for houses and 50 years for flats.

Where the property was first let after 31 March, 1974, the discount may not reduce the price below the cost of the house. The purchaser has a guaranteed right to a mortgage and there are favourable criteria for determining the maximum amount of the loan. If this is insufficient, then a payment of £100 obtains a two-year deferment on completion at the original price. In order to discourage any undesirable practices, if the house is sold within five years of purchase then a proportion of the discount must be repaid.

Nationally during the financial year 1978/79, when about 250 authorities were prepared to sell to their tenants, 37,500 homes were sold, and only just over 1% were flats. This rose to a total of 53,500 in the financial year 1979/80.

The financial consequences for an individual authority depend upon the character of the housing stock and changes in local government grants. Any attempt to show that the aggregate net effects are to the joint financial benefit of local authorities and the Exchequer requires so many long-term assumptions as to be virtually meaningless.

Housing departments are now presented with quite new problems as they cease to manage "ring fence" estates and have to set up management systems for "pepper pot" estates. This, coupled with the additional work of the statutory notices and procedures for sales, is unlikely to reduce the total work-load of departments. Particular difficulties will be encountered in the management of flats; even if only one tenant in a block acquires a 125 year lease new accounting systems will be needed. Prospective purchasers of flats in complex architectural structures need to take expert professional advice.

Management will have to reconcile the often conflicting characteristics of long leaseholders and existing tenants in the same block for an indefinite period in the future. This could be avoided by offering any tenant of a flat who wishes to become an owner-occupier a transfer to either a flat in a block which is intended to become exclusively long leasehold or even a house, but this could become a negotiating tactic. On the other hand, the G.L.C., faced with several hundred properties requiring considerable maintenance and repair, have solved their problems with the homesteading scheme.

As tenants who have exercised their right to buy in due course resell their houses so the flow of second-hand owner-occupied housing on to the market will become more diverse, with implications for those developers who specialize in building new houses for the first-time buyer. In attractive rural areas these re-sales could become recreational second homes, and to avoid this authorities have powers to approve persons who buy from the original tenant or his successor in title, and a potential buy-back provision in the case of disposals within ten years of the original purhcase.

The Housing Act 1980 seeks to encourage the private rented sector by permitting bi-ennial rather than three-year reviews of fair rents and introducing short hold tenancies at a fair rent, and assured tenancies outside the fair rent regime. The Finance Act 1984 exempts from capital gains tax up to £20,000 of value attributable to a leased flat within an owner-occupier's main residence. It is hoped that this will unlock unused basement and top-floor flats in large older houses in inner urban areas.

The voluntary housing sector represents only a small proportion of the total housing stock with about 125,000 tenants of non-charitable associations and 200,000 in co-ownership and co-operative schemes. However, their distinctive character means that in particular areas they make a major contribution in the refurbishment of older property and in meeting the needs of specialized groups. Tenants of non-charitable associations are in much the same position as local authority tenants with secure status and a right to buy. The Housing and Building Control Act 1984 enables tenants of charitable associations to establish their right to buy and discount, and transfer this to a house owned by a nominated non-charitable association.

The Act, like most rent and housing legislation, contains many provisions which the Opposition of the day has indicated it would seek to repeal. Lack of confidence is likely to inhibit the private sector utilizing some of the provisions in Part II, particularly assured tenancies and possibly shortholds.

The management of public and voluntary sector housing is generally undertaken as an exclusive activity and these can properly be regarded as specialized areas. These have not been considered any further, but many general practice surveyors have some involvement in the private rented sector. The present statutory position is rather similar to that observed by geologists in their study of the earth's crust. Deposits of material have been laid down at different dates and have been subject to weathering by a climate of political, economic and social factors. The result is a deeply fissured landscape exposing layers of material of different dates. In the absence of an ordnance survey map it is proposed to draw attention to some of the more striking features, including those exposed in 1980.

7.2.1 The Private Rented Sector

The long-term implications of rent control and the necessarily associated security of tenure have been recognized for many years. As Scrutton, L.J., observed in *Remon v. City of London Real Property Co. Ltd*, 1921: "*the policy of the statute is a matter for Parliament and not for me, but those who ask for and pass* such legislation should not be surprised if, as one of the effects, existing houses are not let but only offered for sale and no fresh houses are built (for renting) by private enterprise".

Through a series of complex and inter-related Rent Acts and Housing Acts, new types of tenancies have been created with varying degrees of protection from the levels of rent in the subsequently distorted open market, and tenants have enjoyed indefinite security of tenure. When regulated tenancies were created under the Rent Act 1965 to be let at "fair rents", there still remained a large number of controlled tenancies, under the Rent Act 1957, at a historic rent-limit based in most cases on twice the 1956 gross value. Over the years the basis for conversion of controlled to regulated tenancies has been amended with criteria based upon the rateable value of the premises and the provision of standard amenities and the state of repair. The Housing Act 1980, section 64, converted all remaining controlled tenancies; this in no way affects the security of the tenants but does enable the landlord to charge a fair rent.

In 1978 the D.O.E. survey of the privately rented sector showed the stock to be as follows:

Tenancy	Number (1,000s)	%
Controlled	176	7
Regulated—registered	529	22
unregistered	1,078	46
Resident landlord	140	6
Rent free	274	12
Rented with business	136	6
Others	31	1
	2,364	100%

However new lettings did not reflect the balance of the stock, over 20% were by employers to employees, 15% were by resident landlords and 60% were of furnished accommodation to relatively mobile tenants. The vast majority of new lettings, particularly in London are in practice outside the Rent Acts.

As regards rental levels, median unregistered rents were about 25% higher than registered rents, at the higher levels unregistered rents were about 50% higher and in London 100% higher.

Evidence submitted to the House of Commons First Report from the Environment Committee 1981–82, suggests that if tenants were able to pay the rents required by landlords (9% gross return) rather than fair rents (2% to 3% gross return) then the tenant's would be better off as owner-occupiers. thus even if there were no rent control, the privately rented sector generally appears not to be commercial viable.

The caveat must be added that there are major geographical variations in any aggregated statistics in this field, for example the percentage of lettings with registered rents varies from 5% in rural shire counties (Wiltshire) to 46% in urban shire counties (Nottinghamshire) to 58% in North Tyneside.

Local Authorities have substantial reserve powers to control the occupation condition and management of private sector residential property as follows:

Houses in Multiple Occupation—
Management Order, under the Housing Act 1961, appointing a manager to be responsible for enforcing regulations on repair and maintenance, overcrowding, standard amenities and means of escape from fire. Control Order, under the Housing Act 1964, whereby the local authority take over control.
Registration scheme under the Housing Act 1961.
Statutory Nuisances, defined as premises in such a state as to be prejudicial to health or a nuisance, can be dealt with under the Public Health Act 1936 or the Public Health Act 1961.
Unfit houses can under the Housing Act 1957, be the subject of a repairs order or alternatively a demolition or closing order.
Fit houses, in need of substantial repairs excluding internal decorative repair can be served with a repairs notice.
The Housing (Underground Rooms) Act 1959 enables underground rooms to be closed.

7.2.2 Protected and Statutory Tenancies

The Rent Act 1977 Section 1, states that a tenancy under which a dwelling house is let as a separate dwelling is a protected tenancy. Section 2 provides that a statutory tenancy comes into existence on the termination of the protected tenancy.

Various tenancies are specifically excluded from this status by sections 4 to 16A. Two other categories of occupation can also be distinguished, these are restricted contracts and licences and are set out later in 7.2.5 and 7.2.6 respectively. Direct contracting out of the Rent Acts is not permitted.

The Act specifically provides that certain tenancies are exempted from the definition of protected tenancy. The more important of these are where:

After April 1st, 1973, the dwelling house had a rateable value exceeding £1500 in Greater London or £750 elsewhere, (section 4).

No rent is payable or the rent is less than two-thirds of the rateable value, (section 5).

A substantial part of the rent is fairly attributable to the provision of board and attendance on the tenant, (section 7).

The tenancy is granted by a specified educational institution to a person pursuing a course of study provided by that or another institution, (section 8).

The purpose of the tenancy is to confer a right to occupy the premises for a holiday, (section 9).

The dwelling is comprised in an agricultural holding and is occupied by the person responsible for the control of the farming of the holding, (section 10).

The dwelling-house forms part only of a building and the tenancy was granted by a person who occupies as his residence another dwelling-house which forms part of that building, (section 12).

The landlord's interest belongs to the Crown, (section 13). Though this was amended by section 72 of the Housing Act 1980 in respect of properties managed by the Crown Estate Commissioners.

The landlord's interest belongs to a local authority or housing association, (sections 14 and 15).

Assured tenancy (section 16A).

A number of problems have arisen in connection with section 12, the exclusion from protection enjoyed by resident landlords. Before the Rent Act 1974 protection had been on the basis that premises were unfurnished. The Rent Act 1974 was not intended to deprive any then existing tenants of their protection, so when a tenancy had been granted before that Act, a landlord resident on 14 August 1974 and continuously resident thereafter must be able to show that the premises were furnished at the date the tenancy was granted. In *Mann* v. *Conella*, 1980, a tenancy had been granted in January, 1974, of some fairly fully-furnished premises. It was clear that in qualitative terms the premises were furnished but due to the rapid rise in rents relative to second-hand furniture prices the court held that the 9% of rent attributable to furnishings did not form a substantial part of the whole rent as required by the Rent Act 1968. This feature seems likely to cast a shadow forward for many years, rather like the controlled tenancies of the Housing Act 1957 which were only finally put to rest by the Housing Act 1980.

The death of a resident landlord poses further difficulties. In *Landau* v. *Sloane*, 1980, the executors relied on Schedule 2, paragraph 1(c), of the 1977 Act, which required the court to disregard a period of one year's non-residence (extended to two years post, 1980) and served a notice to quit which expired during this executor's year. The Court of Appeal held that since after that year there was still no resident landlord in occupation the tenant became a statutory tenant. This was reversed by the House of Lords giving the executors the status of resident landlords.

After the termination of a protected tenancy, section 2 provides that the person who immediately before the termination was the protected tenant becomes the statutory tenant as long as he occupies the dwelling-house as his residence. The terms of the tenancy are the same as those of the preceding contractual tenancy, consistent with the Act.

It is an offence under Schedule 1, paragraph 12, for a tenant to ask for or receive payment for giving up possession other than from the landlord, and if the tenant requires that furniture must be purchased any excess over a reasonable price is treated as a payment for giving up possession.

Part 1 of Schedule 1 as amended by the Housing Act 1980 provides that a surviving spouse residing with the tenant at the date of his death becomes the statutory tenant. In other cases if a member of the original tenant's family was residing with him for a period of six months or more immediately before the death then that person becomes the statutory tenant. Family is interpreted in a social rather than a narrow legal or genetic sense, but the relationship must have acquired a degree of permanence. This transfer on death can occur on two occasions and is a major cause of the difference between tenanted and vacant possession value.

A statutory tenancy can be brought to an end by the tenant giving up possession. Since the tenant's action is instrumental in providing the landlord with a windfall gain, then the realities of the market place are such that the tenant will expect a share of that gain. Otherwise, apart from changes in the circumstances which take the tenancy outside the Rent Acts, possession can only be obtained with the benefit of an order of the court in accordance with section 98.

7.2.3 Security of Tenure

A protected or statutory tenant enjoys substantial security of tenure and a notice to quit which must give a minimum of four weeks notice, and cannot be enforced unless the landlord gets a possession order from the courts. Over 100,000 residential possession orders were made in 1982 as follows:

Private sector lettings	20,130
Agricultural tied cottages	80
Service tenancies	1,290
Mortgage repossessions	23,650
Repairing covenants	10
Public Sector	58,850
Total	104,010

The grounds upon which a possession order will be granted against a protected or statutory tenant are set out in schedule 15 of the Rent Act 1977. If in Part I of the schedule then the court can only grant possession if it thinks it reasonable to do so. If in Part II, and the tenant was made aware of the grounds before the grant of the tenancy, then the court must grant possession.

Schedule 15   Part I (Discretionary cases)

Case 1   Rent lawfully due is unpaid.
Case 2   Nuisance or annoyance by tenant to adjoining tenant.
Case 3   Physical deterioration due to default by tenant.
Case 4   Ill treatment of furniture by tenant.
Case 5   Tenants notice to quit, acted upon by landlord, who would be seriously prejudiced.
Case 6   Assignment or subletting without landlords consent.
Case 7   Applied to controlled tenancies, not applicable.
Case 8   Required by landlord for service tenancy.
Case 9   Required by landlord for his own domestic purposes.
Case 10   Excessive rent charged by tenant on subtenant.

Part II (Mandatory cases)

Case 11   The landlord previously occupied as his residence and requires it for his occupation (amending legislation 1985).

Case 12   The landlord intends to occupy on his retirement.
Case 13   Tenant occupies out of season holiday property.
Case 14   Letting of student accommodation in vacations.
Case 15   Landlord holds for occupation by minister of religion.
Case 16   Required by landlord for agriculture service tenancy.
Case 17   Required by landlord to assist amalgamation of agricultural holding, having previously been occupied by farm manager.
Case 18   Previously occupied by farm manager.
Case 19   Termination of shorthold tenancy.
Case 20   Letting by serviceman, to be reoccupied as his residence.

Alternatively the landlord can seek to show the court that suitable alternative accommodation is available, and the court must consider it reasonable to grant possession. In *Hill* v. *Rochard*, 1983, the tenants had lived in a large house for 20 years with outbuildings, stable and 1½ acres of land, the court held that a four bedroomed house in a nearby village, with a garden of ⅛ acre was suitable alternative accommodation. However in *Battlesprings Ltd* v. *Gates*, 1983, the court refused to make an order, despite suitable accommodation being available, as the occupier was an elderly widow, who had lived in the property for 35 years.

The criteria to be considered to determine the suitability of the accommodation include:

The area and neighbourhood
Proximity to place of work
Quality and quantity of accommodation
The effect of the new rent.

If housing is to be provided by the Housing Authority a certificate to that effect is regarded as conclusive evidence.

7.2.4 Rents Under Regulated Tenancies

Part III of the Rent Act 1977 deals with the rent which may be charged during the contractual and statutory periods of a regulated tenancy. This is supported by Part IV, which covers the machinery for the registration of a fair rent; both are amended to a significant extent by Part II of the Housing Act 1980.

During a contractual period of a regulated tenancy, if there is a registered rent this sets a contractual rent-limit and any excess which would result from payment of the contractual rent is irrecoverable by the landlord. During a statutory period, when the registered rent has been increased, a notice of increase can be served on the tenant to obtain the payment of the increased rent during the course of a rent-period. When there is no registered rent, the maximum rent recoverable for a statutory period is that for the last contractual period with adjustments for rates, services and improvements.

If a rent agreement with a tenant having security of tenure takes effect after 29 August, 1977, and there is no registered rent then section 51, as amended by section 68 of the Housing Act 1980, provides that it must be in writing, state that the tenant's security of tenure will not be affected if he refuses to enter into the agreement, and that entry into the agreement will not deprive the parties of the right to apply for the registration of a fair rent. Section 68 of the 1980 Act also substitutes a new section 52 into the Rent Act 1977 which deals with rent agreements of regulated tenancies arising from the conversion of controlled tenancies. Section 61 of the 1980 Act substitutes a new section 72 into the 1977 Act, making a registered rent effective from the date of registration rather than as previously, in most cases, from the date of application. A fresh application for registration can now be made two years rather than three years after the previous registration, and Schedule 8 of the 1977 Act is amended to reduce the period of phasing of the new rent. As a result, the increase is in two equal parts, at the start of the period and after one year has elapsed.

The fair rent machinery is supervised by the Secretary of State in consultation with local authorities, though the rent officer forms his opinion independently of the councils, who are reimbursed by central government for the cost of operating the service. The rent officer must keep a register of all fair rents in the area, providing detailed information on the tenancy and the property. An application for registration can be made by either the landlord or the tenant, or jointly; it must be made in the prescribed form (Rent Act 1977 Forms etc. Regulations 1980; 1980 S.I. 1697.), and state the rent which it is sought to register.

Where there is a joint application for registration or no representations are made following an application by only one of the parties, then the rent officer may register the rent without further proceedings if he is satisfied that the rent requested in the application is a fair rent and there can be no reference to a rent assessment committee. In all other cases, if requested, he must give the parties an opportunity to attend a consultation and then inform the parties of his decision as to a fair rent. Within 28 days either of the parties may object and the matter will be referred to the rent assessment committee.

A rent assessment committee consists of a lawyer as chairman together with a surveyor and a layman appointed from a panel by the president of that panel which serves a particular area. The members of the panel are appointed by central government. The parties can either make representations in writing or request a hearing, which is open to members of the public. The committee can either confirm the rent fixed by the rent officer as a fair rent or determine a new fair rent.

Instead of making an application for a fair rent, a landlord may apply for a certificate of fair rent, in order to ascertain what the fair rent would be under various circumstances. There are similar arrangements for consultation and reference to a rent assessment committee, as referred to earlier. When a certificate of fair rent has been issued, an application for registration of a fair rent may be made to the rent officer, who either issues a certificate or informs the applicant that he may within 14 days request that the matter be referred to a rent assessment committee.

A landlord and tenant can make a joint application for the cancellation of a fair rent, subject to various safeguards, and after a consultation with the parties the rent officer may cancel the registration.

A fair rent of a dwelling-house, as defined in section 70 of the 1977 Act, should have regard to all the circumstances (other than personal circumstances), and be on the basis that the number of persons seeking to become tenants of similar dwelling-houses in the locality on the terms (other than those relating to rent) of the regulated tenancy is not substantially greater than the number of such dwelling-houses in the locality which are available for letting on such terms. Various matters are to be disregarded in fixing the fair rent, including disrepair attributable to the tenant or a predecessor in title failing to comply with the terms of the tenancy, and improvements by the tenant other than in pursuance of the terms of the tenancy.

Several methods have been advanced as means of ignoring what is called scarcity value but rather as in rating, comparability is usually a substitute for an elusive correctness. There is some evidence that on average during the latter part of the 1970s rent assessment committees considered fair rents to be higher than the initial determination made by rent officers. The House of Lords judgment in, *Western Heritable Investments*

Ltd. v. *Husband*, 1983, on appeal from the Extra Division of the Court of Session in Scotland contains helpful valuation and legal interpretation.

The Rent Assessment Committee had based its decision on the capital value of the property with vacant possession, had taken 6% as a reasonable return for the landlord and then had regard to the scarcity provision in section 42 of the Rent (Scotland) Act 1971, similar to section 70 in the Rent Act 1977.

From the resulting figure they made deductions for repairs and other expenses and then a deduction of 40% because the property in Glasgow was in an area of relatively high scarcity.

The Scottish Appeal Court had interpreted the Act to mean that it should be presumed that there were no scarcity, irrespective of the facts.

The House of Lords regarded this as an improbable construction, since it defeated the purpose of the legislation, and held that the Committee was correct in law. As to valuation, whether or not the shortage of housing to let had the effect of inflating the price paid for houses with vacant possession was not capable of being precisely demonstrated. It was bad valuation practice to proceed upon a rigid rule of thumb base applying an assumed fair rate of return to vacant possession capital value. However the committee had sufficient expert valuation evidence before it in order to reach the determination they did.

Under the provisions of the Rent Act 1977, before the 1980 amendments, there were about 6,000 registrations a week.

7.2.5 Restricted Contracts

A restricted contract is defined in section 19 of the 1977 Rent Act as a contract whereby one person grants to another, in consideration of a rent which includes payment for the use of furniture or for services, the right to occupy a dwelling as a residence. However distinguished legal authors accept that this is misleading because of the very substantial exemptions. In practical terms restricted contracts are most likely to arise under sections 20 and 21 of the Act.

Section 20 provides that if a tenancy has been precluded from being a protected tenancy solely by section 12 of the Act, then it shall be a restricted contract. Thus encouraging resident landlords to let off surplus accommodation, though the concept is clear, the definitions require very detailed scrutiny to determine their application.

Section 21 provides that where a tenant has the exclusive occupation of any accommodation and the terms of his tenancy include the use of other accommodation in common with his landlord then the tenancy shall have the status of a restricted contract.

Either of the parties or the local authority can refer the contractual rent to the rent tribunal, whose function is transferred to rent assessment committees by the 1980 Act. A local authority cannot validly make a block reference, but must thoroughly investigate each case they wish to put forward, and can refer a contract to the tribunal even if this is opposed by the lessee.

After a hearing, and usually an inspection of the property, the tribunal can approve the rent in the contract, reduce or increase the rent to what they regard as a reasonable sum, or dismiss the reference. There is very little guidance in the Act on what is reasonable, though if there is a registered rent in respect of the dwelling the tribunal cannot reduce the rent below the amount which would be recoverable from the tenant under a regulated tenancy of that dwelling.

The local authority must keep a register of decisions of tribunals on rents of tenancies covered by Part V of the Act and this includes a description of the dwelling.

It is a criminal offence for a landlord to charge more than the reasonable rent once it has been registered and the tenant may recover any excess rent paid. The provisions for review are similar to protected tenancies.

Security of tenure of premises occupied under restricted contracts entered into before the commencement of section 69 of the Housing Act 1980 are covered by sections 103 to 106 of the Rent Act 1977. Where a notice to quit was served after a reference of the contract to the tribunal it shall not have effect for a period of six months after the decision of the tribunal as to a reasonable rent, and the occupier may apply for a deferment of the notice for a period not exceeding six months from the date on which the notice to quit would have had effect. There is no reason why successive applications, should not result in indefinite extensions of the tenancy, though the tribunal should have regard to the balance of hardship between the two parties. For contracts entered into after the commencement of the Housing Act 1980, sections 103 to 106 are expunged by a new section 102A, and replaced by section 106A. This states that when making an order for possession, the court may stay or suspend execution of the order or postpone the date for possession for such periods as it thinks fit but the giving up of possession shall not be postponed more than three months after the making of the order.

Due to earlier legislation any unfurnished tenancy granted by a resident landlord prior to 14 August, 1974 which is still in existence is likely to be a protected tenancy.

7.2.6 Licences

Since a licence conveys no legal estate or interest, but merely gives a right to occupy it is not a tenancy and in general the Rent Acts do not apply—such a device has attractions for landlords.

The problem is defining the term. The courts appear to be much influenced by Lord Denning in *Marchant v. Charters*, 1977, "What is the test to determine whether the occupier of one room in a house is a tenant or a licensee? It does not depend on whether he or she has exclusive occupation or not. It does not depend upon whether the occupation is permanent or temporary. It does not depend upon the label which the parties put upon it. All these are factors which may influence the decision but none of them is conclusive ... Was it intended that the occupier should have a stake in the room or did he only have permission for himself personally to occupy it, whether under contract or not? In the latter case he is a licensee." To illustrate a known form of licence, total sharing may be considered as in *Sturolson v. Weniz*, 1984. Here the landlord enters into a separate contract with each occupier to occupy the accommodation in common with two or more occupiers and clearly there can be no exclusive occupation. This is supported in *Addington Garages v. Fielder*, 1978, though where such an arrangement is a sham, as in *O'Malley v. Seymour*, 1978, this was rejected by the Court. The important House of Lords judgment in *Street v. Mountford*, 1985 offers precise guidance. The occupier in the "licence agreement" which granted exclusive occupation specifically repudiated Rent Act protection. The court held that where there was exclusive occupation and the landlord provided neither attendance nor services, then the occupation was a tenancy.

7.2.7 Rent Book

Where rent is payable weekly then sections 4 and 5 of the Landlord and Tenant Act 1985 requires the landlord to provide a rent book. There is no requirement that payments of rent shall be recorded in the rent book. The book must contain the name and address of the landlord and his agent. Where the landlord is a company, then on the tenants written request, then the company must provide the name and address of every director and the secretary of the company.

The particulars to be included in the rent book are set out in detail in the Rent Book (Forms of Notice) Regulations 1982, S.I. 1982 No. 1474 and vary depending upon whether the tenancy is:

A restricted contract
A protected or statutory tenancy
Covered by the Rent (Agriculture) Act 1976.

Any person who demands or receives rent when there is no rent book is guilty of an offence, subject to the defence that he had no reasonable grounds to suspect the requirements had not been met.

7.2.8 Eviction

At common law a landlord with a right to possession was entitled to re-enter and take possession provided he did not contravene the Statute of Forcible Entry. This was repealed by the criminal Law Act 1977 and a new offence of violence by securing entry was created. However, the position at common law is subject to the provisions of the Protection from Eviction Act 1977, consolidating the provisions of earlier Rent Acts. Section 2 provides that where any premises are let on a lease with a right of re-entry or forfeiture it shall not be lawful to enforce that right while any person is lawfully residing in the premises, without proceedings in the court. Section 1 of the Act creates two criminal offences. The first occurs if a person unlawfully deprives a protected residential occupier of the property, or attempts to do so; he is guilty of an offence unless he proves that he had reasonable cause to believe that the residential occupier had ceased to reside on the premises. The second offence refers to persons who, with the intent of getting the occupier to give up possession, interfere with the peace or comfort of the occupier or persistently withhold services reasonably required for the use of the premises. Occupiers who are outside the full protection of the Rent Acts, such as lessees under restricted contracts and service tenancies, are given some protection by section 3 of the Act, which provides that it shall not be lawful for the owner to enforce his right to recover possession otherwise than by proceedings in the court.

It is perhaps surprising that not until 1984 was a company successfully prosecuted under the 1977 Act. In *Westminster City Council* v. *AMK Property Management*, 1984, the landlords were found guilty of unlawful harrassment and fined £10,000 plus costs of £21,000 (and their own costs). Their conduct included:

Switching off electricity and water
Piling rubble in hallways
Constant noises from drilling.

7.2.9 Long Leases at a Low Rent

The occupier of a dwelling under a tenancy which was originally granted for a term exceeding 21 years at a rent of less than two-thirds of the rateable value of the premises qualifies for protection under Part I of the Landlord and Tenant Act 1954. This provides that the tenancy shall automatically continue unless terminated by not less than one month's notice by the tenant or by a landlord's notice in one of two prescribed forms specifying the date at which the tenancy is to come to an end and enquiring whether the tenant is prepared to give up possession. The procedures and time-periods involved are similar to those that apply to business tenancies covered by Part II of the Act. If the landlord wishes to regain possession he uses the second of the two forms, stating that he proposes to apply to the court for possession on one of the grounds specified in the third schedule of the Act, which are similar to those in Part I of Schedule 15 of the Rent Act 1977. Any dispute can be resolved by the court within a strict time-table of notices by the parties. Alternatively, the landlord's notice can contain the terms for a proposed statutory tenancy and if the parties cannot reach agreement the landlord may apply to the court within a strict time-table, otherwise the original tenancy continues. Where the terms of the statutory tenancy have been agreed between the parties at least two months before the termination date specified, or determined by the court, the long tenancy will continue until the termination date or for three months after the application to the court has been finally disposed of, and any time for appealing has expired, whichever is the later. The tenant then occupies on a regulated tenancy with the usual provisions for fixing the rent.

Many tenants who are covered by Part I of the Landlord and Tenant Act 1954 also qualify under the Leasehold Reform Act 1967. At the time the legislation was passed by the then Labour Government enabling a tenant to purchase compulsorily the freehold interest of his landlord, it was considered in some circles as an unreasonable interference with a private contract.

The facilities offered by the Conservative Government's Housing Act 1980 for local authority tenants to purchase their homes show the change that has occurred. Indeed a number of members of Parliament have suggested that the only remaining anomaly is in the private sector, where all tenants should now have the right to purchase the freehold from their landlord.

An occupier wishing to enfranchise must show that he has been the tenant of a house under a long lease at a low rent for three years and that it satisfies the rateable value limits.

Where the necessary conditions are satisfied then the tenant can serve a notice on the landlord of his intention to acquire the freehold. The landlord is bound to convey the house to the tenant at a price in accordance with section 9 of the Act as amended. The Lands Tribunal have heard a number of cases where various interpretations of the detailed valuation provisions have been considered, and precedents are now established.

The Housing Act 1980, section 142 and Schedule 22, transfers this jurisdiction to rent assessment committees. When exercising this function they are known as leasehold valuation tribunals, from which there is a right of appeal to the Lands Tribunal. Schedule 21 of the Act contains a number of other amendments including a formula for valuing a minor superior tenancy based on the return from $2\frac{1}{2}\%$ Consols. As an alternative to enfranchisement, the tenant can claim a 50 year extension of the lease at a modern ground rent with a review after 25 years.

7.2.10 New Types of Tenure

The Housing Act 1980 introduced two quite new forms of tenure with the aim of making the private rented sector more attractive to landlords. The new shorthold tenancy is designed to give no more security than is agreed by a contract within the fair rent regime. An assured tenancy from an approved landlord is quite outside Rent Act protection and as a commercial transaction is subject to the statutory framework which applies to business tenancies.

A protected shorthold tenancy is created in accordance with section 52 by the landlord granting a lease of between one and five years, and before the commencement of the term giving the tenant a valid notice of the status of the tenancy. Further, either the rent must be registered or an application for registration be made within 28 days of the start of the tenancy. Outside London this requirement was removed by Statutory Instrument in 1981. Section 53 provides that a tenant may terminate the shorthold tenancy before the end of the term by giving one month's notice in the case of a term of less than two years and three month's notice for a term of over two years, and any agreement as to a penalty is void. In order that the landlord can recover possession an additional case 19 is added to Part II of Schedule 15 of the Rent Act 1977, which covers mandatory orders for possession.

An assured tenancy under section 56 can only be granted by an approved body specified by the Secretary of State such as an institution, in respect of a dwelling erected after the effective date which had not been previously occupied other than under an assured tenancy. The principles of Part II of the Landlord and Tenant Act 1954, as amended by the Law of Property Act 1969, apply to the renewal and continuation of the tenancy with the amendments set out in Schedule 5 of the Act.

7.3 Repair

At common law there is no general implied covenant by the landlord that the premises are fit for the purposes for which they are to be used. As a result of the Occupiers' Liability Act 1957 the landlord owes a common duty of care in respect of the parts of a building under his control and following the Defective Premises Act 1972 he is liable for injury resulting from his negligence in respect of repairing covenants in the lease or imposed by statute.

The case of *Rimmer* v. *Liverpool City Council*, 1983, decided by the House of Lords has identified a duty on landlords in common law quite apart from contract or statute. The court held that a builder–owner (as distinct from a bare landlord) owed a duty to the tenant to take reasonable care in designing and constructing a flat so that it would be reasonably safe when let to him.

The most significant statutory provisions are in sections 11 to 17 of the Landlord and Tenant Act 1985. They provide that in leases for less than seven years the landlord is responsible for the repair of the structure and exterior of a dwelling house including drains gutters and external pipes; and to keep in repair and proper working order installations for the supply of hot water, gas and electricity and for sanitation and for space heating and hot water. This overrides any clause in the lease, though the County Court may approve contracting out by the parties. There is also provision for specific performance.

In *Douglas Scott v. Scorgie*, 1984, it was held that the roof of a block of flats whilst not part of the demises to the tenant, was sufficiently related to the demise as to be subject to the statutory clause.

In determining the standard of repair required regard shall be had to the age, character and prospective life of the dwelling house and the locality in which it is situated, further the tenant is required to "do the little jobs about the house that a reasonable tenant would do" *Warren v. Keen*, 1953.

It appears from *O'Brien v. Robinson*, 1973, that the duty only arises when the landlord is advised of the disrepair by the tenant, despite a statutory covenant granting him the right of access to view the condition of the property.

If there is a covenant to repair and the landlord refuses to meet his obligation then in *Calabar Properties Ltd v. Stitcher*, 1983, where the tenant had to move into alternative accommodation the court held that damages should be awarded for; the cost of the alternative accommodation, the cost of any repair paid for by the tenant, and the unpleasantness of living in the deteriorating accommodation. The Housing Act 1980, Section 80 provides that section 32 does not apply to leases granted to various public bodies.

The possibility that tenants of residential property might wish to make improvements had not been regarded as of any significance for many years. The Housing Act 1980, section 81, replaces section 19(2) of the Landlord and Tenant Act 1927 in respect of secure, protected and statutory tenancies. As a result there is an implied covenant that the tenant will not make any alterations without the landlord's consent, but that this is not to be unreasonably withheld and the onus of proof is on the landlord, with presumptions in the tenant's favour. Sections 38 and 39 provide that in the case of a secure tenant the landlord shall at the end of the tenancy have the power to make such payment in respect of the improvement as he considers appropriate and the rent cannot be increased during the tenancy to reflect the improvement.

In *Graystone Property Investments Ltd* v. *Margulies*, 1983, the tenant of a flat wished to remove the false ceiling within a total floor to ceiling height of 18 ft 6 inches and construct a mezzanine floor. The landlord argued that the demise only extended to the underside of the false ceiling. The court rejected this saying there was no sensible reason why the landlord should retain a variety of irregular shaped voids to which he had no access and that the demise extended to the underside of the flat above.

In the latter part of the 1970s the improvement of residential property lost some of its momentum. In 1974 there were 137,350 applications for improvement grants and in the first half of 1979 there were only 24,745. This was due to a combination of reasons; slowness of the approvals system, local authorities adopting a more rigorous approach to the overall standards, including repairs not qualifying for grant, reduced financial viability of the work, and the number of properties already improved. Part VII of the Housing Act 1980 enables tenants to apply for grants under Part VII of the Housing Act 1974 and Schedule 12 amends the detail of the grants system, permitting the Secretary of State to specify different percentages for different kinds of grants.

7.4 Service Charges

A well drafted service charge clause in the lease of a typical mansion-block flat should cover apportionment, services provided, payment, availability of accounts, sinking funds and the procedure for settling disputes. Unfortunately, the combination of the rapidly-rising cost of providing services and the abuses of some landlords have shown that the contractual relationship alone is an unsatisfactory basis for a tenant's occupation of his home. The problem is particularly acute in central London, where mansion-blocks provide the majority of residential accommodation. As a result Members of Parliament have been rather more personally aware of the issues involved. The statutory provisions designed to protect the tenant also increase the cost of managing the flats, which in turn increase the service charge and only a small number of the larger firms are prepared to take on the work.

The Rent Act 1977 provides in section 71(4) that a rent officer or rent assessment committee may register a variable service charge as part of a fair rent if the terms of the variation are reasonable but the most important legislation is that contained in the Housing Finance Act 1972. Section 90 required landlords to provide information on service charges, but did not provide a means by which the tenant could challenge this information. The Housing Act 1974 created a new section 91A in the original Act such that service charges could only be recovered from the tenant in respect of chargeable items provided to a reasonable standard. The landlord was required to obtain two estimates where the cost of work exceeded £250 and where it cost over £2,000 consult with the individual tenants or the tenants' association before commencing the work; the costs and delays of the procedures involved undoubtedly further increased the management charges.

Schedule 19 of the Housing Act 1980 (now to be found in sections 18 to 30 of the Landlord and Tenant Act 1985), replaced sections 90 to 91A in the original Act. A service charge is defined to include costs or estimated costs incurred or to be incurred; this would seem to overcome the problem in *Frobisher (Second Investments) Ltd.* v. *Kiloran Trust Company Ltd. and Another*, 1980, where the court held that in accordance with section 91A,(1)(b), the landlords were not entitled to require interim payments to be made in advance, based on estimated costs.

The landlord can only include costs in the service charge if they were reasonably incurred and if the services provided or works carried out are of a reasonable standard. If the charge is payable before the costs are incurred, necessary adjustments will have to be made. Where the costs involved exceed £25 multiplied by the number of flats or £500, whichever is the greater, the landlord must obtain two estimates, one of which is to be from an independent party. These estimates shall be made available to the tenants and, unless the work is urgent, cannot be commenced until one month has elapsed. A tenant can require the landlord to supply a written summary of the costs in the preceding year and when more than four flats are involved it must be certified by a qualified accountant as a fair summary and sufficiently supported by documents.

The schedule does not apply to service charges payable by a tenant of a flat the rent of which is registered under Part IV of the Housing Act 1977 unless the amount registered is a variable amount under section 71(4).

The problems of apportionment and changes in the services are well illustrated by *Pole Properties Ltd* v. *Feinberg*, 1981.

The lease contained a provision for the tenant to pay $\frac{2}{7}$ of the increase in the cost of fuel for the common solid fuel boiler serving four flats; the proportion was based on the floor area of the flats.

The landlords acquired the adjacent property, which was also converted to flats and installed on oil fired boiler which was connected to both the new flats and the pipes and radiators of the old flats. The landlords claimed that the charges should be based on a revised ratio of the area of each flat to the area of the flats in both properties.

The tenant argued that the quality of heating varied between the properties and hence an aggregate area apportionment was inequitable. An expert gave evidence that a directly heated volume basis of apportionment should be adopted and the calculations showed the tenant's share to be 12·08% of the of the combined cost of heating the two buildings.

The provisions found in the 1980 Housing Act apply to Local Authorities, Development Corporations, Housing Associations and tenant management companies in respect of long leasehold properties.

Prior to the 1980 Act, tenants management companies, the normal way of dealing with long leasehold flats, operated outside any statutory framework. In view of the penalties which can be incurred for failure to comply with the Act, members may be less willing to be officers, and hence subject to fines of up to £500.

7.5 The Sale of Flats

The development of new flats for sale on 999 year leases with a management company consisting of each of the occupiers as a shareholder is a well proved method by which developers can exit from the scene when the last flat has been sold. Ideally, the flats will contain a sufficient range of interested and able occupiers capable of running the management company, as regards both day-to-day matters and the creation of sinking funds to meet longer-term maintenance needs.

Major problems have arisen in the break-up of existing mansion-blocks and their subsequent management. The break-up process needs to be approached in a cautious way; the decision to break-up the block will be influenced by the relationship between the capital value of the income subject to the fair rent legislation and the likely proceeds from sales in say, the first two or three years, less the cost of works to flats and the common parts. The rate of sales will depend upon the age-pattern, occupations, social mobility and incomes of the tenants and the extent to which physical and legal aspects of the property can be combined to create a pattern of rights and duties attractive to both the potential mortgagors and mortgagees.

The timing and phasing of the initial communication with the tenants must be related to the requirements of prudent management. For several years the landlord and his agent will have had the break-up potential under review and as tenants leave the flats will be kept vacant. The tenants that remain may well recognize the signs of an impending disposal of long leases.

Once formally advised of the landlord's intentions, tenants, particularly older tenants of limited means, will probably feel threatened and react in a hostile manner. Tenants unwilling to buy may, through negotiation, be prepared to move to alternative accommodation at a concessionary rent with expenses paid or accept a capital payment for giving the landlord vacant possession. Tenants unwilling either to purchase or move are in a strong position, fortified by the succession rules, and it should be recognized from the start that for some years the block will have to be managed in its hybrid form. Each type of occupier has different perceptions of the flats and expectations as to the extent, standard and cost of the services provided.

In the break-up of mansion-flats or conversion of a large old property it is a difficult equation to decide how much should be spent on the refurbishment and improvement of the individual flats and common parts. To some extent there is a trade-off between carrying out extensive and thorough maintenance and improvement prior to sale and the size of the service charge in the medium and long term. It requires the most careful surveying and management to determine a realistic budget for this work, which often has to be carried out in a building occupied by many tenants, some of whom may not be entirely in sympathy with the landlord's objectives.

The worst possible type of lease for the sale of flats is one based upon the normal landlord and tenant relationship. Since the ground rent is usually modest, with infrequent and uneconomic reviews, the landlord rapidly loses interest and potential mortgagees may be worried about the effective implementation of covenants necessary to preserve the value of the property.

When dealing with a new block of long-leasehold flats the developer can step out of the scene by requiring each tenant to become a shareholder in a management company who hold the freehold or a long-lease interest in the block. This requires either a few conscientious owners to act as officers of the company, though the requirements of the Companies Acts seem somewhat excessive in the light of the limited objectives and scale of most blocks of flats. An alternative is a trustee-administered lease where a trustee is interposed between the lessor and lessee which gives continuity of management; a specialized company, Holding and Management, Ltd., administer 5,000 flats on this basis.

Effective as the sale of flats may be in providing the most favourable financial return to the landlords of mansion-blocks, the continuing loss of rented accommodation in inner urban areas decreases both the general and housing mobility of various groups in the community, particularly young people. This inhibits the movement of labour in response to the pattern of employment opportunities and has other undesirable effects.

7.6 Managing Agents

Whilst the academic, the philosopher, the politician, and the economist can identify, the problems and postulate solutions on an "if" basis, experienced managers are required to operate the system as they find it on a daily basis.

The R.I.C.S. in their Practice Note on "The Responsibilities of Residential Managing Agents" have identified the duties covered by a standard management fee as:

1. Submitting demands and collecting rent, rates, service and other charges at appropriate intervals.
2. Making payments to superior lessors, suppliers, staff, contractors, rating authorities, professional advisers, insurers and others as may be appropriate.
3. Administering building and other insurances.
4. Preparing and submitting statements and accounting for balances at agreed intervals, normally quarterly.
5. Producing and circularizing service charge accounts and supplying such information and details to which tenants and recognized tenants associations are entitled.
6. Producing an annual estimate of expenditure for service charge purposes and contributions to reserves.
7. Administering reserve funds.

8. Where an auditor is required, answering enquiries from auditors.
9. Employing required staff (excluding advertising and agency expenses) and effecting necessary supervision.
10. Arranging and supervising maintenance contracts for all plant and equipment.
11. Making periodical visits to the property to ensure proper day to day running and to inspect the building as to general condition.
12. Attending to normal routine management enquiries from tenants.
13. Dealing with day to day repairs to structure, plant, fixtures, fittings and equipment.
14. Keeping records in relation to tenancies and other relevant matters relating to the property.
15. Checking compliance with terms of leases and statutory requirements.
16. Instructing solicitors in relation to unpaid rent or charges and other matters.
17. Advising generally on management policy.

Other duties for which an additional fee is payable as and when required include:

Preparation of specifications, obtaining tenders, and supervising works of a substantial nature.
Attending court and giving evidence.
Advising on Health, Safety and Fire requirements.
Advising upon landlords consents under the lease.
Fire Insurance Valuations.
Advising upon and acting for the landlord in respect of fair rents.
Preparation of schedules of dilapidations or condition.
Letting and renewals.
Checking inventories.
Advising on insurance claims.
Advising on grants.
Capital and annual valuations.

Some of the problems that can arise in residential management are illustrated by *Murray* v. *Sturgis and Others*, 1981. The owner of a flat was posted to Paris early in 1979 and instructed the agents, Sturgis and Sons, to let and manage his ground floor flat in Chiswick, at a fee of 15% of the total annual rent.
The firm let the flat for two months to a Mr. Bonviss, without

references, at a rent of £75 per week and a deposit of £300; he overstayed his tenancy. A tenancy was subsequently granted to a Mrs. Redding without references, deposit or rent in advance. Following complaints about noise the landlord's agent visited the flat and saw the decorations and furnishings were damaged. Mrs. Redding left the flat early in 1980.

Damages were awarded against the defendants for negligence on the following basis for events occurring between 26 March, 1979 and 30 June, 1980.

Unpaid rent by Mr. Bonviss	£142·45
Unpaid rent by Mr. Bonviss	£488·91
Tenants use of phones, kept in the plaintiff's name	£310·97
Unpaid rent by Mrs. Redding	£645·45
Unpaid rent by Mrs. Redding	£473·33
Unpaid rent by Mrs. Redding	£946·56
Tenant's use of gas kept in the plaintiff's name	£69·12
Dilapidations	£2,810·00
General damages	£100·00
Total	£5,986·79

In *Parkside Knightsbridge Ltd* v. *Horwitz*, 1983, the court considered a dispute on the reasonableness of the in-house management company's claim of £12,800 for the management and supervision of the service charge in a luxury block of flats which totalled around £120,000.

Evidence was given that major practices quoted the following fees for this work:

Jones Lang Wootton 5% of gross rents	£23,000
Chestertons 4% of gross rents	£18,000
Mellersh and Harding 14% of service charge	£19,000

The above excluded rent collection but included V.A.T. It was also said that Rent Officers allowed 12% to 15% of the service charge. The in-house management costs were, not surprisingly, held to be reasonable.

In 1983 the R.I.C.S. published a Report of a Working Party on the Management of Blocks of Flats, relevant to rack rented, partial break-ups and complete long lease schemes, but excluding rent regulation and registration. The recommendation included:

Stronger measures to require identification of the landlord, such that failure to comply with Sections 121 and 122 of the Housing Act 1974 rendered the tenants' obligations unenforceable during the period of non-compliance.

Amendments to Schedule 19 of the 1980 Act; tenants right to challenge appointment of managing agent, regulations for the recognition of tenants associations, provision to create a sinking fund even if the lease is silent.

A system of arbitration for defective leases.

Standard leases or model clauses.

Inland Revenue to clarify treatment of sinking funds.

In 1984 the Minister for Housing and Construction set up the Nugee Committee of Inquiry into the Management of Privately Owned Blocks of Flats. It reported in November 1985, adopting most of the R.I.C.S. recommendations, legislation is likely before 1987.

7.7 Conclusion

It is difficult to reach any firm conclusions on the management of private sector residential premises. The property varies from a single modern house let furnished by its owner when working overseas for a specified period to the large "ring fence" estates built in London during the early part of the nineteenth century. The landlords are as diverse as the Church Commissioners who, to judge from their annual reports, regard their residential property as a painful burden, and small private companies operating rooming houses in the inner cities. Tenants vary from the wealthy itinerant company executives to those with needs far greater than many of those occupying perhaps subsidized local authority housing.

The whole is supervised by a legislative code designed to protect relatively weak tenants from unscrupulous landlords. The fact that many landlords are fair, that many tenants have no perception of their rights and that those tenants determined to exercise all their rights to the letter of the law are in a commanding position casts doubts on the legal concepts underlying the statutes, which are themselves the product of partisan political argument. The statutory fair rents obtained from letting property are not commensurate with the real cost of the resources utilized in providing residential accommodation, with the result that the more responsible landlords reduce their involvement. Much of the market, with the exception of some specialized high-quality accommodation in London, operates in an uneasy truce of short-term expediency and long-term despair.

In 1985 the Conservative government considered the case for deregulating new tenancies. The arguments need to be considered from the point of view of both narrow technical mechanisms and broader macro economics. In particular; the boost to the construction industry, the higher rents (and tax payments by landlords) the higher housing benefits, an assumed trade off of local authority provision for private sector provision, with a consequential reduction in the public sector borrowing requirements; the latter, the most tantilizing of goals.

Fear as to the intentions of any future governments would be likely to frustrate the implementation of the measures by private landlords, and this was not implemented.

Unless there is a fundamental change it seems likely that in absolute terms the private sector will continue to decline faster than the growth of the voluntary sector. The consequences of a continuing decline in the private rented sector could be partly overcome by local authorities adopting a new approach to their tower blocks built during the 1960s. These buildings are unsuitable for families or elderly tenants who look to the local authority to meet their permanent housing need. If the blocks were managed on the basis of providing relatively short-term accommodation at rents reflecting the real disposable income of young people, this could resolve a whole series of problems and result in increased income for the authority.

Sources and Further Reading

Aldridge, The Housing Act 1980, Oyez, 1980.
Appraisal of the Financial Effects of Council House Sales, D.O.E., January 1980.
Doling, Have the Rent Acts become irrelevant? 270 E.G. 1148.
George, The Sale of Flats, Sweet and Maxwell, 1978.
Mainly for Students, Lease or Licence, 253 E.G. 1306.
Manual of Legislation Relating to Rent Regulation and Control, Institute of Rent Officers Educational Trust, 1977.
Nationwide Building Society, Housing Trends, published quarterly.
O'Brien, Giving Tenants the Right to Buy, C.S., May, 1980.
Pettit, Landlord and Tenant under the Rent Act 1977, Butterworths, 1978.
Report of the Working Party on the Management of Blocks of Flats, R.I.C.S., 1983.

The Responsibilities of Residential Managing Agents, R.I.C.S., 1981.
Tonkin, Problem of Administering Sold Flats, C.S., June, 1979.
Tonkin, Management of Flats, 259 E.G. 745, 837.
West, The Law of Dilapidations, Estates Gazette, 1979.
Whitehead, Can Private Renting Survive, 266 E.G. 691.
Williams, Repairs and the Housing Act 1961, 270 E.G. 709.

PART III

Positive Management

Chapter 8

Estates Policy

8.1 Positive Management

The nature of an estate reflects the aggregate effects of the inter-action between the institutional setting of the property market, consisting of economic, social, technical and legal factors, and aims and objectives of the proprietary interest.

The extent to which those aims are defined and the vigour with which they are pursued and monitored will determine the distinctive form and character of the estate, making it more than the sum of the various property interests at a particular instant in time. The time-scales involved, which vary from the long-term implications of new ground-leases on the free-holder's ultimate reversion to the short-term practicalities of day-to-day management, require a flexible approach to decision-making. The range of issues involved, from the technical performance of components of construction to the impact of new government policy on the overall performance of an investment portfolio require breadth of view and the ability to assimilate and react to new situations.

Positive management is more an attitude of mind than just the effective exercise of suitably approved procedures. The achievement of the right balance between the efficient operation of existing procedures and fresh analysis, innovation and its implementation is what distinguishes the exceptionally gifted from the able and technically competent professional.

With hindsight, it is all too easy in a typical annual report to record what has occurred, identify the reasons for it and then make the broadest of statements regarding the likely course of future events, expressing hopes for the future and appreciation of the work of the staff. Perhaps this is the role of a chairman's annual statement and it would be unreasonable to ask for a more definitive form of analysis. Within any corporate body in which property is either the main resource or provides the environment within which operational activities are pursued, much more rigorous internal procedures will be occurring in terms of both management and accounting.

The phrase "positive management" can be used too easily, without the adviser or the client appreciating its full implications. In the context of property generally and investment property in particular, the phrase has only been in general use since the mid-1970s. In fact, positive management has been occurring on the estates of some of the old institutions for several hundred years but only in recent years has it been stated explicitly, almost as an article of faith. The word positive suggests an intention to contrast with some other form of management, hardly negative, since this would be too critical of what by implication had occurred before. Rather positive management as an alternative to passive management, which might best be described as prudent inactivity. The history of property since 1970 is adequate explanation for the emphasis now given to positive management; this can be defined in terms of the application of management concepts discussed in Chapter 2 to the different types of estates, but of equal importance are lively, trained and perceptive minds concerned with the active implementation of the policy.

8.2.1 The National Estate

The concept of a national estate is capable of interpretation in many ways. It can be seen as an informative but passive property record or as the management of land, buildings and infrastructure under varying degrees of control by the State, in the best interests of the public. It involves the links between clear issues of political policy and complex administrative and technical problems, some of which arise from apparently conflicting requirements.

The first stage in a study of the national estate is the identification of a national policy. Are the actions of government simply the aggregate effect of a series of *ad hoc* measures dealing with individual aspects of land and property that surface from time to time in manifestoes and legislation, or is there some case for seeking to establish policy and administrative procedures which encourage a broad approach to the prudent management of land and buildings, irrespective of the nature of the proprietary interest? To some extent this is a political question, but aside from the emphasis which a Minister could give to statutory initiatives, the concepts involved have not enjoyed much discussion outside a narrow legislative setting. However in 1985 a paper was presented to the National Economic Development Office which considered the £10 billion per

annum spent on public sector infrastructure and public buildings. There is concern regarding inadequate regular maintenance and lack of strategy between central and local
government.

In the post-war period alternative Labour and Conservative
governments have resulted in regular and predictable changes
to the setting within which the management, development
and taxation of land occurs. The policies reflected by the 1947
Act, the 1964 Ministry of Land and Natural Resources and
the Land White Paper of 1974 were all subsequently changed
by incoming Conservative governments. In local government,
town planning, though monitored by central government,
operates in a very local way, and indeed more emphasis is being
given to local plans and less to structure plans and their overall
supervision by the Secretary of State.

8.2.2 Department of the Environment

The importance of policy in the area of land administration
was recognized by central government in 1977 by the creation
within the Department of the Environment of a Directorate
of Land Economy, responsible for advising the Secretary of
State on land policies generally, and surveyors were appointed
as senior civil servants with that Directorate. Though small
in number, they can be distinguished from surveyors seconded
to the Department from the Chief Valuer's Office of the Inland
Revenue, who advise on the practical aspects of land valuation,
and those located in Marsham Street or regional offices responsible for the implementation of statutory provisions and particular programmes. The Directorate's area of responsibility
included land economy aspects of planning, housing, transport, agriculture, development agencies and property finance.
Their activities varied from advising on the representations
made by the various pressure groups in this field to the bridging
of the not unknown gulf between policy and detailed implementation.

The most extensive and rigorous analysis of the role and
performance of the D.O.E. was formulated in 1980 in the form
of "Management Information System for Ministers" (MINIS).

This showed that the majority of urban estates policy issues
were located in the Inner Cities Directorate and the Planning
and Land Use Directorate, the latter having absorbed the Land
Economy Directorate.

The Inner Cities Directorate was concerned with the

development and implementation of policy initiatives for inner cities, including:

Industrial Improvement Areas
Enterprise Zones
Links between Commerce, Industry and Local Initiatives
Housing Aspects
Partnership and Programme Area Policy
Urban Development Corporations
Analysis of Urban Trends
Management of Research Programme.

The Planning and Land Use Policy Directorate was organized into five Divisions, dealing with eleven main activities including;

Policy and procedures for public sector land transactions
    relaxation of central control
    amendment to Crichel Down rules (see 10.4.3)
    abolishing selective checking by D.V. (see 10.2.2)
    advice to other government departments
Policy and monitoring of derelict land reclamation
Development control policy
Monitoring and streamlining the planning machine
Policy on supply of development land
    liaison with House Builders Federation (see 10.4.3)
    monitoring features on county basis
    management of research (see 8.3)
Winding up of Community Land Act
Commercial Property Market
    monitor working of 1954 Act (see 6.2)
    shopping policy
    liaison with U.R.P.I.
Property Advisory Group
    structure and activity of property market
    planning gain (see 10.3)
    public/private development partnerships
    property market information (see 3 and 11)
Land Registers
    monitoring operation and land release (see 10.4.3)
Estates Policy
    disposal of public sector assets (see 10.4.3)
    mechanisms of development
    effect of capital allowances on industrial property (see 12.5.2)

professional advice to Inland Revenue (see 12.2)
professional advice on local authority rental income accounting
liaison with private sector including, B.P.F., R.I.C.S., Chambers of Commerce (see 8.2.3)
professional advice on British Rail Property Board and to Ports Directorate (see 4.3.3)
liaison with regional offices.

In 1985 a specialist Land and Property Division was formed under Christopher Howes which was somewhat similar to the Land Economy Directorate of 1977.

8.2.3 Relationships

The function of national estate management is concerned with the relationship between the aggregate value of the return or benefit enjoyed by the occupiers and users of land and buildings and their external effects, compared with the real cost of the resources used in the provision and maintenance of real property. The available resources are a combination of those allocated by the public sector and those available through the financial institutions, reported upon by the Wilson Committee. Apart from their criticism of Building Society interest rates and the accountability of Pension Funds, in general terms the Committee seemed satisfied that there were no major deficiencies in the mechanics of the financial institutions. The problem is that the returns from investment in industry are not sufficiently attractive. It is unlikely that the proposal in a minority report for a new joint fund would in any way improve the situation.

National estate management firstly, requires some subjective political judgment on the social consequences of general economic policy and the discretionary influence exercised by government on the parties concerned with the management of urban property. Over recent years both the channels of communication and the perception of those involved has been much improved.

The second part of a public sector policy for estates is the creation and general supervision of a statutory, administrative and institutional framework conducive to the efficient management of estates, whether in the public or private sector. Statutory aspects such as planning and taxation are the most obvious and the most direct in their effect. Unless there is real evidence that long delays in the granting of planning consents result in better decisions than would otherwise be given, then there is a presumption in favour of quicker decisions.

Apparent abuses of the planning system also need to be considered as is shown by the Town and Country Planning (Compensation) Act 1985 which reversed the effect of *London Borough of Camden* v. *Peaktop Properties (Hampstead) Ltd*, 1983.

The result of the case implied that under sections 165 and 169 and the eighth Schedule of the 1971 Act, the owners of blocks of flats could make application for planning permission for an extension of less than 10% with the hope of a refusal. This would entitle them to compensation. Following the case the London Borough of Kensington and Chelsea received 20 such "penthouse" applications of a compensation nature.

In taxation there is concern that tax-planning considerations caused by the desire to maximize the net financial return have distorted the true resource implications, which is against the public interest. Both new and existing policies need detailed scrutiny to ensure that the intended objectives either do not cause negative side-effects or that the net effect is sufficiently positive to justify their introduction.

In the U.K. there has been a tradition of professional institutions operating not only rules of professional conduct but also policing voluntary agreements which might otherwise be regulated directly or indirectly by statute. This is nowhere better illustrated than by the Guidance Notes prepared by the R.I.C.S. Assets Valuation Standards Committee. The 26 guidance notes and seven background papers extent to 100 pages and provide a manual of good and required practice. These also have implications for determining the extent to which a particular task can be seen to have been performed in a competent manner.

The Committee's functions are as follows:

(1) to advise and assist members on request concerned with the valuation of property assets of companies in meeting the requirements of the Stock Exchange, the City Panel on Take-Overs and Mergers, and Company Law and Accountancy standards;

(2) to keep under continuous review standards of valuation and procedures necessary to keep abreast with public policy and attitudes apart from the requirements set out in (1) above;

(3) to initiate the preparation of Guidance Notes as and when appropriate on valuation standards and procedures related to property assets;

Estates Policy 211

(4) to arrange for valuation of property assets which are published in the Press (e.g., a prospectus for a sale of shares) or referred to in the Press, to be read; in the event of any apparent inconsistency with any R.I.C.S. Guidance Notes, to invite the member concerned to discuss the matter with the Committee; to provide answers to public criticisms of valuations or valuers, as appropriate;

(5) to be responsible for liaison with the Stock Exchange, the Institute of Chartered Accountants, and the City Panel on Take-Overs and Mergers.

So far, only in respect of the valuation of the assets of insurance companies has the Government considered it necessary to provide statutory regulations and the Guidance Notes go on to provide useful commentary on the statutory instrument.

Though rather less than 1% of estate management practice is concerned with the management of the concept of the national estate, the remaining 99% of estate management practice is the management of that disaggregated national estate. Within public sector estates there will probably be more recognition of the national perspective, but the pressures of good neighbourliness and socio-economic change linked to political sensitivity are likely to affect the larger private estates.

8.3 Research

The supporting role of the encouragement of innovation and research is important, but only if the impact of proprietary interests is given due weight both in the design of the research brief, and the interpretation of the results. There is a danger that research expertise and methodology developed within the disciplines of economics and geography and applied in the currently unfashionable field of planning may be used with too many implicit assumptions from the philosophy of planning and the mathematics of aggregation. The diverse and heterogeneous nature of land and buildings means there is no common vehicle or form for assembling information and helping to trace through from cause to effect. The usual research techniques require a considerable time-span for analysis and synthesis, during this time the market can change and with it the impact of particular parameters built into the original research brief, resulting in doubts as to the relevance of the project.

For example, two industrial buildings may appear identical; if one had been developed by a property company and the other by a local authority, their site selection, funding, taxation, management are all likely to be different, but in each case appropriate to the overall terms of reference of the proprietory body. The aggregation of such data masks rather than illuminates the distinctive features contributing to decision-making in both the provision and management of such property.

If research is defined as, "a systematic enquiry to test hypotheses and further the development of both theory and methodology applied both to the procedures involved in the profession (techniques, institutional processes etc.) and the substantial issues", then it is instructive to observe its interpretation by different sectors.

Only the largest fifteen to twenty practices have their own permanent in house research capacity, though this does not prevent other practices from commissioning or undertaking research. Such research may be:

To enhance their capacity to deliver services to clients.
To meet a particular client's need.
To enhance the development of their practice.

Research may well be seen as an element of public relations. There may be some unease between the time horizons of those requiring research and those undertaking research.

In the public sector, research in our areas of interest, has often been planning lead. During the 1980s there has been a move towards crisper more prescribed, shorter timescale tasks with a stronger estates emphasis particularly looking at:

The inner city
Derelict land
Industrial regeneration
Land supply pipeline
The effect of the development control system.

This is indicated by the D.O.E. Directorates areas of responsibility in 8.2.

Academic research was until the late 1970s distinguished by its inability to identify issues in urban property and translate them into good research projects for a variety of reasons. A combination of circumstances was required, and is occurring to change the climate and there are grounds for some optimism that a research capacity is being added to the skills of the property manager, from within his own education through the undergraduate schools.

The role of the R.I.C.S. is to create an environment supportive of research particularly in the fields of education and resources. This will enable surveyors to undertake research that will benefit the profession and for research to be easily translated into practice to benefit surveyors.

The Economic and Social Research Council's Planning and Environmental Committee is responsible for research into problems relating to the spatial structure, development and management of the socio economic and man made environment at national, regional and local levels in the U.K., in other developed countries and elsewhere in the world. Land use studies and planning, housing and residential location are central to its remit. In its Policy Statement of 1983 it made specific reference to "the study of the land development process, land management and land values, the supply of and demand for housing, transport and recreational facilities and the influence of public and quasi public agencies on the pattern of urban and rural development".

The publication of "The Land Market and the Development Process, a Review of Research and Policy" by the School for Advanced Urban Studies in 1978 was an important reference point.

In 1983 two important conferences took place, "Land Policy" sponsored by the then S.S.R.C. and "Land Management Research" sponsored by the Heads of Department of Surveying in Polytechnics. These, together with a widening of the available means of publishing work indicate a major change is occurring. The client need identified in the late 1970s is now being matched by a response from the researchers. As a result a scale leap has been made in the ten years between 1975 and 1985, it will take a further ten years to bear fruit and to assess its full effects. The position is reviewed in "Research and the Urban Estates Surveyor" a discussion paper circulated by the General Practice and Planning and Development Divisions of the R.I.C.S. in 1984.

8.4 Individual Estates

The formulation of estates policy requires good communication between those who hold or represent the proprietary interest and the professional estate manager. The policy need not be a plan in the formal sense of a series of phased consequential events, it could take the form of a position statement with several alternative but not mutually exclusive programmes. The role of policy would then be reviewing the emphasis to be given in the implementation of each programme. The client needs to be well-informed on the significance of the issues which must be decided and the alternatives available. He may well also look for some guidance on the effectiveness of the implementation of estates policy.

Implementation refers to the process whereby a statement of policy subsequently has a direct and specific effect on the management of an individual property interest. This implies an operational structure providing responsibility and account-ability, though to go further and suggest that a particular form is appropriate to a particular type of estate is neither sensible nor possible.

The training and academic disciplines from which the sur-veyor's skills have developed tend to stress the uniqueness of every interest in real property, resulting in individual solu-tions to individual problems. However, the size of the financial resources involved and the complexity of the business environ-ment means that surveyors have to work more closely with other professionals and line management. This has encouraged surveyors to review the link between policy and the conduct of their work, and as a result in private practice the taking of instructions has become more formal and more rigorous reporting styles and monitoring procedures have been adopted.

The long-term consequences of a particular property decision coupled with the indeterminate life of some estates, such as both the old and new institutions, means a view has to be taken, often on rather weak evidence, on the likely outcome of a series of related activities. In this situation the best way of maximizing income in the short-run is usually inconsistent with the agreed long-term policy. For example, the timing of the refurbishment of an office building and the most appro-priate specification to realize the greatest net proceeds is a matter of very fine judgment; it can require intentional voids for some months or even years.

One estate's view of the short, medium and long-term may differ substantially from that of another estate, indeed they may vary in respect of different properties within the same portfolio. Nevertheless, it is a useful guide to consider the short term to be a period of less than a year and particularly the period covered by the various procedures for statutory and contractual notices. The medium-term is then a period of between one and five years, similar to the interval between rent reviews and the review is a useful opportunity for the parties to vary the terms of the lease by agreement. This would also be consistent with the timing of major reinspections and the implementation of changes to the portfolio in the light of analysis of the physical and financial performance of individual properties. In the long-term, that is to say more than five years hence, it is possible for so many parameters to change that the best plan is the one which keeps open as many alternatives as possible and brings forward into the medium-term plan those with the greatest potential consistent with any overriding portfolio requirements.

The overall character of the portfolio is shaped by a complex interaction between functional necessity, institutional factors and the opinion of key management personalities. The functional requirements may be in terms of property as a resource for commerce or industry, or as a source of investment income. As the purpose of the proprietary interest change, so will the use made of the portfolio and the utilization of individual properties. This will be assisted by an efficient records system designed to store, retrieve and manipulate data in the most convenient form.

Changes in the legal, social and economic framework within which property rights are defined and used can be made very quickly by a new government and have a major effect on the management of the estate. The patent form of statutory provisions means that they cannot easily be overlooked, though considerable uncertainty can exist as to their detailed interpretation. Social and economic change are less obvious and require some perception across a broad range of human activity in order to analyse their effect and consequences for the portfolio.

Due to the relatively small staff involved in the management of estates, individuals are able to have a direct impact on the practical management of individual properties. Flair and personal charisma have their role to play, which may or may not succeed in identifying or creating opportunities, but their successful implementation depends upon a positive approach to management, utilizing a wide range of resources and techniques, drawn from both experience and innovation.

Sources and Further Reading

Empty Housing in England (Vacant Property Survey, 1977), H.M.S.O., 1980.
Guidance Notes on the Valuations of Assets, First Edition (1974) and Second Edition (1980), R.I.C.S.

Management Information System for Ministers, Directorate Statements, D.O.E., 1980.

Research and the Urban Estates Surveyor, R.I.C.S., 1984.

Review of the Functioning of Financial Institutions (Wilson Committee), H.M.S.O., 1980.

Schiller, Property Research, 269 E.G. Property Market Review, Supplement 32.

Surveying in Eighties (SITE Report), R.I.C.S., 1980.

The Land Market and the Development Process, S.A.U.S., 1978.

Thorncroft, Principles of Estate Management, Ch. 12 (Estates Gazette, 1965).

Chapter 9

Professional Practice

9.1.1 Property Records

The exercise of estate management skills occurs within an environment shaped by the character of the organization in which the surveyor works, the extent and quality of the information that is available and the nature of the relationship with the client. Statute and case-law have in recent years resulted in a much more rigorous approach to the relationship with the client, in the taking of instructions and the consequences of both written and oral advice. Developments in technology have enabled information to be stored and handled in completely new ways, offering opportunities for more comprehensive and analytical forms of reporting to clients. The surveyor is therefore faced with not only new types of tasks but new ways of performing old tasks, and at the same time constant reminders of the need for the highest levels of technical competence and professional judgment. In meeting the needs of clients, whether in the public or private sector, surveyors are working in large organizations, with delegation and specialization of function. No longer does an individual client receive advice from an individual surveyor; both now operate within some form of corporate structure. The giving of instructions, their acceptance, reporting and associated records are all more formal and less personal than in the past.

The delivery of property management services in a professional office depends firstly upon the effective performance of three types of function:

Professional   knowledge, judgment, experience and personal skills,
Technical   the performance of physical tasks,
Accounting   financial records and action,

and secondly, upon the quality of communication between these functions. In a large organization each task will tend to be carried out by specialized staff. Hence the larger the organization the greater will be the need for the arrangements for communication, interaction and monitoring. Thus, the role of the records system is not just to passively store information but to prompt approved action, monitor the results, and sound the alert when the outcome is unsatisfactory.

9.1.2 Information

Surveyors seldom get the opportunity to set up an ideal records system. Local government re-organization in 1973 meant that some authorities needed a new system but immediate practical problems required immediate practical solutions and it often proved impossible to review the various systems which existed in the several authorities constituting the new local government unit. The creation of an in-house estates department in commerce and industry is another point in time when initiatives could be taken to determine an appropriate records system. In private practice the individual client's portfolios will be operated on systems with as many common features as possible, and if a computer application is introduced then there will be the greatest pressure for a common system. It is possible to make improvements to existing record systems and this will become necessary as commercial practices change, as the client's requirements become more sophisticated, or as a result of recognition of the contribution which computers can make to the practice.

An ideal records system can only be devised when a number of key questions have been answered;

Who needs what information?
Why do they need the information?
How will the information be used?
How quickly is information required and how is it kept up-to-date?
How often is the information used?
How will the various interested parties, lawyer, surveyor, accountant and client be involved in the development of the system?

As the answers to these questions become known, so preliminary conclusions can be reached on the appropriate means for the collection, storage and access of the information. It is important that the approach to information is dynamic rather than static, that is to say the collection and storage of information should, whilst recording the situation at the date of initial entry to the system, emphasize the up-dating of data. Proformas for extracting information should prompt staff to seek out the correct information and capture new information as it becomes available, such as periodic changes in service charge components and rentals.

The kind of information needed for property management is extensive but the primary responsibility is financial accountability to the client. This requires monitoring the exercise of the responsibilities of the two parties and effective action on behalf of the client at certain key dates in the life of the property as specified in the covenants and by statute law. The property records, or what used to be called the "terrier" and is called the data base in computer installations, contains the permanent details necessary to manage the property. A proforma suitable for the collection of this data within a landlord's management system is set out in Appendix E. It consists of sections covering:

The property	address, description, accommodation, details of acquisition, services, user.
The landlord	name, address, account file number.
The tenant	name, address, account file number.
The lease	a summary of the terms of the lease and the implementation of rights under the lease.

The whole being supported by an extensive file of documents containing some, or all of:

Site plan and boundaries.
Original architects drawings and plans together with alterations.
Specification and maintenance manual.
Cost, date and extent of improvement expenditures.
Planning consents.
Photographs and plan showing position from which they were taken and date.
Ordnance Survey plans.
Insurance policies.
Leases.
Other rights and duties in respect of the land.
Other specialist material, consents and licences.

Depending upon the extent of the estate and the nature of the property, some form of summary will be available. It may be visual or geographically based, using Ordnance Survey maps or plans or overlays or simply a schedule, and it will in most cases be indexed primarily on the address of the property. The strength of a typical system based on Ordnance sheets is also its weakness. It usually takes only a few moments to produce the record on any particular property given its address, but if the question is:

How many units do we own in excess of a certain size?
What proportion of our space is vacant?
How many rent-reviews are in excess of seven years?
How many units are occupied by a particular company?
How many rentals are not quarterly in advance?
Which leases have break clauses?
With what company do we have the most insurance cover?
How many leases expire in a certain year?

then the records clerk is likely to indicate that there will be some delay in providing the answer and it is at this point that the computer salesman indicates that he may be able to help.

The above aspects are relevant to the management of property on behalf of a landlord. However, in a predominantly owner-occupied estate or tenanted estate the information needs will be different and the management emphasis will be concentrated on a narrower front. The owner-occupied estate will stress maintenance aspects and costs in use and the tenanted estate will have fewer opportunities for taking initiatives, in the main responding to the action of landlords.

The D.H.S.S. Circular, H.C. 83/22 Estate Management: Underused and Surplus Property in the N.H.S. (which is mainly owner occupied) has proposed an estate data base consisting of:

Title deeds
Up-to-date estate terrier
Tenure information and rateable values
Notional rents
Current use value and any enhanced value
Property assessment—
    functional suitability
    space utilization
    condition of stock
    energy performance
The cost of bringing the property assessment up to the required standard.

The whole supported by:

Estman Code
Land Transactions Handbook

Works Information and Management System, see 11.52.
Mereworth, a training model health district

and reported in the Strategic plans and annual programmes of each district co-ordinated by the Regional Property Surveyor.

During 1984 research began to identify techniques, which would permit comparison between different Regions and Districts on the basis of a matrix of; built area, site areas and quality of accommodation. If implemented, it will represent the most rigorous form of audit of any large owner-occupied estate ever undertaken.

In commerce, particularly retailing, when location is all important, the form of tenure will be less important than the right postion, and most companies will inevitably build up a mixed tenure estate requiring a more complex form of records and estates organization than for an estate of predomirently one form of tenure.

Decisions will have to be taken on the way that the information is kept, and in an attempt to save space, micro-filming has been introduced in the public sector. Unfortunately the staff used to "fillet" the files prior to micro-filming are often not aware of the significance of the content of files and despite the assurance of the management consultants and the savings in space the procedure would seem to be of marginal benefit having regard to the overall effectiveness of the resulting micro-film records.

9.1.3 Action

Property records designed for management purposes may be useful for other purposes. One retail chain worked out which of its shops would be flooded if the threatened Thames Surge should occur before the barrier was completed. Hopefully their plan of action was stored on a shelf above high-water-mark.

The procedures for the management of a property are closely related to those of the accounts department. Unless rent is received and outgoings paid at the required dates and in the correct manner, the work of the lawyer and the surveyor have been to no avail, since the property has failed to perform its function as a secure investment. In order to obtain that income the landlord will have to take action at key dates and in accordance with the terms of the lease generally supervise the physical condition of the property and the use made of it by the tenant.

The data base permits the surveyor to be advised of key dates when action needs to be taken. In smaller portfolios this can conveniently be arranged in a management diary, the process being:

Extraction or determination of key dates.
Selection of appropriate lead time.
Entry in perpetual diary.
Monitoring of diary.
Notification to surveyor.
Action taken and amendment of diary.
Monitoring by principal.

Whether the clerical procedures involved are the responsibility of a records section or the accounts office or individual surveyors depends upon the type of office and many other factors.

The larger the portfolio, the larger the task, and a system of cards can be used for each function referred to each property, recording the action to be taken. As action is taken the card is placed in the correct lead time position for the next cycle of activity. This operation is ideally suited to a computer application and subject to adequate procedures to ensure the integrity of information you provide an automatic diary within the context of a comprehensive computer management system. Key dates can arise in connection with:

Statutes	Notices under the Landlord and Tenant Acts.
Structure	Maintenance schedules and inspection. Procedures to enforce covenants.
Valuation	Portfolio valuation dates.
Lease	Rent-review procedures. Demands and reminders. Options.
Fire insurance	Inspections and valuation dates.

In addition to action under the lease and the exercise of the client's rights as provided for by statute law, the estate manager has to consider broader issues. The performance of individual properties within the portfolio will be viewed in different ways by owner-occupier, tenant or landlord. Opportunities for positive management must be identified, analysed and recommendations made to clients. The portfolio as a whole will be reviewed from time to time and, having regard to the weight attached to various criteria, decisions taken on its management over different time horizons, see Chapter 11.

9.1.4 Accounts

The account procedures used to give effect to the client's instructions will have developed over a period of years reflecting the requirements of:

Clients
The firms business management procedures
The professional bodies.

The surveyor will need to work closely with the accountants department in respect of:

Form, content and amendment of records
Rent demands and arrears
Reporting forms to clients
Service charges, see 9.1.5 and 6.4.7
V.A.T., see 9.1.6 and 12.6
Professional accounting regulations, see 9.1.7
Firms accounts and fees, see 9.4.

The wide variety of estates, and both paper and computer accounting systems render inappropriate any reference to an ideal system of accounts. However whether paper or computer based a system should exhibit the following features:

A facility for rent demands from weekly to annual frequency both in advance and arrear, and rent recovery.
The payment of invoices in respect of approved expenditures.
The daily recording of cash and bank transactions.
Tenants accounts and statements.
Arrears notices and monitoring by the surveyor.
Stop rent procedures, (distinguished from zero rent demands).
Ease of amendment and correction.
Financial security.
Comprehensive reporting forms to client at appropriate frequency; income statement, expenditure statement for individual properties and a summary sheet, unlet units, service charge analysis.
Comprehensive service charge records and apportionment procedures.
Ease of operating audit trails.
Conformity to professional accounting and surveying standards.

A typical route through which an expense incurred in relation to a client's investment property will pass is as follows:

Invoice received in accordance with contract or instructions.
Invoice recorded and individual dealing is noted.
Considered, approved and signed by management surveyor, passed to accounts department.
Client's (landlord's) balance checked to ensure there are sufficient funds for payment. If there is regularly a problem revise arrangements with client.
Cheque drawn and entered in payments cash book.
Client's management ledger debited.
Invoice recorded against the property and apportioned amount posted to individual tenants' service charge account, to be demanded in accordance with the lease provisions, (in arrear or in advance).
Tenant demand procedures; actual accrual, quarterly in arrear, quarterly in advance. The latter whilst apparently attractive has problems in balancing cash flow.
Payment by tenant entered in receipts book and credited to client's management account.
End of year, balancing of in advance payments. Review of service charge year by management surveyor.

The need for rent recovery procedures is an inevitable consequence of the service of rent demands. Typical practice consists of the following;

Normal rent demand before quarter day
Copy rent demand reminder two weeks after quarter day
One phone call one week later
Letter by recorded delivery;

"Our records show that the rent in respect of the above property in the sum of £x which was due to our Client on the 'quarter day' has not been paid despite two applications and a telephone call.

Our Clients have instructed us to advise you that if settlement has not been received at this Office on or before 'date' they reserve the right to take any action open to them to make recovery, including the use of a certificated bailiff, without giving further notice, and recovering any costs of so doing from yourselves; should our Clients decide to instruct a bailiff then you will be responsible not only for the statutory levy fees, but also any additional commission paid by our Clients to the bailiff."

Instruct bailiffs who may recover rent by distraint and if so described (as additional rent) in the lease, service charge.

9.1.5 Service Charges

Service charges must first of all be fully in accordance with the detailed provisions of the lease regarding the service involved, the basis of apportionment, and the frequency of the account; See 6.4.7 for commercial leases and 7.4 for residential leases.

Problems arise which are not covered by the lease, such as the telephone accounts strike of 1979 where services were provided but accounts were not rendered for up to nine months and then on a non-standard pattern for a further six months in equity the service charges should be on a full accruals basis whilst accounts departments tend to work on a cash basis.

If a rating assessment basis is used for apportionment and there are changes in assessments, the notification of the change in assessment, the date from which it came into effect, and the consequential need for adjustment of service charges already paid over a period of several years will not be referred to in the lease. *Moorcroft Estates* v. *Doxford*, 1979, places a heavy burden on surveyors in this situation since it was held that the appropriate ratio of rateable values is that existing at the date each service charge item was incurred.

There needs to be close liaison between the accounts department and the surveyor in the supervision of contractors and the monitoring approving and allocating of suppliers invoices. Upon receipt of an invoice, the surveyor should approve it as being reasonably incurred within the terms of the lease and carried out to a reasonable standard. When paid, the accounts section may need guidance on the apportionment of the sum between different parts of the building or service charge heads, before the individual tenant apportionment calculations are carried out. A clear statement of the principles adopted in the case of unusual variations in charges will undoubtedly avoid queries and delays in payment which can cause the client to put up extra funds.

As part of the positive management of the client's portfolio the managing agents should carry out regular analysis of the cost of the provision of specific services. The accountants will need the surveyor's help in determining the most suitable unit for comparison and his opinion as to the relative quality of service provided having regard to the character of different buildings. Whilst relatively straightforward for regularly recurring expenditure. Irregular or exceptional expenditures may need to be extracted or their annual equivalent calculated to produce worthwhile analysis.

In 1984 Jones Lang Wootton published research based on monitoring of 62 office buildings over the period 1971–82. This showed service charges rose by 15.5% p.a. compound over the period, less than the increase in rates in London, but more than double average rental growth rate.

Average service charges varied significantly with location, at 1982 prices, as follows:

Location	Air conditioned £ (ft²)	Non-air conditioned £ (ft²)
City	3·50	1·76
West End	4·11	1·66
Rest of G.L.C.	2·52	1·39
Provincial	1·90	1·16

This can be analysed as follows:

Cost component	Air conditioned %	Non-air conditioned %
Cleaning	10	14
Heating (and a/c)	16	5
Wages	11	18
Lft	5	6
Security	11	10
Repairs and Insurance	13	13
Energy (see 11.5.3)	22	21
Sundries & Management	12	13

The cost per ft² varied with the size of buildings. Whilst air conditioned costs fell continuously with building size, non air conditioned fell sharply to a size of 10,000 ft² and then tended to be level for larger buildings.

Furbur in a survey of office buildings in Merseyside showed the following pattern of increases in £ ft²:

1975	1977	1979	1981	1983
0·53	0·74	0·98	1·26	1·55

9.1.6 Value Added Tax

Rent will generally be either exempt or zero rated, that is to say leases of less than 21 years (except holiday lettings) are exempt and totally outside the V.A.T. regime, whereas leases of more than 21 years are zero rated.

If in demising the premises the landlord covenants to provide services to the common parts of the building those services will be deemed to form part of the right to occupy the premises i.e. the supply of accommodation with covenanted services is treated as a single supply. The fact that the "rent" may be determined in part by the costs of providing the services would not of itself affect the position.

If a landlord makes a separate charge for services (and it is not described as additional rent) that will be a separate supply which will be taxable at the standard rate unless the services are of a type to which zero rating applies. However, Customs have said that "So long as the contribution made by the tenants, in accordance with 'service charge' arrangements, is towards the upkeep of the building as a whole and is not in consideration for supplies made to a tenant in respect of his particular flat or suite of office, it is regarded as part of the consideration for the right to occupy the premises".

If the landlord prefers he may treat himself as acting as an agent for the tenants. If he does that he must operate a separate fund for the service charges for each individual property. He then recharges to the tenants the actual V.A.T. borne on payments made in respect of the property.

If the landlord appoints an agent to manage the property for him this will not affect the V.A.T. position. As the agent will not be aware of the landlord's V.A.T. position from quarter to quarter it may be impractical in such circumstances to adopt the strict legal position of treating the service charge as rent.

If a landlord is wholly exempt he will be unable to recover V.A.T. input charged on various maintenance contracts and any registered tenants will be unable to reclaim. Some alternative method might enable those tenants to reclaim, if the tenant were directly responsible for the expenditures then he would have been able to recover the V.A.T.

If the landlord is fully registered for V.A.T. purposes, then he will reclaim the V.A.T. on the various individual contracts and the tenants as the final consumer will pay their apportioned amount of the aggregate accounts under the service charge plus the agent's management fee which also includes V.A.T.

9.1.7 Professional Accounting Regulations

The R.I.C.S. issued Accounts Regulations in 1977 with the principal aim of ensuring that clients' money is kept separate from that of the firm, together with proper records of dealings with the clients' money; enforced by the requirement to submit an "Accountant's Certificate" to the Institution each year.

The 13 regulations, based on the earlier Law Society rules, are in four parts:

Part I   Definitions
Part II   Bank accounts
Part III   Books and records
Part IV   Monitoring and enforcement.

The most important regulations include:

From Part I, "Clients money shall mean money held or received by a member, his firm or his company on account of a person from who he, ... as a surveyor, as agent, bailee or in any other capacity including that of stake-holder provided that the expression client's money shall not include money to which the only person beneficially entitled is the member himself".

From Part II, "Drawing money on behalf of a client from a client account when such drawing exceeds the total of the money held on behalf of the client is not permissible".

From Part III, "Every member shall at all times keep properly written up such accounts as may be necessary:

(a) to show his dealings with:
    (i) all money received, held or paid by him; and
    (ii) any other money dealt with by him through a client account
(b) to show separately in respect of each client all client's money which is received held or paid by him on account of such a client.
(2) All dealings referred to in sub para (a) of paragraph 1 of this regulation shall be recorded as appropriate either:
    (a) in a client's cash book, or in a client column in a cash book; or
    (b) in a record of sums transferred from the ledger account of one client to that of another; and in addition, in a client's leger, or in a client's column of a ledger.
(3) Every member shall not less than once in every succeed-

ing period of three months cause the balance of his client's cash book (or client's column of his cash book) to be agreed with his client account bank statements and shall keep in the cash book or other appropriate place a reconciliation statement showing his agreement.

(4) In this regulation the expressions "accounts", "books", "ledgers" shall be deemed to include loose leaf books and such cards or other permanent documents or records as are necessary for the operation of any system of book keeping, mechanical or otherwise, including computer operated systems".

From Part IV "Once in each period of twelve months every member . . . shall deliver to the Institution:
either:

(a) a certificate stating that the member did not receive or hold clients money during the accounting period; or an accountant's certificate set out in the form prescribed by the Institution."

The Accountant's Certificate Regulations set out nine tests which must be carried out on the accounts.

9.2.1 The Client

The general framework within which:

The client, whether public or private, instructs the surveyor,
The surveyor, whether in-house or consultant undertakes the task,
The surveyor reports to the client,
The client responds to the report, and his expectations as to the competence of the surveyor,

has been considered in, "Pleased to Report", published in 1983. As a result, this now permits a more partial and specific approach in this text, concentrating on the property management aspects of that process.

The client, seeking property management services, requires the exercise of professional expertise that lies between that of:

A valuation report which builds towards the pinnacle of a specific figure.
A physical report which considers each element in turn, each part is of equal importance.

Property management is essentially tactical, converting policy into the most appropriate action and monitoring its implementation.

9.2.2 Instructions and Fees

The instructions given by a client and accepted by the surveyor on behalf of his firm create a legal contract between the parties. In the past instructions have not been approached with the priority they now receive, partly due to the Unfair Contracts Terms Act 1977. Also clients are becoming increasingly sophisticated, aware of the subtle relationships between instructions, fees, caveats and standards of competence. Some tasks carried out by the profession are well known, easily described, and the results specific and immediate. In these circumstances instructions and their acceptance should present few problems. However, the more specialist the property, the less routine the task, the more unstable the market, the longer the life of the projects then the greater is the degree of professional expertise required. This has implications as to the calibre and experience of the professional staff involved and the appropriate basis for fees. In these circumstances the original indication of instructions from the client may need refinement and this is often supported with preliminary advice. Such discussions are rather difficult since, at this stage, fee negotiation will also be taking place.

The levels at which management services may be provided are illustrated by the following from the management services brochure, of a major firm:

"The combinations of clients' resources and needs, interacting with the different types of property and terms under which they are occupied, produces a requirement for the provision of different levels of professional management. These include:

Watching brief. The minimum level of management appropriate to vacant property awaiting re-development, where we respond only to statutory notices or similar requirements.

Care and Maintenance. Appropriate for buildings which are vacant for a variety of operational or investment purposes.

Standard Management. Management of an individual building with normal lease covenants and service contracts, rent collection, service charge and accounting work.

Portfolio Management. This implies a comprehensive application of management skills across a number of properties with close liaison with the client leading to the implementation of a plan for the portfolio. Typically, this will include a diary of:

Rent review, insurance, inspection, schedules, action. It is here that we are most able to demonstrate positive management.

Investment Performance Management. This is a logical development of portfolio management and utilizes our capacity for the preparation of analytical reports on the performance of portfolios on both sector and geographical bases. These are then related to appropriate indices enabling recommendations to be made on individual property performance."

Having identified the level of management; the duties and frequency at which different activities should be undertaken can be established. The previously mentioned document refers to:

"The continuing nature of management means that cycles of activity can be identified and this enables a periodic management system to be developed.

Regular action will include:

Daily—Response to tenants' enquiries and emergency action in the case of building or services failure.

Monthly—Monitoring of the quality and efficiency of those services provided.

Quarterly—The issue of rent and service charge demands action on non-payment and reporting and accounting to the client.

Annual—Cycles of inspection for re-decoration, maintenance and repair, together with forward budgeting.

Every four or five years—A major review of policy and implementation, rent reviews and lease renewals."

These are illustrated in detail by Appendix F, which applies to a covered shopping centre.

The result of agreeing the level and frequency of management activity can be a management brief. This is illustrated by the "Duties of Managing Agents of Commercial Property," published by R.I.C.S. in 1985.

"For buildings let in single occupation on a full repairing and insuring lease, for a standard management fee the managing agent should:

Submit demands for and collect rents, insurance licence fees and other charges from lessees on a quarterly basis and forward monies at agreed intervals.

Make payments to superior lessors, professional advisers, insurers or others, subject to R.I.C.S. accounts regulations.

Check that tenant has current building and other insurances, and administer other insurances, such as public liability cover, on behalf of landlord.

Maintain separate clients' accounts and ledgers and prepare and submit statements and accounts with balances and supporting invoices at agreed intervals, normally quarterly.

Inspect property periodically to ensure proper occupation and to check compliance with lease as to decoration and repairs.

Deal with routine management enquiries from tenants.

Keep records in relation to tenancy and other relevant matters relating to the property.

The agent should also advise on obligations to serve statutory or contractual notices, such as rent reviews and lease expiries and options, before the notices fall due. He should instruct solicitors or certified bailiffs on unpaid rent, charges or other matters agreed with the client, including late payment of monies due under the terms of the lease. he will attend court regarding arrears of rent and other monies.

Consider applications by tenants for alterations.

Offer professional services in connection with applications for the lessor's consent to assignments, sub-lettings and changes of use.

Advise on management policy.

Provide inspection reports on general conditions to clients.

Liaise with client's solicitors in relation to leases and other relevant documents.

For buildings in multiple occupation with the landlord responsible for the provision of services, the managing agent should:

Submit demands and collect payments for service charges—quarterly—or to meet lease requirements, deal with annual reconciliation of these charges and administer the charges for residential tenancies.

Pay suppliers, contractors, staff or others providing services.

Administer building and other insurances, including plant and equipment, employer's liability and public liability cover.

Produce and circulate service charge accounts, including

balancing charges or refunds and, where necessary, supply information to tenants and others unless leases require certification by independent auditors.

Where necessary, produce annual estimates of future expenditure for service charge purposes and reserves, administer funds and provide information to auditors.

When instructed by client, engage and supervise staff, detail their duties, and pay wages and attendant expenses.

Arrange and supervise standard maintenance contracts for all plant and equipment, general cleaning, security, landscape maintenance and others.

Inspect property periodically to check day-to-day running and operation.

Deal with routine management enquiries from tenants about services provided.

Deal with day-to-day repairs to structure, plant, fixtures and fittings and equipment, and with emergency repairs.

Keep records on tenancies and other matters relevant to property.

For shopping centres, maintain overall responsibility for promotions and administer promotions account.

Check compliance with terms of leases and statutory requirements.

Arrange for fire alarm system to be tested and for regular fire practices and, where appropriate, arrange annual boiler and lift inspections.

Where appropriate, arrange load tests on cradles, safety eyebolts or other lifting tackle and annual changeover on sprinkler systems from water to air and vice versa.

Submit applications for fire certificates.

Where appropriate, obtain petroleum spirit licences for internal car parking areas.

Maintain on premises accident book, copies of fire certificate and other statutory reports and fire alarm log book, and administer matters arising

Deal with day-to-day matters concerning safety and welfare of people within property arising from statute or other regulations.

Managing agents may agree other duties with clients which fall outside the scope of the standard fee. The agent may

Prepare specifications, obtain competitive tenders and supervise works of substantial nature other than day-to-day repairs.

Give evidence in court on recovery of rent or other charges from tenants, or compliance with lease covenants.
Advise on rating, planning, grant applications, or insurance claims.
Prepare replacement cost valuations for fire insurance purposes.
Prepare schedules of dilapidations or condition, negotiate claim settlements or supervise repairs.
Negotiate rent reviews and submit evidence to arbitration or independent expert.
Effect lettings or renewals of leases or other options and attend court hearings in connection with lease renewals.
Prepare and check inventories of landlords' and tenants' fixtures and fittings.
Prepare and advise on valuations for insurance, capital or rental purposes or capital allowances.
Provide copies of leases, policies, receipts and other documents or additional copies of current or past accounts.
Deal with matters arising in connection with adjoining properties or owners.
Advise on renewal or modification or restrictive covenants.
For residential tenancies, offer traditional professional services on matters arising under Rent or Housing Acts."

The fees charged for commercial management, normally 10% for the management of service charges, included within the service charge accounts to tenants; and around $2\frac{1}{2}$% on incomes received on behalf of clients, do not rival the apparently spectacular fees of agency and investment departments. Management brings with it rent review and renewal, insurance inspections and valuations, maintenance and refurbishment, acquisition and disposals, rating, and other specialist services available from a firm able to provide a comprehensive service, each of which generates its own fees. The certainty and regularity of management work means that it can be staffed efficiently, providing a stable element of the firm's fee income, and since part of the fees, 10% of service charge, is cost-orientated and part, $2\frac{1}{2}$% of income received, is value-orientated there is a further in-built stability.

In *Concorde Graphics Ltd. v. Andromeda Investments S A*, 1982, there was a service charge with a schedule of items which did not specifically include either the managing agents fees or a basis upon which they should be calculated. However the landlords employed the firm of Wimbourne

Martin French and Co who in their accounts to tenants included a charge for management based on 10% of the expenditure incurred by the landlord.

New landlords appointed new agents, Grant and Partners, they adopted a new basis for their managing agents remuneration, namely $7\frac{1}{2}$% of the rental income. The tenant on comparing the old and new management charge and noted the new charge was almost three times higher, and that the management fee element on the new basis which had been agreed with the landlord, was nearly five times higher. It was held that the managing agents were not suitably disinterested to determine the dispute as landlords surveyor.

The fees charged for residential management are illustrated in the case of *Parkside Knightsbridge Ltd v. Horwitz*, 1983, see 7.6.

Tenders are an increasing feature of the granting of management instructions and fee negotiations. In 1984 Electricity Supply Nominees put out to tender the management of half of their £800 million property portfolio, which had for many years been managed for Richard Ellis. The final short list consisted of Hillier Parker, Richard Ellis, and Debenham Tewson and Chinnocks, the last of these obtained the instructions.

From time to time instructions have to be refused. Generally this will be because of some existing client-relationship in the property, though there may be other reasons concerned with personal or family involvement. In these latter cases once the client has been informed he may well be happy for the firm to continue to act. It can sometimes happen that, with the consent of both parties, a firm can act for both parties simultaneously, for example, two partners could hold personal appointments to particular bodies. This tends to happen with the old institutions. Within the robustness of a large firm and with the clear consent of both parties in some formal exchange of letters, a quite adequate professional relationship could exist except upon no more than infrequent occasions.

9.2.3 Inspections

Inspections are a key requirement for a good records system, which is essential for sound management. There are many reasons for property inspection—the majority are related to the creation, enforcement or transfer of rights in the property itself or transactions in financial assets which offer interests in the property. The remainder of inspections are mainly in connection with the physical fabric of the building, though very often they will be as a result of the enforcement of rights and duties between the landlord and tenant. Property inspection is not just a physical matter, it provides an opportunity to make personal contact with the occupier, be he tenant or owner, with whom the property manager will be in regular communication.

No estate manager likes to take decisions in respect of property he has not personally inspected. In large organizations this is often inevitable and in these circumstances the estate manager will need to have confidence in both the ability of the surveyor and the comprehensiveness of procedures to ensure that the right information is available within the management organization. The link between the formulation of policy and its implementation in respect of individual properties needs to be more than a matter of personalities; they come and go, suffer illness and are subject to the normal human failings. In large organizations, to provide job satisfaction and so motivate professional staff to give of their best, the executive manager and the property surveyor need to have an effective form of communication, in both directions. The larger the estates organization, particularly in the public sector, the more likely it is that a technician grade of property referencer is responsible for the detailed referencing and recording of property information and its subsequent storage and access. Some very good surveyors take a very bad reference, concerned only with the information necessary to solve the particular instructions rather than the creation of a good record of all aspects of the property which will serve to provide useful information on several other occasions in the future. At the same time technicians can only be effective with the benefit of detailed professional supervision. Too little use is still made of photographs in recording the character of buildings, which can seldom be achieved by the most copious notes.

The first requirement before a detailed inspection is a clear brief as to its purpose, and existing records should be carefully checked. In the public service or commerce and industry, that is to say, single-client in-house estates departments, this is very much easier than in private practice, where the multiplicity of clients means that the filing systems tend to be client-based rather than property based.

With manual filing systems it is difficult to identify any previous records in connection with a property upon which the firm has been newly-instructed. In the past the property may have been disposed of by an existing client, used as a comparable, investigated on behalf of another client or in one of several other ways already be well known to one or more individuals.

The result is unnecessary time spent on new referencing and lack of information on the history of the property which may be difficult or impossible to obtain at the present time. Accurate measurement based upon the R.I.C.S./I.S.V.A. code of measuring practice is undoubtedly one of the requirements for a successful negotiation. To enter a negotiation knowing that all your measurements are accurate to the nearest three inches or five centimetres can be used to advantage. If differences occur and the other surveyor is not prepared to accept your figures, a joint inspection can have a rather chastening effect, particularly if you indicate that you regard agreed areas as important for your proof of evidence. Better still, the presentation of a complete typed schedule of areas at the very first meeting can impress upon the other party your determination to pursue your client's interests to the full. On the other hand, it is easy to spend far too much of the site visit carrying out meticulous measurement and failing to recognize qualitative and subjective factors which fundamentally affect the valuations and the management advice arising from a report. The pursuit of accuracy of 0·01% in measurements used in calculations, when the accuracy of many of the other factors influencing the decision are around say 5%, introduces a false sense of security into what is not a science, perhaps poorly described as an art and more akin to a craft.

A surveyor will determine the most appropriate procedure for an inspection. In large complexes a preliminary walk about with the benefit of the opinion of site management can be followed with some time with the site engineer, who can usually find copies of plans if these were not already available. The detailed referencing technique is a matter of personal preference. There are some benefits in taking the largest overall measurement possible and then taking out. However, those with experience of steel and paper mills, lard factories and killing lines at meat pie factories tend to adopt a more pragmatic view.

Many of the factors upon which advice is based cannot be measured but some can be monitored on a regular basis. Regular inspections and prompt action to remedy defects can have a positive effect not just on the fabric of the building but on the attitude of the individual tenant involved, as well as protecting the client from various statutory liabilities. The overall integrity of the portfolio depends upon many factors, not least of which is the opinion held by the occupiers of the quality of the management.

9.2.4 Reports

Skill in report writing can only be achieved after years of experience. it is salutary for a surveyor to study a report he wrote several years ago and realize how his style has developed. There is no doubt that a poorly constructed or badly phrased report does detract from the client's appreciation of, and confidence in, the recommendations made in a report. The ability to draft a good report is fundamental to the effective exercise of the surveyor's expertise, it is the main form of communication with the client and, apart from the property itself, the permanent record of fact and opinion upon which further instructions may be taken. The several different types of reports illustrate the range of work associated with the management of individual properties or the estate as a whole.

A valuation report, though requiring adequate descriptive material and some consideration of either the statutory or market setting, tends to turn upon the figure that appears in the last paragraph; there is a measurable financial result and this may be tested in the market place.

A report dealing with the physical condition of a property, such as a structural survey, does not build up so much to a focus, but presents a comprehensive view. A management report lies somewhere between these two types of report. Property management aspects will be considered, as will the potential of the physical structure to meet the needs of occupiers and its suitability for other uses. Several alternative courses of action are usually identified, the report concluding with the reasons for selecting the most appropriate action and identifying possible consequences. There are a number of specialist reports, the most structured being in accordance with the Assets Valuation Standards Committee guidance notes where there is both a recommended format and phraseology for parts of the report.

The report should result in the reader arriving inevitably at the same conclusion as the writer, with a degree of appreciation appropriate to his technical knowledge. The surveyor must have a clear understanding of his client's perception of the issues which are being considered. There is no blueprint that can be used, but the report should be confined to meeting the instructions.

An initial meeting with the client is never wasted in establishing communication and clarifying the scope of instructions far more effectively than correspondence, though a written record of the discussions should be confirmed with the client as soon as possible. Fact and opinion should be sufficiently separate for the client to appreciate the difference, but linked so that opinion can be seen as originating from particular facts. At some stage the weight to be attached to opinion can be analysed, perhaps in the concluding paragraphs. The report should stand as a comprehensive document but this does not mean it must be either lengthy or complex. A short report with several appendices or schedules of fact may be as effective as an apparently longer report.

At various points in the report it will be necessary to digress from the main flow to define or illustrate technical terminology. This is worth doing well once, early in the report for each term, rather than covering somewhat inadequately in a different form of words on each occasion. A covering letter attached to the report enables any necessary personal communication to be achieved. The report itself should be in an impersonal style and verbosity can often be avoided by making sentences short, which prevents the convoluted sentence within which the extravagant use of English seems to flourish; this sentence is showing symptoms of verbosity. Lastly, it concentrates the mind most effectively to say to yourself, "How would this sound in court in a year's time, if I were being sued for professional negligence?"

9.2.5 Competence

The actions of a surveyor in managing an estate or individual property on behalf of his client can be subject to criticism on account of several types of misconduct. If fraud is involved then this would be a criminal matter. The client, if dissatisfied with the service provided, is able to sue for damages on the basis of the contract for the provision of services. Alternatively the surveyor may have been negligent in common law or statute and both the client and third parties will have a remedy in damages. A surveyor whilst conducting his client's affairs and not offending either against the criminal or civil law may offended against the rules of conduct of his own professional body and be subject to some form of disciplinary hearing. Such a hearing would need to be conducted in accordance with the rules of natural justice. Further, when involved in estate agency, the surveyor will be subject to the Estate Agents Act 1979, though there is in it nothing of substance, as regards conduct, which is not already required of members of the leading professional bodies. The proper conduct of the firm's accounts has been dealt with by the R.I.C.S. Accounts Regulations see 9.1.7, issued in November, 1977, which, amplify the basic bye-law requirements to separate clients' money from the firm's money. These are now monitored and enforced by firms having to provide an annual certificate to the R.I.C.S. from an accountant who is a member of one of the approved professional bodies. Gemmell has suggested that, due to the nature of the regulations and the precision with which they are expected to be interpreted, there are going to be a large number of qualified certificates. The regulations are based on the 1975 Solicitor's Account Regulations which may provide some useful precedents for staff responsible for keeping the accounts and for those accountants carrying out the annual monitoring function.

The careful acceptance of instructions and the selection of appropriate caveats should ensure that the surveyor enters into a contract that he is potentially capable of carrying out on behalf of his client. However, problems do occur under the head of negligence. In contract a claim is time-barred after six years, whereas a claim in negligence extends to six years after the date when the loss occurs, which may be several years after the completion of the job. This means that insurers are faced with a long tail before any given year of account can be finalized. A retired partner would be wise to ensure that adequate professional negligence cover remains in force to cover claims arising from when he was in practice.

The standard of care required by a professional man was considered in the case of *Bolam* v. *Friern Hospital Management Company*, 1957, where it was stated that "The test is that of the ordinary skilled man exercising and professing to have that special skill. A man need not possess the highest expert skill: it is well established law that it is sufficient if he exercises skill of an ordinary competent man exercising that particular art." If a surveyor is consulted as a specialist, then *Duchess of Argyll* v. *Beuselinck*, 1972, suggests that the standard of a specialist may be expected.

Until *Hedley Byrne and Co. Ltd. v. Heller and Partners*, 1964, it was understood that a professional firm's liability arose only out of the contractual engagement, but in that case Lord Morris said: "If someone possessed of a special skill undertakes, quite irrespective of contract, to apply that skill for the assistance of another person who relies upon such skill, a duty of care will arise, furthermore if in a sphere in which a person is so placed that others could reasonably rely upon his skill or judgment or upon his ability to make careful enquiry, a person takes it upon himself to give information or advice to, or allows his information to be passed on to, another person, who, as he knows or should know, will place reliance upon it, then a duty of care will arise." In *Anns v. London Borough of Merton*, 1977, which concerned the negligent exercise of a power to enforce building bye-laws, it was held that even though the plaintiffs had not relied upon the inspector's report, this did not prevent damages being awarded against the local authority.

Legal cases on the breach of the necessary standard of care by surveyors number some hundreds and at any one time there are several thousand outstanding claims.

R.I.C.S. Insurance Services insures many firms and analysis of their claims into categories as at November 1983 showed the following:

	Total value %	No. of claims	No. of claims %
Structural Surveys	33	2,646	47
Valuations	18	723	13
Auctioneering	1	118	2
Architectural	14	553	10
Quantity Surveying	3	93	2
Estate Agency	2	353	6
Management (incl. R.R.)	23	687	12
Miscellaneous	6	501	8
Total	100	5,674	100

Some of the most eye catching cases have been in the field of valuation, where the significance of a precise valuation figure permits easier reporting by the press and in structural and building society surveys which perhaps cover the activity of the largest group of surveyors.

The detail of the different types of claims in connection with the various types of work of the survey or is covered in "Pleased

To Report". Though attention should be drawn to *Stevenson v. Nationwide Building Society*, 1984. Here negligence was found on the part of the Building Society staff surveyor, but the society was held to be protected by the disclaimer in the report and valuation. Every case turns on its facts, but at least the limits to *Yianni v. Edwin Evans*, 1981, are now being constructed.

The work of the surveyor in property management can best be illustrated by the following cases. The taking of initiatives under leases is perhaps the most practical example of positive management. The negligence implications of the decision is *United Scientific Instruments Holdings Ltd v. Burnley Borough Council*, 1977, that time was not of the essence, caused many a sigh of relief in lawyers and surveyors offices. Though where time is explicitly of the essence, as in the case of options the financial consequences can be severe. In *Social Workers Pension Fund v. Wood Nash and Winters*, 1983, there was a 21 year lease with an option to break in favour of both parties in the fifteenth year. The solicitors involved failed to advise the fund as to the exercise of the option with the result that whereas market rent could have been obtained, the tenants continued in occupation at a historic rent for a further six years. Damages of £95,000 were awarded.

One question frequently raised is how much a non-legal professional should know of the law in his chosen specialism *BL Holding Ltd v. Robert J Wood and Partners*, 1978, provides some useful guidance. An architect was instructed to design a building within the 10,000 ft^2 exemption from the then Office Development Permits. The defendants were surprised to learn from the Planning Authority that the basement car park and caretaker's flat could be ignored in the calculations but the building was designed and built on this basis. Sadly the building proved impossible to let, since prospective tenants were told that the planning permission was invalid, as the necessary Permit for a building of over 10,000 ft had not been obtained. The High Court held the architects were negligent, as they should have pursued their doubts and advised their clients to obtain expert legal advice. The Court of Appeal, 1979, allowed an appeal on the grounds that, it was a difficult area of law, likely to confuse other architects, and the plaintiff advised by Chartered Surveyors and experienced property developers had independently taken the same view as the defendants. The taking up of references is perhaps regarded as something of a mere formality, this was considered in *Nahhas v. Pier House (Cheyne*

Walk) Management Ltd, 1984; the second defendants were Harold Williams and Partners who were engaged as managing agents. The flats were expensive; in 1984 a one bedroomed flat cost £55,000 and in 1980 a typical service charge was £2,000 p.a. A complex series of events including the occupier's illness, sets of keys, replacement locks etc. resulted in the porters holding the keys to the flat and later it was found that jewellery of considerable value was missing from the flat. One of the porters pleaded guilty and it became clear his profession was that of thief, having served 11 sentences since 1966 with 33 convictions. The court held that the key control system was quite satisfactory but there had been negligence in the recruitment of the porter and particularly in the checking of references since the porters were in effect in a similar position to security guards.

Following on from the breach of the duty of care, the measure of damages and the mitigation of loss need to be considered. Perhaps the most interesting case for the property manager is *Teasdale v. Williams*, 1984. The damages in a negligence case turned on the timing the section 24a notice, and its relationship to a rising market. The landlord's solicitors had served an interim rent notice effective from June 1977, unfortunately despite several requests, the tenant's solicitor failed to advise the tenant's surveyor of this. The latter continued to defer negotiations for a new lease, thinking his client continued to pay the historic rent of £4,500.

If a new five year lease had been agreed with effect from June 1977, when the plaintiffs original term expired, it was estimated the rent would have been £20,000. The rent was not agreed until June 1979 at £26,500 for a seven year lease. The landlord's surveyor was able to negotiate a reduction for the first two years to £19,000. It was held that the consequences of the tenant's solicitors negligence was:

A loss of 3 years × (£26,500 − £20,000) = £19,500
A gain of 2 years × (£20,000 − £19,000) = £ 2,000
£17,500

The defendant had argued that if a rent had been negotiated as at 1977, on a five year term then upon renewal of that lease in 1982 there would have been a saving compared with the actual events that occurred. Since the new hypothetical lease in 1982 would have been at £40,000 p.a. whereas for the first two years the tenant was actually paying £36,500 p.a. However the court held that this possible temporary rental advantage could not be isolated.

It must be acknowledged by even the most experienced and respected senior partner that, despite his own knowledge, the firm may through the excesses, inadequacy or recklessness of one individual, or misfortune, be faced with a claim for negligence. The firm will then read its professional negligence policy with deepening interest.

The Law Society introduced a compulsory scheme in 1975 and by 1983 annual premiums were of the order of £1,500 per partner for a London practice and £1,200 per partner for a provincial practice. The I.S.V.A. introduced a compulsory scheme in 1982 and the R.I.C.S. followed with a requirement after 1 January, 1986, that minimum cover of £100,000 or £250,000 be carried, of an approved specification.

These schemes apply both to private practice and also to those in the public service who undertake private work and those employees in the private sector who, with or without their employers consent, undertake private work.

For the largest partnerships in London, cover of the order of £20 million to £30 million is now common, the premium forming part of the unseen overheads on every job. Reports of a claim against Richard Ellis of £45 million by Electricity Supply Nominees in 1984 in respect of project management work on the Trocadero scheme and other properties indicate the potential scale of risk.

Uncertainty as to the period for which a liability in negligence should run resulted in a report by the Law Reform Committee in 1984 (Latent Damage, Cmnd 9390). This recommended that plaintiffs should be unable to commence any action in negligence more than 15 years from the breach of duty. Subject to this rule, the existing six year period of limitation from the date damage occurred, should be extended to allow plaintiffs a further three years from the date of discovery of damage, (legislation expected in 1986).

It may be thought that many of the preceding matters have little or no relevance to the surveyor in the public service or commerce and industry. This is not so, the standards of competence to be expected are the same for all those who claim to exercise a particular professional skill. It is true that responsibility may be less personal and retribution more diffuse in character, bringing the organization rather than the individual into disrepute. In local government, changes in the political control of the council can bring about in policy changes which result in the acquisition or disposal of land in a manner quite outside the principles of prudent estate management.

The best professional negligence policy is the encouragement of good practice at all levels within the firm. Apart from a sound knowledge of the law, a positive approach to avoid claims and hence keep the premium low would include the following:

Written instructions, acknowledgement and written clarification of any uncertainty, including agreed file notes on meetings.

Standard procedures for standard types of job, using job cards or proformas and progress reports.

The efficient handling of correspondence received is much enhanced by the use of a bring-forward procedure to prevent letters being permanently filed until all their contents have received attention.

Supervision by the principals in some convenient form, either at certain stages during jobs or periodic briefings. In larger practices direct supervision by the principals can sometimes be a problem.

Regular communication with the client by means of interim reports. Clients may assume correctly in some cases that no information from the firm means no action is occurring.

Rigorous diary and accounting procedures which provide an independent form of monitoring the work of junior staff.

The ability to recognize the circumstances in which the client should be recommended to seek specialist advice.

Trust must still be placed in the competence, integrity and sense of professional enquiry of staff. This is undoubtedly one of the attractions of the profession, the ability to use independent thought to resolve client's problems and in so doing develop one's own personal skill in the practical application of professional expertise. It brings with it a heavy responsibility, and the surveyor must appreciate this early in his career. Equally the employer should provide an environment in which a high level of professional competence is encouraged and demonstrated by experienced practitioners.

9.3.1 Computers

Between the mid 1970s and the mid 1980s an essentially scientific instrument became a household product. As a result the general use of computers is becoming well known to those entering higher education and the majority of those completing vocational degrees in many disciplines are fluent in their use.

John Kirkwood of Sheffield Polytechnic in "Information Technology and Land Administration" has elegantly described and separated in Part I of his text the basics of information technology:

Computer hardware
Peripheral devices
Computer software
Programming and problem solving
Systems analysis

from their application to the land in Part II.

A comprehensive estate management computer system makes use of techniques which exist in the application of computers to other property situations. The matching facility of estate agency is equally important in searching the estates database for various purposes including the automatic diary. Valuation programs may be utilized as part of regular portfolio valuation and taken further lead to portfolio performance measurement.

Information technology has had two major effects on estate agency first in the marketing of residential property. Here the creation of large chains during the 1980s with substantial capital resources enabled electronic office and communication systems to challenge the property columns of newspapers as the means of initial contact. Secondly the two key office records systems, the property register and the applicants register are ideally suited to storage on disc. Searching the property register with appropriate parameters permits the matching to applicants' requirements and printing and mailing, with follow up on an automatic diary. The skills of the estate agent of; valuation, obtaining instructions, advising on sale negotiation and marketing are of course still essential. Indeed, the applicant and property data base permits the agent to analyse the nature of his work in hand and transactions in ways such as; success rate, accuracy of valuations, number of visits to properties and contacts with applicants, which may enable him to run his business more effectively. It is now necessary to consider whether registration is necessary under the Data Protection Act 1984.

As regards valuation the potential of computers to handle risk and uncertainty together with the many repetitive calculations necessary for sensitivity analysis has been used for feasibility studies for large scale projects and shopping models. For many years computers have been used for calculation of the published valuations tables, but the advent of micro processors has enabled equated yield analysis to become established practice within a few years of its theoretical exposition. Micro Owl and other specialist financial discounting packages offer an almost infinite range of combinations of the variables found in the half dozen or so sets of published valuation tables. These published tables are now technically obsolete but it will be several years before user requirements change and their relative costs render them financially obsolete. A further application is for investment purposes. Once the details of properties in an investment portfolio have been entered in the data base, they can be re-valued rapidly and at frequent intervals. Research by actuaries and surveyors has lead to a more analytical approach to the measurement of property performance measurement. COMPAS and COMPAS-ON-LINE developed by St. Quintins in conjunction with Chase Econometrics/Interactive Data Corporation is perhaps the most widely known.

Dr. Stephen Hargitay of Bristol Polytechnic has developed a particularly comprehensive system, with four sub-systems around a large database. The data-base contains details of the properties which requires regular updating, together with sub-files which store the results of previous runs of the system.

The operational subsystems consist of:

Database management: to create, update and manipulate database files.

Performance analysis: of historic and prospective performance comprising: Revaluation, Performance and Yield Prospect.

Valuation and Appraisal: this program comprises various traditional and D.C.F. procedures including Development Appraisal and Project Selection.

Utilities Suite: to maintain the system and to create new data-bases.

Property management applications are perhaps less spectacular than agency, development and valuation uses, but more wide ranging in terms of their practical effect. The opportunities afforded by the technology particularly spread sheet formats for recording, extraction and adjustment of property records and accounts means that very large portfolios can now be managed with a greater degree of certainty, rigour and completeness of property and accounting information than was possible in the past. Further, in connection with the review and renewal of tenancies and other action dates, a completely automatic key dates system is available.

Two examples of applications that have been developed by Dick Warren at Bristol Polytechnic illustrate what can be achieved using widely available software packages.

A Development Appraisal worksheet incorporating a Sensitivity Analysis system, with all operations driven automatically by in-built programs. Variable factors and output variables are selected from a menu and the resulting table of results may be printed in a report, analysed graphically or filed on a disk for future reference.

A simple database linked to a display screen, both menu driven by in-built programs. Records can be extracted from the database and transferred to the display screen for viewing or amending. New data can be entered on the display screen and saved into the database. All this involves the transferance of data records from one worksheet to another using temporary files.

Many enhancements can be added; sorting the data, finding and extracting data that matches set criteria and multiple linking of database sets to form a comprehensive data storage and retrieval system.

Today's business computers can now be linked by a network to provide desk top terminals to all the surveyors in an office. Only then will it be possible to create a full database of property records in order to get the benefit of full access to all past and present property information, linked to analytical systems and the work processing and other facilities in the office.

9.3.2 Factors Influencing Design of a System

The process between identifying the usefulness of computers for the storage and manipulation of data and the practical application in the professional office is expensive of time, money and hard-earned experience. As the hardware falls in price and becomes more sophisticated then, even with a printer and visual display unit, the equipment occupies less space and can cost less per annum than a secretary. The greater availability of equipment means that two technical problems have to be faced, firstly the efficient entry to the data base of the file on every property. The extraction of information from hundreds of leases and transfer into the data base is a very boring job for a surveyor but the layman would not be able to appreciate some of the subtle and complex arrangements found in leases. The second major problem is the development of the software, which can now account for 70% of the cost of the total system. The ideal arrangement is in-house analysts and programmers, but only the largest employers can afford these overheads and even when a system has been installed provision must be made for a maintenance programmer. Technical knowledge of the installation, systems analysis and programming is not an essential requirement amongst the professional staff. Recent graduates from a number of estate management courses have had some experience of using packages and writing their own programs for project appraisal, valuation and agency matching. Computer companies are themselves now much more aware of the special requirements of surveyors. However, the greater the appreciation by the surveyors of the issues involved the more effective will be the results of the brief prepared for the computer consultants.

Liaison with the clients is vital. Even if the firm can see the merits of the proposed computer installation, unless the clients have also been sufficiently involved they will be unable to come to the same conclusion. There are three opportunities for involving clients; preliminary advice as to the firm's intentions, detailed discussions on the application of the system to the client's portfolio and an invitation for their comments when they have received a full cycle of the new account report forms.

The overall character of a system will develop from:

Size of the task
Extent of the data base
Frequency of input and output
Need for an inter-active facility
Number and location of access points
Perception of future requirements
Innovatory style of the management
Revenue and capital budget.

Access to the property data-base will be via a hierarchy of files; client, estate (fund or company) properties, tenants or occupiers. Movement between and within files is facilitated by a menu and prompts.

The creation or amendment of programs requires the support of staff, but a balance has to be struck between the involvement of a committee with its bone-grinding procedures and some incisive action by specialist computer staff. The latter's action will need to be subject to continuous review as dummy clients and accounts are used to test the programs.

Care must be taken to avoid the production of too much print-out. In an interactive system, surveyors can at any time obtain the current position in respect of client's accounts, tenant's records and action dates. They can easily be overwhelmed by receiving every month, several inches of thickness of print-out representing the aggregate data and accounts in respect of the portfolios for which they are responsible. They then have to search through to find the exceptions requiring consideration or action. Whenever possible the programs should search for the exceptions and any print-out which arrives on a surveyor's desk which he did not specifically request should arise because of a regular exceptions search in the program. The minimum requirement would seem to be: arrears, voids, changes in the data-base and action dates. if this minimum requirement results in several hundred sheets of print-out arriving each month on the desk of any one individual this would imply a serious problem of either the individual's work-load or performance. This can lead to the potential use of the computer for the management and monitoring of the work of individuals and overall management of the firm.

Lastly, the system must be secure in accounting and information terms against acts, omissions and accidents. The use of passwords can control access to parts of the data-base and changes to the data-base can automatically be made available on a daily or weekly cycle to a manager. Monitoring systems permit a manager to note who has been using the system. Accidents come in various forms; electrical, mechanical, fire or water and other incidents need to be considered, it is normal practice to back up daily and store the disk in a fire proof safe.

9.3.3 Public Sector Systems

In the public sector there are three major types of application of computers to land and buildings; management of the corporate estate, management of the housing estate, and comprehensive property referencing. The management of the corporate estate is not very different from the management of commercial investment portfolios by the larger private practices; the G.L.C. probably developed the most comprehensive system.

The kind of information that needs to be entered on the property masterfile for the local authority housing estate is rather different from that for commercial property management.

Maintenance is in every case the responsibility of the landlord, often undertaken by a direct labour organization. Homes (Housing Maintenance and Evaluation System) designed by South West Systems for Bath City Council is typical of a number of authorities. The hardware included a D.E.C. 11/23 mini computer, two 10M byte removable disk drives with four V.D.Us. and two 180 cps bi-directional logic seeking matrix printers.

When a maintenance request comes in, the operator uses the address to display the property file which gives a basic physical description of the property and a history of work undertaken. A menu procedure is then used to describe the required work in the following hierarchy:

Level 1 (element)   1 Plumbing
                        2 Fabric
                        3 Fittings
                        4 Heating
                        5 Mechanical ventilation
                        6 Electricity
                        7 Gas
                        8 Other services
                        9 Decoration
Level 2 (the different types of fitting)
Level 3 (the parts of the fitting)
Level 4 (the required procedure).

The task is then managed by checking if it is in hand, or referring it for inspection, or allocating the task for action. The task is then allocated to a contractor on the basis of analysed price and workload. Printed material is sent to the contractor and occupier, once the task is completed this is entered and automatically amends the maintenance history in the property file and the contractor's record.

The system provides the additional benefit of ready monitoring of the performance of dwelling types, materials and services and thus contributes to a program of planned maintenance.

Unique to the public sector is the need for a comprehensive form of property referencing system. Land and property records held on local authority computers are identified by a reference number. Often there are a number of individual files each holding details on the same property, each using a different reference number for that unit of information. Within the computer a single integrated file may be achieved by creating a series of links between the individual files. This requires the creation of a master reference number for each unit of property which:

is capable of identifying the smallest unit of property;
is unique;
can accommodate future changes in disposition of land and property;
can be used to generate the postal address.

A system called U.P.R.N. (Unique Property Reference System) has been developed by Leeds City Council and is used in Tameside and Birmingham. This is related to work on the National Gazetteer and is being considered by the Inland Revenue Valuation Office. It takes the form of;

Street code of five digits.
Street sub-division (plot code) of four digits.
Pseudo indicator of one character.
Street sub-sub-division (plot sub-division) of three digits.
Check digit of one digit.

The pseudo digit enables functional properties, such as bus stations, which are not street numbered to be represented. The system cannot be used for "live infrastructure" such as roads, railways or power-transmission facilities. A development of this is the National Gazetteer, based on a basic spatial unit consisting of;

Unique property number
Postal address
Land-use description
12-figure grid reference.

This should enable survey work by local and national bodies to gain access to, and make use of, information in computers rather more easily, including land availability for particular uses, accessing planning and corporate estate files, the creation of property statistics, using rating files and the valuation list and the housing department's property and accounts files.

In 1985 the D.O.E. Land Registers under the 1980 Act were incorporated into a computer data base for access by the public.

9.3.4 Private Sector Systems

Jones Lang Wootton was possibly the first London partnership to introduce a computerized accounts system. Experience of this system and an agency property data base led to the development of a comprehensive estate management system during the mid 1970s. The system runs on an ICL 1903 and was developed jointly with Computer Analysts and Programmers, Ltd., at a cost of several hundred thousand pounds. It is the most comprehensive service available, since it extends from the basic accounts function through portfolio management and re-valuation to the measurement of portfolio performance.

Within property management the system is particularly rigorous in its approach to insurance. Each month a report is produced showing all insurance policies due for renewal three months ahead, with all the current information relevant to the insurance of the property. When a complete re-valuation for insurance purposes has been carried out by a surveyor, the computer will, for a maximum of five years, revise the reinstatement cost on the basis of monthly input of cost data and the contents of the insurance master file for the property.

In 1973 Debenham, Tewson and Chinnocks, with a management portfolio then worth £200 million, introduced a system based on an I.B.M. 370 developed with Cooper and Lybrand Associates, Ltd. During 1980 they transferred to an in-house Hewlett Packard system, made possible by the rapid development in micro-processors. The system is based on a hierarchy of files; landlords, buildings, tenants and tenancy, the last being a very comprehensive data sheet of all information relevant to the management of the property, including special instructions such as rent-stop. A copy is automatically passed to the surveyor when there is any change in the data base for verification and action. The system provides the typical automatic diary, property report forms and accounts programs.

The Computer Management Group has developed a system called PROMAS (Property Management Accounting System) which has been used by Bernard Thorpe and Richard Ellis. In 1979 Bernard Thorpe and C.M.G. launched MANDATA, available on an agency basis or through outright purchase for use on an in-house computer. It provides a wide range of property management programs including a monthly up-date on action dates with an 18 month lead period. Bernard Thorpe uses the system to manage 6,000 tenancies. The cost of using MANDATA on an agency basis with C.M.G. for say, a 25 client,

500 tenant management task, has been quoted at an initial expenditure of £2,000 and £180 per month.

During the early 1970s Cluttons worked for three years with Lowndes-Ajax Computer Services on an estate management accounting system. The system used an I.B.M. 370/158 at Croydon and operated from terminals at Cluttons Data Processing Division at Maidstone, which employs 35 staff. Data was transmitted between the two centres on daily, weekly and monthly cycles. The monthly cycle included;

Changes in the data base during the month
Annual rental budgets
Annual projections of commission
All lettings
Action dates
Rent and other charges, demands and final demands
Accounting and control information;
  Arrears
  Service charges
  V.A.T.
  Clients accounts
  Commission schedules
  Cash books
  Bank balances
  Specialist analysis for clients and in-house use.

More recently a Texas Instruments Minicomputer with a 512k memory and 150 megabyte store has been used, linked to 10 megabyte or 20 megabyte micros in each of the firms offices throughout the country, handling 22,000 tenancies.

Several large provincial firms, including Pearsons and J. P. Sturge, started operating Kiezle 2000 systems in the mid 1970s, at a cost of £10,000 to £15,000 for both the hardware and software development this provided a normal accounts computer adapted to property management.

Sun Alliance estates department manages about 900 properties for various funds funds in the group. In mid 1982 they decided to adopt "PIMS" (Property Investment Management System) written by C.M.G. in conjunction with Scottish Metropolitan Properties. The system runs on the I.B.M. system 36, with a basic hardware cost of £12,500 and software cost of a similar amount.

In order to create the data base, Sun Alliance had to complete about 30,000 proformas to cover all the relevant matters relating to the properties and 2,500 leases. The Sun Alliance system which went live in 1984 combines "pims" with C.M.Gs. "Stacs" accounting package. There are 12 screens at their main office with dedicated lines to Manchester and Bristol.

In 1982 after three years of development, Weatherall Green and Smith installed a NOVA 3 supplied by Data General with software from Fraser Williams. Typically the files occupy the following pages of V.D.U. screen:

Client file   1 page
Property file   2 pages
Lease file   6 pages.

Particular attention has been paid to service charges which are perhaps the single most time consuming part of a property manager's task. There are 100 possible expense categories, and any property may have up to 20 assigned to it, each of which may, or may not, be recoverable. Each lease within a property may have its own percentage attributable to any of the expense categories, the object being to apportion service charge expenses incurred automatically to individual tenant accounts.

St. Quintins acquired a Wang VS 80 in 1981 initially for internal office purposes, with a capacity of 384k, three hard disk drives and 12 terminals. Most of their software has been developed in house covering; investment, appraisal, valuation, performance measurement, property management, investment register, office accounting and word processing, file index, rent review, information and mailing lists. Subsequently the more interactive programs were put on a Motorola 8000 microprocessor with a 15 megabyte fixed Winchester hard disk drive and a 600k floppy disk. This can be net-worked with either up to six or 32 work stations.

The National Freight Corporation was the subject of an employee buy out in 1982 and occupies about 500 transport depots, 250 Pickford Travel shops and 250 specialized properties from cold stores to refuse tips.

In 1982 they appointed Mentor Management Associates who had recently developed a property management system for Unigate to advise them on computer applications. Their system is based on a General Automation Interactor 660 with 80 megabytes of on-line disk storage and peripherals in Bedford, and a V.D.U. and printer in each of their regional offices in London, Leicester, Harrogate and Stroud.

The task was initially accounts lead with an emphasis on the automation of:

Information retrieval problems
Property accounting
Administration.

The system had to have regard to a mixed freehold and leasehold estate, separate operating companies sharing the same site and tenants. Further, as part of the privatization process, new financial discipline was being introduced together with a rigorous review of the portfolio.

Rental accounting is fully integrated with the sales and purchase ledger sub systems as well as the property management data base.

All receivable transactions, whether generated automatically from the property unit and tenancy database, or directly in respect of non-property transactions, are recorded in the appropriate sales ledger. Similarly, regular payments in respect of properties like rents, insurance and easements can be made automatically and, together with all other business expenses; these are all posted to the purchases ledgers.

Expenses which the system identifies as rechargeable to tenants can also be recharged automatically. Links to the nominal ledger and group consolidation can also be performed.

9.4 Management of the Department

Clients, whether a single corporate client, such as a board or elected members, or the diverse range of public and private clients in a professional practice, need managing. Sometimes the inexperienced client needs to be lead into new areas, whereas the thoughts and requirements of the experienced client may need to be anticipated if the client/adviser relationship is to foster. In the context of private practice, clients need to be obtained, serviced and enhanced. A prudent client will from time to time review the service being provided and the fee that is charged.

Managements may be gained and lost by factors quite extraneous to the ability of the Surveyors. The disposal of an investment invariably results in the transfer of the management to the purchaser's company, the same applies to the transfer of the ownership of the portfolio. This aside, management is usually gained as a result of acting for the developer, hence the importance of the management surveyor in acting as a member of the development team.

The undertaking of tasks by staff will be substantially assisted by a regularly updated, standard management manual, essentially the distillation of best practice over the years, this has many benefits. Standard tasks are likely to be considered with greater care. All those in the firm will know how other colleagues have approached work and new staff are likely to be effective more quickly.

In a large estates department it is possible to distinguish:

Partners/Directorate—The management of the business in operational, financial and corporate terms.
The promotion of the department.
The recruitment, development and reward of staff.
Associates/Senior Surveyors—The management of the portfolios.
The demonstration and encouragement of performance.
Surveyors—The management of properties/tenants.

Many aspects have been covered in this chapter, some of which are also relevant to other areas of work of the general practice surveyor. In the context of property management it has been suggested that the application of very recent micro-processor technology will bring direct computer applications within the reach of many more organizations. Whilst the computer is only a tool with which to better meet the requirements of clients, it does tend to alter the way that individual property management tasks are approached. Those most versed in the exercise of traditional skills sometimes find new tools not to their liking, and equally the enthusiasm of the technologist can get him out of his depth in areas of professional practice of which he has only a rudimentary knowledge. The sign of an educated profession is the ability to analyse critically existing practice, test new proposals and apply those that are approved in a sense of positive enquiry.

The extent to which the computer can be used to assist in the management of the work loads of staff and contribute to the financial and general management of the firm is certainly worth careful investigation. As staff costs continue to rise at a rate which demands an accelerating rise in fee income, large private practices may well adopt some of the job evaluation techniques of the public sector. The techniques developed in property management are highly relevant to the management of the people involved in property management. Analysis of the work in the management department can proceed in a number of ways. A starting point is the total fee income from each client; this can then be analysed into service charge management and rental income management and further classified into that arising from the different types of property. It should then be possible for experienced senior staff to determine the relative profitabilities of the various subgroups of specific management work. As a result the fee basis can be amended or changes made in procedures, management practice or staffing to improve the contribution of the work to the overall profitability of the practice.

The other activities generated from regular property management, mentioned earlier, tend, with the exception of rent-reviews to be irregular and thus not as easily analysed as the regular cycle of specific management. This requires a longer time-scale, of at least five years, but it is an important function of the management department, and the partner responsible will want to stress the contribution this makes to the firm as a whole both in fee income and balance of the range of work.

Increases in fee income occur as a result of increases in rent and service charges of which the fees are a percentage. With a computer it is easy to identify all the reviews in each of the next few years and apply to them current open market rental values. This will show the likely fees for both specific management and the negotiation of the reviews. New management work will be obtained in respect of many of the development schemes in which the firm is involved. If typical rentals and service charges are related to realistic occupation dates over the next few years for those buildings where management instructions are likely, then again projected fee income can be calculated.

This is not to suggest that this type of analysis need be a frequent activity, every three to five years would be reasonable, and this is likely to be similar to the time-scale of reviews of other parts of the work of the practice.

The existence of regular reviews will assist in the general adaptation of the firm in response to the changing working environment. it will also enable associates and senior staff to demonstrate wider management skills and assist in their career development. The experience gained within the firm will, in the intervening years, enable job specifications, realistic work-loads and fees to be discussed with more certainty as to their impact on the aggregate activity of the practice. It may be of some interest that in 1983 property management accounted for 28% of the fee income of Drivas Jonas.

There will be some costs involved but the returns in terms of the more efficient use of staff and the contribution to medium-term financial management are such as to make this a necessity in a well-run practice. the techniques have been expressed in terms of private practice but with some adaptation are suitable and helpful in the overall management of many other sectors of activity.

In 1985 the R.I.C.S. published a report, "Competition and the Chartered Surveyor", which identified practice management skills as the key area for development in order for surveyors to compete effectively. The report was partial in as much it concentrated on private practice as the leading edge of the profession in terms of its proximity to markets and need to respond to changing client demand.

In terms of services to existing commercial property (as opposed to development) total fees were estimated as follows:

Agency	£200 m p.a.
Estate Management	£120 m p.a.
Valuation	£50 m p.a.
Rent review	£30 m p.a.
Building survey	£30 m p.a.

In respect of all the above, attention was concentrated on three distinctive roles of partners as;

Business entrepreneurs, creating opportunity and resources to earn profits.

Managers across a wide range of functions, personnel, finance, technical.

Experts in a narrow area of professional expertise.

This lead to questioning of the extent to which medium sized practices would be able to perform these increasingly specialized functions.

Sources and Further Reading

Property Records:
Furber, Office Service Charge Data, 272 E.G. 1036, 1142.
Gemmell, R.I.C.S. Accounts Regulations, Oyez, 1979.
Scarrett, Property Management, Spon, 1983.
Urry, V.A.T. and Property Transactions, 265 E.G. 375.
Wyldbore-Smith, Savings in Service Changes, Property Management, Vol. 3, No. 1, Henry Stewart.

The Client:
Jess, A Guide to Insurance of Professional Negligence Risks, Butterworth, 1982.
Stapleton, Pleased To Report, E.G., 1983.

260 *Estate Management Practice*

Computers:
Hunt, Briefing: Computers, series in C.S.W. 1984.
Kirkwood, Information Technology and Land Administration, E.G., 1984.

The Department:
Allsopp, Management in the Professions, Business Book, 1979.
R.I.C.S., Competition and the Chartered Surveyor, 1985.

Chapter 10

Acquisition and Disposal

10.1 Motivation of the Parties

The buying or selling of property may be an isolated transaction in the life of an individual or of a small company, but in a larger corporate body the frequency of such transactions will lead to these being conducted within formal procedures as part of the general management of the organization. Before examining these procedures and their consequences it is worth considering the motivation of purchasers and vendors. In very few circumstances is it ever essential to sell or buy a particular property; the decision to initiate the transaction will usually develop as a result of a careful analysis of many factors, and a number of possible properties may be identified, a transaction in any one of them being all that is required.

Since one man's acquisition is another man's disposal, the best transaction is one where both vendor and purchaser are well satisfied. That is to say, having regard to all aspects of the property, the vendor considers he obtained a good price and the purchaser believes he has paid a reasonable sum. This can arise through various circumstances, partly as a result of different opinions as to the future of the market in general and the particular property. In the investment market, the existence of specialist management expertise, the potential of marriage value, an over concern, with historic costs or the need to change the balance of a portfolio can all act as the catalyst to initiate the sale. The mere pressure of functional requirements accounts for most transactions by tenants and owner-occupiers adjusting to technical and economic change in their sphere of activity. Subject to the constraints of specialist users, the rate of change in relation to the financial structure of the occupier's business will determine the emphasis between renting and owner-occupation of either fully developed sites or new development.

Prior to the commencement of development there may be years of site-assembly and holding management before the complex of negotiations, design and financing can be presented as a coherent and feasible package, meeting the requirements of investor, occupiers and public sector controls.

The client is represented by a team of advisers and their selection, monitoring, cohesion and supervision of areas of responsibility requires considerable personal skills on his part. They for their part will be involved in negotiations and discussions with public and private bodies and in their reporting may be influenced by factors other than solely the successful negotiation of the current transaction. The background, discipline and personality of the client's representative will influence the overall conduct of the negotiations and the significance attached to the opinions of the advisers in the various disciplines.

10.2.1 Acquisition

Acquisition can be for the purposes of development, occupation or investment, the same general process is involved for each of these:

Policy, leading to brief and then instructions.
Search for suitable property, site finding.
Preparation and investigation of short list.
Detailed investigation—physical
                                     appraisal
                                     acquisition
                                     finance
                                     taxation
                                     legal
                                     management
Agreement, subject to contract.
Recommendation and decision process.
Approval and financing.
Documentation.
Implementation.
Entry to portfolio.
Physical and tenurial adjustment.
User.
Management and monitoring.

Where properties are being acquired regularly then this process will itself be monitored and supervised to ensure that the best use is made of the financial resources, and that analysis of the extent to which the brief has been met is fed back to the policy-making unit.

Where occupation is involved, particularly the occupation of a large unit, with considerable employment generation, then not only are political and social factors involved but the occupier will be interested in the general environment and infrastructure associated with a particular location. The weight be attached to these and the trade-off between individual properties and the locational features they provide are not capable of precise measurement. Financial incentives as part of government programmes may prove less permanent than the features they are designed to overcome. The range of issues which need to be considered when advising clients in a comprehensive way on location and alternative forms of tenure are wider than those normally provided in property reports, but well within the expertise of the surveyor.

A potential occupier can buy or rent an existing unit, take a pre-let from a developer or develop to meet his own requirements. The latter is particularly true of the public sector and the more specialized types of occupiers in the private sector.

A potential investor can buy an existing investment, develop on a pre-let reflecting to some extent occupiers' requirements, or develop speculatively. In the case of industrial development sponsored by the public sector the euphemism "advance" factory is used to indicate that it is speculative but for the best of reasons.

Both occupiers and investors increase the scale of their activities and their property holdings by take-overs and mergers. Local authorities, Institutions, property companies, retail chains and manufacturing companies are all involved, and in the wake of such activities comes rationalization and reorganization of function and resources. There is a tendency to seek new and more centralized offices for the headquarters activities. At the same time the operational assets will need the most careful analysis and review to ensure that the accident of ownership of the aggregate estate does not become the justification for continued use.

10.2.2 Public Sector Acquisition

In 1972 the Borner Committee was appointed to consider the use of valuers in the public service and particularly the requirements which had existed since 1920 for the District Valuer to approve the price paid by local authorities in the acquisition of land, using funds arising from specific grant or loan sanction. The Greater London Council had only been subject to this approval in respect of funds from specific grants. The report recommended a new procedure of selective checks by the District Valuer and this seemed to work well, with only a very small number of cases referred to the Secretary of State. Local authorities point out that this does not mean that their figure is wrong, rather that there is at least a difference of professional opinion. The problem is to what extent, if any, local political aspects have influenced the local authority's opinion? The selective checks were removed by a Circular in 1980.

In 1984 there was a further review of Government Valuation Services (The Dalton Committee, see 4.2), to which the R.I.C.S. submitted the following recommendations:

1. Merger of D.V./V.O. and P.S.A. organized into separate Valuation and Management functions.
2. The Crown Estate and Statutory Undertakers to retain their separate estates function.
3. The merged service to regard its user departments and authorities as identified clients, who would be charged for the services provided.
4. A greater range of public sector work should be available for private practice to undertake, subject to essential safeguards such as confidentiality.

In the case of acquisitions of land or buildings from local authorities, purchasers may find signs of some tension between the estates department and the planning department as they seek to negotiate both price and planning consent with the two departments of the vendor council.

It can be even more difficult when acting for a client buying from a shire county which is having a disagreement with the district council that exercises planning control. Every additional £1 of planning gain negotiated by the district can only mean £1 less to be offered to the vendor county, or vice versa, depending upon which council's offices you are negotiating in during an apparently unending series of meetings.

10.3 Land Holding

Acquisition and disposal are in many circumstances quite unrelated, only a minority of acquisitions are made for the specific purpose of a subsequent disposal as part of a process of land assembly, with or without the provision of infrastructure. This is one of the functions of the builder/developer and is in its most sophisticated form in the case of residential land banks which seek to:

ensure continuity of production;
allow a flexible response to changes in market demand;
provide for unforeseen delays on other sites;
achieve a partial monopoly in certain areas;
provide benefit from rising land values.

Many builders consider that three years supply is a normal requirement, but some land can be in the bank for many years before being developed. One of the major complaints of builders is that local authorities are not granting consents on enough land. This is partly due to the use of different criteria; the local authority tends to look at the aggregate land supply rather than the patterns of ownership of individual builders. A builder assesses each site in the light of its physical and financial suitability for his type of development, whereas the planning authority lack the incentive to consider the financial feasibility of sites which are available in a physical sense.

Research has shown that in many cases councils have over-stated the land that is practically available by 15% to 20% in aggregate, which means by very much more in specific locations. In Circular 9/80 the Secretary of State asked local authorities to ensure that five years' supply of land was continually available. This land must be free or easily freed from planning, physical and ownership constraints and be capable of being economically developed. The identification of the five-year land bank will require close liaison between authorities, builders and landowners. Any local deficiency in the identification of sufficient land will be a factor in the determination of planning appeals. Development land is expensive to hold and one way of reducing the cost is for the builder to purchase an option, that is to say for a small sum acquire the exclusive right to buy the land within a specified period at an agreed price. The Community Land Act 1975 made the function of bringing land forward for development a duty of the local authority, and the system of accounts and procedures highlighted many aspects involved in land assembly, whether carried out by the public or private sectors. However, for political, financial and technical reasons the measure only lasted for five years, although in the hybrid form of the Land Authority for Wales it has proved a success.

The time-cost of holding land for site-assembly is often hidden. If an interest charge is included within the feasibility study, the decision-makers are made more than aware of the costs of delay, whether caused by administrative, proprietary or economic factors. This was recognized in the Development Land Tax 1976, which provides for a special addition of up to 15% per annum for four years to cover the costs of holding development land. Only in a limited number of cases will the land acquired be a vacant serviced greenfield site. If it is residential property, steps will have to be taken to secure it against squatters or to go through the due process of law to remove any squatters. In urban areas fly tipping is a constant problem and on the urban–rural fringe such land can quickly become an unofficial gypsy site.

Where land is being acquired for development, then the outline or detailed consent will be the single most important factor, very often these negotiations will take place in an environment in which the planning authority seek some planning gain, using section 52 of the 1971 Act. In October 1981 the Property Advisory Group published a report on this subject, this was followed by a draft circular in March 1983 which generated substantial comment and a Circular 22/83. The circular states that authorities are not entitled to treat an applicant's need for planning permission as an opportunity to obtain wholly extraneous benefits from the developer. The reasonableness of the obligations can be tested by:

Is the planning gain needed for the development to proceed? In the case of financial payments will they assist this purpose?

Is the gain clearly related to the development?

Where related to a mixed development, is the condition imposed to secure an acceptable balance of uses?

Is the condition related to the scale of the development?

A developer is entitled to refuse unreasonable conditions and appeal to the Secretary of State. Indeed in *Westminster Renslade Ltd* v. *S of S for the Environment*, 1983, the High Court quashed a decision of the Minister refusing consent because no planning gain was offered to the local authority. The inspector had refused consent because insufficient car park space under public control had been provided.

The parties to section 52 agreements have assumed them to be of a permanent nature, but the Lands Tribunal in *Re Beecham Group Ltd's Application*, 1980, were asked to discharge an agreement made under Section 37 of the 1962 Act (the predecessor of section 52). Although the agreement was only ten years old and the applicants were the original covenantees, for various reasons including the Inspector's reasoning in a planning appeal, the Tribunal approved the application.

In a similar context to the validity of section 52 agreements, in 1985 the D.O.E. published circular 1/85, "The Use of Conditions in Planning Permissions", in which it is said that conditions should be both necessary and reasonable, as well as enforceable, precise and relevant both to planning and to the development which is to be permitted.

10.4.1 Disposal

There is a natural inertia against the disposal of interests in property. There are many reasons for this, some explained perhaps more by psychology than estate management. In large functional organizations, including statutory undertakers, it may be difficult to find an individual prepared to say, "We will never need that property again", and if you take the alternative approach you can never be proved wrong. In the financial Institutions disposals average around 2% or 3% per annum of the total value of the portfolio. The measurement of portfolio performance is introducing a new discipline and thus more incentive to see disposal as a normal part of portfolio management.

One of the reasons for disposals is the realization of a capital profit. In the 1960s and 1970s companies recorded their assets at historic costs. This was often convenient, since the return on assets employed appeared more attractive than the reality of the situation. Such companies were liable to be identified by asset-strippers, whose *raison d'être* was redistributing the ownership of assets to those able to obtain a higher financial return. Unfortunately the consequential changes in employment opportunities and social implications meant that their private sector restructuring of British industry was no more popular than that carried out on a much larger scale by the Conservative government elected in 1979.

10.4.2 Methods of Disposal

The alternative means of marketing interests, private negotiations, auction or tender, each possess particular features which make them suitable for different circumstances. When the market for property is unstable or the vendor wishes to exercise some control over the identity of the purchaser tenders can be invited, possibly in excess of a specified figure. If the site has development potential and the disposal is linked to a design brief then the potential purchaser's bid will be a combination of price and detailed scheme. Unless they have access to considerable development expertise vendors have difficulty in determining which of the combinations of price and project should be accepted. Even if the best proposal can be identified in a quantitative way, the purchaser's ability effectively to implement the scheme and manage the overall project needs to be carefully considered in the light of their track-record. The alternative approaches include a preliminary tender and then negotiations with several short-listed potential purchasers, which gives an opportunity to assess their performance. Tenders can be abused by purchasers who use them to get "their foot in the door" and then steadily renegotiate the terms. Auctions can be very useful in certain circumstances. A well organized auction should absolve any vendors acting in a trustee capacity from criticism as to either their general conduct or the price realized. The date, venue and form of the auction need to be carefully planned to prove attractive to what are seen as the typical purchasers, avoiding bank holiday and other holiday periods. The benefit to a vendor is that a successful bid is immediately followed by the signing of a contract and the payment of the deposit, but this could deter some potential purchasers when credit is difficult to arrange.

The recommendation of a reserve by the auctioneers is never an easy task, and even then the client may issue other instructions. A sale at a price well in excess of the reserve reflects poorly on the auctioneer's knowledge of the market; failure to reach the reserve is possibly indicative of other problems.

During the first half of the 1980s auctions steadily increased in popularity as a means of selling commercial investments. The table developed by Chartered Surveyors Weekly shows the value of and structure of sales by the ten major firms in 1984.

Firm	Value Realized £m	Number of Auctions	Lots Offered	Success Rate
Allsop and Co.	56	7	465	91
Barnard Marcus	48	12	2,302	78
Willmotts	34	12	1,706	78
Harman Healey	33	6	462	94
Hilliyers	27	19	1,037	N/A
Healey and Baker	11	7	N/A	78
Longden and Cook	10	14	636	75
Hillier Parker	10	4	69	80
Conrad Ritblat	10	4	126	90
Jones Lang Wotton	10	4	45	85

The firms fall into two distinct groups, five (the low number of lots offered) are major national commercial practices whose auctioneering is growing rapidly from a small base and the remaining five are known primarily as specialist auctioneers of residential and low value commercial property.

A convincing explanation of why auctions are back in fashion is difficult, but is probably related to the rapid expansion of trading in secondary properties, together with the extensive overhaul of major institutional portfolios, made possible by the analytical techniques developed by major practices in the late 1970s.

The vast majority of properties are sold through private negotiations but the period of time involved can vary from hours to years. In the case of prime investments, the relatively small numbers of surveyors that act on behalf of the Institutions and property companies rely on personal knowledge of those in the market. What would appear to be a permanent shortage of the prime property investment means that for much of the time a seller's market exists as Institutions seek to place part of their continually growing income into these properties. Apart from this specialized market, disposals require a carefully planned advertising programme using the various alternative media to publicize the property to best advantage. The selection of the best method for a particular sale and its effective implementation is a function of the character of the property and the motivation of the vendor. In the case of a public sector client, there may be a preference for auction or tender and the agent involved should expect to keep a more formal record of all aspects that are involved in working towards a disposal. No method is exclusive; an unsuccessful auction is often followed by a private sale, and a sale where offers are invited in excess of a specified sum can sometimes only be resolved fairly between several potential purchasers by the introduction of an informal tender procedure.

Tenders can result in a higher price than that obtained by other means but some potential purchasers may indicate unwillingness to take part. An auction is organized to realize a price one bid over that of the second highest bidder and in private negotations there is sufficient feed-back of information and opportunity to make a series of bids for the purchaser to ensure that he pays no more than he need to obtain the property. However, a tender provides the opportunity for one fixed specific bid only by a certain date, made in ignorance of any other bid by any other party; such a bid can only be the highest the purchaser is prepared to offer. The vendor is not, of course, bound to accept the highest tender and there are circumstances when it would be prudent to accept a lower bid, and this possibility should be made clear in the tender documents.

In recent years development has been accepted as not only an activity but a study in its own right, and this is reflected by a growing volume of research, analysis and information, the existence of which has permitted this text to leave unmentioned the effect of the various factors which contribute to the development process. There are, however, some particular types of transactions within the development process which are an integral part of estate management.

A ground lease, typically for 125 years, represents an ideal way for development to occur within a comprehensive framework controlled by the ground landlord. There is a natural tendency for the developer to seek a better package of terms from his occupying tenant than he is prepared to agree with the ground landlord. To some extent this is essential, since without the resulting profit there would be no developer and no development. The return which the landlord receives is a ground rent, reviewed at certain intervals, related to the rents achieved for the completed building, typically between 10% and 20% of the full rent. One of the highest percentages was the reported 28.25% paid by Legal and General to the City Corporation for an office site in Leadenhall Market. Rather than agree a fixed review period for the ground rent of say five years, a landlord can seek an "as and when" basis, that is to say, as occupation rents are actually reviewed or renewed, so the ground rent rises in proportion. Clearly this will result in more complex accounts but it is likely to lead to a more attractive cash-flow and as occupation leases terminate and shorter frequency rent reviews are agreed, this is automatically reflected in the frequency of ground rent reviews. To what extent it is necessary or possible to agree an over-riding provision to protect the landlord against any downside risk is a matter for negotiation.

In *Freehold and Leasehold Shop Properties Ltd* v. *Friends Provident Life Office*, 1984 271 E.G. 451 the rent payable to the ground landlord was $17\frac{1}{2}$% of; the rack rent (if the property was let as a whole) or the aggregate total of rentals payable in respect of lettings current at the review date and agreed rentals in respect of any parts then vacant, whichever is the greater. It would be in the interests of the head lessee to negotiate with his underlessees payment of a premium in lieu of rent, hence reducing the payment to the ground landlord to a minimum.

A developer will be anxious to obtain pre-lets to neutralize risk and facilitate the financing of the project and the potential occupier who is able to provide a pre-let is in a strong position. In signing the agreement to take a lease it is possible to agree a single specific rental figure. Alternatively, a formula can be agreed to share the "overage", the occupier paying as a minimum the rent which the then hypothetical premises would command at the date of the agreement plus say half the increase in market rent up to the date when he goes into occupation. The occupier should be well pleased, having obtained the premises cheaper than if he had simply taken a finished unit. The developer has almost entirely removed the risk at a cost of say half the rise in rental value during the period of construction, which for industrial property can be between six and nine months. To be effective this would require some machinery to resolve any dispute as to the rental value of the completed premises. Section 55 of the Finance Act 1977 dealt with the tax problems that arose under D.L.T. and is referred to in Chapter 12.

All formulae in leases and their components should be subject to careful study and tested to ensure that figures used are substantiated by the market and that there is no unexpected sensitivity, as values and costs change during the life of a building.

10.4.3 Public Sector Disposals

The normal market factors which influence disposals are complicated by several other factors in the public sector. In both central and local government there are political issues and the Conservative government elected in 1979 had as strong a political will to dispose of land as the Labour government elected in 1974 had to acquire land. There are also technical aspects— the scale of operation is large, having economic effects beyond those of just land transactions, and the accountability required of the public sector may require some particular procedures to be followed.

The political philosophy behind the Conservative government's programme of disposals has been explained by the Secretary of State as based upon a number of objects that coincide as follows: "First we have a very large public sector borrowing requirement and to the extent that we can release assets we are able to reduce the borrowing requirement. Second, we are trying to ensure that assets are used as effectively as we can, particularly in terms of land. Therefore where the public sector has got land that is not used as effectively as we would like, we are very anxious to ensure that it is put on the market and sold to people who have a use for it. Third, we are determined to change the balance between the public and private sector by extending the private sector. So for all those three reasons we are examining the assets in State ownership with a view to disposing of them where we think it practicable and desirable to do so."

Whether that philosophy appeals or not, its implementation by surveyors in the public service and consultants represents a strategic operation and presents new problems. The most striking programme has been that for the New Towns where the objective was to sell assets worth £100 million within one year of gaining office, with the aim of a further £200 million to be sold. In the summer of 1979, Healey and Baker, the consultants appointed to advise the Minister, were given a month to report on the following terms of reference:

"To advise the Secretary of State as to the disposable value of the commercial land and buildings held by the Commission and as to a sensible programme for realising the assets remaining after those already earmarked by the New Towns for disposal in the current financial year, and in particular to assess the total value to serve as a basis for decisions on future disposals; advise on which assets were suitable for immediate disposal, which would be suitable for disposal on a given time-scale and which assets are unsaleable; propose a programme for disposals in the light of this information and to advise on the means of disposal to be adopted; consider the programme of disposals proposed by the New Towns and to advise whether any adjustments were necessary to fit in with long-term proposals."

The challenging task involved has been explained by Paul Orchard-Lisle in "Selling Surplus Public Property", a supplement to "The Chartered Surveyor" of April 1980.

Each generation of new towns had a distinctive estate in physical and terminal terms and since the estates had not been developed with the intention of sale, the expectation of the politicians for rapid results were not always consistent with prudent management and valuation advice. Properties were first offered to the occupier then to intermediate lessees to take advantage of marriage value, which was never realized on less than a pro rata basis from the point of view of the vendor. The table shows disposals in the first three years.

	79/80 £m	80/81 £m	81/82 £m	Total £m
New Town Dev. Corp.	43·4	68·1	74·1	185·6
Commission for New Towns	5·7	34·7	59·4	99·8
Total	49·1	102·8	133·5	285·4

As at March 1985, The Commission for New Towns, responsible for the eight completed towns, mostly around London, had made disposals of £317 m. The majority of these were to tenants. Bracknell and Crawley each contributed £70 m. Despite the disposals, the Commission's rental income in 1984/5 was £26 m.

The specialist nature of some public sector property is shown by the instructions given to Richard Ellis to dispose of 125 year leases on the 38 Motorway Service Areas, which represent a capital investment of over £40 million. Many of the sales are likely to be to the current operators, most of whom hold leases with between 30 and 50 years unexpired. The diversity of the property involved in the public sector is shown by the sales of assets by the Property Services Agency, which include almost every type of property all over the world.

The disposal of urban land has been much easier since July 1979 with the removal of the redundant land and accommodation procedures, which required land to be offered to a hierarchy of public sector bodies.

The scale of the disposals raises a number of issues which last arose on the sale of land surplus to requirements after 1945. The Crichel Down case concerned the sale of agricultural land acquired for a bombing range before the war which the previous owner discovered had been sold to the Commissioners of Crown Lands. After a lengthy campaign to re-purchase the land the Minister made a statement in Parliament in 1954 that, "The Government has now made the important new decision that where a former owner or his successors can establish a special personal claim, he will, where possible, be given a special opportunity to buy back the land when it is no longer wanted for Government purposes ... at a price to be assessed by the district valuer as being the current market price".

In 1980 the P.S.A. started to dispose of the Bloomsbury site acquired for the proposed British Library during the 1960s. George Allen and Unwin wished to buy back their freehold which had been acquired in 1963, and only after a most vociferous campaign were the Government forced to honour the commitments which had been given to this effect at the date the premises were acquired.

New rules were introduced by the D.O.E. in 1981 whereby former owners will be given a first opportunity to repurchase land provided it has not been materially changes in character since acquisition. This general obligation to offer back will not apply if the land becomes surplus more than 25 years after the date of acquisition.

The offer back will normally be made to the freeholder, however if the land was subject to a long lease at the time of acquisition and a long period remains at the time of disposal (say 21 years) then the leaseholder may qualify. Exceptions to this offer back are of two types, firstly where some other public body has some essential need for the land and secondly for technical land management reasons. Full advertisement procedures are set out, in order to ensure that proper steps are taken to trace former owners.

As the State's disposal of public sector land gathered momentum, the fact that the Crown was not covered by the planning legislation, and therefore could not sell with the benefit of planning consent, for the most advantageous use, became a problem. The Town and Country Planning Act 1984 was passed to overcome the deficiencies in Circular 49/63 which came to light in R v. Worthing Borough Council ex P Birch, 1983.

Many public sector bodies have been active in the identification and disposal of surplus land. In order to identify surplus public sector land in a comprehensive way the Local Government, Planning and Land Act 1980 enables the Secretary of State to maintain a register of under-used land in the area covered by a district council or London borough. The Secretary of State has power to direct any of the public sector bodies concerned to dispose of land, including the method and terms of disposal.

The body has a right to make representations but there is no formal appeal. Initially 21 District Council areas were identified, this was extended to 35 and by the end of 1981, 2,500 sites with an area of 22,000 acres were included in the Registers.

By February 1983 over 100,000 acres had been identified on the registers all over the country. The House Builders Federation has examined all the sites on a sample of 63 registers and out of 26,000 acres identified 2,900 acres physically capable of being developed for housing purposes.

Around London 66 sites in the Metropolitan Green Belt were investigated, of which 26 were found not to be meeting any of the Green Belt criteria, in many cases scrub land which had been heavily fly-tipped.

In Bristol the Federation asked the Minister to bring pressure on the Council to dispose of 17 sites suitable for housing.

In 1982 the balance of ownership of land on the register was:

Local Authorities	63%	
Statutory undertakers	32%	(British Rail 13%)
Nationalized industries	3%	
Crown Land	2%	

In view of the very extensive estate of the P.S.A., which accounts for Crown land one can conclude that either it is managed in a supremely efficient manner, or the discretion to include Crown land has been exercised in only the most exceptional circumstances.

As at 1 July, 1984, 18,000 acres of registered land had been sold and several thousand acres had been removed from the register having been brought into use. In 1985 the Minister began the process of forcing authorities to dispose of 388 acres on 50 sites by using the powers in section 99 of the 1980 Act.

The appropriateness of limiting the register only to publicly-owned land has been questioned, as has the means which can be used to describe the land to be entered on the register. The degree of under-use of land is a function of its perceived potential in relation to its planning background and the solution to many planning problems is outside the control of an individual public or private landowner. What appears to be a large holding may have been acquired at different dates, be of different tenure and split up by used or disused roads, railways or canals, whereas a very small site may possess considerable potential marriage value. It would be wrong to think such a register will in itself solve problems; it may help to identify problems whose solution requires the expenditure of large capital sums on infrastructure and the re-arrangement of the ownership of various interests. One possible consequence of the greater availability of land which had previously proved inaccessible would be a fall in land values, with other unexpected results.

Arising from government policy the D.H.S.S. commissioned a report "Underused and Surplus Property in the National Health Service". The Minister's decisions are to be found in H.C. 83/22, (and H.C. 85/26) the contents of which are typical of the approach introduced across the whole of the public sector.

Each District to undertake a survey of the condition and utilization of the stock of buildings.

Each District in consultation with the District Valuer or private firms to value the stock, with detailed work on possible sites for disposal.

Records of maintenance and replacement costs.

A policy of bridging finance to assist cost saving schemes.

Notional rents based on rateable values in consultation with the Treasury Valuer, a form of weighting to be developed by an Advisory Group on Estate Management to reflect factors such as service worth.

A Regional Property Surveyor (possibly filled by secondment from the Valuation Office) and Advisory Panel.

A National Property Advisory Group to monitor the implementation of the report and advise as requested.

The development of standard procedures using the EstMan code and Land Transactions Handbook.

A survey of N.H.S. accommodation identified 112,000 residential units. The report recommended that only 29,000 for first year nurses and 11,000 for junior doctors should be retained. The strategy for disposal should start with free standing properties outside hospital precincts which could raise £170 million. Though about 20% of the total number of units were empty, those were not necessarily the most easily disposed units. However, if it has been customary for poorly paid medical staff to have access to cheap hospital housing, the removal of the housing will quite properly affect their aspirations as to pay.

In local government the scale of acquisition and disposal is very much influenced by the broad policy of the elected members within the constraints of the availability of finance. Through statute central government is able to specify the terms upon which local authorities can dispose of land. The Local Government Act 1972, section 123, commences with a brief statement that a council may dispose of land in any way that they wish. This is then limited in various ways, for example, any disposal other than a lease for less than seven years must be at the best consideration that can reasonably be obtained. Letting property at a concessionary rent is not to be encouraged; it is far better to let at a full open market rent and find some other way of encouraging the particular occupier, by an interest-free loan or a grant. Once concessionary rents are known to be paid, the estates department will find pressure from elected members and others can grow, and the whole integrity of the rent-roll can be challenged. Further, as small business, originally encouraged by the assistance, prospers and is able to pay the market rent, the size of the increase from a concessionary rent is likely to be criticized.

Local government officers have needed a certain lightness of foot in order to keep up with the changes in the regulation by central government of disposals by their authorities. The Land White Paper of 1974, reflecting the philosophy of the 1947 and 1967 legislation, was enacted as the Community Land Act 1975. This introduced a new section 123(a) into the 1972 Act which prevented disposals of any interest other than leases for less than seven years without the approval of the Secretary of State. Under the Community Land Act, Circular 6, of March 1976, a general consent was given to dispose of the freehold in land for owner-occupied housing and 99 year leases for most other purposes. This caused considerable difficulties, since some Institutions refused to fund developments on the basis of a 99 year lease. The grounds for their action were not totally justified, since as long as land is acquired at a price fully reflecting the implications of such a lease, a development can still be feasible. In December 1977, the general consent was slightly relaxed to include the freehold of up to 0·5 hectare with a value of less than £25,000. The previous limit had been £500. In May 1979, the Conservative government removed these controls and returned to the status quo of the Local Government Act 1972. Some further relaxation was introduced by the Local Government, Planning and Land Act 1980.

10.5 Marriage Value

The concept of the whole being worth more (or less) than the sum of the parts is not just a feature of property. In industry, mergers between companies are often justified on the basis that the two companies involved each possess specialist technical, financial or marketing skills of a semi-monopolistic character which would, if exercised jointly, be to the mutual benefit of both companies. In the event this may not always prove to be the case. Similarly, in personal terms, a group of individuals with a common purpose may form a coherent team or a bickering committee. In real property marriage value consists of tenurial and physical aspects and both can be present to varying degrees. Consider the successful and well-established tenant farmer who has the opportunity to buy the freehold vacant possession interest in land adjoining his tenanted farm. Because he can farm this with no increase in his capital equipment, his fixed costs can be spread over a larger acreage and that land is worth more to him than to some other potential purchasers because of his existing leasehold interest. In fact, the new land need not adjoin his present farm but merely be conveniently located. At the other extreme the developer with 99% of a carefully assembled site will be very anxious to acquire the final outstanding property and only he will know its true value, having acquired, ideally, a freehold interest. The scheme usually requires the demolition of any buildings on the site.

The concept of marriage value has been recognized in statute and case law for many years in the fields of compensation and taxation, for example in the formula used to adjust costs on the part-disposal of an interest for capital taxation purposes.

Tenurial marriage value generally arises from the differing approaches for the valuation of freehold and leasehold interests. As long as dual rate tax-adjusted tables are used to value leasehold interests and single rate tables for freeholds, then the combination and merger of the component interests will result in a higher value than the aggregate of the component interests. The distribution of the surplus between the parties will depend upon their relative negotiating strengths and perception of the position of the other parties. The extent of this is most marked in the residential field, where tenants enjoy security of tenure and either party on obtaining the right to dispose of the property with vacant possession can make a substantial and possibly tax-free gain. In the commercial field the tenant in occupation may also be prepared to offer more for the freehold or long leasehold interest in his property than would be obtained if it were sold as just one of a number of properties in an investment portfolio.

The break-up of an interest can result in greater aggregate proceeds than if the whole interest were sold as one lot, though consideration must be given to the extra time and costs involved. An investment consisting of a very large, fully developed site comprising a number of distinctive buildings might be worth more if available in the market as several lots. The principle was articulated in *Ellesmere v. Inland Revenue Commissioners*, 1918, in connection with the break-up value of an agricultural estate. This gave rise to the phrase "prudent lotting" as one of the valuation rules for the then estate duty and is equally relevant to capital transfer tax valuations. To the extent that this is the opposite of marriage value, it can be called divorce value.

The re-arrangement of interests and the terms upon which they are held is the practical application of marriage value concepts to detailed portfolio management. An important feature of a commercial investment is a "clear" lease, all the outgoings being the direct responsibility of the tenant or at least the financial responsibility through a comprehensive service charge. It will be in the landlord's interest to offer his tenant who holds on old-type lease terms, some encouragement to alter the terms at review or renewal.

Sources and Further Reading

Armon Jones, Marketing, Estate Times, 30.3.84.
Auctioneers lose their reserve, C.S., 5.1.84.
D.O.E. Circular 26/76, Community Land Act Circular 6.
D.O.E. Circular 9/80, Land for Private Housebuilding.
Realising the new town assets, C.S., 14.4.83.
Releasing Land for Building Development, R.T.P.I., 1978.
Report of the Committee on the Use of Valuers in the Public Service Borner Report, H.M.S.O. Comnd 5518.
Report on Initial Land Register Inspections, House Builders Federation, 1983.
Selling Surplus Public Property, Supplement to C.S., April 1980.
Study of the Availability of Private House-building Land in Greater Manchester, 1978–81, D.O.E., 1978.
Stungo, Public Sector Land, 269 E.G. 291.
The Land Market and the Development Process, S.A.U.S., 1978.
Underused and Surplus Property in the National Health Services, Ceri Davies Report, H.M.S.O., 1983.

Chapter 11

Portfolio Performance

11.1.1 Introduction

The measurement of portfolio performance presents challenging conceptual and technical problems. Measurement is not an end in itself, rather a means to an end, that of the improvement of the performance of the portfolio, which requires the application of a wide range of skills to the management of the underlying assets.

Performance can be defined as achievement relative to objectives. Chapter 8 considered the factors influencing estates policy, the way that policy develops and its expression in terms of objectives. If achievement can be measured, then the extent to which it has been possible to meet the objectives can be expressed in a quantitative sense. If the objective has not been achieved this does not automatically imply a failure on the part of those responsible for the implementation of the objectives. Unforeseeable changes in conditions, lack of resources, or doubts as to the quality of the system of measurement should all be carefully considered. All these features and many more can be seen in respect of objectives expressed in terms of the cost of the occupation of real property and the returns from investment in real property.

Occupiers, particularly owner-occupiers, are not only concerned about the cost in use of their buildings but by careful design, maintenance, refurbishment and use of buildings they can significantly reduce these costs. The Property Services Agency are responsible for the largest urban estate in the U.K. and therefore possess both motivation and the resources necessary to consider this in some depth. Considerable research is taking place, sponsored by various agencies, in the field of cost in use and the development and application of techniques to make the best use of capital and revenue budgets related to the quality of services provided. This is related to a consideration of the effects of the high cost of energy on the urban fabric and the whole subject has been given the name terotechnology.

The investment portfolios considered in Chapters 3 and 5

were managed to meet the requirement of investors subject to varying parameters. The differences between income and liabilities, the relative attractiveness of income or capital growth and the alternative mediums for investment have made the job of the analysts difficult, and the results liable to criticism on various grounds. In the late 1960s techniques were developed in the U.S.A., and in 1972 the Society of Investment Analysts published a report called "The Measurement of Portfolio Performance for Pension Funds". Until very recently the application of these techniques has been confined to the gilt and equity portfolios of Institutions.

11.1.2 Activity Rates

Activity rates vary significantly between the different types of assets and different types of Institutions. The level of activity of private sector funds in the gilt and, particularly the equity, markets is higher than for the public sector pension funds. There are many possible explanations, varying from the brokers' commission being based on turnover to the fact that market activity by the very large public sector pension funds can result in their dealing against their own best interests.

Activity Rates, annual percentage

	Prop.		Gilts		Equities	
	I	P	I	P	I	P
1978	2·8	1·8	81·6	66·7	9·8	12·2
1979	2·6	1·7	90·4	81·2	10·7	13·2
1980	1·5	1·5	79·2	48·2	14·3	11·0
1981	1·6	1·8	80·1	45·5	15·1	14·2
1982	2·2	1·7	86·3	70·7	17·5	18·3
1983	3·1	3·2	76·2	56·4	20·1	22·5

I = Insurance Companies   P = Pension Funds
Source: D.T.C. Money Into Property 1984

A paper read to the British Institute of Actuaries Students' Society in January, 1980, revealed that between 1970 and 1978 three-quarters of all pension fund equity portfolios failed to out-perform the F.T.-Actuaries all-share index before allowing for expenses. According to "The Economist", a report on local authority portfolio performance showed that in 1977–78 only eight out of 78 local authority pension funds out-performed the index. Further, the worst eight performing funds contained five of the six most active dealing funds in gilt-edged investments, which does tend to raise issues such as what are advisers being paid for, since better performance could be achieved by simply holding a typical portfolio.

The estate manager, either in-house or consultant, cannot possess all the conceptual ability, professional skill and technical knowledge to advise across the breadth and depth of the issues involved in the continuing management responsibility for an urban estate. His function is in many ways similar to that of a project manager leading and co-ordinating not just the development period but a continuing role throughout the life of the estate.

This can be seen in a definition of project management adopted by an R.I.C.S. working party, "Leading the planning, monitoring and co-ordinating of a project involving the use or development of land and buildings in accordance with financial or other objectives and controlling the contributions of various professional advisers and others needed to initiate, design, construct and, where appropriate, dispose or manage."

The long-term use of the properties for occupation or investment purposes will only be interrupted on very infrequent occasions for refurbishment or redevelopment. Regular programmed maintenance should ensure that the periods of quiet enjoyment by the occupiers are as long as possible, providing the highest possible returns in actual or notional rent.

On the entry of a property to the portfolio a rigorous maintenance survey should be commissioned to determine a programme of repairs and maintenance and identify opportunities for physical improvements. The property should then be re-inspected in detail at regular intervals, every three to five years, in order to determine the aggregate effects of the individual parts of the maintenance programme and adjust to changing circumstances. All the aspects of the maintenance of the building can be entered in a maintenance manual which is both a record of the technical nature of both the structure and services of the building and a means of monitoring the implementation of minor works and programmed maintenance. This can also be used to forecast costs and so contribute to the positive management of both investment and owner-occupied properties.

11.1.3 General Portfolio Balance

Property has to compete with all the alternative investments for the attention of the fund managers of Insurance Companies and Pension Funds. The table shows a relative stability for property compared with, a fall in the annual purchasers of gilts due to reduced government borrowing, and the increase in overseas securities following the removal of exchange control. Thus external factors appear to be as important as the individual performance of sectors.

Percentage Allocation of Funds

	1978		1981		1983	
	I	P	I	P	I	P
British Government Securities	60	34	40	27	32	35
U.K. Company Securities	18	30	19	28	26	21
Overseas Securities	3	9	12	24	19	18
Indirect Property Involvement	2	5	1	0	1	0
Direct Property Investment	12	13	15	11	12	7
Other	5	9	13	10	10	19
	100	100	100	100	100	100
Total £m	4,431	4,681	7,305	6,841	7,333	7,428

I = Insurance Companies
P = Pension Funds
Source: D.T.C. Money Into Property 1984

Disenchantment with property in 1983 is evident from a fall in Insurance Company and Pension Fund allocations to direct property investment to only 12% and 7%, respectively the lowest for many years, and 1985 showed no improvement. The fall in the stock of property within the general portfolio is shown by Willis Faber's survey of managed funds with average property holdings falling; 1982, 8·8%; 1983, 7·5%; 1984, 7%; due partly to the poorer capital performance.

11.1.4 General Portfolio Performance

The case for the surveyor having some familiarity with the alternative investments to property rests upon his need to be able to explain the role of property in a general portfolio. The case for property rests upon:

Diversity, the wider the range of assets in the general portfolio then the lower the overall risk.

Stability, property has generally shown less volatility than equities and gilts.

Regeneration, property unlike other investments lends itself to holding management rather than, trading management. With the opportunity of the benefits of positive management; though against this the problems of depreciation are not as fully considered as they should be.

Security, life as we know it requires commercial (and agricultural) property, though the rate of change of user requirements is accelerating, this creates both difficulties and opportunities.

Whilst both property shares and property unit trusts offer access to property in a more manageable investment vehicle, the indirectness and the inability to influence its management distinguish these alternatives from direct property investment. The means by which syndication may be applied to large investments £20 million plus in the U.K. is under active consideration.

Property, apart from the ill fated sortie into *objet d'art* by several major pension funds, offers all the psychological attributes of ownership of the physical—an indefinable security. Despite these features (and its elements) real property will only hold a permanent and significant role in institutional portfolios if in the long term it provides an acceptable return. This is conveniently demonstrated by Jones Lang Woottons graph of "Overall Performance Combined Capital and Income", in their quarterly property index.

With the exception of the common catastrophe period of 1973/4, property has until recently performed satisfactorily; between the start of 1982 and mid 1985 property was disappointing.

To those who hold property as a long term asset, rises in capital value whilst welcome are of no real assistance in paying annual liabilities and it must be stated that a substantial part of property's combined capital and income performance is due to the continuous fall in yields from 1976 to 1982. Healey and Baker's prime commercial property yield for shops has fallen from 6½% to 3½% during this period. In other words the Y.P. has increased from 15·38 to 28·57, that is to say an 85% rise in capital value of a type which cannot be repeated indefinitely in the future. In fairness it must be said that the definition of prime has applied to a changing and perhaps reducing number of properties each year.

The implications of this have been demonstrated in two stages by Rowe and Pitman in their March 1984 Property Research, Issue No. 27. The first stage shows the required rental growth per annum from property to equate with gilts.

	Yield %	Annual growth required %
15 year gilts	10·81	—
Shops	3·50	8·25
Offices	4·75	6·97
Industrial	7·00	4·51
Allshare yield	4·51	—
Offices/Allshare yield gap	0·29	—

The second stage converts the rental growth into office rents in principal types of centres:

	Rent per ft²			
	1984 £	1989 £	1994 £	1999 £
City	30	40	59	83
Windsor	16	23	32	44
Epsom	12	17	24	33
Newbury	8	12	16	22
Edinburgh ⎱ Bristol ⎰	6	9	12	17

As Michael Mallinson, the chief surveyor to the Prudential Assurance Company, observed in 1984, "A shop at 3·5% with five yearly reviews must cover some ground if it is to match gilts at 10·5%".

A further problem has been the convention that property shall in fact show 2% over gilts to reflect its "hassle factor". The case against this in 1985 was made by Will Frazer in "Gilt Yields and Property Target Return".

11.2 Property Portfolio Management

The preceding parts of this chapter can only be implemented through the selection, acquisition, development, management and measurement, improvement and disposal of individual properties.

Investors assess these and determine their acquisition and disposal policy between sectors in the light of their expectations. This has been demonstrated by Rowe and Pitmans Property Research Issue No. 26, which analysed a survey of seventy investing institutions who were asked to indicate their preference for each sector in terms of their planned priorities for acquisitions in 1984.

Sector	*Choice*				
	1	2	3	4	No expenditure
Shops	93%	5%	—	—	2%
Offices	14%	49%	22%	3%	12%
Industrials	7%	28%	24%	7%	34%
Agriculture	—	3%	7%	18%	72%

This direction was confirmed by a survey by Debenham Tewson and Chinnocks of 90 funds at the same time. They found that 62% of funds wished to increase their holdings of shops and only 12% were looking for an increase in their industrial holdings.

To the extent that this is achieved and for the period of time the flow of cash is directed in this way and assuming the turnover rates remain as low as 2%; then it would be possible to calculate the rate at which the underlying balance of the investment stock will change.

Rowe and Pitman then went down to the next tier of decision making and analysed the funds requirements within sectors against criteria such as:

rental
location
positive and negative attributes.

The results for industrial property can be shown by ranking the aggregate of first and second choices by the fund managers for the most preferred building type:

Factory with 40% offices	26%
Two storey computer building	20%
Warehouse with 10% offices	16%
Terrace 4 × 5,000 ft²	14%
1960s factory	11%
Retail Warehouse	10%
Terrace 16 × 1,250 ft²	3%

The size of the fund has very significant implication for the size and character of its property sector and hence the nature and scale of the management task:

Pension Funds: Percentage of Assets Held in
Property Investments—1982

Size of fund (£m)	Number in sample	Weighted average* %
0–10	276	8·0
10–20	94	9·3
20–50	128	11·1
50–100	79	11·7
100–200	60	14·2
200–300	22	17·0
300–400	5	23·6
400–500	3	25·0
500–1,000	13	20·5
1,000+	13	27·3
Total	693	20·1

*Weighted by size of pension fund.
Source: D.T.C. Money Into Property 1983

Some interesting trends have emerged, as the funds get larger, the proportion of offices increases and the proportion of industrial property decreases. The largest funds also have a larger proportion of shopping than the smaller funds.

As more research is carried out, so the diversity of funds becomes apparent; this combined with the different approaches to management is likely to result in widely differing performances. It is important that as comparison of performance develops, so knowledge of the underlying reasons develops as fast or faster.

The reasons for the emphasis of Institutions on freeholds rather than long leaseholds was analysed by Bowie in 1984. He identifies that long term building leases, however appropriate they may be when granted have within them the seeds of quite severe problems, as evidenced by substantial marriage value transactions, which is the market's recognition of the price which will be paid to overcome the problems. This is illustrated by Rowe and Pitman's Survey of March 1984, which identified that 37% of funds were less inclined to buy leaseholds, than four years before.

The freeholder, letting directly to occupational tenants, is in a much better position to react to external changes which affect the property and determine the timing and scale of the most effective expenditures to react to depreciation. Whereas, after a number of years the intermediate long leaseholder with a rent geared to a modern ground rent only has a depreciating building with poor rental growth with which to pay it. Hence the capital value of the difference between these two income flows is not very attractive and could become negative.

The renegotiation of the various leases between landlord, ground lessee, tenants and subtenants, in order to redevelop or refurbish is easily frustrated by any one of many factors. Advantageous as these problems may be to professional advisors, long term investors are likely to seek extensive safeguards as ground lessees, with a common refurbishment/redevelopment date built into the occupational tenancies or the freeholder may have to accept a 60 or 65 year ground lease with a significantly lower ground rental or premium.

11.3.1 Investment Properties

Portfolio objectives can only be achieved by acquisition/management/disposal of individual properties. Irrespective of the balance between shops, offices and industrial property, the investment quality of the assets may vary; the age of properties will reflect the date the portfolio was first created, the ratio of new funds and the turnover rate.

Since the late 1970s there has been some evidence of a more rapid ageing process of investment properties with technical obsolescence, leading to social obsolescence, leading to economic obsolescence. This raises the problem as to at what stage and at what scale refurbishment or redevelopment should take place?

The consequence of this has been a debate, but as yet no conclusions for practice, on depreciation, how it should be allowed for in valuation and its differential effect on different types of property. Norman Bowie has suggested that after allowing for depreciation the relationship between buying yields and true yields might be as follows:

	Buying yield %	*True yield* %
Shops	3·5	3·25
Offices	5·0	3·9
Industrials	7·5	5·5

The variation is due to the shorter life of industrials and the higher percentage of site value attributable to shops and offices. This type of market view of depreciation can be distinguished from the formal accounting approach through Standard Statements of Accounting Practice and the R.I.C.S. Assets Valuation Standards Committee.

This discussion has coincided with the lowest U.K. inflation rates for many years, for example in 1984 only 6%. The lower the rate of inflation, the poorer the case for equity investments and the greater the emphasis on current income, as opposed to reversionary income.

The central point of this chapter is the need for the surveyor to be able to move fluently between the mechanisms of the management of individual properties and the broader portfolio issues during a time when the parameters of property investment are changing very rapidly.

A considerable amount of comment on investment properties is in terms of prime property, demonstrated by four principal elements:

The best location for the particular land use.
The best physical structure on the site.
The lease form and income flow should represent best current commercial practice.
The tenant offers the best covenant.

The prime characteristics are not intrinsic to a property investment:

The 100% pitch in a retail location can change as new development occurs.
A building can suffer technical obsolescence as it ages.
Lease clauses develop over time and the best characteristics of one generation are the embarrassment of the next.
The stock market's opinion of trading companies can change quickly for many reasons, altering the quality of the covenant.

In their 1984 Annual Report Richard Ellis analysed a typical institutional portfolio as comprising property of the following types:

prime 21%; standard 61% and secondary 18%

and this terminology was defined by a pattern of yield bands as at March 1983:

Average yield	Offices %	Shops %	Industrials %
Prime	4·8	3·9	6·6
Standard	5·9	5·0	7·9
Secondary	9·6	9·3	11·6
Limit of yields			
Prime	below 5¼%	below 4¼%	below 7¼%
Standard	5¼–7½%	4¼–6%	7¼–10%
Secondary	over 7½%	over 6%	over 10%

They also considered the ranking of each type of property as regards rental growth between 1981 and 1983. Offices reflected the expected order of prime, standard and then secondary, whereas shops showed the reverse order (see Russell Schiller's work in 11.3.2).

Whilst the portfolio as a whole requires management, each individual property requires management and it is in this field that well tried and proven techniques exist:

Physical improvement—extension, refurbishment, redevelopment.
Letting tactics.
Change of use.
Enforcement of covenants.
Legal improvement—covenants, access.
Acquisition/disposal of companies rather than properties.
Tenurial and physical marriage/divorce.
Trading.
Monitoring of maintenance and outgoings.
Lease renegotiation.
Sale and leaseback.

The three principal types of property have particular characteristics which lend themselves to the application of techniques in different ways, these are considered below.

11.3.2 Retail

·The management of enclosed shopping centres requires a spectrum of activity from the monitoring of the cleaning of the public and services areas to the prevention of any form of obsolescence occurring within what is a very specific user. The different views on tenant-mix illustrate the complex and interrelated issues. Specialization has shown itself to be successful. Burlington Arcade demonstrates that covered malls are not the prerogative of the developers of the latter half of the twentieth century and similar facilities can be found in a number of towns developed at the end of the eighteenth century. Much the same theme can be seen in the speciality centre created at Covent Garden. In the design of modern shopping malls the architect creates and distributes patterns of values around the centre, related to pedestrian flows and the access points to the centre and individual units. Tenant-mix is a combination of the range of size of units, location of units the public's perception of specific retailers, and level and basis of rents.

The methods used by individual retailers in their estimation of the rent they can afford to pay, and by surveyors in their feasibility study for the centre, may be very different. They include residual, comparison, using several different techniques, turn-over and rate of return on capital employed. In 1975 a CALUS study of 18 new shopping malls found that open market rent as a percentage of turnover varied from an average of 1·3% for food retailers to an average of 9·6% for clothing and shoes. This implies a higher profit margin on the durable goods and can be seen in the trading policy for edge-of-town superstores. Customers are attracted in by food price competition but the operators devote a growing proportion of space to durable goods and are anxious to see a high proportion of sales of this type. Subject to special terms initially for anchor tenants, when the development is completed the rents for the majority of the units will be pitched at such a level as to ensure that the space will let in a reasonable period of time. If lettings or occupations are slow, a long period during which unlet units blight the centre can be avoided by sensitive hoardings, displays and promotion activity within the centre.

As the first rent-reviews approach, something of a combative atmosphere may develop as the landlord tries to buy-in and re-let to establish open market value and negotiates with the tenant with whom he thinks he can obtain the highest basis. The tenants who compete against each other in their trading can find a common interest in their negotiations with the landlord.

The selection of tenants and the design and size of units is related partly to the function of the centre and partly to its size. It would be truer in some cases to say that the tenants select the shopping centre. The larger the population served, the more emphasis there will be on durable and fashion goods and the greater the proportion of larger units.

It should not be assumed that there is always a case for very specific user clauses. They sometimes arise more from bureaucratic paternalism than a carefully considered commercial view. Large stores are able to change the balance of the goods sold on both an annual cycle and a permanent basis. This can be achieved by both adjustment of the floor areas of departments and relocation of departments within the premises. Tight user clauses can also cause difficulties at rent-reviews, since tenants argue that open market rental value for the specialized use is less than an unqualified use. During 1980 the Office of Fair Trading commenced a preliminary investigation into restrictive user clauses on the basis that they create a quasi-monopoly, distort competition and increase prices. It is likely that legislation will enhance the capacity of the office to investigate both the general nature and particular application of such clauses.

As any vacancies occur this may provide an opportunity either to establish open market rental value prior to a cycle of rent reviews or to alter the size of units, tenant mix and refurbish in response to changing retail requirements. The table of national percentages of floor space and units provides some background on the overall pattern of use and unit size.

The C.A.C.I. Survey of 998 Shopping Centres in Great Britain in 1984 showed the following pattern of occupation:

	% of units	%	% of floor space	%
Bakers, butchers and general provisions	11·3		14·0	
Confectionary, tobacco and newsagents	3·8		2·6	
Convenience goods		15·1		16·6
Clothing and footwear	15·8		12·0	
Household goods	10·2		14·7	
Other non food	23·1		15·0	
Department stores	2·3		14·0	
Comparison goods		51·4		55·7
Restaurants and cafes	7·5		5·3	
Other services	15·0		12·8	
Services		22·5		18·1
Unclassified		3·0		1·8
Vacant		8·0		7·8
		100		100

This together with A.C.O.R.N. (A Classification Of Residential Neighbourhoods) which classifies areas into 38 consumer categories and WORKFORCE, which classifies people working in a given area are examples of the growing range of data systems highly relevant to retail forecasting, location, design and management.

For many years there has been a steady fall in the number of grocery and food retail outlets and the units have got larger. This is illustrated in Chapter 3 in respect of Tesco, and more generally by the table of reductions in shop numbers between 1971 and 1978.

Number of shops	1971 £	1978 £	% change	Sales per shop 1978 £
Co-operatives	16,480	10,370	−37·1	295,950
Multiples	71,162	66,343	− 6·8	315,165
Large independents	83,966	67,886	−19·1	95,911
One-shop independents	338,210	245,000	−27·6	59,105
All traders	509,818	389,599	−23·6	115,426

During the same period that primarily food-orientated superstores were being developed on green field sites, units on industrial estates were undergoing a change of use, for the sale of durable goods and as D.I.Y. centres. The largest covered malls with a regional catchment have as much as 85% or more of their sales area devoted to durable goods, whereas district centres, particularly those serving newer residential areas, are closer to the national average for the use of retail space. Care has to be taken in interpreting the pattern of retail trade in New Towns because of the phased development, the planning philosophy current at the date of the master plan and the impact on existing residential and shopping centres. They show exceptional variations about the national average figures.

Russell Schiller in "Shopping Trends as they affect the Investor" has reached some interesting and surprising conclusions on the relationship between yield and rental growth in different size centres. These are that the largest centres with the lowest yields have enjoyed poorer rental growth than the lower rank towns, (see top of next page).

There are a number of points for concern about retail property:

Will rental growth justify the very low yields on prime properties?

	Population change 71–81 %	Yield %	Rental growth 72–83	81–83
Top 20 towns (e.g. Leeds)	−8·8	3·7	205	9·7
Middle 10 towns (e.g. Brighton)	−4·0	3·9	271	11·0
Lower 8 towns (e.g. Colchester)	3·8	3·9	332˙	5·9
Bottom 11 towns (e.g. Newbury)	18·2	5·0	327	28·6

How will the rate and service charge burden influence rentals?
What will the effects be of electronic shopping?
How much further will the shift to edge of town one stop shopping go?
What depreciation and maintenance problems are likely to arise on large enclosed centres?
What will be the effect of Sunday opening?

Clearly the role of the property manager extends far beyond lease covenants. In 1984 the Henley Centre for Forecasting estimated that there were 375 superstores (sales area of over 25,000 ft^2) and that by 1990 there would be 740, with 110 in Greater London and 130 in the rest of the South East. The rigour and determination of the major groups to achieve their own programmes of store opening are demonstrated in many ways including publications by Tesco and Asda on retail patterns, parking and superstore developments.

At the end of 1981 Asda had 56 stores, Tesco 40, Fine Fare 28, Mainstop 11, and half of all 57 outstanding planning consents were in the south east and south west, making up for the relative under representation compared with the Midlands and the North. At the end of 1984 Asda's total had risen to 83 and that of Tesco's to 61, but the latter had more sites with planning permission.

If the Henley Centre for Forecasting estimate is to be achieved then some tentative conclusions can be made:

If outstanding planning consents are a guide then hypermarkets are likely to be built in the ratio of 1:10 with superstores.
Between 1978 and 1981 the average number of new stores

per annum was 30 to 40. This suggests a faster opening rate, initially through the market leaders and later possibly by a large number of groups.
The expansion of the D.I.Y. groups and their ever widening range of goods may mean that boundaries between super-stores and D.I.Y. warehouses become less clear.

The above will have significant implications for the long term rental growth of established shopping centres and suburban parades which are vulnerable to either the direct effect of a superstore taking customers or the indirect effects such as parking or traffic flows.

11.3.3 Retail Refurbishment

Changes in the pattern of rental trade, due to demographic factors and alternative retail facilities mean that after 10 or 15 years, shopping centres can show signs of obsolescence. This may be physical, in terms of poor weathering of the structural envelope, or difficulty with the maintenance and cleaning of internal finishes, particularly the floor. The design may have provided what are now unsuitable-sized units and the pattern of trade may be different from that which generated the original tenants. Under those circumstances assignment and sub-letting should be encouraged with the aim of maintaining the trading vitality of the centre.

Experience from North America shows very extensive refurbishment expenditures are necessary to retain the viability of their shopping centres. In the U.K. the 1960s centres are now ageing to a similar point. In 1984 the Prudential sold four of such centres for £55 million, using the funds to improve other centres. The purchasers, Pos Tel saw the properties as a way of improving their exposure in the retail market and the necessary improvements providing a good return on capital. The changes in the balance between the different types of shopping centres of 50,000 ft² gross or greater can be seen in the Hillier Parker survey.

	65–69	70–74	75–79	80–82
Open	72%	51%	35%	32%
Covered	20%	21%	14%	23%
Enclosed	8%	28%	51%	45%
Number	84	158	158	88
Area m ft²	10.4	22·4	27·8	14·3

This shows the percentage of type by floor area and the number of centres developed in each period. The rate at which new schemes are opening is now falling rapidly, 1982 was the lowest year since 1968.

The purposes of refurbishment expenditure are related to:

Extension or enclosure, as is in the case of Basildon.
Maintenance of external envelope.
Remedy of building defects, of which water penetration may be a principal cause.
Layout and fitting of circulation areas.
Arrangement of retail space.
Services and energy conservation.
Finishings—walls, floor and ceilings.
Shop fronts and fascias.
Security and safety.

The extent to which this is possible will depend upon negotiations with tenants and it will be necessary to establish what proportion of the cost is attributable to the service charge. This can then lead to the renegotiation of the occupational lease and the institutional finance.

The distribution of new shopping centres in the 1970s varies substantially, consider three towns of relatively similar size:

Nottingham $1 \cdot 27$ m ft^2 in three central schemes
Leeds $1 \cdot 60$ m ft^2 in four central schemes and nine suburban schemes
Bristol $0 \cdot 43$ m ft^2 in five suburban schemes.

Thus in some areas refurbishment may be concentrated on the rearrangement and refitting of older department stores to provide smaller units with a substantial increase in the aggregate of the rentals.

Due to the nature of immediate post war redevelopment, many city councils have a substantial corporate estate including retail property, the 99 year fixed rent ground leases appropriate for their development in the 1950s now offer neither corporate landlord nor institution a suitable basis for the future. For example the site of the Debenhams store in Bristol was originally let to Legal and General for a fixed term expiring in 2056 at a fixed ground rent of £12,500 p.a. The City Council agreed a surrender and renewal in 1982 of a 125 year lease at a peppercorn, for a premium of £1·6 million. This provides a substantial sum for the freeholder, for greater than the value of the fixed income and much deferred reversion. The institution has a 125 year term at a peppercorn as opposed to a 74 year term; very close to a freehold permitting a complete revision of the valuation of the income from the occupying tenant (marriage value released to the advantage of both parties) and encouraging the institution and occupying tenant to enter into negotiations as to the scale of, and contribution towards refurbishment.

11.3.4 Offices

A comprehensive review of the management/investment aspects of offices remains a tantalizing goal. However the reality is that whilst the potential of information technology is known and being demonstrated in isolated cases its effect on the stock of office property and the character and utilization of the new flow is not yet clear.

The indication so far point to:

Concern about long term rental performance, see 11.1.4.

The disposal of somewhat grandiose HQ buildings in London, as much related to changes in industrial management as technology.

The construction of a small number of large specialist decentralized HQs, particularly in the "Western Corridor", orientated to the use of information technology.

Growing awareness of the sensitivity of the work performance of staff to the humidity level of the air flow in air conditioned buildings. The vulnerability of the system to infection by bacteria.

Very considerable interest in "name over the door" self contained low rise office buildings of 10,000 to 30,000 ft².

A lack of interest in being a tenant of several floors in a tower block, particularly "thin" towers.

At the end of 1982 some major funds decided to reduce their holdings of London office properties. The Post Office Staff Superannuation Fund considered the 56% offices content of its £1 billion portfolio too high and favoured a move to 40%. The Prudential was seeking to dispose of two major office blocks.

Central Cross Court, Tottenham Court Road, and 21 Moorfields, Moorgate Station with a combined asking price of the order of £70 million.

An alternative approach was demonstrated earlier that year by Legal and General whose London offices portfolio contained many typical 1960s buildings. In Bucklesbury House, Walbrook E.C.4, with a total of 325,000 ft² they bought out 94,000 ft² of space let to Bankers Trust and Lloyds Bank at historic rents on infrequent reviews, for £10 million. The space was refurbished and let on current rack rental lease terms.

One recent phenomena is the different ways that are being devised to respond to the need for small suites. On greenfield campus sites this can be achieved by a two storey building with columns on a grid in a "high tech" building with provision for multiple access and perimter ring services. By means of easily demountable partitioning and interchangeable walling/glazing panels, suites down to the size of no more than literally a single room can be formed within days with low adaption costs. Such accommodation enjoys substantial car parking, which is a key selling point since the number of separate identities is high, each requiring a car space. This is well demonstrated at Cherry Orchard on Sun Alliance's Kembrey Park Scheme in Swindon.

In the centre of towns, business facilities are being created, often in a refurbished building with degrees of presence providing:

Grades of office space:
Office suites
Individual offices   payable quarterly, monthly
Open plan work stations   or weekly.

A range of office services:
Telephone with switchboard service
Word processing
Typing
Prestel
Telex
Facsimile
24 hour answerphone
Photocopying
Direct mail facilities
Printing
Video
Postal address
Portering
Information centre
Supported by additional accommodation when needed for:
Conferences
Audio visual presentations

Exhibitions
Catering.

The term "office hotel" has been used to describe the above, it requires hotel type on-site management. Users pay an annual membership fee and then an accommodation charge levied perhaps monthly to cover:

traditional rent
rates
traditional service charge items.

There is then an office services tariff for using the facilities that directly support the users operational activities, probably levied weekly. Typically the status of the occupiers will be that of licencees. Thus it is necessary to separate the property from the entreprenurial management company that converts the bare property into a business centre. Such a management company could be jointly owned by a property company and a business equipment company.

In conclusion as greater recognition is given to user require-ments it is helpful to consider the results of research by J.L.W. in 1985 which shows the take up of space by principal types of users in their 50 centre offices survey between 1983 and 1985:

Business sector	South East %	Other %	Total %
Raw Materials	4	1	4
High Tech	22	7	18
Other Trades	16	6	14
Property	4	0	3
Hotels/Catering	2	2	2
Transport and Communica-tions	5	25*	10
Banking and Finance	16	19	17
Insurance	11	10	10
Public Administration	8	15	10

*British Telecom established as a special factor.

11.3.5 Office Refurbishment

Over a period of years the date for the expiry of individual leases within a building may cease to be co-terminous and inhi-bit refurbishment or redevelopment. Negotiations with one or two key tenants can unlock important opportunities, and as St. Quintin observed in their 1979 Report, "In cases where office property requires refurbishment following acquisition by an Institutional client and there are sitting tenants within the building, it requires tact, perseverance and fortitude by the property manager to marry the concept of quiet enjoyment with a need for property portfolio improvement". The high environmental standards now required by tenants mean that buildings originally constructed in the 1920s and 1930s need major refurbishment in order to justify their continued existence in the investment portfolios of the major Institutions.

This is well illustrated by Berkeley Square House, with a gross area of 500,000 ft². This was the largest office building in Europe when constructed in the late 1930s. By 1978 there were 67 tenancies including major international companies. Obtaining comprehensive vacant possession would have been prohibitively expensive and decanting the tenants impractical due to the needs for extensive vertical access. The only alternative was an in-situ approach and the principal elements were as follows:

Central heating, new boiler house (24 m B.T.U.) ring main on roof and drilling throughout the building for new flow and return pipes. Replacement radiators combined with new tinted double glazed aluminium window; installation by working from external cradles behind a temporary screen providing 1 metre of internal working space.

False ceilings including new electrical wiring and lighting, possible only because of the lofty ceilings of the 1930s. Common parts: W.C. cores, and plant rooms, kitchenettes, staircases, lifts, lobbies and halls, all refurbished or renewed, whilst maintaining an operating building, and making more efficient use of space.

The main problems were those of managing the tenants, the contractors and the users of the building, particularly the safety of the occupiers during the works. Maximum use had to be made of evening and weekend work and the entire project depended upon the cohesiveness of the team of:

house staff
joint contractors (Laing/Matthew Hall partnership)
professional team
project manager (J.L.W.)

The project managers were based in the building and were able to respond to any problems immediately throughout the two and a half year project period. During this time 100,000 ft^2 of space was bought in from tenants in order to enhance the revenue earning potential of the capital works.

In a building of similar size, The Adelphi, fronting the Embankment, constructed in 1938, Town and City spent £20 million during 15 months on a comprehensive refurbishment. A slightly smaller building Triton Court, owned by the Royal London Insurance Society, was subject to a spectacular refurbishment during 1983/84. The result was 200,000 ft^2 of lettable space together with an attrium formed by glazing over a vast lightwell providing the landscaped hanging gardens ambience of the newest office buildings.

It has been suggested that the strength of the older property companies, their properties held at historic cost may become their weakness. Unless they can find substantial sums each year for modernization the yields on the annual capitalization of incomes are likely to rise. Between 1973 and 1984 Land Securities has been running a "closed portfolio" strategy. Investing fresh money in adjacent properties and buying in intermediate interests rather than new areas. As a consequence, the portfolio is geared to large blocks of higher cost city centre property, with low exposure to new growth areas in the Home Counties. Total debt has been run down consistently, and now stands at under 10% of assets. Ten years ago, it equalled 49% of assets.

The combination of these two factors has obliged the group to use equity issues or asset sales to generate funds. Between 1975 and 1984, Land Securities raised £126 million from two rights issues, and £275 million from property disposal.

Perhaps a big debenture issue is the only way to break the vicious circle of rising operating expense, debt reduction and property sales. But the group might prove unable to earn enough on the fresh capital to cover the costs of the debt, hence threatening the buoyancy of earnings.

Buildings constructed during the 1950s and 1960s are also now being subjected to major refurbishment, requiring quite different techniques to interwar buildings. Most refurbishment requires the creation of a false ceiling for services and lighting and a false floor or screed for laying three core conduit to service boxes on a suitable grid. Many 1960s buildings fail a feasibility study because the net floor to ceiling height remaining is inadequate to meet building regulation requirements. The question which must be asked with greater care, determination and analysis is how is the potential obsolescence of this type of building being reflected in the capitalization of the current income?

Richard Ellis have, as a model, considered an office building in the West End of 10,000 ft² constructed in the 1960s. This was subject in 1970 to a minor refurbishment (improvements to common parts and suspended ceilings) and 1980 (air conditioning, major refitting of offices and common parts); the rental consequences were as follows:

Condition	1960	1970	1980	1984
Original building	£1·50 ft²	£3·50 ft²	£11 ft²	£12 ft²
Building + 1970 works	—	£5·50	£13·50	£14·50
Building + 1980 works	—	—	£16·25	£18·00

In each case the cost of the refurbishment together with the rental loss were significantly less than the increase in capital value, at the date of the works, and in 1984 the effect of the capital expenditures were both still magnified in the capital value.

The change in the importance of refurbishment is illustrated by the fact that in the City, at the end of 1982 only 12% of newly started schemes were refurbishments, one year later the figure had risen to 75%.

11.3.6 Industrial

Older industrial properties suffer from many defects that make them unattractive to the major institutions, for example:

Over developed site.
Poor access for heavy vehicles.
Restricted parking and manoeuvring space.
Restricted circulation.
Inflexible layout for users.
Poor insulation, particularly roofs.
High maintenance costs, particularly roofs.
Drainage and maintenance problems in valley gutters.
Poor services.
Difficult subdivision.
Poor appearance.

All the above create management problems and restrict rental growth and changes to meet the operational needs of users.

The pre 1940s north light building, tends to be a greater problem than the 1960s industrial shed, the latter was improved during the 1970s. These properties occur in greater percentages in the portfolios of the smaller funds.

King and Cos survey of vacant space shows an increase from 1979 of 54 million ft² to a peak of 178 million ft² in 1983, falling to 153 million ft² in 1984. The greatest fall was in Avon/ South-West region where a 20% reduction took warehousing down to 3·19 million ft². The survey excluded multi-storey mills and semi derelict property. The vacant space arises from three principal reasons:

Redundancies resulting in surplus space.
Obsolete property—unlikely to ever let again.
New units not yet let.

In 1984, Hillier Parker's survey of industrial voids among 39 funds holding £1 billion of industrial property showed the latter had become serious. They reported that of those developments completed in the last 12 months, 34% were vacant, compared with only 10% at the same time last year. This is confirmed by the answers to the following questions asked of institutional funds:

Average speed of letting	1983	1984
now	9·1 months	12·1 months
a year ago	6·7 months	12·4 months

By the early 1980s a new type of multi-use building began to appear very often described as a "high tech" within a science or business park campus, with distinctive features:

Walls on a steel frame, with hook on, interchangeable glazing or infill panels.
Highly insulated flat roof on deep lattice beams, capable of taking all services with ready access.
A perimeter service trench around the building, enabling services to be tapped at any point.
Toilets and stairs in external moveable modules.
Atrium bays within the building permitting daylight walls/ courtyards to be adjusted.
Easily installed mezzanine floors.
High landscape environment with extensive parking.
Selective tenant mix.

The challenge these represent to the development industry has been recognized by their mismatch with the use classes order, which was subject to review in 1985.

11.3.7 Overseas Property

During the 1960s a small number of firms pioneered overseas offices. One of the first of these Jones Lang Wootton now has 23 offices in 11 countries and Richard Ellis has 25 offices in a similar number of countries.

The early 1970s witnessed an invasion of the major E.E.C. countries by British developers and professional advisers but the collapse of the commercial property market, with serious over-supply of offices in the capital cities was as severe in Europe as in the U.K. This was followed by a period of relative inactivity which has now been replaced by a more analytical and sympathetic involvement by firms acting on behalf of both their U.K. and international client base in Europe, America and Australasia.

In many countries there are administrative procedures regulating the investment of funds by non-nationals and the transfer of income and capital is subject to a complex tax-treaty network and arrangements for double taxation relief. In the other major countries in the E.E.C. the transfer of land is subject to onerous registration charges which tend to discourage land transactions, and there is a less monolithic involvement by the Institutions.

The relaxation of U.K. exchange control coupled with generally higher overseas yields has sharpened awareness of opportunities, though changes in exchange rates distort the real characteristics of the performance of property investments in different countries. Most factors in an investment equation stem from politics and economics and there remains the conundrum that many properties in the U.K., the country with the lowest rate of economic growth, show some of the best capital appreciation.

Whilst overseas activity by U.K.-based practices was originally based on development and investment, the resulting portfolios required management in a form acceptable to the U.K. Institutions. Slowly the type of work carried out by professional offices overseas is becoming more balanced, including acting on behalf of the occupational interests of both domestic and international companies.

In France, Germany and Holland commercial leases generally place fewer obligations on the tenants and are either for shorter periods than in the U.K. or contain a tenant's option to break at intervals similar to or shorter than U.K. rent-reviews. This, together with annual indexation based on costs, results in a less sharply-stepped income profile than with a typical U.K. property investment. The relationship between indexed rent and open market rent influences tenants in the exercise of their frequent options to break.

Debenham Tewsons survey of Money into Property in 1983 found that the U.S.A. accounted for 69% by value and offices 71% by use, with industrials only 1%. Clearly the U.S.A. dominates overseas property investment, it is therefore important to recognize some major differences both in terms of the market and property management:

The range of investment opportunities is wider, including hotels and residential property.

The yields tend to be higher.

The life cycle of buildings tends to be shorter.

The construction period is significantly shorter.

Tenants are in a stronger position and tend to occupy for shorter periods.

Occupation rights are a product to be marketed, in a highly competitive environment.

Landlords tend to let on a gross basis covering all costs associated with occupation up to specified "stops", tenants paying an "excess" in future years if necessary.

Pension funds beneficiaries enjoy greater rights to disclosure.

Generous Tax depreciation.

Large high value properties are managed in a more positive and responsive manner:

rapid response to maintenance and repair by in-house management personal regular refurbishment.

greater use of computer technology in the management of buildings.

Not all aspects of the U.S. market are successful, between March 1981 and September 1985, Coldwell Banker's office vacancy index rose from 3·8% of the stock to 16·5%.

The management of the growing number of portfolios with a significant content of overseas property requires surveyors prepared to think outside the relatively narrow and restrictive domestic institutional structure and to assimilate quite new parameters in the exercise of their estate management skills. In so doing they may well find this provides the unexpected benefit of a new perspective on their property activities in the U.K.

11.4.1 Investment Performance

The last half of the 1970s saw the creation of several indices reflecting various features of the property investment market. Rental and capital value surveys have become more sophisticated, with weighted sampling on a regional basis for different types of property, and these have formed the base for property portfolio performance indices.

The concept of an index is simply the conversion of a measure of some quantifiable feature in a chosen base year to 100, for ease of comparison. The cost of living index is familiar, the overall change in the cost of a selected, weighted basket of the typical family's budget. This index can be interpreted in a number of ways to give different annual rates of inflation:

Year-on-year (the 12 months that have just elapsed).
Financial year.
Calendar year.
Average monthly, forward (the next 12 months, assuming the particular month is representative of the year to come).
Monthly extrapolated (the future 12 months, assuming the trend of the last few months still continues).

In a typical year of changing monthly figures each of the above is likely to give a different answer, something which has not escaped the attention of politicians.

Within the investment market it is easy to assume that since representative daily published figures of the performance of gilts and equities exist, any property performance figures are equally representative and authoritative.

For many years leading agents have produced annual reports on aspects of the commercial and industrial property markets. As clients' requirements have become more sophisticated and competition for investment work more intense, so the previously rather bland reports have become more specialized vehicles for demonstrating the analytical skills of agents. Some of the statistical sampling problems can be avoided by seeking opinions of the direction of change in market indicators rather than their absolute level, and this type of poll is complementary to quantitative surveys of rental and capital values. A comprehensive property portfolio performance index devised from market surveys requires statistical, sampling and investment analysis techniques not normally reflected in the philosophy or expertise of the surveying profession, which has never had much of a liking for applied statistics. This has led to growth in the use of specialist research agencies and a greater awareness of the role of technical support. One of the incidental results is that only a few provincial partnerships are now likely to be in a position to offer comprehensive in-house investment advice comparable to that available from the resources of major London practices.

Any portfolio at a particular date has its own unique mix of characteristics; type of property, age, location, tenants, value, size, tenure and pattern of rent-reviews. There is a considerable problem in carrying out a statistical survey of every fund's holdings in order to produce a suitably weighted "warts and all" average current portfolio. The warts would include secondary investments, vacant property, the effects of reviews, property held with the hope of marriage value, essential cash balances, and proceeds awaiting re-investment, development properties, partial voids and unallocated service charges.

11.4.2 Indices

The following are the main published indices, based upon a report by Rowe and Pitman in 1983.

CAPITAL GROWTH INDICES

J.L.W. PROPERTY INDEX	This index is based upon the increase in value of the properties held in the J.L.W. Property Index Portfolio. The portfolio is designed and managed to represent a typical institutional portfolio in terms of the distribution of capital value by region and use. New monies are invested annually at a constant proportion of the global amount of money going into property. As an actual portfolio it is actively managed and properties are subject to further improvement, regearing etc. and may be sold. These decisions are largely those of the clients so the "management" of the fund is to some extent independent of J.L.W. All the properties are known to J.L.W. who value quarterly. The index is published in February, May, August and November. Note that Agricultural Property is included in the All Property Index. Shops 29%, Offices 48%, Industrial 18%, Agriculture 5%

J.L.W. AGGRE-GATE FUND INDEX

The J.L.W. Aggregate Fund Index represents the sum total of all funds within J.L.W.'s Property Performance and Analysis Service. This includes funds advised by J.L.W. and funds managed and valued by others. The Fund consists of properties that are valued monthly, quarterly and annually. As the bulk are valued on the March quarter day, the Aggregate Fund Index and the statistics quoted are based solely on that set of properties, although of course the total Fund is considerably larger. The Fund is increasing in size as more portfolios are processed and J.L.W. will not enter data into the system until they are sure of its authenticity and accuracy. This data has been produced as part of a comprehensive performance measurement service and has not been published in index form before, although we hope that J.L.W. will make available to us future data to update our index on a regular basis. Note that Agricultural, Miscellaneous and Shops with an Office content are included in the All Property Index.

Shops 15%, Offices/Shops 17%, Offices 33%, Industrial 20%, Other 15%

MICHAEL LAURIE/ E.I.U. CAPITAL VALUE INDEX

As described in the Rental Growth Index Table below, this index is based upon the views of local agents of the rental values of average institutional-type properties within their areas. These rental values are then capitalized, again using an average prime yield for each sector. For instance, in their latest valuation, the following capitalizing rates were applied: Shops—5%, Offices—5·5%, Industrial—7%. A half-yearly index is produced but only published annually in July. The data is selected from 17 regional centres and the data is weighted to reflect institutional views. Currently London and the South East carry a 40% weighting whilst the 8 remaining regions have weightings ranging from 5–15% each.

Shops 33·3%, Offices 33·3%, Industrial 33·3%

MICHAEL LAURIE E.I.U. PROPERTY PERFORMANCE INDEX

This index is another based upon the performance of an aggregate fund, made up of all the subscribers to the service. Of all the portfolios discussed in this paper, it is the largest and is estimated to represent 25% of current institutional property holdings. The portfolio covers a wide selection of property and is by no means confined to prime property alone. Michael Laurie have no input by way of valuation, these being done by the subscribers' own in-house valuers or independent firms. The valuation date is 31 December but in some cases, where a portfolio is valued at another date, the data has to be adjusted to comply. A quarterly index is produced by interpolation but is only published annually in July.
Shops 27%, Offices 55%, Industrial 18%

RICHARD ELLIS PROPERTY MARKET INDICATORS

This index, whilst similar to the two other aggregate fund indices, certainly in size, differs in one essential characteristic. Constituent properties, which are drawn from over 30 portfolios where Richard Ellis act in some professional manner, must conform to certain criteria. Property has to be institutional but excludes all properties which have, between the two year end valuation dates, been refurbishments or developments; or are 50 year or less leasehold interests, or had further capital investment or suffered any change in the lease structure which may have affected capital or rental values. Weighting of the portfolio by sector and region is also designed to reflect general institutional preferences—71·6% by value lies in the City, Greater London and the South East. Presently no Agricultural property is measured. Valuations are carried out at/or around the March quarter date but not all the properties are valued by Richard Ellis. This index is published in September.
Shops 24%, Offices 49%, Industrial 27%

RENTAL GROWTH INDICES

J.L.W. PROPERTY INDEX

This index is based upon the increase in estimated rental values of the properties held in the J.L.W. Property Index Portfolio. The portfolio is designed and managed to represent a typical institutional portfolio in terms of the distribution of capital value by region and use. New monies are invested annually at a constant proportion of the global amount of going into property. As an actual portfolio it is actively managed and properties are subject to further improvement, regearing etc. and may be sold. These decisions are largely those of the clients so the "management" of the fund is to some extent independent of J.L.W. All the properties are known to J.L.W. who value quarterly. The index is published in February, May, August and November. Note that Agricultural Property is included in the All Property Index. Shops 29%, Offices 48%, Industrial 18%, Agricultural 5%

INVESTORS' CHRONICLE/ HILLIER PARKER MAY & ROWDEN RENT INDEX

The concept of this index differs from the one above. A sample of rents (Rent Points) is taken from all regions of the country and these are weighted to reflect an "institutional" portfolio. Rental values are estimated by the firm assuming a standard shop unit in the 100% pitch, new offices of over 20,000 sq ft in the provinces but an average suite of about 5,000 sq ft in Central London and new industrial units of 15,000 sq ft, in prime locations at each Rent Point. The weighting of the portfolio was arrived at after a survey and analysis of Pension Funds, Unit Trusts and Insurance Companies and is therefore intended to be an average "institutional" portfolio. The valuations are carried out half-yearly, as at 1 May and 1 November and the index is published later each month. Shops 30%, Offices 45%, Industrial 25%

HEALEY AND BAKER RENTAL GROWTH INDEX

H. & B. employ much the same concept as the H.P.M.R. Index, assuming prime "institutional" property in the 100% locations. A wide sample of generally accepted institutional towns is selected, and an index calculated for each location. These indices are then aggregated and averaged to form an index for each sector. This is an essential difference to

H.P.M.R.'s index, for it assumes that rental growth in any location is equally important to any other. Rental values are estimated by the firm half-yearly as at 1 June and 1 December and the index is published in July and February.

MICHAEL LAURIE/ E.I.U. AVERAGE RENT INDEX

In the course of calculating their Capital Value Index, rental values are collected from a number of towns. These values are the opinions of local agents and are only intended as a general reflection of average rents being achieved. The data is collected in January but local agents are asked to supply values for the previous July. Michael Laurie do not publish an index as such but an average rent weighted to reflect the institutional view of each rent point is calculated and this data has been used to create the R. & P. Adjusted Index.

Shops 33·3%, Offices 33·3%, Industrial 33·3%

RICHARD ELLIS PROPERTY MARKET INDICATORS

This measures the annual increase in rental values of selected institutional property drawn from over 30 portfolios where Richard Ellis act in some manner. Rental value increases are intended to reflect changes in supply and demand alone for the reasons set out in the Capital Growth Index Table above. Valuations are similarly carried out annual at/or around the March Quarter date. The weighting of the index by regions also reflects general institutional preferences—71·6% by value is located in the City, Greater London and the South East.

Shops 20%, Offices 47%, Industrial 33%

R.I.C.S./ INSTITUTE OF ACTUARIES

A panel's opinion of rental movements for a typical unit of office accommodation in London and major provincial centres.

In 1984 the four leading practices:
  Richard Ellis
  Healey and Baker
  Hillier Parker
  Jones Lang Wootton

combined to produce a joint Property Market Index, with a sample size of £4 billion. The scheme includes capital and rental performance of six subsections—shops, offices, industrial and warehouses, agricultural, development and refurbishment properties, and actively managed properties. The problem of the classification of retail warehouses is resolved by the basis of the rent review clause which tend to be either retail or warehouse based. Initially the index will be published annually by an independent agency in parallel with the firms own individual existing publications. At a later stage more contribution may join and firms may suspend their own individual indices. At the end of 1984 six other practices announced an investment property data bank, backed by £7 billion of property portfolios, to be published quarterly. In 1985 both groups agreed to collaborate under the auspices of the R.I.C.S. The firms' initiative represents an important and significant stage in the development of the profession, though competing indices may be counter productive.

The property type balance of a portfolio is only the first step in its analysis. The dynamics only become apparent upon consideration of the relative youth or maturity of the fund, one aspect of this can be illustrated by comparing the most desired portfolio balance of 1972, referred to in Chapter 3:

shops 20%   offices 70%   industrials 10%

with say the 1978 Investors' Chronicle/Hillier Parker balance of:

shops 30%   offices 45%   industrials 25%

then the implications for two rather different types of funds (assuming values did not change between 1972 and 1978) can be shown by analysis of a reasonably large and established property fund of £100 million in 1972 growing at a rate of £8 million per annum and a relatively small new fund in 1972 of £20 million growing at a rate of £4 million per annum. The established fund, growing at £8 million per annum:

	Shops £m	Offices £m	Industrials £m	Totals £m
1972 split	20	70	10	100
1978 split	44	67	37	148
Portfolio change	+24	−3	+27	+48

It would be impossible to move from one desired portfolio in 1972 to the other desired portfolio in 1978 without disposals.

The new fund, growing at £4 million per annum:

	Shops £m	Offices £m	Industrials £m	Totals £m
1972 split	4	14	2	20
1978 split	13	20	11	44
Portfolio change	+9	+6	+9	+24

In this case the relatively new and faster-growing fund is lighter on its feet, and also operating in a market where there is a greater variety of suitable investment properties. The actual figures are not of great importance, what matters is the trend implication of the need for a disposal policy in the first case.

11.4.3 Measuring Performance

Any portfolio performance measuring system needs to try and provide for the following:

To measure past performance.
To measure the levels of risk associated with that performance.
To identify whether the performance can be considered to be good or bad, in both property and general investment terms.
To explain the reasons for the performance and to identify the critical factors which need to be tackled to improve performance.
To provide a basis for taking a view as to likely future performance and risk.
To enable the portfolio to be balanced and structured to meet the particular characteristics and objectives of individual funds.
To enable property portfolios to be compared with other investments such as gilts and equities.

In order to do this the agency involved requires detailed information about the clients portfolio:

Historic cash flows for each property.
Regular capital revaluations.
Specific information from the management record systems (legal, physical, financial, etc.).

Together with an appropriate set of measuring indices, both property based and general.

Performance is measured in the traditional way, by finding out the rate of return which equates the flow of revenues to the flow of costs, taking into account the timing of both receipts and costs.

The Hillier Parker Portfolio Analysis System presents a comprehensive view of the portfolio through ten schedules:

Schedule 1   Structure of portfolio.
            2   Geographical spread by capital value.
            3   Anticipated income over the next ten years.
            4   Historic rental income growth.
            5   Historic rental value growth.
            6   Historic capital value growth.
            7   Internal rate of return.
            8   Long term performance.
            9   Comparison of rental growth with I.C.H.P. index.
         10   Comparison with other investments.

Consideration of the above enables the experienced investment surveyor to prepare a report and hence portfolio strategy which in broad terms proposes future tenure sector and geographical activity and in narrow terms identifies properties which have performed badly, the causes and the remedies.

The technical procedure can be undertaken on either a money weighted (the discount rate which equates the initial outlay and cash flows at the dates they occur to the final value of the investment) or time weighted (the geometric mean of the returns in each period of time under consideration) rate of return. The latter is to be preferred and most published indices are on that basis.

The time period over which performance is measured affects the annual rate of return and also the relative merits of one sector or sub-sector of a portfolio compared with another.

The annual rate of return is not the sole criteria upon which judgment should be made. The risk of not achieving this can be measured by considering the volatility at intermediate dates during the period of study. Calculation of the standard deviation enables the risk to be associated with the yield of each sub-sector. Thus acquisitions and disposals can be assessed both in terms of individual properties and the effect on the overall portfolio financial balance as regards yield and risk. A number of the above points are illustrated by the table of Total Returns of Sectors published by Jones Lang Wootton.

11.4.4 The Future

The assumptions underlying portfolio performance measurement can be subject to a number of criticisms.

The extent to which valuations are proved in the market place is the most serious, since if these are not accurate, conclusions based upon quarterly, half yearly or annual analyis will not command respect. The small percentage turnover in property funds provides an inadequate basis to test the integrity of the valuations.

The relevance of the classification of property into categories for the purpose of analysis is being challenged by the nature of high technology buildings. A typical computer company taking a unit on an industrial estate requires about 25% offices, 15% testing or research space which looks like offices, 30% light assembly, 20% storage. Such a unit is much more akin to the offices sector, though located on an industrial estate.

Different investors have different requirements and liabilities and so need to pursue different investment policies, even if their portfolio property type balance appears similar to the index. Where the subject portfolio has a different property profile to the index then though analysis across the whole portfolio may not be suitable, sub-sector analysis will still be possible which can then be adjusted to equate with the property type balance of the subject portfolio.

Whatever the merits, mechanism and historical conclusions which can be drawn from a study of past performance, including the significant improvements in methodology since the late 1970s, the only reason for making an investment is a future expectation of an income flow. Hence property performance analysis leads inevitably to the estimation of future changes in the factors influencing values. These fall into two categories national macro economic factors and local factors related to individual properties and their environs. Study of the former is relatively well advanced in general economic models. This is reflected in the success of Hillier Parker's shop and industrial rental projections, which over a few years have been successful.

The quantitative analysis of factors influencing values locally is still in its infancy. Short term supply aspects, that is to say land and property availability—local authority and practices registers of space—are widely reported.

The retail sector has made more progress than other sectors due to the significance of population, social composition and earning statistics. This can be illustrated by the recognition given to Cathedral towns in 1982/3. The combination of a relatively wealthy population plus tourism with often a restricted central area shopping policy was seen as generating long term rental growth, as a result yields fell particularly sharply.

As property performance measurement achieves some maturity during the latter half of the 1980s it is likely that increasing attention will be paid to the search for an analytical basis to estimate future changes in property values.

It would be wrong to directly equate the performance of the property portfolio with the performance of the managers (or even the performance of the trustees). For example a property manager might hold back from the market, not using his allocation and permitting money to temporarily be used in another sector of the portfolio, to better effect; or the trustees might delay or frustrate a particular property proposal.

11.5.1 Owner Occupation

Owner occupation arises either through necessity, where property is specialized and not capable of being provided by an investment market economy; or through choice, the latter can arise through the client seeking a new building, typically provided by developers, but with detailing, quality or features which meet user requirements or by the purchase of a second-hand building with vacant possession. In the early 1980s the fall in the real value of properties except shops, resulted in a growth in the purchase of smaller office buildings and industrials for owner occupation. A final group of owner-occupiers arises from tenants purchasing their freehold or long leasehold, this was temporarily accelerated by the disposals by public sector bodies. Somewhat related to the above is a tenant who enters into a pre-let agreement of an entire building early in the construction period, exerting considerable influence on elements of the structure, including arrangements to "rent-alize" additional items of capital expenditure.

Owner occupiers are concerned with the long term costs of occupation. Most of these are determined at the stages of design and specification of construction detailing and services. Despite the highest standards at these stages it will be necessary to monitor carefully the exercise of construction skills and the quality of components to ensure that the brief has been properly executed. The consequences are apparent to surveyors who regularly have the opportunity to inspect offices built for owner-occupation and those built for leasing. In the latter case, the comprehensive service charges paid by tenants result in a tenuous link between those responsible for design and project management, and the tenants bearing the financial responsibility for the long-term consequences through service charges, of the maintenance and use of the building.

Owner occupiers of properties which are normally let or sold in the market place can readily adopt market evidence so that each trading "profit centre" can be charged a notional or actual rent on an equitable basis. Indeed one trading manager of a profit centre is known to have been so insensed by the notional rent which the group surveyor wished to charge, that he instructed his own consultant surveyor to negotiate the notional rental. Thus user decisions are tested in the rental market place. In capital terms, values are important as the security behind the loans raised to promote business activity, and A.V.S.C. requirements have reinforced the need for regular revaluations. Increasingly, owner-occupiers form a property holding subsidiary which assesses their interests against market interest and advises upon redevelopment of other matters which would otherwise be masked by operational requirements.

Operational activities in the public sector can be grouped together in decreasing comparability with the private sector:

Industries—Oil
          Mines
          New Towns
          Royal Ordnance Factories (privatized 1986)
          English Estates
          Development Corporations
Utilities   —Telecom (privatized 1985)
          Gas (privatized 1986)
          Electricity
          Post
          Railways
Services —Health
          Education
          Welfare
          Defence
          Housing.

Policies of privatization have since 1979 sought to:

Transfer elements to the private sector as trading operations.
Dispose of surplus assets.

Introduce shadow rents to reflect the costs of occupation. Undertake capital valuations, distinguishing replacement cost and open market value.

This, together with work on the annual equivalent cost of providing units of accommodation, and the design of monitoring and audit systems have introduced a new discipline to the use of property by the public sector.

11.5.2 Maintenance

The object of maintenance is to keep a building in a condition to fulfil its function within broad financial and economic criteria. At the heart of this is the balancing of the technically possible with the financially prudent. It is possible to extend the structural life of a building indefinitely, well beyond the point of financial profitability for its current use and the economic and social life of the building in terms of alternative uses of the building or its site.

Building surveyors have acquired an enviable skill in the technology of maintenance. However their skill needs to be used in conjunction with quantity surveyors, whose impact on the birth of the building and the estate manager concerned with the overall health of the property, represent the wider decision making environment.

The term "Terotechnology" has been used to embrace the life cycle requirements of buildings, "A combination of management, financial engineering and other practices applied to physical assets in pursuit of economic life cycle costs. It is concerned with the specification and design for reliability and ease of maintenance of plant, machinery, equipment, buildings and structures with their installation, commissioning maintenance, modification and replacement and with feed back of information on design, performance and costs. It is a technology that takes into account the marketing and observance of design—maintenance—cost practice of all assets, the conservation of resources and the promotion of controlled and calculated life span of assets as against built in or unpredictable obsolescence."

With experience of the performance of alternative components and service installations, cost in use techniques can be used at the design stage to ensure that at that date the balance between capital costs and annual costs results in an acceptable cost over the projected life of the building. Changes in the real cost of energy, the availability of materials and the relationships between costs of material and labour mean that we are trying to solve problems in the maintenance and use of existing buildings which could not have been foreseen at the design stage. Further, changes in the cost of money during the life of building from that prevailing at the date of the design stage mean that the present value calculations used to bring all the costs to a common base year shift the significance of capital and annual payments. Thus whatever the developments in terotechnology, maintenance will continue to be a major activity in the construction industry, currently representing over a third of its total output, and estate managers are part of the team acting for the client in the planning and management of the maintenance. In some cases direct labour is involved; the practical aspects of direct and contract labour have become partially obscured by political issues. It is more a question of "horses for courses" than either system possessing different intrinsic qualities; in time of tightening maintenance budgets the estate manager who relies upon direct labour should ensure that he is well versed in all aspects of industrial relations and employment protection legislation.

The need for maintenance can arise from:

Servicing—planned on a regular cycle, most of the activities involving cleaning of internal and external elements of the structure and service facilities.

Rectification—a response to inherent defects in the design, construction or installation stages of the building process. This provides an opportunity to "trade off" current capital expenditure against future maintenance costs. To the extent that the defects were avoidable this supports the need for more effective management and specification during the project and may have implications for the liability of those involved in the work.

Replacement—both building systems and materials are subject to attack from a variety of sources (user, environmental, physical stress, chemical and biological). The selection of the most appropriate solution requires a breadth of view of the likely prospects for the building.

A possible fourth category is renovation, but this constitutes the interface with improvement and refurbishment, the relevance to which in respect of particular types of properties has been considered under 11.3.1.

The response to the need for maintenance can be classified as:

Planned preventative maintenance—work designed to prevent failure or defect occurring.
Planned corrective maintenance—work in order to restore a facility to an acceptable standard.
Unplanned maintenance—response to unforeseen failure or damage due to external factors.

In practice something between the first two categories may be more realistic with appropriate cycles of inspection for different purposes grouped together to strike the best balance between the costs of inspection and preventation compared with repair keeping across a large estate can result in extensive maintenance cost records. The effective analysis of which may require skills not readily found amongst those involved in the day to day management of the estate.

The R.I.C.S. Building Maintenance Cost Information Service has had considerable success in improving communication between maintenance managers, property occupiers and the design team. Its publications include:

Building Maintenance Price Book, an annual guide for estimating building maintenance work across all the trades.
Briefing of Maintenance Costs, a quarterly commentary on costs; with indices including forecasts over the next 12 months.
Average Occupancy Costs, an analysis across a range of building types.
Energy Consumption, an analysis of the use and cost of energy across a range of building types.

A new report form for property occupancy costs was published in 1985, which it is hoped will encourage subscribers to create a sufficiently large data bank. These developments if carried to conclusion will mean owner-occupiers should be able to assess performance in a similar way to investors.

Their objectives will be assisted by the work of the Building Research Establishment. Their publication "Performance Specifications for Whole Buildings" seeks to bring together all the elements of a building:

Structural
Environmental and Services
Running Costs
Safety and Security
Layout and User

as a brief for the designer and to show the roles and relationships between those various interests that contribute to the execution of the brief.

In recognition of the need for an integrated and comprehensive approach to the physical management of buildings, the R.I.C.S. published a practice note on "Building Management Manuals" in 1981. The contents of which should refer to:

General Information
  brief description
  future extension arrangements
  structural limitations
  service installations
  responsibilities during defects period
  insurance
  public utilities
  demolition constraints
Day to Day Administration
  maintenance, contracts and approvals
  meter controls
  environmental control
  rights over the property
  accessability
  user requirements
Security
Safety
  fire, protection and escape
  emergency procedures
Housekeeping/Maintenance
  functions and cycles of activity
  planned maintenance
  emergency repairs
Appendix
  plans
  consents
  manufacturers leaflets
  project team and sub contractors
  maintenance.

The way these may be co-ordinated together is shown by W.I.M.S. (Works information and management system) developed by the D.H.S.S., consisting of eight modules:

Property—property management data base.
Condition Appraisal—the condition of the building with estimates of the upgrading costs in the longer term.

Annual Maintenance—currently planned maintenance and
analysis of workload over a shorter term.
Assets Management.
Stock/Purchase Order.
Energy Management
Redecoration.
Budget Commitment Account.

11.5.3 Energy Management

Over the last few years substantial field trials have been undertaken by major property users encouraged by the Department
of Energy including:

W. H. Smith in Rotherham who have reduced energy costs
from £10 m^2 to £6 m^2 per annum for an extra capital cost
of £4,500, giving a pay back over 18 months.
Rank Leisure in Hounslow who used an infra red sensor to
monitor CO^2 in the ventilation exhaust and adjusted rate
of air change to reflect actual occupancy, with a 20% saving
in energy cost.
Tesco at Chelmsford who estimate that a 10% saving in
energy through Monitoring and Targeting systems would be
equivalent to a 4% to 5% increase in net profit.
Local authorities who have installed environment and activity programmed switches on lighting circuits with savings
in excess of 40%.

In the case of new building substantial opportunities exist
for the design of an integrated system of energy management
in the design of the building and the selection, installation
and use of the services. However more frequently the property
manager will be concerned with seeking to reduce the energy
used in an existing building and will be looking for a relatively
short payback period on the capital cost. For example in the
P.S.A. there has been some very real success in energy conservation. By 1978/79 fuel consumption had fallen to two-thirds
of the 1972/73 level. This was achieved by prudent action by
the occupiers, capital expenditure, improved plant management and a rigorous purchasing policy.
In the field of lighting initiatives include:

A reduction in the fittings provided.
Programmed time switches off at strategic times.
Reorganization of the lighting system into background and
task lighting over individual work areas.

In the field of heating initiatives include:

The identification of zones with different heating requirements.

Perimeter/access heating systems closely linked to censors recording the external environment.

Modernization and improved maintenance of energy sources.

Enhancement of the insulation quality of the external envelope.

Separation of heating and hot water systems.

Flexible and sensitive control systems, which may be part of a comprehensive fire, security and plant management system.

Research has shown that in the least energy efficient buildings, energy costs can be cut by about half by applying skills and expertise to better control requiring minimal capital expenditure.

Essential to any system is rigorous monitoring and targeting. This requires the technical skills and the communication skills to gain the support and interest of the users of the building.

11.5.4 Conclusion

External factors such as the listing of a building as being of historical or architectural interest can pre-empt some options for its positive management, but in many cases there is a complex legal liability/cost/time/value/risk equation with so many apparent unknowns as to be incapable of a single prescribed solution. The estate manager's role is to create a framework for analysis and discussion within which contributions form various disciplines can produce alternative proposals for consideration by the client. Decisions on the scale and timing of the refurbishment of, say industrial buildings, are influenced by the rate of technical change within that industry and the significance of the particular buildings within a continuous or linked industrial process. Thus good estates decisions can only be taken within the context of the corporate management of the particular profit centre of which the site forms a part.

The effect of grants or tax-planning can cause significant differences between the cost in terms of real resources and financial cost to a particular occupier of maintenance, refurbishment or redevelopment proposal; this is one field where communication problems between accountants and surveyors become very clear. The apparent savings from conducting maintenance or project works in a particular way by phasing, or any other change, in what would be the normal technical procedure needs to be carefully checked to ensure that other costs or uncertainty are not introduced, off-setting the apparent benefits.

The client may well be subject to constraints other than those identified by the advisors who have prepared the alternative technical proposals, and whilst accepting the influence of the various factors involved the client may wish to give a different weight to these or select a proposal on the basis of minimum risk. The estate manager needs to breadth of view that permits him to see beyond the merits of specific technical solutions to issues arising in respect of individual properties. Until he has a clear and dynamic view of his client's operational activities he cannot hope to provide an estates service that makes the best use of the available resources.

Sources and Further Reading

A Forecast of Shop Rents, Hillier Parker Research, Annual. —
A Hyper-active Bank Can Damage Your Pension, the Economist, 2.2.80.
Bamfield, The Changing Face of British Retailing, National Westminster Bank Quarterly Review, May 1980.
Blundell, Prime Yields, A Dangerous Market Barometer, Estate Times, 11.11.83.
Bowie, The Institutional Drift to Freehold Ownership, 270 E.G. 20.
British Shopping Developments 1965–1982 Hillier Parker, 1983.
Brown, Explaining Portfolio Performance, 276 E.G. 1335. —
CALUS Research Report—Rent Assessment and Tenant Mix in Planned Shopping Centres, 1975.
Carr-Jones, Maximizing the Performance of Property Assets, 272 E.G. 20.
Chapman, Wyatt and Thompson, Measuring Portfolio Performance, C.S., May 1980.
Chapman, Your Disobedient Servant, Chatto and Windus, 1978.
Davey, Profile of a faceless landlord, C.S. January 1979.
Department of Industry, Terotechnology—An Introduction to the Management of Physical Resources, H.M.S.O., 1975.
Energy Management, October 1984, monthly.
Estate Management: Underused and Surplus Property in the N.H.S., H.C. (83) 22.
Evans, Retailers' Property Requirements, 276 E.G. 1342.
Finlay, Refurbishment on the Grand Scale, C.S., 7.4.83.
Furbur, Office Service Charge Data, 272 E.G. 413.

Fraser, Gilt Yields and Property's Target Return, 273 E.G. 1291.

Health Service Management, Operation of the Property and Works Function, H.C. (85) 26.

Hetherington, Money and time weighted rates of returns, 256 E.G. 1164.

Hetherington, Property Performance Measurement Systems, 271 E.G. 261.

J.L.W. Occasional Paper, Property Investment Performance over 20 years, Summer 1982.

Martin, Shopping Centre Management, Spon, 1982.

Pension Fund Management and Investment Supplement to Local Government Chronicle, 6.4.79.

Performance Specification for Whole Buildings, B.R.E., 1984.

Property Investment—Green Paper, R.I.C.S. Annual Conference, 1980.

Property Services Agency Annual Report, H.M.S.O., 1979.

Ratcliffe, An Introduction to Urban Land Administration, Chs 8 and 16, Estates Gazette, 1978.

R.I.C.S., Building Management Manual, 1981.

Schiller, Shopping Trends as they affect the Investor, 267 E.G. 420.

Seeley, Building Maintenance, Macmillan, 1976.

The Growth and Impact of Instutitional Investors, Briston and Dobbins, Institute of Chartered Accountants, 1978.

Whelan, The Triton Titan, C.S.W. 28.6.84.

Chapter 12

Tax Planning

12.1 Introduction

Tax planning is a relatively new field for the general practice surveyor but it is now a fundamental part of the positive management of estates in the private sector and to a limited extent also a role of the public sector.

Knowledge of the nature of the individual taxes as they affect landed property is only the first step in tax planning. What is required is a detailed understanding of their aggregate and inter-active effects on each of possibly several alternative ways in which a transfer in land or a project can be structured. The full extent of a liability may not be know conclusively until a considerable time after the event which triggers off the liability, and the mitigation of that liability will require contributions from lawyers, accountants and surveyors, acting for a common client but not always achieving very successful communication between each other.

Central government is also involved in tax planning, both in macro-economic terms predicting revenue from land taxation and the detailed drafting of legislation to give effect to policy in a complex climate of tax avoidance.

Until the Development Land Tax Act in 1976, local government had never been required to be involved in national taxation, but their involvement in local taxation and its role within the overall pattern of financing local government has resulted in the acquisition of specialist skills in the estimation of revenue from rates and the management of the rating system.

In broad terms, tax planning can be justified as giving certainty as to the consequences of carrying through a specific transaction. Tax-payers are under no obligation to pay more tax than they need and it would be unwise for the government to introduce legislation without an appreciation of its consequences or potential revenue.

Where uncertainty remains, problems arise as to whether a particular action is avoidance or evasion and it may only be resolved by an appeal through the courts. If taxpayers perceive a particular tax to be excessive or unfair then the greater will be their tax planning and the more the resources used for what appears to some observers to be at best unproductive activity. Tax planning is a symptom of high tax rates, though as a rider it must be said that money not paid in tax, through tax planning, can be used to create more wealth with a multiplier effect for the economy as a whole and taxation in particular.

12.2 Central Government

There are three government departments involved in the taxation of land transactions. The Department of the Environment, formulating land policy, and able to advise upon the effects of particular taxes on the management and development of land; the Inland Revenue, responsible for the detailed content of the legislation and the process of assessment, valuation and collection necessary to give effect to the provisions of the legislation; and the Treasury, involved in the consequences of the aggregate income and expenditure of government.

When new tax proposals are being considered, an estimate of the net annual increase in revenue can only be made with a detailed knowledge of the draft Bill, and the state of the market, and allowance must be made for inter-action which could reduce the revenue from other taxes. The consequence of new taxes are difficult to predict, since taxpayers perception of the tax may differ from its reality. Various pressure groups and professional bodies take initiatives to lobby government on taxation, and make detailed comments on Bills, and the assessment and, where necessary, response to such memoranda requires detailed knowledge of the motivation of the authors. Unfortunately, more open discussion of possible legislation is often not compatible with the tight parliamentary time-table required to maintain the political momentum. The challenge offered by this work is as great as or greater than that of advising an individual client contemplating the largest of development projects, and it is important that the profession demonstrates its ability to make an appropriate contribution to the public sector. Inevitably, once enacted, the new legislation will be subject to the effects of changes in the property market, in the economy as a whole and in due course a new administration.

As a result it may be repealed or alternatively become harmonized into the statutory framework as part of the setting within which estate management decisions are taken. These decisions are not just those taken by corporate taxpayers and their advisers. Changes in the provision of tax-relief for residential mortgages affects not only builders, house and land prices but the family budgets of the majority of householders in the country, and hence aggregate consumer-demand.

12.3 Local Authorities

The absence of local government from involvement in national taxation does not mean that it is not affected by national taxation. Most large authorities are active in the development of industrial property, and such property is also provided by the private sector. The availability and extent of capital allowances was a factor in determining the minimum initial rent acceptable to the private sector whose units are in competition with those provided by the local authority.

Net-of-tax purchasing, introduced by section 39 of the Development Land Act 1976, involved authorities directly in the national tax system. Attractive as the idea may have seemed at White Paper stage, its application was complex and bureaucratic in the extreme. In enabling local authorities to pay the net-of-tax price for all land acquired after 1 August, 1976, vendors of land with development value, accounting for no more than 5% of acqusitions by local authorities, became involved in completely new procedures. The authorities suddenly found themselves with the potential to buy land cheaply on the basis of a lucky dip, unaware of the necessary detail to determine which of several possible sites offered the greatest windfall saving. Informal qualitative advice was available from the District Valuer, but there was no guarantee that he possessed all the necessary information, and full disclosure was inconsistent with the accepted standards of privacy of an individual's tax affairs.

There was an incentive for vendors to co-operate in providing the information necessary to calculate a specific deduction. The alternative way of calculating the consideration was based on a relatively harsh formula deduction. The only merit was that any excess of deduction over the correct amount of tax was subsequently repaid with tax-free interest, representing a very attractive gross rate for high-rate taxpayers. The section was repealed with effect from 5 August, 1980 by the Finance Act 1980.

The rating system was subject to almost continuous review during the 1970s, but its removal creates almost insuperable problems, particularly for a Conservative government committed to reducing direct taxation; despite the resolve of politicians, it seems to have acquired an embarrassing permanence.

Rates account for about 60% of the total revenue of local government and aggregate rateable values are used in determining some of the central government grants which provide almost all the remainder of the funding for local government. In order to estimate the product of a one penny rate, which is the basis for calculating the poundage and precepts, the valuation list has to be analysed in terms of various sub-groups representing the different types of property reflecting the differential poundages. The effects of changes in assessments as a result of appeals and new construction and changes in liability as a result of new legislation, need to be estimated from year to year and incorporated into the authorities' budgets.

The discretionary power to charge rates on the owners of empty property and the now ineffective surcharge on unoccupied commercial property involve only a small number of hereditaments, but they are often amongst the most valuable within the list. The results of negotiations and appeals on the largest assessments are significant within a financial climate of cash-limits in central government's funding of local government.

12.4.1 The Tax-payer's Strategy

Tax planning in terms of the individual or corporate taxpayer can be defined as, "The holding, dealing, transferring, selling, developing, letting, licensing or granting of options in property in such a way as to maximize the present value of the net proceeds after tax from the point of view of investor or occupier, who may have the status of: individual, partnership, company, institution or charity." This includes making arrangements for the payment of tax liabilities in the most convenient way. The legal environment within which this work is carried out requires an attempt to make the clearest distinction between tax-avoidance (the limitation of tax liability within the law) and evasion (illegal activity or inactivity reducing a tax liability).

Unfortunately, there is blurring between the two, arising from the loose connection between the legal and the moral, resulting in tax "avoision" which is the minimization of liability practised by the taxpayer who has difficulty in equating the legal with the moral and the illegal with the immoral.

In 1979 the Chairman of the Inland Revenue estimated that the total of tax evaded amounted to £3 to £3·5 billion per annum. The practical difficulty in studying tax planning is how to avoid moving too rapidly from the broad definition to the minutiae of the interpretation of specific situations or statutory provisions which each individually offer some possibility of tax saving.

Every year revenue law becomes more complex, avenues are closed and others are opened and a clear understanding of the implications of legislation can only develop after considering its effect on a number of transactions by different types of taxpayers. Some legislation is specifically for anti-avoidance purposes. The Income and Corporation Taxes Act 1970, section 488, enables the Inland Revenue to tax as income any gains from land if it was acquired or developed with the sole or main object of realizing a gain from a disposal, perhaps coming to greater prominence as a result of the repeal of Development Land Tax.

In *Page* v. *Lowther*, 1983, the Court of Appeal criticised the misleading side note in the Act, "artificial transactions in land". They held that it applied to Trustees who sold a 99 year building lease for a total of £1,126,934, the premium paid by the developers, Trafalgar House being linked to the price obtained for underleases of the houses and flats built upon the 2·6 acre site in Kensington. On the other hand there is a published Inland Revenue booklet of nearly 100 extra-statutory concessions, which represent the practical and equitable relaxation of the otherwise harsh effects of legislation.

The success or failure of tax planning measures may not be known for many years. The occurrence of some future event such as death or the completion of some procedures may be certain though the date at which these will occur is uncertain. Despite the many uncertainties involved, the potential savings are sufficient to encourage the prudent taxpayer to distinguish between gross returns and net-of-tax returns from land transactions.

The disposal of an interest in land can result in liability for one or more of income tax, capital gains tax and capital transfer tax. That disposal can be the grant, surrender, assignment or part disposal of a lease; the transfer of a freehold; sale and lease-back; the grant of an option; or the grant or surrender or some rights over land.

The complexity of these is a study in its own right and a

pre-requisite for considering tax planning. A strategy for tax planning builds upon a detailed knowledge of taxation and property transactions. A combination of a key concepts approach and an assets approach can generate the perception necessary, in the analysis of the impact of taxation upon transactions, to identify opportunities for maximizing the net proceeds.

However complex the transactions may seem and baffling the work of the parliamentary draftsman, most tax planning revolves around no more than half-a-dozen key concepts; the status of the parties, the character of the transaction in relation to the whole process, timing, the exercise of options and notification requirements, the inter-action of taxes and valuation.

12.4.2 The Status of the Parties

The legal status of the parties to a transaction is determined partly by their formal title and partly by their conduct. A partnership need not necessarily be created by a written document, it can be assumed by the conduct of the parties. Charities have traditionally enjoyed tax-free status, though this was temporarily removed between 1976 and 1980 in respect of some liability to development land tax. The status of property companies is of great importance on the disposal of properties. A dealing company is liable to tax on the basis that properties are trading stock and subject to corporation tax, an investment company is taxed under the less onerous capital gains regime.

In *Simmons* v. *Inland Revenue Commissioners*, 1979, the liquidation of several unquoted property companies involved the disposal of nine blocks of offices and flats. The Court of Appeal supported the Special Commissioners in using the motives and intentions deduced from the available facts to decide that only some of the properties had acquired the status of investments. It is therefore important that newly-formed property companies use all means possible to specify and demonstrate the desired status of all properties entering the portfolio. Formal resolutions recorded in the minutes of meetings, the presentation of the accounts, and the creation of a specific dealing company within the group help to avoid tainting the investment company with dealing profits.

In *Arndale Properties Ltd.* v. *Coates*, 1982, connected taxpayers sought to obtain group relief for a trading loss under section 258 of I.C.T.A. 1970 by changing the status of a lease from a capital asset to a trading asset.

The three connected parties were described as, "Arndale Properties Ltd. are members of the same group as Sovereign Property Investments (Newport) Ltd. and the Arndale Property Trust Ltd., Sovereign is a Property Development Company, Arndale Properties are a Property Dealing Company." The Arndale Centre at Newport had been developed at a cost of £5·3 million, but was only worth £3·1 million in 1973. It was held that Arndale had no intention of trading, the lease and the arrangements were a "timid veil" and therefore they had not acquired the lease as trading stock. This was confirmed by the House of Lords in 1984.

12.4.3 The Character of the Transaction

Income from land can be taxed under various schedules. The extent of other income and losses and their source means that there are benefits in seeking to direct the income towards the most advantageous schedule and case.

The right to deduct expenses from property income is restricted both as to the period of time involved and the source of the income. As regards the period involved the basis rule is that expenses can only be offset against the income from the lease during which they were incurred.

The exception to this is that expenses of a previous qualifying period may be deducted as long as there has not been an intervening non-qualifying period. Qualifying periods are defined as a previous lease at a full rent by the same landlord, or a void, following such a lease. Thus accumulated losses may be carried forward, but a period of owner occupation or a letting at less than a full rent wipe out previous accumulated expenditure.

For tax purposes a full rent means a rent (including any premium) which, taking one year with another, exceeds the lesson expenses under the lease, very different from full rental value.

The above has been in the context of the lease or leases relating to the same property, the second stage is to consider the extent to which income and expenditure may be pooled between different properties, the following classification can be adopted:

Pool 1, let at a full rent, not on tenants repairing leases. Rents and expenditure are aggregated, excess expenditure can be carried forward indefinitely within pool 1.

Pool 2, let at full rent on tenants repair leases. Rent and

expenditure are aggregated and excess expenditure set against pool 1 and/or carried forward indefinitely within pools 2 or 1.

Pool 3, let at less than a full rent. No aggregation and excess expenditure can only be carried forward against the particular property during the currency of the lease.

Income from the letting of furnished premises can initially be divided between that which enjoys ancillary services and that where the provisions of services is an integral part of the facilities provided. If the Revenue can be satisfied on this point the income is taxed under Schedule D, Case I. The provisions of meals and cleaning of rooms is generally regarded as sufficient to show a serviced furnished letting. The income from a normal furnished letting is taxed under Schedule D, Case VI, but the taxpayer can elect to be taxed under Schedule A on the income attributable to the bare property and under Schedule D, Case VI, for the furnishings. The case for making the election will depend upon the location of the taxpayer's other profits and losses.

The case of *Griffiths* v. *Jackson and Peaman*, 1983 resulted in income from the holiday letting of cottages, bungalows, caravans, flats and chalets being subject to a more onerous regime, losing the right to have the income taxed as a business under D Case I. As a result a wife's share would no longer enjoy her allowance, separate earnings election was not available and investment income surcharged applied.

As a result of intensive lobbying the Finance Act 1984 substantially changed the effective nature of such transactions from those of "property" to "business", back-dated to 6 April, 1982. To qualify holiday accommodation must be available for letting to the public for 140 days a year, actually let for 70 days and for seven months of the year not occupied by the same tenant for more than 31 days. If more than one property is owned, the 70 days may be averaged.

The benefits are:

The income is treated as earned, which is of particular benefit to a married couple where the wife runs the lettings.

The income ranks as relevant earnings for pension purposes.

A more generous approach can be taken in the identification of allowable expenses.

Interest on loans is deductible.

Income losses can be relieved against other income, and carried back.

Roll-over and retirement reliefs are available under capital gains tax.

Options have been used for many years to reserve a land bank or rights at modest cost in times of uncertainty. The basic type of option is one way, an option for the developer to purchase. However in recent years cross-options have become more common. Here the potential vendor has the benefit of an option to sell and the potential purchaser has the benefit of an option to buy (known as put and call options). Thus a commercial transaction can be secured which can be activated by either party. This can be distanced in time from the legal transaction, being the contract.

A somewhat similar situation can arise with a conditional contract, again designed to manage uncertainty, frequently arising from the planning system. A contract is entered into conditional upon the grant of a specified planning permission. Quite elaborate conditions and procedures may be provided; for example, what conditions attaching to the consent will or will not be acceptable, the professional advisors to be involved, the time limits at various stages and the use of an arbitrator. Again the commercial transactions will be distanced some months or even years from the legal transaction, when the condition is satisfied.

12.4.4 Timing

The order in which events occur can affect the aggregate tax liability of one or more of the taxpayers involved. Also, legislation contains specific dates, or provides that particular periods during which land is held or occupied, qualify for some form of relief. A residential owner-occupier's exemption from capital gains tax exhibits several of these features and is examined later in the Chapter.

Sale and lease-backs are not only a legitimate way for occupiers to raise funds for the purposes of their business but also enable Institutions to create investments out of the existing stock of property with the benefit of the covenant of the existing occupier. The rent paid by the occupier is a normal deduction from the gross income of the business. This led to loans being "dressed up" as sale and lease backs with a rent and capital sum in excess of the true value of the property involved. The Income and the Corporation Taxes Act 1970, section 491, restrict the rent qualifying for deduction from the profits to a normal commercial rent of the premises. Where the original interest was for less than 50 years and the lease-back for less than 15, then the Finance Act 1972, section 80 provides that part of the capital sum received shall be taxed as income.

The softening of capital transfer tax by the Conservative government elected in 1979 means that ten yearly accumulation periods replace life-time accumulations. Other capital transfer tax points on timing include the right to substitute the actual proceeds of disposal of land for the valuation on death, if the sale occurs within three years of death, and the carry forward for one year only of any unused annual exemptions.

12.4.5 Elections and Notifications

Various opportunities exist to select which of two alternative methods should be adopted as the basis for the assessment of a tax-liability. A number of these affect agriculture and forestry, where a decision on one piece of land affects the tax-treatment of other land. Generally this is not the case for urban property.

A situation where the surveyor's advice is essential is the assessment of capital gains tax on land owned on 6 April, 1965. The normal basis is on time-apportionment, that is to say the total gain is spread evenly over the total period of ownership after 6 April, 1945, and that part attributable to ownership after 6 April, 1965 is charged to tax. Alternatively the Capital Gains Tax Act 1979, Schedule 5, provides that the assessment can be based on the value of the land as at April, 1965. Before making the election, which is irrevocable, the surveyor should have strong evidence to support the figures he anticipates agreeing with the District Valuer. In the case of land having development value there is no choice, the April, 1965 basis must be adopted.

12.4.6 Inter-action of Taxes

Both students and practitioners should expect this to be an unpleasant minefield. The depth of knowledge necessary to report with confidence to a client on any but the simplest situation is only found amongst the specialists. There is a survival kit available against any professional negligence claims. It consists of two elements, firstly an explicit assumption that the client's accountant is likely to possess more relevant information than any other adviser, secondly, if the surveyor considers that there could be a possibility of an inter-action, a caveat in a preliminary report along the following lines: "It will be necessary to liaise with both the accountants and lawyers involved in this matter to determine the extent to which inter-action of taxes has an effect on a precedent or subsequent transaction in the land."

A situation that frequently arises is the payment of a premium for a lease of less than 50 years. The longer the lease the more the premium has the character of a capital sum, whilst a "premium" on the grant of a lease for one year only is just rent. The sum charged to income tax is the premium less one-fiftieth of the premium for every year by which the term of lease exceeds one year—the rest is charged to capital gains tax. Where the lease obliges the tenant to improve the property, then in accordance with section 80 of the Income and Corporation Taxes Act 1970 the increase in value of the landlord's interest (not the cost incurred) is treated as a premium. Leases now usually contain a covenant by the tenant to remove the improvement at the end of the term, reducing the value of the benefit to the landlord to nil. The fact that the tenant will generally be quite pleased to avoid the expense of removing the improvement, if the landlord does not require him to do so, does not seem to prevent the operation of this tax-avoidance mechanism by the landlord.

12.4.7 Valuation

To some extent valuation is related to inter-actions, since a high or low valuation can have the effect of changing the extent to which a particular tax affects the transaction. Where there has not been an arms-length transaction, legislation requires a valuation, "On the basis of what the interest might reasonably be expected to fetch on a sale in the open market," or some similar phrase.

In *Re Hayes Will Trust, Pattinson v. Hayes,* 1971, it was said, "It does not mean that the price to be fixed by valuation is the highest possible price that might be obtained. It has been established time and again in these courts ... that there is a range of price in some cases wide, which competent valuers would recognize as the price which, property would fetch if sold in the open market. The section does not require that the top price of that range should be the price fixed ... That price together with the lowest price in the range may be expected to be the least likely price within the range, to be obtained in the open market. The most likely price, in the absence of consultation between the valuers representing conflicting interests, would presumably be the mean price."

Valuations are required across the whole range of national taxation. Gifts and sales at an undervalue can create problems for both the donor and donee. Valuations will be required and, in the case of capital transfers tax, the liability is based upon the diminution in value of the donor's estate. The presence of marriage value or divorce value can result in a figure very different from that which is the basis for the capital gains tax liability, which is simply the open market value of the interest. The Finance Act 1980 has recognized the inequity of this double liability and where both the donor and donee agree the capital gains liability can be rolled over.

As an antithesis to the many cases where valuations are required where there is no market transaction, in *Wilcon Homes Ltd.* v. *Commissioners of Inland Revenue*, 1983, the Revenue claimed that an arms length transaction was not on a market value basis.

The sale of 4·19 acres was arranged in 1978 by an unqualified valuer, who advertised the land by private circulation (he was deceased at the date of the hearing), at a price of £45,000. The purchaser claimed the benefit of section 18 of the 1976 D.L.T.A. being the exemption for a project begun within three years of purchase at a full development value. The Revenue contended the price should have been £105,000. The Lands Tribunal held that it was for the party alleging that the actual price was not open market value to establish their case, and the comparables produced by the Revenue did not show a sufficiently clear pattern of value.

With increasingly complex interaction of taxes and chains of transaction between various related parties the results of a particular valuation (either by agreement or by the Lands Tribunal) or tax determination (by the Special Commissioners or an appeal by the Higher Courts) can have a direct effect on other transactions of that taxpayer or other taxpayers in transaction chain.

On occasions the taxpayer's valuer may be tempted to seek agreement at the higher or lower extremity of the band in order to create tax-saving on another anticipated transaction in that asset. This may well prove to be in the interests of the client, but the surveyor could well find the basis agreed a considerable embarrassment on other occasions in negotiations with the District Valuer. The problem of achieving the very best for a client at the expense of possibly damaging professional credibility on numerous subsequent negotiations is one which each professional man or woman has to resolve for him or her self.

In 1982 the Revenue at last recognized the inequity for assets owned for some years of taxing money, rather than real gains for capital gains tax purposes. They introduced indexation for rises in value after 1982, but based upon 1965 value or subsequent acquisition costs. In 1985, a 1982 base was introduced for the purposes of indexation after that date. However the unfairness remains in as much that no indexation is available for the money rise in value between 1965 and 1982.

To the several thousand 1965 valuations agreed by the Inland Revenue each year will be added a need for a similar number of valuations as at 1982, though there will be a good chance that at least one of the parties to that negotiation will have some personal relevant market experience, the lack of which makes 1965 valuations increasingly hypothetical.

12.4.8 Development Land Tax

This tax introduced in 1976 and abolished in 1985 contained perhaps the most complex assessment and valuation procedures of any land tax.

There were substantial opportunities for the mitigation of liability:

The initiative rested with the taxpayer in the identification, notification and phasing of projects which were treated as deemed disposals. The use of advanced notice of a deemed disposal offered further possibilities. Enhancement expenditure could, subject to the date the property was acquired, exert up to 160% leverage on the base value.

The definition of current use value interacted in a complex way with planning law requiring a strong interdisciplinary approach, in order to determine the full extent of tolerances.

A cubic measuring code meant that old, lofty, poorly arranged buildings, could produce a modern equivalent of much greater useable floor area, free of the tax.

Each different type of leasing transaction required an amendment to the assessment procedures which could produce anomalies.

Considerable experience was gained both by the Revenue and taxpayers advisors in the interpretation of tax legislation and its impact on highly complex transactions. Only a small

number of cases reached the courts but some important interpretation is to be found in *R.* v. *Commissioners of Inland Revenue, ex-parte Harrow LBC,* 1983. The case arose under section
39 of the 1976 Act, acquisition by local authorities at a price
net of D.L.T., (repealed by the 1980 Finance Act). In order to
seek to establish the commencement of a project of material
development, Gerald Eve and Co. submitted a certified record
in connection with a 15 mm copper pipe unconnected to anything in a three foot deep hole; this would have prevented
the net of tax acquisition basis. The Court held that the works
were "colourable operations", undertaken solely to avoid tax,
there being no reasonable expectation of being able to carry
out the development to completion and thus there had been
no project. Whilst the route by which the issue arose is unlikely
to arise again, the issue itself is of general application, particularly in the light of the doctrine of in *Furniss* v. *Dawson,* 1984.

The comprehensive abolition of the tax with effect from 19
March, 1985, came as something of a surprise, as evidenced
by the number of transactions subject to the tax in the few
weeks before the chancellor's statement. However whilst
D.L.T. existed section 488 of the Income and Corporation Taxes
Act 1970 effectively fell into abeyance. This section may now
be used to assess taxpayers to income as opposed capital taxes,
which in the case of individuals could result in the highest
income tax rate, 60%.

12.5.1 Assets Approach

Allied with the key concepts approach is the need to be aware
of the pattern of exemptions and reliefs afforded to particular
types of assets. Agriculture and forestry have enjoyed very substantial relief from taxes on both income and capital. This can
affect the value of such assets, though there is a danger of
falling into a circular argument, the relief afforded making such
assets relatively expensive and any new investor seeking the
benefit of the tax haven pays dearly in purchasing an asset
offering tax benefits. To the extent that a significant amount
of agricultural land is purchase by the Institutions, who are
unable to take advantage of capital transfer tax relief enjoyed
by individuals, this aspect is now less important in agriculture.

Leaving aside agricultural land and buildings and forestry
as a major but specialist area of study, business assets as a
whole, and particularly industrial buildings and plant, benefit
from an extensive range of reliefs designed to encourage invest-

ment. An owner-occupier's main residence, which is interpreted broadly, qualifies for exemption from capital gains tax. A growing awareness of the problems of the maintenance and management of heritage property has resulted in it enjoying much greater relief than was available in the early 1970s. The introduction of Enterprise Zones means that for the first time national taxation is also being used for the purposes of regional economic planning, since the effect of tax reliefs in the designated zones is similar to some of the incentives administered by the Department of Industry.

12.5.2 Business Assets

Business assets enjoy relief from capital taxes. When capital transfer tax was introduced to replace estate duty, it was feared that its effect on lifetime and death transfers would cause the break-up of family businesses. Valuation relief is now available, varying from 20% to 50%, depending upon the status of the assets, and this, together with the careful redistribution of the assets over periods of ten years, can overcome most of the problems. It cannot be claimed in addition to the 50% or 30% valuation relief on the agricultural value of agricultural land, but it is an alternative for agricultural land which fails to satisfy the conditions as to its use, ownership, extent or value.

In order to encourage investment in new assets, capital gains tax liability is deferred on the disposal of business assets if the proceeds are used to purchase replacement assets, which must be acquired in the period of one year before, to three years after, the disposal. What would otherwise be the chargeable gain on the disposal of the asset is deducted from the acquisition cost of the new asset, thus rolling over the liability as long as the business continues to operate. Retirement relief is available to the proprietor of a business on its sale, if he is over 60, up to a maximum of £100,000, and can be used to avoid the deferred liability arising from previous roll-over relief. Whilst this applies to the disposal of a business or an interest in a business it does not apply to the disposal of an individual asset. In *McGregor* v. *Adcock*, 1977, the taxpayer (a farmer) who sold some of his land which he used for his business was held not to have sold part of his business and so was not entitled to relief.

Before the 1984 Finance Act, Capital Allowances had been a significant, and it was thought, permanent feature of the tax landscape, as follows:

Type of asset	Capital Allowance Initial %	Annual %
All industrial buildings	75	4
Industrials less than 1,250 sq ft	100	(25)
Enterprise zones	100	(25)
Hotels	20	4
Agricultural buildings	20	10
Assured tenancies	20	4
Plant and machinery	100	(25)

The application of which depended upon detail rules as to the:

Status of the occupier
Qualifying trade
Status of owner
Qualifying amount

As a result the tax benefit influenced the appraisal, funding, development, design and marketing of occupational and investment interests. Further the annual accounts of development companies, particularly industrial developers showed capital allowances making a significant contribution to profits and by implication acting as a factor in the price of shares. Indeed the 1983 Finance Act extended capital allowances, responding to high tech buildings, by increasing from 10% to 25% the proportion of offices which qualify in an industrial building.

The 1984 Finance Act represented a fundamental shift whereby both the rate of Corporation Tax and the rate of initial capital allowances, except for Enterprize Zones, were to be progressively reduced as follows:

Date	Initial capital allowances P. & M. %	Industrial buildings and assured tenancies %	Corporation Tax (normal) %
Before 14 March 84	100	75	50
After 14 March 84	75	50	45
After 1 April 85	50	25	40
After 1 April 86	0	0	35

In shorthand, the Chancellor described this as trying to ensure that prudent investment decisions are made on the basis of commercial market assessments not tax assessments. It may be too simplistic to suggest that the result will be capital intensive industries qualifying for allowances having a greater taxable profit but paying a similar amount of tax and the services sector having similar taxable profits and paying less tax. On balance the measures are beneficial to the property company sector, compared with other sectors of the equity market.

Whilst annual capital allowances remain at 25% on the reducing balance for plant and machinery and 4% on industrial buildings, on agricultural buildings and hotels their impact will be increased, since previously most capital allowances were taken in the first year and little remained to be written off in later years.

A company incurring building costs will still try to show that as much as possible of the cost is attributable to plant and machinery as distinct from the structure and finishes. Since plant and machinery are not defined in statute law, distinguishing them from land and buildings has resulted in considerable case law. *J. Lyons and Co. Ltd* v. *Attorney-General*, 1944, stated the principle that if plant is the apparatus which a business man uses for carrying on his business it must therefore exclude the place in which he carries on the business. The interpretation of this principle is not easy. Apparatus to provide, electric light or power, hot water, central heating, ventilation or air-conditioning and, fire alarm and sprinkler systems all qualify as plant but in *Hampton* v. *Forte Autogrill Ltd*, 1980, it was held that expenditure on false ceilings to provide cladding to such services was ineligible.

The line between shop fitting and the property itself was partly clarified by *Leeds Permanent Building Society* v. *Proctor*, 1982. The case concerned free standing screens between the window and the office area, upon which displays could be mounted, it was held that they were similar to fascia boards and projecting signs and qualified as plant.

In *Stokes* v. *Costain Property Investments*, 1984, the tenant, with a lease of 99 years, failed to obtain capital allowances on £500,000 spent on lifts and central heating since it was held that the plant and machinery could only belong to the freeholder. Whereas the freeholder could not enjoy the capital allowances, since he had not incurred the expenditure. This was reversed by clause 56 of the 1985 Finance Bill, by identifying a range of alternative circumstances in which persons with an interest in the land could enjoy the allowance.

Since refurbishment of office properties can entail a higher percentage of expenditure on plant and machinery than a new building, a comparison of the relative merits of two schemes can result in an understatement of the former, since the net cost is substantially reduced, if the various qualifying conditions are met.

12.5.3 Owner-occupier's Main Residence

An owner-occupier's main residence is totally exempt from capital gains tax and the Capital Gains Tax Act 1979 provides for generous periods of absence for various purposes before the owner becomes liable to the tax. The Finance Act 1980 has (as amended) extended the exemption to include up to a maximum of £20,000 of value attributable to a let portion of an owner-occupier's main residence as long as the let portion represents the minority of the total value of the asset. This should act as an incentive for the better use of some of the older large houses in inner cities and remove one of the disincentives from declaring income from this type of letting. In *Makins* v. *Elson*, 1977, a residential caravan of a semi-permanent nature together with its plot was held to qualify as an owner-occupied dwellinghouse.

Absence is permitted for long periods of time without affecting the exemption. Any period of absence when working overseas qualifies, and also up to four years when working elsewhere in the U.K. In addition up to a further three years' absence is permitted, but in all cases the taxpayer must have resided in the house before and after the periods of absence. Provisions also exist to enable the exemption to be enjoyed in respect of land which is purchased as a building plot upon which the taxpayer then builds his main residence and also a period of up to two years immediately preceding the sale of the property, to cover the very practical problems encountered when moving house.

With regard to both taxes a house owned by the taxpayer but occupied by a dependent relative as a main residence also qualifies for exemption. In the case of *Varty* v. *Lines*, 1976, the taxpayer sold his house before and separately from his garden. As a consequence what was sold by the vendor as a garden was in reality a parcel of bare land enjoying no exemptions or reliefs.

12.5.4 National Heritage Assets

The preservation of the national heritage is a goal supported by all, and it can best be achieved by a balance of ownership between the public, private and voluntary sectors. Opening a private house which has been a family home for several hundred years brings in revenue but also results in additional costs to meet the needs of visitors. These include lavatories, refreshment facilities, car parks, fire, safety and security arrangements and various minor works.

Where occupation by the owner is the dominant user, net visitor-income (income less expenses directly incurred in opening the house) is assessed under Schedule D, Case VI. Where occupation by the owner is of secondary importance and the enterprise is managed on a commercial basis with the view to the realization of a profit then the income is assessed under Schedule D, Case 1 and all outgoings associated with the property can be set-off against income.

Capital taxation of heritage property has been a contentious subject for many years. There are now extensive exemptions from capital transfer tax in respect of land and buildings which the Treasury accept as being of outstanding historic interest, subject to reasonable steps being taken for their preservation and access by the public. In addition, gifts to designated national bodies or non-profit making organizations are exempt from both capital gains tax and capital transfer tax, though undertakings can be required as to the use, disposal, preservation and access to any of the assets involved. Substantial funds are necessary in order to maintain the property involved and the creation of a maintenance settlement is exempt from capital transfer tax as long as when it comes to an end the funds can only be used for some similar purpose by a national body or a charity.

The re-structuring during 1980 of the National Land Fund to form the National Heritage Fund together with its initial capital of £15·5 million and annual income of £5·5 million will be used mainly for the making of grants and loans to assist in the preservation of heritage property both personal and real. A secondary use will be to re-imbuse the Revenue when they accept property of pre-eminent importance in lieu of the payment of capital transfer tax.

In 1984 the Fund enabled the National Trust to purchase and endow Belton House. In the same year Calke Abbey illustrated the various issues. The owner of the house, park and

14,000 acres of farmland was faced with capital transfer tax of £10 million, with interest of £1,300 per day. The maximum proceeds would be raised by a piecemeal disposal of the real and personal property. The Trust was keen to accept the entire property with the income from the farmland as the endorsement for maintenance and repair. The Treasury was unwilling to designate all the farmland as demonstrating the necessary criteria. Finally the £8 million required for repairs and the endowment was cobbled together by a joint scheme involving:

The National Heritage Memorial Fund	£4·5 m
Trustees of the Estate	£1·0 m
Historic Building Council (now part of the Historic Buildings and Monuments Commission for England)	£1·0 m
National Trust	£1·0 m
An increase to the endowment land of	1,100 acres

Though the trustees will still have to sell a substantial part of the estate to pay the balance of the capital transfer tax.

12.6 Value Added Tax

Value Added Tax is administered by Customs and Excise in perhaps a more adversarial role than that adopted by the Inspector of Taxes. Group 8 of Schedule 4 of the Finance Act 1972, provided that the supply in the course of construction, alteration or demolition of any building . . . of any services other than the services of an architect, surveyor or consultant was zero rated unless the work could be described as "repair or maintenance", in which case it was standard rated. The House of Lords ruled in *ACT Construction Ltd*. v. *C. and E. Commissioners*, 1982, that underpinning was new construction work, extending the building in a downward direction—hence zero rated.

The same Court has ruled in *C. and E. Commissioners* v. *Viva Gas Appliances*, 1983, that the provision of gas fires in place of solid fuel fireplaces, though not a "substantial" nor "structural" alteration was nevertheless a "sufficient" alteration, and hence should be zero rated.

The V.A.T. status of the recovering of roofs was a matter of considerable debate. In 1982 a V.A.T. Tribunal held that complete replacement of slate by tile and clay by concrete coverings was zero rated. This was reversed by the High Court, *C. and E. Commissioners* v. *Sutton Housing Trust*, 1983, and has been criticized. However J. Lindsey Thomas reports in the Chartered Surveyor Weekly of 16.6.83 and the C. and E. has agreed to zero rate his replacement of cedarwood shingles by artificial slate tiles.

The 1984 Finance Act substantially changed the law, except for "protected buildings". After 1 June, 1984, all work to existing buildings, whether maintenance and repair or alteration, is standard rated. The Common Market is putting pressure on the government to levy V.A.T. on new commercial and industrial buildings, which would at least have the merit of equality.

The demolition of a complete building remains zero rated; where only a single facade remains, then the construction of a new building will be zero rated, but where the outer walls remain, all new work is standard rated.

Protected buildings, that is to say listed buildings and ancient monuments, still qualify for zero rating in the following circumstances:

Alterations (but not maintenance and repair) requiring and having received listed building consent.

Sale or long lease of listed building by a person substantially reconstructing it, (60% of the cost of entire reconstruction qualifying as zero alterations).

The provisions of the 1984 Finance Act significantly affected the financial characteristics of many proposed refurbishment schemes and there were reports that companies, including Haselmere, renegotiated their acquisition price of buildings downwards.

Other aspects of V.A.T. which will affect the property manager include:

The granting of the freehold or of a lease for a period of over 21 years by a taxpayer constructing a building in order to qualify for zero rating, rather than exemption, and so enjoy credit for related input tax. A taxpayer is a constructor, if he owns the land and as a minimum, commissions a contractor to develop the land over which he has control. Incidentally, the insertion of a break clause does not affect the 21 year rule.

If the fund takes an interest directly from the vendor and the developer is a mere project manager under a development agreement, then his services will be subject to V.A.T.

The election under Section 21 of the Finance Act 1972 as

amended, for two or more companies to be treated as members of a group, and effectively pool their input and output tax.

In conclusion it is important to distinguish between services given by builders, which are either standard rated (work to existing buildings) or zero rated (completely new buildings) and the disposal or letting of such buildings, which are either zero rated (freehold or lease for more than 21 years) or exempt (lease of less than 21 years).

12.7 Rates

Rate payments are a function of valuation, poundage and liability, each is a study in its own right. Debenham Tewson and Chinnock's annual survey of rent and rates points to the relationship between these, which becomes distorted the longer a revaluation is delayed. Overall rate payments were found to be increasing when expressed as a percentage of rent:

1981	51%
1982	53%
1983	56%

This is powerfully demonstrated during the period 1973 to 1983 on average when adjusted for inflation, rentals have declined by 45% and rates risen by 32%.

This has now been considered by the Land Tribunal in *Sadick v. Dumbell*, 1984, and *Newman (PC) Business Equipment Ltd. v. Dumbell*, 1984. The ratepayers surveyor suggested that between 1973 and 1982 rates, as a percentage of rental value in the appeal premises road, had more than doubled to just over 100% but in an adjoining shopping area had reduced by about a third to 34%. The Lands Tribunal held that "the same state" in section 20 (tone of the list) of the 1967 General Rate Act meant the same physical state, so that the change in rate burden cannot be taken into consideration. However, to the extent that this has influenced rentals, then at a revaluation it will be taken into account. Conversely where rents have risen more than average, then after a revaluation, rate burden will be substantially increased and hence possibly depress future rental growth.

Despite several hundred years of rating practice, the law of valuation is still being developed. The House of Lords in *K Shoes Shops Ltd.* v. *Hardy*, 1983, had to consider the date at which premises were to be valued for the purposes of the current valuation list, being that introduced in 1 April, 1973. The ratepayers claimed that the list was based on:

Information sought from the public in 1970.
Supplied to the Valuation Office in 1971.
Estimates prepared in 1972.

Hence the list was in fact based upon 1970 levels of values and therefore 1973 rental evidence was inadmissible. The Court held that the common valuation date was 1 April, 1983, and there was nothing in the 1967 Act to indicate the contrary.

For over 300 years rating was primarily a tax on occupiers and the liability to pay rates also an obligation on the tenant in the lease. Since 1966 Rating Authorities have had the power, if they so resolved, to charge rates on the owners of empty property.

The Local Government Act 1974, amending Schedule 1 of the 1967 General Rate Act permitted a charge of up to 100% on designated types of property in parts of the rating area. The Local Government Planning and Land Act 1980 enables the Secretary of State to set a ceiling to the percentage which may be charged for different types of property and the resulting Unoccupied Property Rate (Variation of current ceiling) Order 1980 No. 2012 limited the charge on non-domestic property to 50%.

The Rating (Exemption of Unoccupied Industrial Hereditaments) Regulations 1984 No. 221 exempted from empty rates premises constructed or adapted for use wholly or mainly for industrial purposes. However the archaic rating language adopted failed to have regard to reality. In fact industrial sheds are built speculatively with consent for various classes of development including both Class III (light industrial) and Class X (warehousing); much uncertainty was created. As a result from 1 April 1985 a new order was made extending the exemption to storage and mineral hereditaments.

Hereditaments are permitted to be vacant for three months before the empty rate charge is levied and six months in the case of newly-completed dwellings. Empty dwellings are charged at the commercial poundage, so in areas where 100% empty-rate charge is levied, it may be better to claim that such property is occupied and so benefit from the lower domestic poundage.

The completion notice procedure in Schedule 1 of the General Rate Act 1967 enables authorities to bring new buildings within the charge if they could reasonably be completed within three months. Owners may be able to agree a later date than that specified in the completion notice but unless an appeal is made to the County Court within 21 days of the service of the completion notice there is no way of challenging the date in the completion notice and the consequential rate liability. The decision of the County Court can be challenged in the Court of Appeal.

There have been a number of appeals concerned with the criteria for determinating when a building is completed. *Ravenseft Properties Ltd.* v. *Newham Borough Council,* 1975, established that the test was whether a building was capable of occupation for its intended purpose, thought it is difficult to interpret this principle in respect of individual elements of building services and finishes.

In practice it may be possible for an owner of a newly-erected building to reach an agreement with an authority on a payment considerably less than the sum demanded as an alternative to the uncertainty and cost of proceeding through the courts. The contents of D.o.E. circular 34/78, which emphasized the discretion available to authorities in broadly defined cases of hardship, has undoubtedly helped ratepayers.

When hereditaments which have been occupied become vacant, the landlord can be faced with some difficult problems. If, as sometimes happens, the tenant vacated several months before the end of the lease, then the tenant's advisers will have already made use of the three-month exemption from empty rates and this will not be available to the landlord. This can be overcome by the landlord going into occupation, or an agent doing so on his behalf, for a minimum period of six weeks, paying rates on the normal basis, thus creating a new occupation which can subsequently qualify for a further three months exemption.

The alternative situation, where a landlord has benefited from the three-month exemption prior to letting a newly-completed office building, was considered in the case of *London Borough of Brent* v. *Ladbroke Rentals Ltd.,* 1979. It was held that a tenant could not then claim a further three month void from the date the lease commenced.

The empty rate charge can be avoided in various circumstances including:

Where occupation prohibited by law.
Listed buildings, though not all authorities ensure that the

list from the Town Planning Department is fed through to
the Treasurers Department, so demands are sometimes made
on listed buildings.

Where the hereditament is held vacant for a minister of
religion.

Bankruptcy and liquidation reasons.

The interaction of planning law and rating were considered
in *Hailbury Investment Ltd.* v. *City of Westminster*, 1983.
Premises were described in the Valuation List as offices, they
were unoccupied because the offices planning consent had
expired. The Court held that the owner was prohibited by law
from occupying the premises for the purpose described in the
Valuation List.

In *Providence Properties Ltd.* v. *Liverpool City Council*, 1980,
it was held that as the curtillage of a listed building fell entirely
within the curtillage of the larger hereditament no exemption
was available. Clearly, where possible any listed building
should be the subject of a separate proposal. It is likely that
where a facade is listed and the building behind demolished
and a new building constructed in its place, then a case can
be made for the exemption applying.

The ratepayers' position has been strengthened by *Deben-*
ham PLC v. *Westminster City Council*, 1985. Here the detailed
provisions of listed building law enabled the Court to define
listed buildings so as to include other property, forming the
hereditament, joined to the postal address building that was
listed and so overturn a distress warrant issued by a stipendiary
magistrate for the sum of £70,000 in respect of the old Hamleys
toy shop.

If refurbishment or re-development is planned, the design
and project management should be sufficiently advanced to
permit the commencement of some work immediately the
premises are vacated, and as long as these works are part
of the overall project, and a proposal is served at the appropriate time, a nominal assessment should be obtained. In the
case of old premises awaiting re-development then applying
the *rebus sic stantibus* concept, one way to avoid empty rates
is to remove substantial areas of the roof-covering to arrive
at a nominal assessment.

The economic climate has changed from that prevailing at
the time the Local Government Act 1974 was being drafted.
The new sections, 17A and 17B, that Act inserted in the 1967
Act created a mandatory cumulative rating surcharge on the

owners of unused commercial buildings. This was repealed by an order under the Local Government Planning and Land Act 1980.

Since the latter part of the 1960s surveyors have become much more involved in the overall liability of clients for rates as distinct from the previous more limited responsibilities for rating valuation. This requires detailed discussions with both the Inland Revenue Valuation Office and the rating section of the Treasurer's Department. Though staffed by individuals, each has a distinctive character and role which must be clearly understood in order to obtain the best for the client.

12.8 Caveats

The fundamental points which the preceding review of private sector tax planning has sought to make is that a detailed knowledge of individual taxes is not enough. What is needed is an analysis of the various ways in which a transaction may be structured, or a potential liability crystallize into a taxable event. With the exception of Mellows, most texts fail to adopt a transaction or assets-orientated approach, causing tax planning to appear both disjointed and anecdotal. There are a number of problems in applying tax planning on behalf of clients. Avoidance and evasion are not always distinct, the correct interpretation of legislation is a matter for the courts and until a relevant case has been heard and possibly a decision given on an appeal, the law cannot be said to be clear. Even when the law is clear the appropriateness of a particular route, procedure or transaction must be considered carefully. To distort an activity for tax savings purposes is justified if the resulting transaction is still a reasonable commercial activity, but if the distortion becomes excessive so as to create uncertainty and change the whole nature of the transaction it may become difficult to quantify the extent of the saving. The possibility of annual or more frequent changes in taxation legislation, together with admittedly infrequent, retrospective enactments casts doubts upon any arrangements which cannot be implemented and completed within a short period.

To be effective, tax planning requires a relatively sophisticated client able to select, control and monitor a team of professional advisers appropriate to the particular task under consideration. This is not just a matter of the services of the right professional partnership, it is one of the co-ordination of the right individuals. The fees incurred in obtaining advice, implementing the recommendations and if necessary pursuing the matter before the courts are such as to require the high probability of a many fold payback over the total cost incurred. There is also the question of the whole ethics of the subject. In many fields of law the legal and the moral do not coincide and interpretation of the moral is a matter of personal judgment as are the means of giving it effect. Avoidance of one tax may be at the expense of a liability to another tax in respect of the taxable event or a subsequent taxable event. The tax-saving is therefore only the margin between the particular tax avoidance and the alternative liability, whether current or prospective.

Any tax planning arrangements must now satisfy the criteria in *Ramsay Ltd.* v. *CIR*, 1982, where Lord Wilberforce identified the following features of transactions which can be taken to be a fiscal nullity:

The scheme is prepackaged, planned in accordance with a timetable.
The transactions whilst real, have no significance except as steps in the whole process.
Whilst actual sums of money are involved the gains and losses have no commercial reality, the instigator's financial position at the end being unaltered, save for fees incurred.
The transactions have no commercial motive, being designed only to avoid tax.

The later case of *Furniss* v. *Dawson*, 1984, is much more than an endorsement of Ramsey. Now any steps in a transaction which have no commercial advantage other than to avoid or deter a tax liability will be disregarded for fiscal purposes. The definition of the bounds of this new doctrine may take some years to establish. The Inland Revenue have reviewed several Development Land Tax situations including the spreading of a sale over several years to enjoy the annual exemptions, this could have involved the use of cross options (see 12.4.3), whereby the commercial deal is secured but the tax events are phased.

12.9 Payment

In the case of capital transfer tax, the tax is in general payable six months after the end of the month in which the chargeable transfer was made, and capital gains tax is payable three months after the end of the year of assessment in which the disposal took place. Under certain circumstances both taxes can also be paid in instalments. The likelihood of liability for large capital tax payments is often known many years ahead of the event triggering off the liability. Every opportunity should be taken to utilize the intervening years to the full by making use of any annual allowances which are available and building up a fund in order to avoid having to break up the balanced business or assets which give rise to the charge. Many family businesses are still exposed to capital transfer tax. Apparently good tax planning proposals can be frustrated due to the personalities of the proprietors, often with unfortunate results for their dependants and employees.

Sources and Further Reading

Commercial Property, The unoccupied rate and the rating surcharge, R 385 R.I.C.S. Abstracts, November, 1976.
Darlow, Tax and Holiday Property, 272 EG 24.
Dawson, Opening Houses to the Public, C.S. Rural Quarterly, Vol. 2, No. 2, 1974.
Debenham Tewson and Chinnocks, Office Rents and Rates, Annual.
Emeny, Principles and Practice of Rating Valuation, Estates Gazette, 1984.
Empty Property Rate, D.O.E. Circular 34/78.
Extra-Statutory Concessions in Operation at 30th September, 1976, and Annual Supplements, Board of Inland Revenue.
Holroyd-Pearce and Avery-Jones, Gains from Property Transactions— The Attack on Tax Avoidance, Blundell Memorial Lectures, 1980.
Inland Revenue Statistics H.M.S.O., Annual.
King, VAT on Construction and Development Work, Granada, 1984.
Mellows, Taxation of Land Transactions, Butterworths, 1978.
Parte, Budget Proposals Strike Rebuild Schemes Twice, ET 27.4.84.
R.I.C.S. Handbook of CLA and DLT, Kluwer-Harrup, 1976.
Soares, Land and Tax Planning, Oyez Longman, 1983.
Stapleton, Capital Allowances, 266 EG 499.
Stapleton, Relief from Empty Rates, 270 EG 1252.
Tax Avoision, Institute of Economic Affairs, 1979.
The Property Development Process, Taxation Aspects of Property Development, C.A.L.U.S., 1976.
Urry, VAT and Property Transactions, II 264 EG 518, III 264 EG 904, IV 265 EG 113, V 265 EG 375.

Appendix A
Corporate Strategy

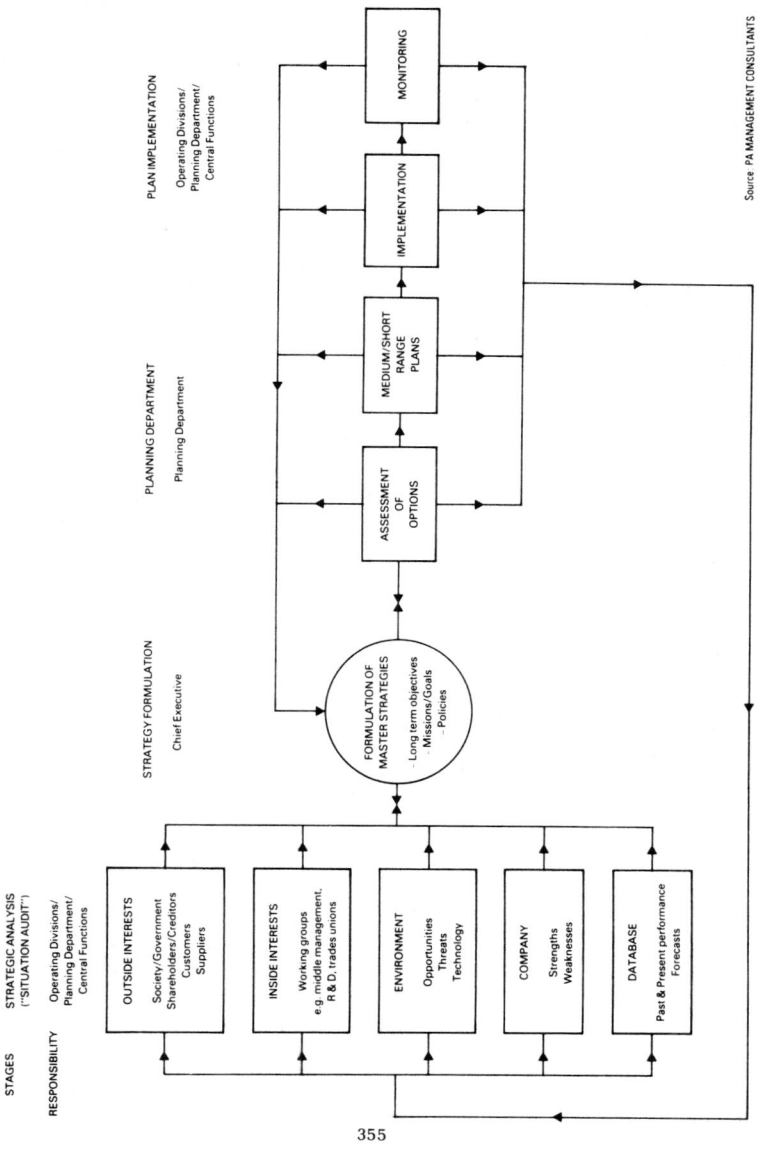

Source PA MANAGEMENT CONSULTANTS

Appendix B

Home Civil Estate (areas in 1,000 m²)

	April 1978 Freehold		April 1978 Leasehold		April 1979 Freehold		April 1979 Leasehold	
	Area	Holdings	Area	Holdings	Area	Holdings	Area	Holdings
OFFICE								
London	691	162	1,791	923	858	241	2,001	886
Other	1,524	1,157	2,627	4,303	2,220	1,463	2,695	3,573
STORAGE								
London	129	18	187	76	204	18	128	31
Other	1,113	175	258	182	1,403	259	171	146
MISC.								
London	276	104	107	74	330	67	107	54
Other	1,381	773	351	577	1,849	1,212	220	601
TOTAL	5,114	2,389	5,321	6,135	6,864	3,260	5,322	5,291
LAND								
London	330	24	50	11	70	11	80	35
Other	15,060	380	3,870	267	47,180	1,154	8,080	865
TOTAL	15,390	404	3,920	278	47,250	1,165	8,160	900

Source: P.S.A. Annual Reports

357

Appendix C

Flow-chart through Landlord and Tenant Act 1954—Part II

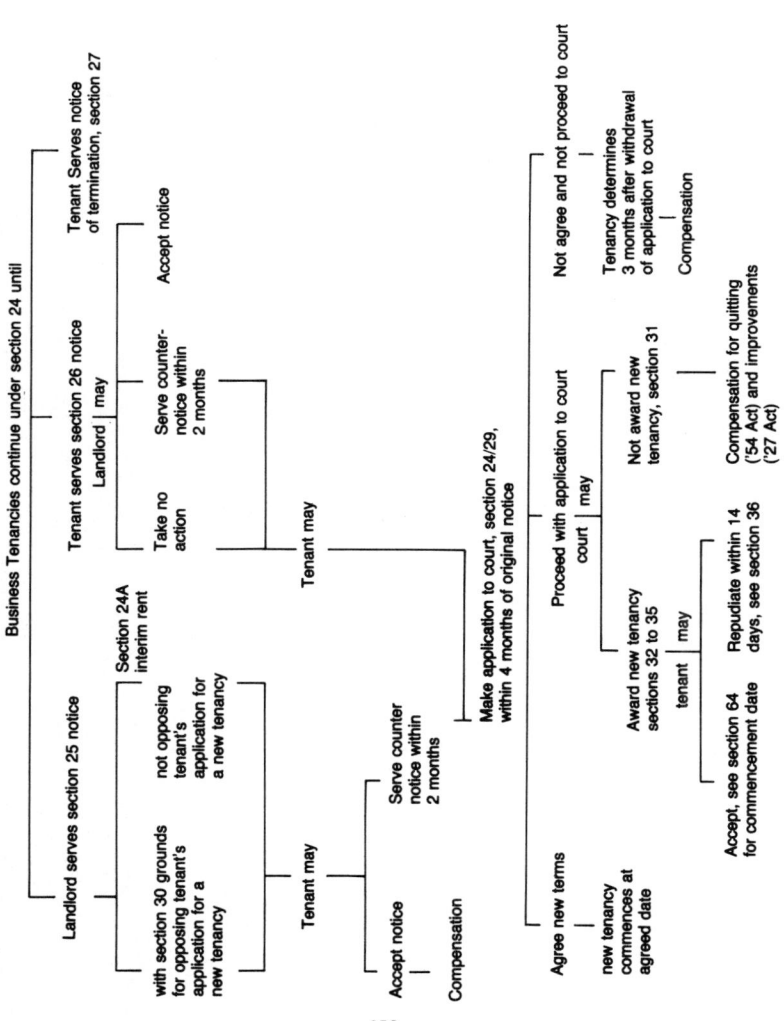

359

Appendix D
Model Rent Review Clause (1980)

... yielding and paying to the landlord yearly rents ascertained in accordance with the next four clauses hereof without any deduction by equal quarterly payments in advance on the usual quarterdays the first payment (being an apportioned sum) to be made on the date hereof

Clause 1

Definitions

In this deed "review date" means the   day of   in the year 19   and in every   year thereafter and "review period" means the period starting with any review date up to the next review date or starting with the last review date up to the end of the term hereof.

Clause 2

The yearly rent shall be:

(A) until the first review date the rent of £   and

Provisions for revision of rent (see Note 1)

(B) during each successive review period *a* rent equal to the rent previously payable hereunder or such revised rent as may be ascertained as herein provided *whichever be the greater* and

Additional sub-clause for upwards/downwards reviews only

(C) in the event of a revised rent not being ascertained as herein provided the rent payable for the relevant review period shall be the rent payable immediately prior to the commencement of such period.

NOTE 1

If the reviews are to be "upwards/downwards" the word in italics should be omitted and paragraph (C) should be added.

361

Clause 3

Ascertainment of amount at landlord's option by arbitrator or independent valuer (see Notes 2 and 3)

Such revised rent for any review period may be agreed at any time between the landlord and the tenant or (in the absence of agreement) determined not earlier than the relevant review date at the option of the landlord either by an arbitrator or by an independent valuer (acting as an expert and not as an arbitrator) such arbitrator or valuer to be nominated in the absence of agreement by or on behalf of the president for the time being of the Royal Institution of Chartered Surveyors on the application of the landlord made not earlier than six months before the relevant review date *but not later than the end of the relevant review period* and so that in the case of such arbitration or valuation the revised rent to be awarded or determined by the arbitrator or valuer shall be such as he shall decide should be the yearly rent at the relevant review date for the demised premises.

NOTE 2

Only one of the three commencing paragraphs given for Clause 3 should be used. The essential differences are that the first gives the landlord alone the right to opt for arbitration or independent valuation. The second and third provide respectively for arbitration only and for independent valuation only but both allow either the landlord or the tenant to initiate the process. If the words in italics are included in the commencing paragraph there will be a time limit after which a review can no longer be initiated.

Clause 3

— OR —

Ascertainment of amount by arbitrator (see Notes 2 and 3)

Such revised rent for any review period may be agreed at any time between the landlord and the tenant or (in the absence of agreement) determined not earlier than the relevant review date by an arbitrator such arbitrator to be nominated in the absence of agreement by or on behalf of the president for the time being of the Royal Institution of Chartered Surveyors on the application of the landlord or the tenant made not earlier than six months before the relevant review date *but not later than the end of the relevant review period* and so that in the case of such arbitration the revised rent to be awarded by the arbitrator shall be such as he shall decide should be the yearly rent at the relevant review date for the demised premises

— OR —

Clause 3

Ascertainment of amount by independent valuer (see Notes 2 and 3)

Such revised rent for any review period may be agreed at any time between the landlord and the tenant or (in the absence of agreement) determined not earlier than the relevant review date by an independent valuer (acting as an expert and not as an arbitrator) such valuer to be nominated in the absence of agreement by or on behalf of the president for the time being of the Royal Institution of Chartered Surveyors on the application of the landlord or the tenant made not earlier than six months before the relevant review date *but not later than the end of the relevant review period* and so that in the case of such valuation the revised rent to be determined by the valuer shall be such as he shall decide should be the yearly rent at the relevant review date for the demised premises

Provisions applicable in all versions of clause 3

(A) On the following assumptions at that date:
(i) that the demised premises are fit for immediate occupation and use and that no work has been carried out thereon by the tenant its sub-tenants or their predecessors in title during the said term which has diminished the rental value of the demised premises and that in case the demised

premises have been destroyed or damaged they have been fully restored
(ii) that the demised premises are available to let by a willing landlord to a willing tenant as a whole without a premium but with vacant possession and subject to the provisions of this lease (other than the amount of the rent hereby reserved but including the provisions for rent review) for a term equal to the original term of this lease
(iii) that the covenants herein contained on the part of the tenant have been fully performed and observed
AND having regard to open market rental values current at the relevant review date

(B) But disregarding:
(i) any effect on rent of the fact that the tenant its subtenants or their respective predecessors in title have been in occupation of the demised premises
(ii) any goodwill attached to the demised premises by reason of the carrying on thereat of the business of the tenant its sub-tenants or their predecessors in title in their respective businesses and
(iii) any increase in rental value of the demised premises attributable to the existence at the relevant review date of any improvement to the demised premises or any part thereof carried out with consent where required otherwise than in pursuance of an obligation to the landlord or its predecessors in title
either (a) by the tenant its sub-tenants or their respective predecessors in title during the said term or during any period of occupation prior thereto arising out of an agreement to grant such term

or (b) by any tenant or sub-tenant of the demised premises before the commencement of the term hereby granted so long as the landlord or its predecessors in title have not since the improvement was carried out had vacant possession of the relevant part of the demised premises [AND the improvement was completed

not more than twenty-one years before the
relevant review date]

NOTE 3
Paragraph (B) (iii) (b) may be applicable
only on a renewal. Additionally the words
in square brackets may be omitted or
amended if the twenty-one year period is
not appropriate.

Clause 4

Further provisions
as to arbitration
(see Note4)

IT IS HEREBY FURTHER PROVIDED in
relation to the said revised rent as follows:
(A) *(in the case of arbitration)* the arbitration shall be conducted in accordance
with the Arbitration Act 1950 or any statutory modification or re-enactment thereof
for the time being in force

As to independent valuation
(see Note 4)

(B) *(in the case of determination by a*
valuer)
(i) the fees and expenses of the valuer
including the cost of his appointment
shall be borne equally by the landlord and
the tenant who shall otherwise each bear
their own costs and
(ii) *the valuer shall afford to each of the*
parties hereto an opportunity to make
representations to him and
(iii) if the valuer shall die, delay or become
unwilling or incapable of acting or if for
any other reason the president for the time
being of the Royal Institution of Chartered
Surveyors or the person acting on his
behalf shall in his absolute discretion
think fit he may be writing discharge the
valuer and appoint another in his place

As to memoranda of
ascertainment

(C) When the amount of any rent to be
ascertained as hereinbefore provided shall
have been so ascertained memoranda
thereof shall thereupon be signed by or on
behalf of the landlord and the tenant and
annexed to this lease and counterpart
thereof and the parties shall bear their
own costs in respect thereof

As to interim payment and final adjustments (see Note 5)

(D) (i) if the revised rent payable on and from any review date has not been agreed by that review date rent shall continue to be payable at the rate previously payable and forthwith upon the revised rent being ascertained the tenant shall pay to the landlord any shortfall between the rent and the revised rent *or as the case may be the landlord shall pay to the tenant any excess of the rent paid over the revised rent* payable up to and on the preceding quarter day
(ii) for the purposes of this proviso the revised rent shall be deemed to have been ascertained on the date when the same has been agreed between the parties or as the case may be the date of the award of the arbitrator or of the determination by the valuer

As to notice by the tenant where appointment of arbitrator or independent valuer is at the landlord's option (see Note 6)

(E) Whenever a revised rent in respect of any review period has not been agreed between the landlord and the tenant before the relevant review date and the landlord has not made any application to the president for the time being of the Royal Institution of Chartered Surveyors as hereinbefore provided the tenant may serve on the landlord notice in writing containing a proposal as to the amount of such revised rent *not being less than the rent payable immediately before the commencement of the relevant review period* and the amount so proposed shall be deemed to have been agreed by the parties as the revised rent for the relevant review period and sub-clause

(D) (i) hereof shall apply accordingly unless the landlord shall make such application as aforesaid within three months after service of such notice by the tenant

NOTE 4
If the first version of Clause 3 is used (arbitrator or independent valuer) both (A) and (B) apply. If the second version (arbitrator) is used (B) should be omitted and if the third version (independent valuer) is

used (A) should be omitted. (B) (ii) is optional as regards an independent valuer.

NOTE 5
The words in italics should be omitted if the reviews are "upwards only".

NOTE 6
The words in italics should be included if the reviews are "upwards only".

Source: Joint R.I.C.S./Law Society Working Party

Note: a revised model clause in three variations, was issued in January 1986, annotated December 1985.

Section 1: THE PROPERTY

1 ADDRESS

2 PROPERTY TYPE

3 DATE OF CONSTRUCTION

4 DATE REFURBISHED

5 RATING
GV
RV

6 AREA *GEA, GIA, NIA

7 DATE PURCHASED

8 PURCHASE PRICE

9 INITIAL YIELD

10 REMARKS (Air conditioned, Central heating, Floor loadings, etc.)

Section 2: THE LANDLORD   (Client)*

1 NAME

2 ADDRESS (Registered Company)

3 TELEPHONE
Day   Night

4 REMARKS

5 ACCOUNT FILE NUMBER

Section 3: THE TENANT   (Client)*

1 NAME

2 ADDRESS (Registered Company)

3 TELEPHONE
Day   Night

4 REMARKS

5 ACCOUNT FILE NUMBER

Appendix E

Property Proforma

Section 4: THE LEASE

1 DATE MADE	2 PERIOD	3 COMMENCEMENT	4 EXPIRY
5 RENT PER ANNUM	6 PAYMENT PERIOD	7 DATES	
8 RENT FREE PERIOD	9 RENT REVIEWS	10 DATE	
		RENT	
11 ASSIGNMENT/SUBLETTING		12 REPAIRS	13 BREAK CLAUSE
14 INSURANCE	COMPANY	POLICY NUMBER	PREMIUM DATE
15 INSURANCE REVAL	Date		
	Val		
16 SERVICE CHARGE	BASIS	APPORTIONMENT	17 USER

Section 5: MANAGEMENT NOTES

1 SURVEYOR	2 PROPERTY FILE	3 BUILDING MAINTENANCE MANUAL	4 SPECIAL FILE
5 LAST INSPECTION	date		
	initials		
6 REMARKS			

369

Appendix F

Maintenance Programme, Covered Shopping Centre

EVERY 24 HOURS (Assuming security on a separate contract)

Feature	During opening hours	Outside opening hours
Pavement	Sweep	Wash down
Entrance doors	—	Clean and polish
Malls	Sweep	Clean and polish
Toilets	Inspect	Clean and restock
Lifts	Sweep	Clean and relamp
Service corridors	Sweep	Clean and relamp
Car parks	Sweep	Clean, relamp and re-ticket
Management offices	—	Sweep, clean, restock
P + M	Notify defects	Rectify defects

EACH WEEK
Clean walls
Clean escalator pit
Test emergency generator and alarm systems
Check fuel supply

EACH MONTH
Check stock levels of toilet and cleaning supplies
Clean plant rooms and carry out P + M maintenance procedures
Check stock levels of lamps and other spares

EVERY SIX MONTHS (spring and autumn)
Clean drain gullies
Minor repainting
Detailed internal inspection and arrange for repairs
Review programme of work on landscaping

ANNUALLY
Renew furnishings as necessary
Detailed external inspection and arrange for repairs
Renew all annual licenses and certificates
Monitor statutory or contractual inspections

ANNUALLY THEREAFTER
Implement lease covenants, subject to discussions and negotiations between the parties
Monitor performance of plant and machinery and implement replacement cycle

Table of Cases

Index

378 *Index*

384 Index

Tenancy, *contd.*
- regulated ... 182
- renewal ... 133
- secure ... 173
- service ... 181
- shorthold ... 191
- statutory ... 178

Tenant, mix ... 292
- notice ... 114
- sub ... 115

Tender ... 268
Terrier ... 219
Tesco ... 59, 323
Terotechnology ... 319
Town and Country Planning Act 1984 ... 274
Town and Country Planning (Compensation) Act 1985 ... 210
Trespass ... 128
Trustee Act 1925 ... 67
Trustee Act 1961 ... 68
Trustees ... 67
Turnover ratios ... 39

Unfair Contracts Terms Act 1977 ... 128, 230
Unilever ... 63
University ... 8
Urban Development Corporations ... 84
User covenants ... 151, 162

Vacant possession ... 163, 169, 180, 185
Valuation, bracket ... 338
- external ... 57
- independent ... 51, 160
Value, divorce ... 42
- marriage ... 41, 277
Valuation Office ... 77, 264
VAT ... 227, 346

Waiver ... 155
Weatherall Green and Smith ... 75
Welsh Development Agency ... 85
Woolworth ... 60

Yield, all risks ... 160, 289, 291
- equated ... 160